CW01573055

Governance of Intellectual Property Rights in China and Europe

ELGAR INTELLECTUAL PROPERTY AND GLOBAL DEVELOPMENT

Series Editor: Peter K. Yu, *Professor of Law and Co-Director of the Center for Law and Intellectual Property at Texas A&M University School of Law, USA*

Rapid global economic integration and the increasing importance of technology and information goods have created the need for a broader, deeper and more critical understanding of intellectual property laws and policies. This uniquely designed book series provides an interdisciplinary forum for advancing the debate on the global intellectual property system and related issues that intersect with transnational politics, international governance, and global economic, social, cultural and technological development. The series features the works of established experts and emerging voices in the academy as well as those practising on the frontlines. The series' high-quality, informed and accessible volumes include a wide range of materials such as historical narratives, theoretical explanations, substantive discussions, critical evaluations, empirical analyses, comparative studies, and formulations of practical solutions and best practices. The series will appeal to academics, policy makers, judges, practitioners, transnational lawyers and civil society groups as well as students of law, politics, culture, political economy, international relations and development studies.

Titles in the series include:

Genetic Resources and Traditional Knowledge
Case Studies and Conflicting Interests
Edited by Tania Bubela and E. Richard Gold

The Global Governance of HIV/AIDS
Intellectual Property and Access to Essential Medicines
Edited by Obijiofor Aginam, John Harrington and Peter K. Yu

Access to Information and Knowledge
21st Century Challenges in Intellectual Property and Knowledge Governance
Edited by Dana Beldiman

Trademark Protection and Territoriality Challenges in a Global Economy
Edited by Irene Calboli and Edward Lee

Governance of Intellectual Property Rights in China and Europe
Edited by Nari Lee, Niklas Bruun and Mingde Li

Governance of Intellectual Property Rights in China and Europe

Edited by

Nari Lee

Hanken School of Economics, Helsinki, Finland

Niklas Bruun

Hanken School of Economics, Helsinki, Finland

Mingde Li

Chinese Academy of Social Sciences, China

ELGAR INTELLECTUAL PROPERTY AND GLOBAL
DEVELOPMENT

Cheltenham, UK • Northampton, MA, USA

Published by
Edward Elgar Publishing Limited
The Lypiatts
15 Lansdown Road
Cheltenham
Glos GL50 2JA
UK

Edward Elgar Publishing, Inc.
William Pratt House
9 Dewey Court
Northampton
Massachusetts 01060
USA

A catalogue record for this book
is available from the British Library

Library of Congress Control Number: 2015950510

This book is available electronically in the **Elgar**online
Law subject collection
DOI 10.4337/9781783478217

ISBN 978 1 78347 820 0 (cased)
ISBN 978 1 78347 821 7 (eBook)

Typeset by Servis Filmsetting Ltd, Stockport, Cheshire

Printed and bound in Great Britain by
TJ International Ltd, Padstow, Cornwall

Contents

Contributors

Daniel Opoku Acquah is a doctoral researcher at the University of Turku, Finland and at the Institute for European Studies (IES), Vrije University of Brussels, Belgium.

Rosa Maria Ballardini is an assistant professor in the Department of Accounting and Commercial Law, Hanken School of Economics, Helsinki, Finland.

Niklas Bruun is a professor of intellectual property law at Hanken School of Economics and the director of IPR University Center, Helsinki, Finland. He is also the project leader of the Finnish Academy project 'Legal Transplant For Innovation and Creativity – A Sino-Finnish Comparative Study on the Governance of Intellectual Property Rights' (TranSIP) on behalf of the University of Helsinki.

Yuying Guan is a professor at the Intellectual Property Centre, Chinese Academy of Social Sciences.

Kan He is a candidate for Dr.jur. at the University of Munich (LMU), Germany and TranSIP project researcher at Hanken School of Economics, Helsinki, Finland since 2013. He was a scholarship holder at the Max-Planck Institute for Innovation and Competition in Munich from 2010 to 2013.

Kelli Larson is a PhD candidate and a project researcher (TranSIP) at the Department of Accounting and Commercial Law, Hanken School of Economics, Helsinki, Finland.

Nari Lee is a professor of intellectual property law at Hanken School of Economics, Helsinki, Finland. She is the Consortium Leader of the Academy project 'Legal Transplant For Innovation and Creativity – A Sino-Finnish Comparative Study on the Governance of Intellectual Property Rights (TranSIP).

Mingde Li is the director and professor at the Intellectual Property Center of Chinese Academy of Social Sciences, Beijing, China. He has been the principal investigator and the leader of the research group in China for the research project TranSIP.

Yang Li is a professor at Shenzhen University Law School, China. Professor Li has a PhD from Peking University Law School and is a Visiting Scholar of Hokkaido University Law School, Japan and Drake University Law School, USA. Professor Li also worked as a visiting scholar (2013–14) to the research project TranSIP at the Hanken School of Economics, Helsinki, Finland.

Max Oker-Blom is an adjunct professor at the Hanken School of Economics, Helsinki, Finland. He worked for almost two decades as Senior Vice President, legal, at Fazer group, a Nordic food service group of companies. Previous to that he was a tax partner with PriceWaterhouseCoopers. He is past President of ECTA and currently Secretary General of the same European organization.

Benjamin Pi-Wei Liu served as an assistant professor at John Marshall Law School, USA, after practising law with Stroock & Stroock & Lavan LLP in New York, and in private practice as an IP attorney in Chicago. Broadly interested in comparative patent law and enforcement in East Asia and beyond, particularly in the fields of technology and pharmaceuticals, he was an active member of the extended research team of the TranSIP project. He passed away on 1 December 2014 after a sudden illness.

Laura Tammenlehto is an LL.D candidate in the University of Eastern Finland Law School and was a TranSIP project researcher at the Hanken School of Economics, Helsinki, Finland during 2013–2014.

Weiguang Wu is an associate professor, Tsinghua University Law School, Beijing, China, who specializes in IP and IT law, has a BE and Masters degree in civil and commercial law from Tsinghua University, a European law diploma from EU-China Legal and Judicial Program, LL.M from SMU University Law School, USA, and a PhD in IP law from the Chinese Academy of Social Sciences.

Peter K. Yu is a professor of law and co-director of the Center for Law and Intellectual Property at Texas A&M University School of Law, USA. He has served as Wenlan Scholar Chair Professor at Zhongnan University of Economics and Law in Wuhan, China and as a visiting professor of law at the University of Hong Kong.

Liguo Zhang is a postdoctoral researcher at the Faculty of Law, University of Helsinki, Finland. He received his LL.D from University of Helsinki in 2013 and his LL.M in intellectual property and competition law from Munich Intellectual Property Law Center, Germany in 2006. His research focuses on innovation-related legal issues.

Qi-shan Zhao is a postdoctoral fellow of the Institute of Law, Chinese Academy of Social Sciences. She worked in the Law School of Shanghai University from 2004 to 2012 as an instructor, teaching intellectual property law, patent law and competition law. She gained her Bachelor degree from Chinese Petroleum University, and her LL.M and JSD from Peking University, Beijing, China.

Yajie Zhao is undertaking doctoral research on the comparative study of Chinese and EU intellectual property law at the Faculty of Law, University of Helsinki, Finland.

Lin Zhou is a professor at the Law Institute of Chinese Academy of Social Sciences. He has made extraordinary contributions to the IP field, especially in the area of copyright law and is one of the pioneers of art law research in China.

Acknowledgements

This book is the outcome of a larger comparative law research project financed by the Academy of Finland 'Legal Transplant For Innovation and Creativity – A Sino-Finnish Comparative Study on the Governance of Intellectual Property Rights' (TranSIP), which aims to fill the gaps in research on IP law governance and enforcement in China and Europe. The research project has collaborated with two leading Chinese research institutions, the Institute of Law of the Chinese Academy of Social Sciences (CASS) and Shenzhen University. We are grateful for financial support from the Academy of Finland and the Chinese Academy of Social Sciences. The editors of this book thank Chelsea Foxwell for allowing us to publish Benjamin Pi-Wei Liu's chapter. Benjamin, who passed away on 1 December 2014, was a much valued member of the extended research group, whose participation in the research project conferences enlivened the discussion greatly. We will miss him and his work. The editors also thank Daniel Jongsma, Kenneth O'Connor and Dr Dhanay Cadillo Chandler. The book could not have been completed without their excellent assistance.

Introduction

Nari Lee and Niklas Bruun

Intellectual property (IP) law performs a number of complex functions in society. One important purpose of IP is to foster innovation and creativity in a society. In meeting this important purpose, the system of IP has evolved where international models and international treaties have become important, although the significant decision making for institutional design and norms is in the hands of national authorities and policymakers. In contemporary history, the legal development of IP law, which is marked by 'an import' of foreign legal institutions and concepts from elsewhere, has often been described as legal transplant. As the norms of international IP are increasingly connected to culturally and locally sensitive resources, the debate on the suitability and consequences of legal transplants has become a sensitive issue debated at a global level.

Scholars of IP law have only sporadically attempted to provide an analysis of legal transplants and their anecdotal consequences. The definitions as well as the measurement of success or failure of legal transplants, as well as what follows after, have not been fully explored. The literature may present the recipient nation's successful legislative changes as evidences of a successful legal transplant. To understand the impact in full, their efficacy in achieving the objectives that they are devised to achieve needs further exploration. Moreover, the influence of foreign norms, institutions and practice needs to be critically analysed from a comparative law perspective, to assess how they function in the local socio-economic environments, after initial transplant.

Chinese IP law has been the topic of much interest of recent scholarship. While emerging works are impressive, often they remain descriptive. From a more analytical perspective, this volume examines the series of IP law and system reforms in China as statutory and textual resources to study legal transplants. The adoption of international standards as the law in the books has to be followed by transformation, implementation and enforcement, in order for them to become local practices of governance.

To explore analytically the ongoing changes in Chinese IP law, contributors in this volume use the metaphor of legal transplants to study a series of past and current transformations in IP rights and their governance in China and Europe. From a comparative perspective, the contributors explore how Chinese stakeholder institutions – the legislature, the administration, courts and the market – have dealt with, indigenised and transformed the transplanted norms. Furthermore, to compare Chinese and European IP governance in full, most of the chapters are written jointly by a pair of Chinese and non-Chinese authors.

The book is divided into three parts. Part I, 'Intellectual property for innovation and creativity in China', contains four theoretical chapters that set the framework for the discussion and subsequent comparisons within the volume. These chapters focus on IP law in China and present a history of legal transplants in China and a governance thesis to explain further transformation.

Part II, 'Comparing concepts and norms in Chinese and European IP law', contains six chapters that compare concepts and norms in the IP law of China and Europe. The joint Chinese and European contributors focus on selected topics where transformation is currently ongoing, both in China and in Europe, in three areas of IP law – copyright law, patent law and trademark law, and also in the context of implementing national and regional intellectual property rights (IPR) strategies.

Part III, 'Governance of practices and IP enforcement', contains nine chapters focusing on the transformation in governance of practices and enforcement of IP rights in China and Europe. Jointly, contributors explore governance of practices in the areas of copyright (collective rights management), patent (non-practising entities, standard essential patent licensing) and IP enforcement through courts and the administration, including customs authorities, in China and Europe. These chapters highlight the evolving contours of IPR practices and enforcement in China but also present a great internal divergence in technological and economic developments in different parts of China.

PART I

Intellectual property for innovation and creativity in China

1. Intellectual property law in China – from legal transplant to governance

Nari Lee

1. INTRODUCTION

Intellectual property (IP) law aims to foster innovation and creativity in a society by granting private rights excluding others from using information defined as the object of such rights. Due to the role they play in generating added value in international trade, IP laws are increasingly made and influenced by international norms imposed by conditions set in international agreements, such as the TRIPs Agreement.[1] More and more, governments are seen to be actively using the rhetoric of intellectual property rights (IPR) as an instrument of innovation and cultural policy to improve national competitiveness in the global economy.[2] Due to the importance of IPR and the added value they generate, innovation seems to take a central place in national economic policy in Asia and Europe alike.[3]

The economic importance of IP invites a form of norm competition, as different norms, laws and standards on the protection and uses of IP compete with each other internationally – which is sometimes referred to as IP arbitrage.[4] The norm competition is made clearly visible in the

---

[1] Agreement on Trade-Related Aspects of Intellectual Property Rights, 15 April 1994, 33 ILM 81 (hereinafter TRIPs Agreement).

[2] For example, the EU IP Strategy 2011: European Commission, *Communication from the Commission to the European Parliament, the Council, the European Economic and Social Committee and the Committee of the Regions. A Single Market for Intellectual Property Rights. Boosting Creativity and Innovation to Provide Economic Growth, High Quality Jobs and First Class Products and Services in Europe* (Brussels, 24 May 2011, COM (2011) 287 final).

[3] See, for example, Liguo Zhang, 'Recent IP Legal Reforms in China and the EU in light of Implementing IPR Strategies', Chapter 10 in this volume.

[4] P. Samuelson, 'Intellectual Property Arbitrage: How Foreign Rules Can Affect Domestic Protections' (2004) 71 University of Chicago Law Review 223–239.

context of new international trade treaty negotiations in various forums.[5] As these regulatory competitions show, the nature and foundation of IP law still remain contested, despite the acceptance of IPR as a pragmatic instrument to further the economic growth of a nation. Notably, the discussion on the origin of modern IP law may be one topic that rehashes the differences on the foundation of IP. Modern IP law is often pictured and presented to be an invention as well as an outcome of historical evolution and deliberate interventions by political authorities in the legal tradition of a certain nation or 'the West', despite the attempt to show the contingency of the current IPR institutions with property rights over mental objects.[6]

As seen in the discussions of traditional knowledge and expression, framing traditional knowledge in the context of a private property right has caused controversies.[7] Even in less contentious subject matters, the expanding boundary of IP highlights the inherent tension between nations with heterogeneous economic interests and traditions.

Such conflicts and tension raised during the process of IP law harmonization present serious concerns. Fundamentally, the question is about the *origin of IP norms and the genealogy of law and whether they matter in efficient implementation of IP laws.* Law reforms even within Europe, from where modern IP law is said to originate, are not entirely without controversy. Indeed, convergence of norms in European harmonization projects has had its share of critics.[8] Notably, in an essay published in 1996,

---

[5]   See, for example, Peter K. Yu, 'TPP and Trans-Pacific Perplexities' (2013) 37 Fordham Int'l LJ 1129, showing how some regions are excluded from the treaties, to include some trade terms that were rejected by them earlier. See also, what Dinwoodie and Dreyfuss described as regulatory competition in G. Dinwoodie and R.C. Dreyfuss, 'Designing a Global Intellectual Property System Responsive to Change: The WTO, WIPO, and Beyond' (2009) 46 Houston Law Review 1187.

[6]   See generally, Brad Sherman and Lionel Bently, *The Making of Modern Intellectual Property Law: The British Experience, 1760–1911* (Cambridge University Press 1999). However, they highlight the contingent nature of the law, which resulted from a 'complex and changing set of circumstances' at 6.

[7]   In the context of traditional cultural expression and traditional knowledge and patent claims, Gunther Teubner and Andreas Fischer-Lescano, 'Cannibalizing Epistemes: Will Modern Law Protect Traditional Cultural Expressions?' in Christoph Graber and Mira Burri-Nenova (eds), *Traditional Cultural Expressions in a Digital Environment* (Edward Elgar Publishing 2008).

[8]   G. Teubner, 'Legal Irritants: Good Faith in British Law or How Unifying Law Ends Up in New Differences' (1998) 6 Modern Law Review 111–132; W. Van Gerven, 'Comparative Law in a Texture of Communitarization of National Laws and Europeanization of Community Law' in D. O'Keeffe and A. Bavasso (eds), *Judicial Review In European Union Law – Liber Amicorum in Honour of Lord Slynn of Hadley* 1 (Kluwer Law International 2000) 433.

Legrand observed that all efforts at convergence actually failed to produce a harmonized system of European law, based on the fundamental differences in legal culture and legal systems in Europe.[9] The observation is still relevant in the implementation of EU IP laws and ongoing initiatives of the EU IP law unification agenda.[10] Arguably, the problem of origin may not be as great a concern as for a country where the norms are transplanted. It would be more difficult, for example, to raise a culturally relativist claim in the implementation of IP laws in a European Member State, such as those made by Alford on Chinese copyright law, that IP infringement may be somewhat culturally justifiable.[11] A common understanding that 'intellectual property shall be protected'[12] seems to exist in Europe and there is some common rationality for an individual private property right as well as the belief that creations of mind and abstract objects may be protected, regardless of justification – natural right or utilitarian rationality.

In contrast, various nations in Asia, by design as well as by force, have received laws and systems of laws from Europe. For example, foreign laws and legal systems' influence on modern Japanese law has been well documented.[13] In particular, transplantation of the European law into the Japanese system has even generally been viewed as positive and successfully integrated in the local social order.[14] In contrast, the introduction

---

[9]   Pierre Legrand, 'European Legal Systems Are Not Converging' (1996) 45(1) International and Comparative Law Quarterly 52–81.

[10]   See, for example, on the problems of Europeanization of IP right, Justine Pila. 'The European Patent: An Old and Vexing Problem' (2013) 62(4) International and Comparative Law Quarterly 917–940; B. Hugenholtz, 'Why the Copyright Directive Is Unimportant, and Possibly Invalid' (2000) 22(11) European Intellectual Property Review 499–505; L.R. Helfer, 'The New Innovation Frontier? Intellectual Property and the European Court of Human Rights' (2008) 49 Harvard International Law Journal 1. See also for an overview, J. Pila and A. Ohly (eds), *The Europeanization of Intellectual Property Law: Towards a European Legal Methodology* (Oxford University Press 2014).

[11]   William P. Alford, *To Steal a Book Is an Elegant Offense: Intellectual Property Law in Chinese Civilization* (Stanford University Press 1995).

[12]   See, however, C. Geiger, 'Intellectual Property Shall be Protected!? Article 17(2) of the Charter of Fundamental Rights of the European Union: a Mysterious Provision with an Unclear Scope' (2009) 31(3) European Intellectual Property Review 113–117.

[13]   See, for example, Hiroshi Oda, *Japanese Law* (Oxford University Press 2009). On the European influence on Japanese civil law, see, for example, Zentaro Kitagawa and Karl Riesenhuber (eds), *The Identity of German and Japanese Civil Law in Comparative Perspectives/Die Identität des deutschen und des japanischen Zivilrechts in vergleichender Betrachtung* (De Gruyter 2007).

[14]   Oda (*supra*, n 13), who argues that despite the mystifying argument of disparity between local norms and transplanted law, foreign laws were received by

of the Western system of laws into China and Korea coincides with the marred history of colonialism as well as Japanese imperialism and thus such success is rarely claimed.[15] As such, predominance of narratives of the legal transplant in the discussion of Asian IP law may seem a logical extension of the debates on the origin of the modern legal system and the rule of law in Asia.[16]

The introduction of modern IP law to China provides one example of legal transplant of a system which originates from Europe, documenting a process of adaptation and rejection of transplanted systems and norms across cultures.[17] This chapter argues that the perspective of governance needs to be added to the comparative study of Chinese and European IP law. If legal transplant is a narrative to explain the first wave of normative changes in Chinese IP law and IP law reforms, often resulting from foreign forces and external pressures, this chapter argues that a perspective of governance may better explain the second wave of normative changes in Chinese IP law.

2.   NARRATIVE OF LEGAL TRANSPLANT APPLIED TO CHINESE IP LAW

2.1   Legal Transplant as a Narrative

Legal transplant as a theory in comparative law to explain norm and systemic interactions in laws, across different cultures, is not without

---

Japan without much resistance, as the need for modernization was locally felt. He also highlighted the fact that absence of colonial rulers imposing foreign rule has made the reception smoother as there was broader political support for its reception. Additionally, selective reception as witnessed by the Civil Code, which is a concoction of German, French and English law, has also smoothed the process. Finally, as the transplanted laws were modified to suit the existing customs and conventions, including commercial practices, he considered Japanese legal transplant to be successful.

[15]   See Alford (*supra*, n 11) at 30–55, where he describes it as 'learning the law at gunpoint'.

[16]   See also, Deming Liu, 'The Transplant Effect of the Chinese Patent Law' (2006) 5(3) Chinese Journal of International Law 733–752.

[17]   See Peter Yu, 'The transplant and transformation of intellectual property laws in China', Chapter 2 in this volume. See also Paul Edward Geller, 'Legal Transplants in International Copyright: Some Problems of Method' (1995) 13 UCLA Pacific Basin Law Journal 199; Wei Shi, 'Globalization and Indigenization: Legal Transplant of a Universal TRIPS Regime in a Multicultural World' (2010) 47(3) American Business Law Journal 455–507.

controversy. Various comparative lawyers have assessed and identified negative and positive aspects of borrowing or transplanting legal concepts and systems into a different cultural context.[18] Starting from the very notion of law rooted in the soil of the nature, some have been more negative about the idea,[19] while others seem more positive, leaving room for such legislative experimentation.[20] Notably, if the law is there to recognize a pre-existing normative order, without localization, the laws that are introduced to a foreign culture may only be implemented successfully as a matter of an 'unusual and accidental coincidence' as noted by Montesquieu.[21] If the origin of the law is so important in the implementation of the legal norms, then the system of IP based on IP laws with foreign norms would likely fail. Or, as believed by Watson, laws may be autonomous and as such be transplanted,[22] while the correctness of the metaphor of legal transplantation may be questioned.[23] Some may question the behavioural dynamics induced by the transplanted law,[24] and while some may question the very possibility of comparison, at least among those that accept such possibilities of comparison, the necessity to adapt or modify the transplanted systems to local conditions are highlighted.[25] Taking his cue from Watson, Mattei, for example, highlighted economic efficiency

---

[18]   See for a cogent summary of the history of the theory, John W. Cairns, 'Watson, Walton, and the History of Legal Transplants' (2012) 41 Georgia Journal of International & Comparative Law 637.

[19]   See, for example, F.K. von Savigny, *Vom Beruf unserer Zeit für Gesetzgebung und Rechtswissenschaft* [Of the Vocation of our Age for Legislation and Jurisprudence] (Abraham Hayward tr, first published 1814, The Law Book Exchange 2002).

[20]   See among others, A. Watson, *Legal Transplants: An Approach to Comparative Law* (University of Georgia Press 1974). See also A. Watson, 'Legal Transplants and European Private Law' (2000) 4.4 Electronic Journal of Comparative Law, <http://www.ejcl.org/44/art44-2.html> accessed 10 December 2014.

[21]   Charles de Secondat, Baron de La Brède et de Montesquieu, *The Spirit of Laws* (1748) Book. I, ch. 3, para. [12]. He notably argued that 'que c'est un grand hazard si celles d'une nation peuvent convenir à une autre' ('it is very unlikely for those of one nation to be proper for another'). The English translation is from David Wallace Carrithers (ed), *The Spirit of Laws: A Compendium of the First English Edition* (University of California Press 1977) at 105.

[22]   Watson (*supra*, n 20).

[23]   Teubner (*supra*, n 8) has notably used the term 'legal irritants'.

[24]   Ann W. Seidman and R.B. Seidman, *State and Law in the Development Process: Problem Solving and Institutional Change in the Third World* (St Martin's Press 1994).

[25]   K. Zweigert and H. Kötz, *Introduction to Comparative Law* (Tony Weir tr, 3rd edn, Clarendon Press 1998).

in legal transplant.[26] In between the extremes of impossibility and the ease of legal transplant, Kahn-Freund submits that there are degrees of transferability. According to him, the success of a transplant depends on how closely a foreign institution or law is connected with a distribution of power in the foreign country that is not shared in the recipient country, and how it is likely to be received by organized interest groups in its new setting.[27]

Researchers working on the topic of Chinese law are also warned of the possibility that the concept of law may be so different in China that an eager application of so-called functional comparison would lead to an incorrect observation or conclusion.[28] This warning may very well be worth considering in cases that are so fundamentally local in nature, and where the legal or regulatory arrangement may evolve without particularly using the same rationalities and doctrinal concepts as used and accepted elsewhere.[29] In contrast, if infrastructural institutions are in place and transplanted and used as a means to emulate new norms, insistence on fundamental differences based on cultural relativism may be misleadingly mystifying.

However, once the mystifying claims for a difference are cleared, there are actual and real problems in using legal transplant as a method to induce changes in a society. As noted by Seidman and Seidman, it is hard to verify the causality of outcome of the changes in a society: 'inevitably, people choose how to behave, not only in response to the law, but also to social, economic, political, physical and subject factors arising in their own countries from custom, geography, history, technology and other non legal circumstances'.[30] The changes may very well have been caused by factors external to law such as power relations, politics, technology and culture. Indeed, the failure of law and development projects that ambitiously asked the question whether law matters in economic development highlight the difficulty of the task of assessing the impact of the law.[31] As it

---

[26]   Ugo Mattei, 'Efficiency in Legal Transplants: An Essay in Comparative Law and Economics' (1994) 14(1) International Review of Law and Economics 3–19.

[27]   Otto Kahn-Freund, 'On Uses and Misuses of Comparative Law' (1974) 37(1) Modern Law Review 1–27.

[28]   See, for example, Teemu Ruskola, *Legal Orientalism* (Harvard University Press 2014) 33–36. Legal realists may likewise challenge the notion of functional comparison of superficial similarities as the substantive legal relations underlying them may well be entirely different.

[29]   Alf Ross, 'Tû-Tû' (1957) 70 Harvard Law Review 5, 812–825.

[30]   Seidman and Seidman (*supra*, n 24) at 45.

[31]   See, for examples of such criticism, Tom Ginsburg, 'Does Law Matter for Economic Development? Evidence From East Asia' (2000) 34(3) Law & Society

is unclear what impacts on behavioural changes should be examined, this also makes it hard to measure the success of transplant. Unlike organic transplant, the measurement of a successful legal transplant of a social construct may be impossible as binary causality is impossible to establish in a complex social system.

2.2 Legal Transplant of IP Law Norms to China

When applied to the development of Chinese IP laws, comparative law debates seem to be dominated by more negative than positive narratives of legal transplant.[32] If one looks only at the reports of challenges to enforcement of IPR, one may well concur with such an observation on the failure of transplantation of alien norms to Chinese soil.[33] On a closer look, however, it is possible to note that the narrative of legal transplant may provide only a partial explanation of IP norm interactions in China.[34] IP law reforms in China in recent years seem to be going beyond the local adaptation of the received norms, but are also driven by indigenous demands for new norms to govern and to be governed.

In the area of IP laws alone, various scholars and commentators have argued that it is nearly impossible to say with certainty what impact IP law has on technological, creative or aesthetic progress, as it purports to do. Economists have also convincingly shown that we do not even know whether it is a good idea to try to influence production and use of non-rival and non-excludable knowledge goods with an artificially constructed regime of scarcity – and exclusivity.[35] As such, trying to measure the

---

Review 829–856; Kevin Davis and Michael Trebilcock, 'The Relationship between Law and Development: Optimists vs. Sceptics' (2008) 56 American Journal of Comparative Law 895.

[32] Alford (*supra*, n 11). See for an example of criticism, Shi Wei, 'Cultural Perplexity in Intellectual Property: Is Stealing a Book an Elegant Offense?' (2006) 32 North Carolina Journal of International Law and Commercial Regulation 1, 11.

[33] For example, United States Trade Representative (USTR), *2015 Special 301 Report* (2015) at 33–43 <https://ustr.gov/sites/default/files/2015-Special-301-Report-FINAL.pdf> accessed 31 May 2015.

[34] See, for example, Yu (*supra*, n 17) and Benjamin Liu, 'The glocalization of patent linkage in China', Chapter 9 in this volume.

[35] Fritz Machlup, *An Economic Review of the Patent System: Study of the Subcommittee on Patents, Trademarks, and Copyrights of the Committee on the Judiciary, United States, Senate; Eighty-fifth Congress, Second Session; Pursuant to S. Res. 236* (US Government Printing Office 1958). Fritz Machlup and Edith Penrose 'The Patent Controversy in the Nineteenth Century' (1950) 10(1) Journal of Economic History 1–29. Compare James Bessen and Michael James

impact of transplanted IP law on the local economy is predetermined to be an unclear project.

Nevertheless, if a society may be ruled by the law, introduction of specific regulations should produce some changes at least observable through changed behaviours of the directly regulated target group. Likewise, the success or failure of a legal transplant may be measured through the changes or the absences in the behaviours, before and after the introduction of the norm. Likewise, it is possible to argue that a transplanted norm may be considered rejected, not only when it is vocally opposed by the locals, but also when it remains as irrelevant dead letters in the law book, not referred to, respected or used in practice.[36] In contrast, one may argue that the success may be measured if the new norms are accepted and used by the locals efficiently to settle disputes, instead of the alternatives, or to generate more norms (to make more norms) to introduce further changes,[37] or to otherwise regulate and coordinate conduct of the governed, in the domain regulated by the introduced norm.[38]

Legal transplant highlights origins in the law. In other words, when viewed through the lens of legal transplant, it is the genealogy of a norm, rather than what it regulates, and how it functions in the present tends to become highlighted. Some scholars who study the political economy of the law have pointed out, for example, that the development is a continuation of colonialist history or imperialism, imposed by way of *external pressure*,[39] while others have postulated that such legal transplant is based on *deliberate local motivation* of the recipient country.[40] In the history of

---

Meurer, *Patent Failure: How Judges, Bureaucrats, and Lawyers Put Innovators at Risk* (Princeton University Press 2008).

[36] See, for example, Weiguang Wu, 'China's CMC system and its problems from the Copyright Law of 1990 to its third amendment', Chapter 11 in this volume.

[37] As documented in Lionel Bently, 'The "Extraordinary Multiplicity" of Intellectual Property Laws in the British Colonies in the Nineteenth Century' (2011) 12 Theoretical Inquiries in Law 161–200.

[38] As observed on Chinese copyright businesses in Lucy Montgomery, *China's Creative Industries: Copyright, Social Network Markets and the Business of Culture in a Digital Age* (Edward Elgar Publishing 2010).

[39] See, for example, Alexander Peukert, 'The Colonial Legacy of the International Copyright System' forthcoming in Mamadou Diawara and Ute Röschenthaler (eds), *Staging the Immaterial. Rights, Style and Performance in Sub-Saharan Africa* (Sean Kingston, forthcoming); A. Samuel Oddi, 'TRIPS – Natural Rights and a Polite Form of Economic Imperialism' (1996) 29 Vanderbilt Journal of Transnational Law 415.

[40] See Peter K. Yu, 'Intellectual Property, Economic Development, and the China Puzzle' in Daniel J. Gervais (ed), *Intellectual Property, Trade and*

colonialism, it is argued that legal transplant of copyright law may have been used as a deliberate and calculated means of governance and may hint at a mentality of governing.[41]

Literature presenting the recipient nation's successful statutory implementation of international treaty obligations as evidence of a successful legal transplant does exist.[42] For example, the recent induction of China into the World Trade Organization trading system has transformed China from 'a norm breaker to a norm taker, shaker and a maker'.[43] Scholars also claim that the deliberate and continued introduction and transplantation of obviously foreign legal concepts and doctrines can be motivated by local policies for innovation and creation strategy.[44] However, despite the legislative efforts and enactment of the statutes in the book, the implementation of the law in practice and the law enforcement mechanisms seem to remain a concern in China. Liu, for example, paints a pessimistic picture of the legal transplant of the patent system in China.[45]

3. GOVERNANCE PERSPECTIVE AND CHINESE IP LAWS

The perplexing explanation of simultaneously successful and failed legal transplant of an IP system to Chinese soil seems to indicate that the research on Chinese IP law may need to transit from the path-dependent narratives of norm transplants to that of governance through IPR. In particular the governance thesis may explain how foreign and local doctrines and norms influence and interact with each other, after the initial phase

---

Development: Strategies to Optimize Economic Development in a TRIPS Plus Era (Oxford University Press 2007) 173–220.

[41] See Peukert (*supra*, n 39). See also, A. Rahmatian, 'Neo-Colonial Aspects of Global Intellectual Property Protection' (2009) 12 Journal of World Intellectual Property 40–74.

[42] For example, Yahong Li, 'Transplantation and Transformation – 30 Years of Development of Chinese IP System' in Guanghua Yu (ed), *The Development of the Chinese Legal System: Change and Challenges* (Routledge 2011) 138–154. See also Andrea Wechsler, *Intellectual Property Law in the P.R. China: A Powerful Economic Tool for Innovation and Development* (12 November 2008, Max Planck Institute for Intellectual Property, Competition & Tax Law Research Paper No. 09-02) <http://ssrn.com/abstract=1354546> accessed 31 March 2014.

[43] Peter K. Yu, 'The Middle Kingdom and the Intellectual Property World' (2011) 26 Oregon Review of International Law 209–262.

[44] Yu (*supra*, n 40) and Wechsler (*supra*, n 42).

[45] Liu (*supra*, n 16).

of system transplant, to emulate new norms. By framing the discussion as that of governance, the perpetual debates on the genealogy of Chinese IP law may move away from the question of the cultural and geographical origins of the IP laws to the exploration of how they are used in practice, and who and what they govern.

Governance is a concept we find in the context of a variety of social sciences, to mean any structured form of management of courses of events in a social system, or management of resources and capacities. As a perspective to study any social system, governance seems to be receiving renewed attention among researchers in the field of business studies as well as political scientists and legal scholars.[46] In the context of law in general, governance perspectives highlight the institutional structure underlying a legal system, and tend to be used to understand the rule of law.

A more relevant and useful application of governance perspectives may perhaps be found in the discussions of institutional arrangements of IP law and practices – and the process – highlighting that in IP discourse, substantive norm discussions in the epistemic community itself are equally important as the process of governance that creates such norms, by the institutions and actors in the decision-making process. This is more so in an area where not only the doctrines themselves, but also the facts to which such doctrines are applied, require understanding and knowledge of persons skilled in the art. Academic debates set only in such a context would be likely to be geared inwards among the epistemic community of experts, and normative recommendations resulting from such discussions would be likely to be fed back into a self-referential autopoietic system, and thus may make its rationality immune to criticisms that are normally pitted against a social construct. As the governance perspective opens up the discourse and brings in the *technology of government* to the discussion of IP law, it highlights the *process* of implementation of the law as well as the *institutions* of implementing the law, including the market.

Building upon the governmentality perspective,[47] the governance perspective may highlight that governance may be done through IPR by channelling certain decision making to the market. The governance perspective is often used in two contexts. Some commentators use it more as an economic term to highlight the fact that IPR govern use of resources. Thus the governance perspective used in this manner highlights

---

[46]   Lewis A. Kornhauser, 'Governance Structures, Legal Systems, and the Concept of Law' (2004) 79 Chicago Kent Law Review 355.
[47]   Mitchell Dean, *Governmentality: Power and Rule in Modern Society* (Sage Publications 2010).

the role that an exclusive right of property and the institutions of IP play in the governance of common knowledge resources.[48] Using this type of governance perspective, commentators often compare IPR as private exclusive rights to govern the use of resources with alternative regimes and explore whether the private property regime based on exclusivity is the most suitable or efficient means to govern innovation and knowledge resources. A variation of this approach is also noted by the commentators who compare a contractual or liability-based regime to the property rules of IP.[49] A common theoretical starting point is that they use the concept that *IPR govern* the use of resources through the market. As a corollary, IPR allow non-state actors to participate in the governance on the use of resources through exercising their private rights through a functioning market.

In contrast, taking the governance perspective from the political sciences, there are those who use the governance perspective, focusing on the process of how the norms of IP are formed and on the institutions that are entrusted with the task of governance.[50] Commonly, they start from the observation that the current property arrangement (normative set-up) is contingent as well as the nature of the rights. As the rights themselves may be contingent and thus can be recalibrated to suit particular purposes, the process is highlighted: as process is important, legitimacy of the process as well as efficiency of intervention into the normal workings of the patent market justifies the law/system/institution as well as the substance of the norm. Additionally, these commentators highlight information and

---

[48] See, for example, Brett M. Frischmann, Michael J. Madison and Katherine J. Strandburg (eds), *Governing Knowledge Commons* (Oxford University Press 2014).

[49] J.H. Reichman, 'Legal Hybrids Between the Patent and Copyright Paradigms' (1994) 94 Columbia Law Review, 2432–2558. See also Henry E. Smith, 'Intellectual Property as Property: Delineating Entitlements in Information' (2007) 116 Yale Law Journal 1742.

[50] See, for example, Ingrid Schneider, 'Governing the Patent System in Europe: the EPO's Supranational Autonomy and its Need for a Regulatory Perspective' (2009) 36(8) Science and Public Policy 619–629; Antonina Bakardjieva Engelbrekt, 'Copyright from an Institutional Perspective: Actors, Interests, Stakes and the Logic of Participation' (2007) 4 Review of Economic Research on Copyright Issues 65; Robert P. Merges, 'Contracting into Liability Rules: Intellectual Property Rights and Collective Rights Organizations' (1996) 84 California Law Review 1293; Arti Rai, 'Engaging Facts and Policy: a Multi-institutional Approach to Patent System Reform' (2003) 103 Columbia Law Review 1035; Yoshiyuki Tamura, 'Towards the New Paradigm of Intellectual Property Law. The Law and Policy of Intellectual Property: Building a New Framework' (2008) 20 Intellectual Property Law and Policy Journal 1, 11–20.

limited capacity institutions that are involved in the governance of IP and institutional interdependence/network formation through formation of clusters or nodes, as a result. As Burris, Drahos and Shearing have noted:

> No one network, public or private, has information omniscience. The response of actors to this complexity has been to find ways to link networks to produce new structures of governance, a response that can be labeled nodal governance. These structures do not bring information omniscience to actors, *but they do bring more information, and importantly, resources and technologies, which enable actors to become centers of governance.* Nodes in the networked world are organizational centers in time and space from which the actions of governance flow (emphasis added).[51]

In other words, 'development in knowledge and powers of expertise' are closely connected to the idea of governance, highlighting that not only the state, but also other actors who have capacity and resources to collect necessary information, may participate in the governance.[52] In sum, these commentators seem to share a belief that *IP rights and the institution of 'epistemic communities' of experts need to be governed* as well. Expertise, and inclusion of the process as against the exclusive process highlights that the institutional arrangements in IPR governance cannot ignore the fact that some IP institutions are better at collecting information, and this capacity of an institution to gather information may define the competence of the institution. This aspect of capacity for information collection should be a factor in deciding which governance institution should be given authority to decide.

Using these lines of argument, the governance perspective allows exploration of IP institutions at a peer position in terms of governing IP rights – the legislature, the judiciary the administration and the market – and their interactions. Introduction of changes in one of these institutions through IP system reform would likely affect the operations of the other institutions.[53] For example, introduction of a change in the collective management of copyright or resale rights in Chinese copyright law would need to consider the copyright licensing market and the art market in China.[54]

---

[51]   Scott Burris, Peter Drahos and Clifford Shearing, 'Nodal Governance' (2005) 30 Australian Journal of Legal Philosophy 30.

[52]   N. Rose and P. Miller, 'Political Power Beyond the State: Problematics of Government' (1992) British Journal of Sociology 173–205, 175.

[53]   Neil K. Komesar, *Imperfect Alternatives: Choosing Institutions in Law, Economics, and Public Policy* (University of Chicago Press 1994).

[54]   See Merges (*supra*, n 50); Nari Lee and Yang Li, 'Collective rights management in China and Europe: between market and authority', Chapter 12 in this

Similarly, judicial reform also needs to consider the dynamic between the administration and the courts and to what extent deference may be given to administrative decision making.[55] In principle, a specialized court with a centralized jurisdiction to hear IP disputes may seem an efficient instance of IP governance, by channelling complex cases to expert or specialist judges. The Chinese example of the new special IP court may be a case where this is indeed called for.[56] In contrast, in Europe, such courts as the unified patent court seem to raise a concern as to governance of IPR in Europe.[57]

A more important change to be noted in the context of China and the governance thesis is the observation that governance occurs not only occur through political process, but also through exercise of private rights. The very fact that IP rights govern resources empowers private entities to participate in the process of governance. As IP governs use of resources, not only the institutions that have traditionally been considered a part of the political system (legislative, judicial and administrative), but also the *market* function as governing institutions. IPR are used as instances of governmentality allowing regulation through individuals and entrepreneurs. As noted by Montgomery, 'IP law represents the point of contact between mechanisms of domination – the coercive power of formal law, and techniques of the self: self regulation'.[58] National IP strategies are further instances where such contacts are further built upon the accepted rationalities and technology of governance through IP law and used as means to manage entrepreneurial activities.[59]

---

volume; Lin Zhou and Rosa Maria Ballardini, 'Art law and resale rights in Europe and China', Chapter 7 in this volume.

[55] See for example, Rai (*supra*, n 50).

[56] See Mingde Li, 'Special intellectual property courts in China', Chapter 16 in this volume.

[57] Regulation (EU) 1257/2012 (2012) Implementing enhanced cooperation in the area of the creation of unitary patent protection, published OJEU L361/1-8; Regulation (EU) 1260/2012, Implementing enhanced cooperation in the area of the creation of unitary patent protection with regard to the application translation arrangement, published OJEU L361/89-92; Agreement on a Unified Patent Court, Document no. 16351/12 (11 January 2013). See also a commentary on the background of the agreement, H. Ullrich, 'Harmonizing Patent Law: The Untamable Union Patent' in M.-C. Janssens and G. Van Overwalle (eds), *Harmonisation of European IP Law: From European Rules To Belgian Law And Practice* (Bruylant 2012) 243–294.

[58] Montgomery (*supra*, n 38) at 13.

[59] See Zhang (*supra*, n 3).

4. CONCLUDING REMARKS

As explored in the above, developments in IP law in China include the process of transplant rejection or modification but also the emergence of new norms out of local necessity. As other chapters in this volume show, in some areas of Chinese IP law reforms, external pressures still seem to be heavily present and visible. In other areas, however, the influences for normative changes are muted, or the initiatives for change seem to be based on indigenous local demand.[60] The observation shows that China simultaneously takes the role of being an IP norm taker (or a recipient of legal transplants) as well as a norm maker.[61]

Recent IP law reform in China shows that China increasingly takes the role of 'norm maker' to govern local actors employing deliberate techniques and strategies to make inventors and creators 'governable' as exemplified by the national IP strategy,[62] and utilizes concrete performance measurement[63] in selected areas. At the same time, it is still visibly taking a passive role of 'norm taker' where some legislative experimentations seem to be ongoing.[64]

The governance perspective may explain why IP law norm and practice development in China is now based on a mix of local as well as foreign norms and systems. Indeed it allows us to make a comparison between how the two systems of laws function rather than looking into the origin of the IP law for the sake of creating doctrines and conceptual genealogy. At the same time, when norms and systems become more indigenous, similar problems of origin that we see in Europe may be experienced later in China as well. As more decisions are channelled to the market and self-regulation outside states, through private IP rights, the concerns

---

[60]   See Mingde Li, 'Intellectual property law revision in China: transplantation and transformation,' Chapter 4 in this volume. See also Yuying Guan, 'Orphan works in China and Europe', Chapter 6 in this volume.

[61]   See Niklas Bruun and Liguo Zhang, 'Legal transplant of intellectual property rights in China: norm taker or norm maker?', Chapter 3 in this volume.

[62]   Zhang (*supra*, n 3).

[63]   See, for example, Jiachun Wen, Yongtao Zhou and Xuezhong Zhu, 'Research on Patent Fees Subsided by Local Government in China' (2008) International Conference on Information Management, Innovation Management and Industrial Engineering (ICIII2008) Vol. 3, 269–274; Xibao Li, 'Behind the Recent Surge of Chinese Patenting: An Institutional View' (2012) 41(1) Research Policy 236–249. Compare, Brad Sherman, 'Governing Science-Patents and Public-Sector Research in the United Kingdom' (1995) 26(1) IIC-International Review of Industrial Property and Copyright Law 15–40.

[64]   See for example, Lin and Ballardini (*supra*, n 54).

for informational nodes as well as coordination may become a problem. Some decision making channels that role simply to the market and makes the market take the coordinator's role. The market may take the role of resource governor but the market-based decision-making process may be too opaque and amorphous. Governance perspectives allow us to explore not only the genealogy of norms, but also how further norms and practice evolve, and thus provide a useful analytical tool to explore what happens after the initial transplant in terms of innovation and creativity. As the transplanted system in China matures, this may be precisely what is needed for a comparative law research project.

2. The transplant and transformation of intellectual property laws in China

Peter K. Yu*

1. INTRODUCTION

The history of intellectual property laws in China is a history of legal transplants. From the introduction of intellectual property laws during the late Qing dynasty and the Republican era to the recent laws and amendments adopted by the People's Republic, legal transplant was the primary means by which the modern Chinese intellectual property regime was established.[1] It is indeed no surprise that legal transplants were a key focus of William Alford's seminal work, *To Steal a Book Is an Elegant Offense*.[2] Peter Feng also used the term 'second coming' to describe the introduction of intellectual property laws in China in the 1980s and the early 1990s.[3]

This chapter begins with a brief history of the transplant of intellectual property laws in China. It then examines the drawbacks and benefits of legal transplants. The chapter further discusses four key questions that policymakers should consider when transplanting laws from abroad. The answers to these questions, in turn, may result in not only transplant, but

* This chapter draws on research from the author's earlier works in the *Intellectual Property Journal*, the *University of Louisville Law Review* and *The WIPO Journal*. The author is grateful to La'Cee Groetken and Brooke Yang for excellent research and editorial assistance.

[1] Peter K. Yu, 'Building the Ladder: Three Decades of Development of the Chinese Patent System' (2013) 5 WIPO J 1 ('Building the Ladder'); Peter K. Yu, 'Intellectual Property, Economic Development, and the China Puzzle' in Daniel J. Gervais (ed.), *Intellectual Property, Trade and Development: Strategies to Optimize Economic Development in a TRIPS Plus Era* (1st edn, Oxford University Press 2007) 185–8 ('China Puzzle').

[2] William P. Alford, *To Steal a Book Is an Elegant Offense: Intellectual Property Law in Chinese Civilization* (Stanford University Press 1995) 30–55.

[3] Peter Feng, *Intellectual Property in China* (2nd edn, Sweet & Maxwell Asia 2003) 3.

also transformation – or what Pitman Potter has referred to as 'selective adaptation'.[4] Although this chapter and the larger volume focus on China, the discussion here is likely to be relevant to other jurisdictions.

2.   A BRIEF HISTORY OF LEGAL TRANSPLANTS IN CHINA

For a country with more than 4,000 years of history and a large number of inventions, including the compass, gunpowder, papermaking and wood-block printing,[5] locating the origin of a system that incentivizes invention and innovation is always a challenge. If the global and British patent systems owe their origin to the Venetian Republic in the 15th century and the Statute of Monopolies of 1624, respectively, one can trace the development of Chinese patent rights to 'over 2,000 years ago when the emperors granted individual merchants the right to smelt iron, distill salt, and mint coin'.[6]

Since then, other emperors or territorial rulers had experimented with the introduction of patents on Chinese soil in various historical periods. For example, commentators recounted the push for the patent system during the Taiping Rebellion (1850–1864).[7] A few decades later, a late Qing emperor also attempted to introduce the Regulations to Promote Industrial Technology in 1898, during the famous 'Hundred Days Reform' towards the end of imperial rule.[8] As the name of the reform movement suggests, this ill-fated movement failed in only a few short months, causing its leaders to either be executed or retreat in exile.

In addition to patents, other forms of intellectual property rights were found in imperial China. For example, dynastic codes not only 'restricted

---

[4]   Pitman B. Potter, 'China and the International Legal System: Challenges of Participation' in Donald C. Clarke (ed.), *China's Legal System: New Developments, New Challenges* (Cambridge University Press 2008) 147–8.

[5]   On Chinese scientific developments, see Benjamin A. Elman, *On Their Own Terms: Science in China, 1550–1900* (Harvard University Press 2005); Joseph Needham, *Science and Civilisation in China* (Cambridge University Press 1956–2004), Vols 1–7; Robert Temple, *The Genius of China: 3,000 Years of Science, Discovery, and Invention* (3rd edn, Andre Deutsch 2007).

[6]   Flora Wang, 'An Overview of the Development of the Chinese Patent System' in Mark A. Cohen, A. Elizabeth Bang and Stephanie J. Mitchell (eds), *Chinese Intellectual Property Law and Practice* (Kluwer Law International 1999) 3.

[7]   Ibid.

[8]   Zheng Chengsi with Michael D. Pendleton, *Chinese Intellectual Property and Technology Transfer Law* (Sweet & Maxwell 1987) 52.

the use of certain symbols associated with either the imperial family . . . or officialdom', but also 'barred the imitation of marks used by the ceramists of Jingdezhen and others making goods for exclusive imperial use'.[9] In addition, guild regulations, clan rules and local laws protected producers of tea, silk, cloth, paper and medicines by registering their brand names and symbols.[10] Tight family control and screening of employees were also used to protect the confidentiality of vital manufacturing processes, which today will certainly implicate trade secret laws.[11]

At the turn of the 20th century, China finally introduced its first set of modern intellectual property laws, after much pressure from colonial powers and its foreign trading partners. In 1903, the United States used its military and economic strengths to induce China to sign the Treaty between the United States and China for the Extension of the Commercial Relations between Them. Building upon the newly adopted Paris Convention for the Protection of Industrial Property, to which the United States acceded in 1887, this treaty granted copyright, patent and trademark protection to Americans in return for reciprocal protection to the Chinese.[12]

Pursuant to this turn-of-the-century commercial treaty, China introduced a substantive copyright law in 1910, the year before the fall of the Qing dynasty. Although the patent law was adopted two years later, following the end of imperial rule, the trademark law did not come into existence until 1923, more than a decade after the introduction of both copyright and patent laws. The implementation of these laws was especially difficult, because China remained a semi-colony at that time, and many of these laws were introduced against the wishes of Chinese nationals. As Professor Feng recounted, substantive intellectual property protection arrived 'with such inventions and novel ideas as the gunboat, opium, "most favoured nation" trading status and extraterritoriality'.[13]

During the Republican era, intellectual property rights managed to receive some legislative attention. Shortly after the Nationalist Party (*Kuomintang*) took power in 1928, China introduced a new copyright law, affording protection to books, music, photographs, designs, sculptures and other technical, literary and artistic works.[14] The country also issued a new trademark law and promulgated the Measures to Encourage

---

[9]   Alford (*supra*, n 2) 15.
[10]   Ibid 16.
[11]   Ibid.
[12]   Ibid 37–8.
[13]   Feng (*supra*, n 3) 3.
[14]   Alford (*supra*, n 2) 50.

Industrial Arts, thereby affording protection to indigenous inventions.[15] Notwithstanding these well-intentioned efforts, 'the decades of incessant wars, famines and revolutions scarcely lent [intellectual property rights] a chance to take root in China'.[16] The challenge of protecting and enforcing these rights was exacerbated by the fact that intellectual property laws were transplanted from abroad with scant alteration; the laws also wrongly presumed the existence in China of a certain legal structure and legal consciousness.[17]

In 1949, the Chinese Communist Party established the People's Republic of China. A year later, China introduced the Provisional Regulations Governing Invention and Patent Rights, which covered both inventors' certificates (*fāmíng zhèngshū*) and patents.[18] The country also adopted the Provisional Regulations on Trademark Registration, along with the procedures for dealing with trademarks registered with the previous government.[19] As to copyright law developments, the new Communist government did not offer much protection to authors, other than through occasional regulations concerning *gǎofèi* (basic payment for writings and manuscripts) and contracts between authors and state organs.[20] Regardless of the scope of these protections, retrenchment began a few years later, and virtually all intellectual property regulations were abolished, modified or replaced with transplants from the Soviet Union.[21]

With the launch of the Cultural Revolution in the mid-1960s, formal law and administrative bureaucracy were denounced, and scientists, engineers and members of the intelligentsia were discredited, demoted or dismissed from their positions. In such a politico-juridical environment, there was understandably neither protection nor respect for any form of intellectual property right. As a comrade would question during the Cultural Revolution: 'Is it necessary for a steel worker to put his name on a steel ingot that he produces in the course of his duty? If not, why should

---

[15] Ibid 51–2; Zheng with Pendleton (*supra*, n 8) 52.

[16] Feng (*supra*, n 3) 3.

[17] Alford (*supra*, n 2) 53.

[18] On these regulations and other patent prototypes, see Barden N. Gale, 'The Concept of Intellectual Property in the People's Republic of China: Inventors and Inventions' (1978) 74 China Q 334; Hsia Tao-tai and Kathryn A. Haun, 'Laws of the People's Republic of China on Industrial and Intellectual Property' (1973) 38 L and Contemporary Problems 274, 275–84.

[19] Alford (*supra*, n 2) 59.

[20] Ibid.

[21] Ibid 59–63; Yu, 'Building the Ladder' (*supra*, n 1) 5.

a member of the intelligentsia enjoy the privilege of putting his name on what he produces?'[22]

Given these sentiments, it is therefore no surprise that the modern Chinese intellectual property system was not established until after China re-opened its market to foreign trade in the late 1970s. Putting science and technology in command, as opposed to Mao Zedong's 'politics in command', Chinese leaders, led by Deng Xiaoping, vigorously pushed for the Four Modernizations to develop China's world-class strengths in agriculture, industry, science and technology, and national defence.[23] The establishment of a modern intellectual property system was considered an essential policy tool to help China play economic and technological catch-up.

In July 1979, China and the United States signed the Agreement on Trade Relations between the United States of America and the People's Republic of China. Among other things, the agreement called for reciprocal protection of copyrights, patents and trademarks owned by the nationals of the other party. From an international law standpoint, the agreement was interesting, because it caused China to 'assume[] an international legal obligation for intellectual property rights protection [even] before it had established a domestic intellectual property protection system'.[24] Moreover, the development of the new system was fraught with challenges and ideological debates. Although China quickly began drafting the Patent Law – to both promote economic development and bring in foreign investment – the debate over the law was so intense and controversial that the law was not adopted until 1984, two years after the introduction of the Trademark Law.[25]

Shortly after the adoption of these two laws, the United States and other foreign countries began to exert greater pressure on China to undertake further reform of its intellectual property system. While US firms showed patience shortly after China's re-opening, their patience soon dissipated. As Warren Maruyama, the former general counsel of the US Trade Representative (USTR), recounted: 'At a 1985 meeting to the U.S.–China Joint Committee on Commerce and Trade (JCCT), the U.S. for the first time expressed concerns about weak Chinese IPR [intellectual property

---

[22]   Alford (*supra*, n 2) 65.
[23]   Peter K. Yu, 'Piracy, Prejudice, and Perspectives: An Attempt to Use Shakespeare to Reconfigure the U.S.–China Intellectual Property Debate' (2001) 19 Boston U Intl L J 1, 27.
[24]   Xue Hong and Zheng Chengsi, *Software Protection in China: A Complete Guide* (Sweet & Maxwell Asia 1999) 5.
[25]   Yu, 'Building the Ladder' (*supra*, n 1) 6.

rights] standards. In 1987, the U.S. put IPR protection on the agenda for U.S.–China market access talks.'[26]

At that time, the United States' main intellectual property concern was copyrights, not patents. Although China had already adopted new trademark and patent laws a few years before, it had yet to introduce a new copyright law. Part of the delay was caused by the need for censorship and control of information flows in China. The lack of copyright protection was particularly problematic, as a lack of both copyright protection and market access had made it difficult for the politically powerful US movie, music and software industries to protect their content.

From the mid-1980s, the entertainment industries actively lobbied the USTR to put more pressure on China to reform its intellectual property system. In the late 1980s and early 1990s, the US government repeatedly threatened China with a series of economic sanctions, trade wars, non-renewal of most-favoured-nation status and opposition to China's entry into the World Trade Organization (WTO).[27] Such threats eventually led to the signing of the memorandum of understanding in 1989. This memorandum was seldom mentioned because it was negotiated amidst student protests in Tiananmen Square, but it paved the way for the eventual adoption of the Copyright Law in 1990 and a separate set of computer software regulations the year after.[28]

In January 1992, China and the United States reached another memorandum of understanding, which became the 'first full bilateral IPR agreement' between the two countries.[29] In retrospect, this second memorandum has been rather effective in revamping the Chinese intellectual property system. Pursuant to this memorandum, China acceded to the Berne Convention for the Protection of Literary and Artistic Works and ratified the Geneva Convention for the Protection of Producers of Phonograms against Unauthorized Duplication of Their Phonograms. In 1993, China also amended the Patent Law while adopting the Law against Unfair Competition, which remains in force today.

---

[26] Warren H. Maruyama, 'U.S.–China IPR Negotiations: Trade, Intellectual Property, and the Rule of Law in a Global Economy' in Cohen, Bang and Mitchell (*supra*, n 6) 186.
[27] Peter K. Yu, 'From Pirates to Partners: Protecting Intellectual Property in China in the Twenty-first Century' (2000) 50 American U L Rev 131, 140–51.
[28] This memorandum was reprinted in 'PRC Agrees to Push for Copyright Law that Will Protect Computer Software', *World Intellectual Property Report* (July 1989) 151.
[29] Joseph A. Massey, 'The Emperor Is Far Away: China's Enforcement of Intellectual Property Rights Protection, 1986–2006' (2006) 7 Chicago J Intl L 231, 235.

In 2000, China again amended its intellectual property laws. A major impetus behind these 'millennium amendments' was China's accession to the WTO.[30] China had been petitioning for membership since the founding of this international trading body. After exhaustive negotiations for more than 15 years, China finally joined the WTO on 11 December 2001. Among all the three main branches of intellectual property law, the Patent Law was the first to be revised, with amendments entering into force on 1 July 2001. Amendments to the Copyright Law took effect four months later, while the amendments to the Trademark Law did not come into existence until 10 days before the WTO accession.[31]

For most observers, these 'millennium amendments' were adopted to conform the Chinese intellectual property system to WTO standards. The need for such conformity was understandable considering China's willingness to make significant sacrifices to join the WTO. As Samuel Kim put it, China was eager 'to gain WTO entry at almost any price'.[32] Indeed, many Chinese leaders and members of the public considered the WTO membership not only as an economic issue, but also as an issue affecting national pride. In their view, the accession to the WTO concerned China's rightful place in the world after experiencing 'a century of humiliation', during which foreign imperial powers literally carved the country up into a semi-colony.

Notwithstanding the importance of conforming to WTO standards, many provisions in these amendments were introduced primarily to respond to the country's rapidly changing local conditions (*guóqíng*).[33] Being as much about customization as they were about standardization, these amendments reflected the Chinese leaders' changing attitude towards the rule of law, the emergence of private property rights and local stakeholders, the increasing concerns about ambiguities over relationships in state-owned enterprises and the government's active push for modernization.[34]

From the mid-2000s, the Chinese government began paying greater attention to the development of an innovation- and knowledge-based economy. Such a focus was greatly needed to facilitate continued economic

---

[30]   Peter K. Yu, 'From Pirates to Partners (Episode II): Protecting Intellectual Property in Post-WTO China' (2006) 55 American U L Rev 901, 906–23.

[31]   Ibid 909–10.

[32]   Samuel S. Kim, 'China in World Politics' in Barry Buzan and Rosemary Foot (eds), *Does China Matter? A Reassessment: Essays in Memory of Gerald Segal* (Routledge 2004) 49.

[33]   Yu (*supra*, n 30) 914–23.

[34]   Ibid 908.

growth in areas that could no longer rely on either agriculture or manufacturing. By changing the focus of its development strategy, China also sought to avoid what policymakers and commentators have described as the 'middle-income trap' – the proverbial state of development at which a country is stuck after it has attained a certain level of wealth, but has yet to catch up with its more developed counterparts.[35]

In addition, a stronger focus on intellectual property developments fits within the incremental approach that Chinese leaders have carefully implemented over the years, which some commentators have referred to as 'groping for stones to cross the river' (*mōzhe shítóu guòhé*). In the National Long-term Scientific and Technological Development Program released in February 2006, the State Council formally declared its commitment to turn China into an innovation-based economy within 15 years.[36] Since then, top Chinese leaders have increasingly recognized the economic and strategic significance of a well-functioning intellectual property system.[37]

In June 2008, the State Council released the Outline of the National Intellectual Property Strategy. This pioneering strategy provided a comprehensive plan to improve the protection and management of intellectual property rights while emphasizing the need for active development of independent or self-controlled intellectual property (*zìzhǔ zhīshì chǎnquán*). A few months later, China adopted the Third Amendment to the Patent Law, which completely revamped the Chinese patent system for the third time.

Unlike its predecessors, the 2008 amendment was not about compliance with external norms, such as those established through the WTO or other multilateral agreements. Instead, China, for the first time, adjusted

---

[35]   Peter K. Yu, 'The Middle Intellectual Property Powers' in Randall Peerenboom and Tom Ginsburg (eds), *Law and Development in Middle-Income Countries: Avoiding the Middle-Income Trap* (Cambridge University Press 2014) 105.

[36]   Cao Cong, Richard P. Suttmeier and Denis Fred Simon, 'China's 15-Year Science and Technology Plan' (December 2006) *Physics Today* 38–43; Feng Xiaoqing, 'The Interaction between Enhancing the Capacity for Independent Innovation and Patent Protection: A Perspective on the Third Amendment to the Patent Law of the P.R. China' (2008) 9 Pittsburgh J Technology L and Policy 1 [7]; Mark Liang, 'Chinese Patent Quality: Running the Numbers and Possible Remedies' (2012) 11 John Marshall Rev Intellectual Property L 478, 483–4.

[37]   State Intellectual Property Office, 'China's Intellectual Property Protection in 2008' <http://english.sipo.gov.cn/laws/whitepapers/200904/t20090427_457167. html> accessed 30 March 2015; Wu Handong, 'One Hundred Years of Progress: The Development of the Intellectual Property System in China' (2009) 1 WIPO J 117, 120.

its patent standards based on its own needs. As Guo He observed: 'The impetus for the early amendments came from outside, whilst the need for the third amendment [to the Patent Law] originated from within China, that is to say, the majority of the third amendment was to meet the needs of the development of the domestic economy and technology originating in China.'[38]

In August 2013, China adopted the Third Amendment to the Trademark Law, which entered into effect the following year. As of this writing, China is still in the process of completing its amendment to the Copyright Law. Although three drafts have already been publicly released and commented upon, it remains to be seen when this amendment will be finally adopted.

Notwithstanding this recent set of amendments or proposed amendments, the levels of protection and enforcement of intellectual property rights in China have yet to completely satisfy foreign rights holders and their supportive governments. Virtually every year, the USTR puts China on its Watch List or Priority Watch List.[39] The piracy and counterfeiting problems in China also remain the target of new international intellectual property enforcement initiatives, such as the Anti-Counterfeiting Trade Agreement and the intellectual property chapter in the Trans-Pacific Partnership Agreement.

In 2011, the International Trade Commission released a highly critical report estimating that 'firms in the U.S. [intellectual property]-intensive economy that conducted business in China in 2009 reported losses of approximately $48.2 billion in sales, royalties, or license fees due to IPR infringement in China'.[40] In the past few years, the USTR has also begun paying greater attention to the inadequate protection of trade secrets and other confidential business, technical and scientific information in China.[41]

Given the continuously high volume of intellectual property-related losses suffered by foreign industries and the USTR's increasing attention on intellectual property developments outside the traditional areas of

---

[38]   Guo He, 'Patents' in Rohan Kariyawasam (ed.), *Chinese Intellectual Property and Technology Laws* (Edward Elgar Publishing 2011) 28.
[39]   The notable exception was during the honeymoon period following China's accession to the WTO in December 2001. In April 2005, the USTR elevated China back to the Priority Watch List.
[40]   US International Trade Commission, *China: Effects of Intellectual Property Infringement and Indigenous Innovation Policies on the U.S. Economy* (US International Trade Commission 2011) xiv.
[41]   Office of the US Trade Representative, *2014 Special 301 Report* (Office of the US Trade Representative 2014) 32–3.

copyrights, patents and trademarks, it remains to be seen whether US and other foreign intellectual property laws will continue to be transplanted to China. Nevertheless, as we ponder the future development of the Chinese intellectual property system, we cannot lose sight of the rapid change of the international economic and intellectual property landscapes.

Moreover, the recent years have seen the rise of the BRICS countries (Brazil, Russia, India, China and South Africa), along with greater cohesion within the African Group, a negotiation bloc filled with China's geopolitical allies. Although China was not as active as Brazil and India in the international arena before joining the WTO in 2001 and has maintained a rather low profile in the first few years following its accession, the country has now become much more assertive in the international intellectual property arena. As I have noted in earlier works, China is no longer content to be only a passive 'taker' of international intellectual property norms; it has also slowly assumed the additional roles of both a 'shaker' and a 'maker' of these norms.[42] Given the country's growing efforts in shaking and making international intellectual property norms, one has to wonder what these efforts will portend for the future transplant of intellectual property laws to China.

3. DRAWBACKS OF LEGAL TRANSPLANTS

Legal transplants are very common in the intellectual property arena. From the Berne Convention to the Agreement on Trade-Related Aspects of Intellectual Property Rights (TRIPS Agreement) to the 1996 Internet Treaties of the World Intellectual Property Organization (WIPO), international intellectual property agreements are filled with standards that are transplanted from major intellectual property-exporting countries.[43] Although developing countries fought hard to retain their sovereignty, autonomy and limited policy space, developed countries pushed

---

[42]   Peter K. Yu, 'The First Decade of TRIPS in China' in Zeng Ka and Liang Wei (eds), *China and Global Trade Governance: China's First Decade in the World Trade Organization* (Routledge 2013); Peter K. Yu, 'The Middle Kingdom and the Intellectual Property World' (2011) 13 Oregon Rev Intl L 209 ('Middle Kingdom'). Henry Gao made a similar observation in Henry Gao, 'China's Ascent in Global Trade Governance: From Rule Taker to Rule Shaker and, Maybe Rule Maker?' in Carolyn Deere-Birkbeck (ed.), *Making Global Trade Governance Work for Development: Perspectives and Priorities from Developing Countries* (Cambridge University Press 2011).

[43]   Peter K. Yu, 'The International Enclosure Movement' (2007) 82 Indiana L J 827, 855–72.

aggressively for the much higher standards of protection and enforcement found in their own countries. In the end, the weaker and poorer countries are often forced to transplant laws from abroad regardless of whether those laws match their local needs, interests, conditions or priorities.

In view of these inequitable conditions, intellectual property commentators have always been wary about legal transplants. As I have noted in earlier works, hastily transplanted laws could harm developing countries in at least four different ways. First, as we have learned from the failed 'law and development' movement in the 1960s and early 1970s, legal transplants tend to be insensitive to the local environment.[44] Because of the differences in economic conditions, imitative or innovative capacity, and research and development productivities, an innovative model that works well in one country does not always suit the needs and interests of another.[45] Unquestioned adoption of foreign intellectual property laws therefore may not only fail to result in greater innovative efforts, industrial progress and technology transfer, but may also drain away the resources needed for dealing with the socio-economic and public health problems created by the new legislation.

Worse still, such adoption would exacerbate the dire economic plight of many developing countries, as the new laws would enable foreign rights holders to crush local industries through threats, or even the actual use, of litigation.[46] Even if the new laws were beneficial in the long run, many of these countries might not have the wealth, infrastructure and technological base to take advantage of the opportunities created by the system in the short run.[47] For countries with urgent and desperate public policy needs and a population dying due to a lack of access to essential medicines, the realization of the hope for a brighter long-term future seems far away, if not unrealistic. If protection is strengthened beyond the point of appropriate balance, the present population undoubtedly would greatly suffer.

Second, although promoting uniform rules may be beneficial, greater harmonization of legal standards could take away the valuable

---

[44]   James A. Gardner, *Legal Imperialism: American Lawyers and Foreign Aid in Latin America* (University of Wisconsin Press 1980).

[45]   Claudio R. Frischtak, 'Harmonization Versus Differentiation in Intellectual Property Rights Regimes' in Mitchel B. Wallerstein, Mary Ellen Mogee and Roberta A. Schoen (eds), *Global Dimensions of Intellectual Property Rights in Science and Technology* (National Academy Press 1993) 97; Yu (*supra*, n 43) 889.

[46]   Ellen 't Hoen, 'TRIPS, Pharmaceutical Patents, and Access to Essential Medicines: A Long Way from Seattle to Doha' (2002) 3 Chicago J Intl L 27, 30–31.

[47]   Keith E. Maskus, *Intellectual Property Rights in the Global Economy* (Institute for International Economics 2000) 237.

opportunities for experimentation with new regulatory and economic policies.[48] The creation of diversified rules could also facilitate competition among jurisdictions, thereby rendering the lawmaking process more accountable to the local populations by allowing them to decide for themselves what rules and systems they want to adopt.[49] In the digital age, when laws are introduced quickly and often without convincing empirical evidence, greater experimentation and competition are indeed badly needed.[50]

Third, legal transplants – especially those involving controversial laws and policies – could bring to the recipient countries problems from the source countries. These tag-along problems are particularly troubling for developing countries because they have very limited expertise in assessing the potential problems and unintended consequences caused by the ill-advised transplants. Even worse, many of these countries do not have the resources needed to put in place mechanisms that will help them correct the system should the transplants upset its balance.[51] Because reforms based on foreign models always incur political costs for those pushing for reforms, policymakers may also have limited political capital to introduce additional reform after their initial reforms have failed.[52] As Otto Kahn-Freund reminded us, transplanted laws often bring with them foreign values. They may therefore upset long-standing traditions in the recipient countries while at the same time undermining institutions that are 'closely linked with the structure and organization of political power and social power in their own environment'.[53]

Finally, even when laws are transplanted verbatim, different outcomes may result. Laws tend to be applied or interpreted by reference to domestic market conditions, social contexts and local practices.[54] Factual differences in social practices, competitive conditions or consumer attitudes could also

---

[48]   John F. Duffy, 'Harmony and Diversity in Global Patent Law' (2002) 17 Berkeley Technology L J 685, 707–8.

[49]   Ibid 706–7.

[50]   Peter K. Yu, 'Anticircumvention and Anti-anticircumvention' (2006) 84 Denver U L Rev 13, 40–58.

[51]   Commission on Intellectual Property Rights, *Integrating Intellectual Property Rights and Development Policy: Report of the Commission on Intellectual Property Rights* (Commission on Intellectual Property Rights 2002) 4; Yu (*supra*, n 43) 890.

[52]   Yu (*supra*, n 43) 890.

[53]   O. Kahn-Freund, 'On Uses and Misuses of Comparative Law' (1974) 37 MLR 1, 24.

[54]   Graeme B. Dinwoodie, 'International Intellectual Property Litigation: A Vehicle for Resurgent Comparativist Thought' (2001) 49 American J Comparative

affect legal conclusions, especially those resting on factual findings.[55] As noted by Alan Watson, father of the study of legal transplants:

> [A] voluntary reception or transplant almost always – always in the case of a major transplant – involves a change in the law, which can be due to any number of factors, such as climate, economic conditions, religious outlook . . . or even chance largely unconnected either with particular factors operating within the society as a whole or with the general historical trend.[56]

Thus, the unquestioned transplant of foreign laws is unlikely to result in the sustained development of intellectual property protection in a country lacking in a tradition or a legal culture of such protection. In fact, insensitive and ineffective legal transplants provided some of the key reasons why efforts to introduce intellectual property laws failed spectacularly in the late Qing dynasty and the Republican era.[57] It is indeed no surprise that Montesquieu warned us many centuries ago about the danger of overlooking environmental factors in developing laws. As he wrote in *The Spirit of Laws*:

> [T]he political and civil laws of each nation . . . should be in relation to the climate of each country, to the quality of its soil, to its situation and extent, to the principal occupation of the natives, whether husbandmen, huntsmen, or shepherds: they should have relation to the degree of liberty which the constitution will bear; to the religion of the inhabitants, to their inclinations, riches, numbers, commerce, manners, and customs. In fine, they have relations to each other, as also to their origin, to the intent of the legislator, and to the order of things on which they are established; in all of which different lights they ought to be considered.[58]

4.   BENEFITS OF LEGAL TRANSPLANTS

Notwithstanding their many shortcomings, legal transplants can offer at least four benefits, especially if they are carefully selected and appropriately customized. First, legal transplants allow countries, especially those with limited resources, to take a free ride on the legislative efforts of other,

---

L 429, 436; Paul Edward Geller, 'Legal Transplants in International Copyright: Some Problems of Method' (1994) 13 UCLA Pacific Basin L J 199, 207–9.

[55]   Dinwoodie (*supra*, n 54) 436–7.

[56]   Alan Watson, *Legal Transplants: An Approach to Comparative Law* (2nd edn, University of Georgia Press 1993) 97.

[57]   Alford (*supra*, n 2) 53.

[58]   Montesquieu, *The Spirit of Laws* bk. I, ch. 3.

usually more economically and technologically developed, countries. Efforts to prepare intellectual property laws and regulations can be difficult, time consuming and costly; they may require detailed research and analysis, sophisticated drafting skills and lengthy legislative deliberation.

To reduce the burden on developing countries, Article 67 of the TRIPS Agreement specifically requires developed countries to provide technical and financial cooperation, which includes 'assistance in the preparation of laws and regulations on the protection and enforcement of intellectual property rights as well as on the prevention of their abuse'. To be sure, technical assistance does not always help developing countries, especially when such assistance is narrowly conceived or when it ignores the divergent local conditions in the recipient countries.[59] Nevertheless, the challenge of selecting appropriate technical assistance is no more daunting than the challenge of finding the right model for legal transplant.

Second, legal transplants can provide standards that have served as time-tested solutions to similar problems, drawing on lessons learned from the experiences in the source countries – both positive and negative. As the Hong Kong government noted in one of its consultation papers on digital copyright reform:

> For each of the [consultation] issues, we have outlined the situations in other jurisdictions (such as the UK, the US, Singapore and Australia). We may draw reference from the experience of different jurisdictions when formulating a solution unique to Hong Kong. This could create a model that best suits Hong Kong's needs. On the other hand, we may formulate our solution based on an existing overseas model. The advantage of the latter approach is that our courts could make reference to the case law of that particular jurisdiction when deciding cases before them. This would result in more certainty and predictability in our law.[60]

Indeed, in a small jurisdiction that has limited case law development in the intellectual property area such as Hong Kong, the transplant of intellectual property laws and regulations, if appropriate, could be quite beneficial.

Third, legal transplants may help provide pre-emptive defences to countries that face repeated or intense pressure from their more powerful trading partners, not to mention the strong likelihood that the laws in these powerful countries will eventually become international standards

---

[59] Peter K. Yu, 'Enforcement, Enforcement, What Enforcement?' (2012) 52 IDEA 239, 277–9.

[60] Commerce, Industry and Technology Bureau (Hong Kong), *Copyright Protection in the Digital Environment* (Commerce, Industry and Technology Bureau 2006) v.

by virtue of the source countries' sheer economic and political might.[61] It is no coincidence that many developing countries have adopted US standards in part to avoid the continuous pressure from US intellectual property industries and their supportive governments. Even if external pressure does not come from the United States – for example, when it comes from the European Union instead – having US standards in place could help deflate the pressure by transforming a one-sided battle into a more even-handed global dispute.

Nevertheless, depending on the recipient countries' geopolitical power, it is not uncommon for weaker countries to be induced, or even coerced, into adopting standards from more than one powerful trading partner – for example, standards from both the European Union and the United States. When these standards conflict with each other, the recipient countries will not only be required to adopt standards that are insensitive to their local conditions, but will also be forced to juggle two sets of conflicting international obligations that are hard to honour. Thus, unless legal transplants are needed to deflate intense foreign pressure, countries are advised not to transplant inappropriate standards from powerful countries just for the sake of pre-empting the external pressure for legal transplant.

Finally, if a substantial portion of the international community has already adopted the transplanted laws, such transplants will promote benefits that are derived from greater harmonization. For example, they will make the business environment more predictable, thus reducing the transaction costs of conducting business across borders.[62] By creating the expectations that foreign nationals will be protected from arbitrary government actions, the transplants will also help signal the country's favourable investment climate to foreign firms.[63] In addition, the transplanted laws will result in the development of common rules that facilitate collaboration among trading partners while promoting economies of scale in the governance and administration of the affected rights.[64] By fostering uniformity and thereby reducing destructive protectionism, those laws will also promote free trade and stability in the international community as a whole.[65]

---

[61]   Peter K. Yu, 'Digital Copyright Reform and Legal Transplants in Hong Kong' (2010) 48 U Louisville L Rev 693, 755.

[62]   Peter K. Yu, 'Toward a Nonzero-Sum Approach to Resolving Global Intellectual Property Disputes: What We Can Learn from Mediators, Business Strategists, and International Relations Theorists' (2002) 70 U Cincinnati L Rev 569, 606–8.

[63]   Frischtak (*supra*, n 45) 99–100.

[64]   Duffy (*supra*, n 48) 699–701.

[65]   Ibid 702–3.

In sum, legal transplants have both benefits and drawbacks. Whether the transplanted laws will become effective and successful will depend on the process by which they are transplanted. Before the transplant, policymakers should identify what they seek to achieve through law reform. They should not just transplant laws for the sake of transplantation, pre-emption or even harmonization. Instead, they should evaluate local conditions and select a model that would best fit these specific conditions. They should further explore whether adaptations are needed to make the transplanted laws effective. Finally, after the laws' adoption, they should determine whether further adjustments are needed at the implementation stage to assimilate these laws to local conditions.

5. FOUR QUESTIONS POLICYMAKERS SHOULD ASK

Given the many benefits and drawbacks of legal transplants, if policymakers need to borrow laws from abroad, they need to think seriously about the five questions of when, why, what, where and how: When to borrow? Why to borrow? What to borrow? From where to borrow? And how to borrow? After all, like the transplant of plants or human organs, legal transplant is an elaborate process of evaluation, selection, adaptation and assimilation. It requires care, attention, sensitivity, evidence-based research and human, economic and technical resources.

To help policymakers think through some of the hard questions concerning legal transplants, this chapter advances four key questions that policymakers should consider when transplanting laws from abroad. Although these questions will be discussed and elaborated in the context of intellectual property reforms in China, the discussions are equally relevant to policymakers in other jurisdictions who are tasked with similar reforms.

5.1 What Future Do They Envision?

The first question policymakers need to ask is: What should China's future look like? If the intellectual property reforms in the country are to be effective, policymakers need to be clear about what they want.

As mentioned earlier, the State Council released the Outline of the National Intellectual Property Strategy in June 2008. Paragraph 7 specifically emphasized the need for active development of *zìzhǔ zhīshì chǎnquán*. Since the release of this Outline, US policymakers have translated the term as 'indigenous intellectual property', suggesting China's intention 'to encourage domestic or "indigenous" innovation at the cost of foreign innovation and technologies'.[66] Nevertheless, when the term is put in the right cultural, linguistic and historic contexts, it is more correctly translated and understood as 'independent intellectual property'. As I pointed out in an earlier article:

> [T]he term '*zizhu*' intellectual property certainly covers more than 'indigenous' or 'homegrown' intellectual property. Although the term 'independent intellectual property' does not provide a direct translation, it accurately reflects that '*zizhu*' intellectual property can be developed or acquired from abroad or involve China-based entities with minority foreign ownership. The key to identifying certain intellectual property as '*zizhu*' is whether such an asset is independently controlled by Chinese individuals, firms, or the government.[67]

Beyond *zìzhǔ zhīshì chǎnquán*, however, coming up with a vision of China's future becomes much more challenging. China is a large country with rapidly changing socio-economic conditions and vast disparities in economic and technological growth. The type of intellectual property standards that work well for major cities (such as Beijing, Shanghai and Guangzhou) may not work well for the countryside.[68] Likewise, standards that suit the prosperous coastal areas may be inappropriate for the poor rural west.

Consider, for example, the 2013 figures on invention patents provided by the State Intellectual Property Office in China. Jiangsu, Guangdong and Shandong provinces – the three provinces with the largest volumes of applications – had a total of 141,259, 68,990 and 67,642, respectively.[69] By contrast, Yunnan, Jiangxi and Gansu provinces had a total of only 3,961, 3,931 and 3,735, respectively. The latter figures were about 1/20 of the figure in Guangdong or Shandong province and 1/40 of the figure in Jiangsu province. If one includes Xinjiang, Inner Mongolia, Ningxia, Hainan, Qinghai and Tibet provinces in the latter group, the contrast between the statistics in the two groups becomes even sharper.

From a standpoint of envisioning China's future, having highly uneven sub-national developments could create major challenges for intellectual

---

[66]   Office of the US Trade Representative, *2010 National Trade Estimate Report on Foreign Trade Barriers* (Office of the US Trade Representative 2010) 69.

[67]   Peter K. Yu, 'Five Oft-repeated Questions about China's Recent Rise as a Patent Power' (2013) Cardozo L Rev De Novo 78, 94–5.

[68]   Yu, 'China Puzzle' (*supra*, n 1) 203.

[69]   State Intellectual Property Office, 'Table 2 Distribution of Applications for Inventions Received from Home 2013' <http://english.sipo.gov.cn/statistics/2013/12/201402/t20140217_905142.html> accessed 3 December 2014.

property policymakers. If they seek to tailor protection to the divergent economic and technological conditions in different regions, they likely will have to come up with a 'schizophrenic' nationwide intellectual property policy.[70] Under such a policy, protection will have to be tighter in the fast-growing and technologically proficient regions, but weaker in their less-developed counterparts. If policymakers do not seek to tailor protection to these divergent conditions, and instead accept uniform nationwide standards, they will have to develop a system that is either too strong or too weak for some regions. Or worse, they will have to adopt a system that is unsuitable for all regions – for example, when the system grants only mid-level protection that would be too low for the fast-growing regions but too high for the less-developed regions.

5.2   What Other Opportunities Are Available?

The next question concerns the potential opportunities that arise as a result of intellectual property reforms. Although legal transplant is a process wherein laws migrate from one country to another, it is important not to ignore the important opportunities the transplant process provides for improvements, experiments and new developments.

As Professor Watson reminded us, 'a time of transplant is often a moment when reforms can be introduced'.[71] Likewise, Jeremy Bentham observed more than two centuries ago, '[t]hat a system might be devised, which, while it would be better for Bengal, would also be better even for England'.[72] Because legal transplants provide an opportunity to reform laws and make them more sophisticated, they also 'give[] the recipient society a fine opportunity to become a donor in its turn'.[73]

Taking advantage of the opportunities legal transplants provide is especially important to China. Although the country, along with Brazil and India, remains a key leader of the developing world, its interests sometimes diverge from those of its developing country partners. As I noted in a recent book chapter, China is a 'middle intellectual property power'; it possesses a large and fast-growing aggregate economy and high technological and innovative capabilities.[74] As a result, it obtains benefits

---

[70]   Peter K. Yu, 'International Enclosure, the Regime Complex, and Intellectual Property Schizophrenia' (2007) Michigan State L Rev 1, 25–6.

[71]   Watson (*supra*, n 56) 35.

[72]   Jeremy Bentham, 'Of the Influence of Time and Place in Matters of Legislation' in *The Works of Jeremy Bentham* (Adamant Media 2005) (1843) 185.

[73]   Watson (*supra*, n 56) 99.

[74]   Yu (*supra*, n 35).

from the existing international intellectual property regime even though it continues to question the appropriateness of the regime's high protection and enforcement standards.

Notwithstanding these potential benefits, China still aligns more closely with the developing world than with the developed world, due in large part to the country's continuous struggle with internal problems, uneven regional, sectoral and technological developments, limited resources on a per capita basis, and other reasons unrelated to intellectual property protection and enforcement (such as the retention of leadership in the developing world).[75] In fact, China remains reluctant to increase intellectual property protection for pharmaceuticals, chemicals, fertilizers, seeds and foodstuffs, notwithstanding its already fast-growing industries in entertainment, software, semiconductors and selected areas of biotechnology.[76]

Thus far, it remains unclear what international intellectual property system China will ultimately prefer. As I observed in the inaugural issue of *The WIPO Journal*:

> Although intellectual property protections in [emerging countries such as Brazil, China and India] will no doubt improve in the near future, there is no guarantee that these countries will be interested in retaining the existing intellectual property system once they cross over to the other side of the intellectual property divide. Instead, these 'new champions' may want to develop something different – something that builds upon their historical traditions and cultural backgrounds and that takes account of their drastically different socio-economic conditions.[77]

Thus, China needs to carefully consider the opportunities and constraints legal transplants provide, lest it lose its ability to adopt intellectual property reforms that better align with the country's historical traditions, cultural backgrounds, socio-economic conditions, ideological values and policy preferences.

5.3   How Much Should the Transplanted Laws Be Adapted?

A successful transplant is usually one that is sensitive to the local environment. In order for the transplanted laws to be effective, they may need to undergo a careful evaluation and rigorous adaptation process. When

---

[75]   Yu (*supra*, n 70) 21–32; Yu, 'Middle Kingdom' (*supra*, n 42) 234.

[76]   Yu (*supra*, n 70) 25–6.

[77]   Peter K. Yu, 'The Global Intellectual Property Order and Its Undetermined Future' (2009) 1 WIPO J 1, 13.

they do not undergo such a process – for example, when the transplants originate from a legal environment that is distinctively different from that of China – the effectiveness and expediency of the transplanted laws are questionable.

A case in point is the amendment China made to Article 27 of the Regulations on Customs Protection of Intellectual Property Rights (Customs Regulations) in March 2010. To comply with the WTO panel report in *China – Measures Affecting the Protection and Enforcement of Intellectual Property Rights*, Article 27 was amended to reflect the language used in Article 46 of the TRIPS Agreement. Such direct transcription is intriguing from a legislative standpoint, because the relevant TRIPS language was taken verbatim from the 'A' text proposed by developed countries during the TRIPS negotiations, as opposed to the 'B' text advanced by developing countries.[78] The transcribed TRIPS language also differs significantly from the language used in other parts of the Chinese Customs Regulations.

To be sure, the TRIPS Agreement and the WTO panel report do not dictate how the non-complying laws and regulations are to be amended. Nevertheless, China eventually transcribed the TRIPS language for two reasons. First, the use of such language protected China from future compliance challenges before the WTO with respect to this particular provision. The amendment therefore put an end to the US–China WTO dispute over the inconsistencies between the Chinese Customs Regulations and the TRIPS Agreement.[79] Second, the adopted language showed the country's good-faith effort in bringing its laws into conformity with the TRIPS Agreement. It sent a strong signal to the international community that China takes its WTO obligations seriously. It also allowed the country to earn goodwill despite its continuous struggle to improve intellectual property protection.

From an enforcement standpoint, however, the transcribed language has raised some implementation challenges. Whether the adopted language will provide effective protection to rights holders will depend on how effectively the Chinese authorities implement this language and whether those authorities can fully internalize the underlying values based on language that may be foreign to them and that may not have a standard interpretation in the Chinese legal or regulatory system.

---

[78]   Daniel J. Gervais, 'Intellectual Property, Trade & Development: The State of Play' (2005) 74 Fordham L Rev 505, 508.

[79]   Peter K. Yu, 'The TRIPS Enforcement Dispute' (2011) 89 Nebraska L Rev 1046, 1069–75.

5.4   What Complementary Measures Need to Be Introduced?

In addition to undertaking intellectual property reforms, it is worth exploring whether introducing complementary measures would enhance the protection offered through these reforms. As I have repeatedly mentioned, successful enforcement of intellectual property rights depends on the existence of an 'enabling environment for effective intellectual property protection'.[80] While intellectual property rights remain an important part of the system for providing incentives to intellectual property rights holders, the effectiveness of the system depends on how well the laws are enforced.

In fact, many of the factors affecting intellectual property protection and enforcement may be found outside the intellectual property system. For example, a well-functioning enforcement system depends on the existence of a consciousness of legal rights, respect for the rule of law, an effective and independent judiciary, a well-functioning innovation and competition system, basic infrastructure, established business practices and a critical mass of local stakeholders. Thus, even if intellectual property reforms are undertaken, complementary measures may still be needed to enhance the protection of the interests of intellectual property rights holders.

Moreover, legal reform may not respond well to rapid technological change. Because of the slow and lengthy deliberative process used by the legislature, outdated legislation that stifles creativity and innovation usually remains on the books even though technology has evolved. Thus, to address the reform challenges posed by the Internet and new communications technologies, such as to combat the unauthorized copying problem in the digital environment, policymakers need to explore policy options that meet consumer needs while taking into account both the evolving technological architectures and the Internet users' changing social norms.[81]

Finally, because of the importance of retaining balance in the intellectual property system, the introduction of complementary measures is sometimes needed when intellectual property protection has been ratcheted up to address new problems and challenges. Because intellectual property laws seek to strike the proper balance between proprietary control and public access needs, limitations and exceptions are just as

---

[80]   Yu, 'China Puzzle' (*supra*, n 1) 213–16.
[81]   Peter K. Yu, 'P2P and the Future of Private Copying' (2005) 76 U Colorado L Rev 653, 764.

important as rights.[82] If these laws are to properly function, rights often need to be balanced by corresponding obligations.

6. CONCLUSION

Legal transplants can benefit or harm the recipient countries. When laws are hastily adopted without careful evaluation and adaptation, they may be both ineffective and insensitive to local conditions. They may also stifle local development, upset the existing local tradition and bring problems from abroad. By contrast, when these transplants are carefully selected and appropriately customized, they may provide time-tested models that help solve problems within the country. They may also provide attractive models for improvements, experiments and new developments, earning appreciation and respect from other jurisdictions.

To be sure, some of the transplants China needs may be unique to the country, given its large size, diverse and uneven developments and heavy involvement of the public sector in the intellectual property area. Nevertheless, its experience could provide important lessons concerning legal transplants for other parts of the world. To some extent, intellectual property developments in China have raised the same question as in recent debates concerning China's role in the international policy arena: Does Beijing provide an attractive alternative model for other developing countries that are struggling to catch up economically and technologically in the present international economic system?[83]

This question will bring us back to the beginning of this chapter. It is important to look at the history of the transplant of intellectual property laws in China to understand why countries transplant laws from abroad. It is also important to appreciate the strengths and weaknesses of the transplant process as well as the correction and complementary measures that can be put in place as part of this process. As Professor Watson reminded us, 'Transplanting frequently, perhaps always, involves legal transformation'.[84]

Legal transplant involves not only selection and adoption, but also adaptation and rejection. It 'come[s] in all shapes and sizes . . . [including] imposed reception, solicited imposition, penetration, infiltra-

---

[82]   James Boyle, *Shamans, Software, and Spleens: Law and the Construction of the Information Society* (Harvard University Press 1996) 138.

[83]   Peter K. Yu, 'Sinic Trade Agreements' (2011) 44 UC Davis L Rev 953, 1018–22.

[84]   Watson (*supra*, n 56) 116.

tion, crypto-reception, [and] inoculation'.[85] Thus, as much as we are eager to focus on the various intellectual property laws that have been transplanted to China in the past three decades, we cannot lose sight of the important modifications China has made to those laws, not to mention its rejection of other laws that were once candidates for legal transplant. Hopefully, the choices China has made will provide important lessons for not only those developing countries that are constantly under intense pressure to introduce legal transplants, but also those other countries that continue to advocate the transplant of intellectual property laws to foreign soil.

---

[85]   Ibid 30.

3. Legal transplant of intellectual property rights in China: norm taker or norm maker?

Niklas Bruun and Liguo Zhang

1. INTRODUCTION

The English Statute of Anne and Statute of Monopolies were passed in 1710 and 1624 respectively, and can generally be regarded as the origin of modern intellectual property (IP) law. Accordingly, intellectual property rights (IPRs) have had some roots in the Western world for over 300 years. China first attempted to establish its IP regime about 100 years ago as part of a plan to modernize, or otherwise westernize, its legal system with the intention of transforming the Qing Empire into a modern nation. Nonetheless, this effort eventually failed when the Qing Empire collapsed, and China's current IPR system has only been developed since the end of the 1970s.

Since the 1970s, China has successfully established its new IP legal system. In the last decade, the number of granted patents and registered trademarks in China has increased significantly. This development is testament to the successful transplantation of a modern IP regime into China. When a country has no prior relevant experience locally available in a specific legal area, it is natural to borrow successful models from other countries. The process of establishing a Chinese IP regime demonstrates a vivid model of legal transplantation, whereby the introduction of laws from foreign models is made, in order to achieve desired outcomes.[1]

When we discuss IPRs in China, are we talking about exactly the same thing as we are talking about when we discuss IPRs in the European Union or the US? This chapter examines how China's IP regime has been shaped and how the legal transplant of IP norms has been interacting with the norms of Chinese society. A central hypothesis is that China's IP

---

[1] Natalie P Stoianoff, 'The Influence of the WTO over China's Intellectual Property Regime' (2012) 34 Sydney Law Review 65, 73.

legal transplant and IP norm building is not a passive process of accepting Western rules; rather it is a dynamic process. Law makers had to deal with resistance from traditional ideologies and relevant interested parties in the process of introducing and implementing a new legal regime of IPRs. The process also involves interaction between legislative bodies, judicial institutions, administrative authorities, political and academic elites, the ruling party leaders, state-owned companies and private companies. Furthermore, foreign government and international institutions and consumers actually are also shaping Chinese IP norms.[2] In this process, China is not only a norm taker, but also a norm maker. Norms are more than simply a body of rules or institutions; they are also a social practice incorporating cultural and political practices, customs and traditions and many other elements. Therefore, a common terminology used in different countries does not necessarily carry the same meaning in each context.[3] The process of legal transplant and development of IP norms in China also shows that China not only accepts and adheres to dominant international norms, but also provides an alternative set of justifications and practices for its own IP norms.

Furthermore, this chapter argues that the rapid transplant of IP rules in China has led to the dissonance between formal IP rules and operational IP norms as they are followed in practice. This dissonance has resulted in a number of practical problems in term of IPRs in China. The difficulty with the enforcement of IPRs in China is a profound issue among many others. China needs to narrow the gap between the formal IP law and operational IP norms in practice in order to improve its IPR protection and be fully compatible with international IP norms.

2.   RESISTANCE TO AND ADOPTION OF IPRS IN THE PROCESS OF LEGAL TRANSPLANTATION

2.1   The Motivation for Transplanting IP Law into China

There were three main reasons for China to introduce IP laws based on Western models, even though in China, there still remained a significant hostility towards IPRs.

---

[2]   Nir Kshetri, 'Institutionalization of Intellectual Property Rights in China' (2009) 27 European Management Journal 155, 157.

[3]   William Alford, *To Steal a Book Is an Elegant Offense* (Stanford University Press 1997) 5.

Foreign pressures have been the main impetus for China to transplant IP law. In 1979, after China and the US established diplomatic relations, when the two counties were negotiating trade treaties the US insisted on adding IP provisions into the treaties. Even though there was no IP law at that time in China, the Chinese government promised to provide protection for IPRs. This led to China's entry into the World Intellectual Property Organization in 1980 and to the ratification of the Paris Convention in 1984 and the enactment of a Trademark Act in 1982 and Patent Act in 1984. The trade negotiations between China and the US in 1991 prompted China to update its IP law systematically. The US alleged that China had failed to provide sufficient IP protection for US products and put China in the Special 301 Priority Foreign Countries Report from 1989 onwards, therefore threatening to impose trade sanctions. The US and China continually negotiated on these issues. Finally, the negotiation resulted in a Memorandum of Understanding on IPRs in 1992, as well as China joining the Berne Convention and the Universal Copyright Convention in 1992. The US and China Memorandum of Understanding on IPRs in 1992 required only that China improve its IP legislation and the Chinese government did so. The Patent Act was amended in 1992 and the Trademark Act was amended in 1993. However, soon the US government found that these IP laws were not effectively implemented. In 1994, the US again put China into the Special 301 Priority Foreign Countries Report and urged China to improve its enforcement of IPRs. The subsequent negotiation resulted in Accord 1995, which required China to open Chinese markets to certain US copyright products and to create a mechanism guaranteeing the vigorous enforcement of China's IP laws. Based on the 1995 Accord, China took actions cracking down on piracy of US companies' movies, music and software and made the Regulation on the Custom Protection for Intellectual Property. In the negotiations regarding China's entry into the World Trade Organization (WTO), the US and other countries actively blocked China's entry on the ground of China's deficiencies in protection of IPRs. China therefore had to agree to revise its IP legislation to meet the requirements of the Agreement on Trade-Related Aspects of Intellectual Property Rights (TRIPs). As a result, there was a series of revisions of IP laws during 2000–2001 in China.

China's legal transplant of IP laws was not exclusively a response to Western pressure. The pressure from the West alone could not have made China transplant IP rules into its legal system. Instead, the inherent demand for a new IP regime was a very important factor for China to do so. In 1978, the Chinese government initiated reform which steered national policy from the Cultural Revolution's emphasis on politics and ideology to improving the economy and the people's livelihoods, and opening the economy to the outside world. In this context, building a patent and trademark regime became necessary for attracting foreign direct investment. Second, there was a demand from internal Chinese society to establish an IP regime with the aim of rewarding inventive and creative activities and promoting economic prosperity. Because there was no sufficient resource of IP law in the Chinese legal tradition, the easiest way to build up an IP system was to borrow rules from other countries. The use of transplants in the IP legislation has been a natural way to go forward in the process.

2.2 The Soil for Transplantation of IP Law in China

The transplant of IP law in China is an arduous process, not without resistance. Obviously the legal transplant of IP law in China led to conceptual and practical difficulties, as indicated by William Alford when discussing a 'western subject in an eastern context'.[4] The modern copyright and patent law originate from England, and later they were transplanted into many European countries and the US. These countries basically share the same, or similar, cultural and religious backgrounds. The legal transplant of IP law in China is to some extent a lack of cultural recognition.[5] The local norms inherently resisted the transplant of IP laws, which had been growing and functioning in a completely different cultural environment.

This chapter identifies three elements that contributed to the resistance most, namely cultural, political and economic elements. China has a long history of being among the world's most scientifically and technologically advanced countries. However, China did not independently develop a regime to protect intellectual creations during its history that was equivalent to the IP protection in Western societies.[6] It was only in the 20th century that China had to transplant IP protection from the Western world under international pressure. The proprietary right to intellectual creations is not an indigenous concept in Chinese history and culture, and leads to difficulties in the adoption of basic ideas when transplanting IP law into China.

In China's history, Confucianism has exerted a profound influence on China's political culture, as well as on Chinese spiritual life. For over 2000 years, Confucian ethical values have served as guiding principles

---

[4]   Ibid 7.
    [5]   吴汉东, '知识产权法律构造与移植的文化解释' (2007) 6 中国法学5, 56 (Wu Handong, 'A Cultural Explanation of Composition and Transfer of IP Law' (2007) 6 China Legal Science 5, 56).
    [6]   Alford (*supra*, n 3) 3.

for human interaction at all levels – individual, communal and national – leaving an 'indelible mark' on Chinese culture and society.[7] In modern China, Confucian culture still impacts the Chinese intelligentsia in an unacknowledged, sometimes unconscious way, at every level of life: behaviour, attitude, belief and commitment.[8] In Confucian societies, the creation of intellectual achievements was only a process of self-cultivation, and the outcomes of intellectual creation could not be owned for selfish purposes.[9] Imitation and reproduction of ideas, art and scholarship were an essential way to learn. A scholar's work being broadly imitated or reproduced was considered a token of honour and respect.[10] Disseminating as much as possible of one's works might let the public know that the author's thoughts were compatible with the Confucian master. This did not bring any economic benefit for authors, but it might bring about political benefit, for example the author might get an important position in the government system.[11] Therefore, within this cultural context, the idea of IPRs hardly fits into a Confucian society, where being copied and imitated is considered an honourable act.[12] The famous story of how 'paper becomes expensive in Luoyang' told that Mr Zuo Si's poetry, 'San du fu', was highly renowned upon its release, and later became overwhelmingly popular because many people were copying his work. As a result, the price of paper in Luoyang was said to have risen. This later gave rise to the popular Chinese idiom *Luoyang zhigui* ('Paper is Expensive in Luoyang City'), today used to praise a literary work.

If the potential influence of Confucianism on the legal transplantation of IP law in China was unperceivable, the impact from socialist ideology was real and evident. Since 1949, the Chinese Communist Party (CCP) has ruled China and socialist ideology has been established as an orthodoxy in China. During the period of 1949–58, the newly established government took measures aimed at abolishing private property rights step by step. During this period, to avoid major turbulence, the government tended to

---

[7] Wei-ming Tu, 'The Confucian Tradition in Chinese History' in P Ropp (ed), *Heritage of China: Contemporary Perspectives on Chinese Civilization* (University of California Press 1990) 113.

[8] Ibid 137.

[9] 吴汉东 (Wu Handong) (*supra*, n 5) 55, 56.

[10] Nils Victor Montan, *Trademark Anticounterfeiting in Asia and the Pacific Rim* (International Trademark Association 2001) 23.

[11] 李雨峰, '理性的宰制——关于帝制中国版权问题的省思' (2006) 23 政法论坛: 中国政法大学学报 57, 63, 64 (Li Yufeng, 'Rational Restriction – The Discussion on Copyright in Imperial China' (2006) 23 Tribune of Political Science and Law (Journal of China University of Political Science and Law) 57, 63, 64).

[12] Montan (*supra*, n 10) 23.

provide a certain level of remuneration for authors and inventors as part of its broader effort to spur the intelligentsia to meet the vast scientific and intellectual needs of a state seeking to recover from decades of revolution and war.[13] The legal system was largely transplanted from the model of the Soviet Union. Intellectual creation was regarded as an outcome of human intellectual labour and the common wealth of human society, thus echoing the Confucian view.[14] In 1950, the government made several provisional laws which regulated IP, such as the Provisional Regulations on the Protection of Invention Rights and Patent Rights, the Procedures for Dealing with Trademarks Registered at the Trademark Office of the former Kuomintang government and the Provisional Regulations on Trademark Registration. The former invalidated all registrations by the former Kuomintang government, while the latter provided for the establishment of a new registration-based trademark system.[15] Nonetheless, these regulations had nothing to do with protection of IPRs, but were to encourage people to carry out technological inventions through patent regulation and to regulate commercial and market order through trademark regulation.[16] Up to 1963, when the patent regulation was abolished, only four patents were granted under the regulation.[17]

By 1958, the socialist transformation of the economy essentially eliminated private ownership and IPRs became unnecessary. In 1963, the Chinese government promulgated the Invention Reward Statute and Technology Improvement Statute to replace the Provisional Regulations on the Protection of Invention Rights and Patent Rights of 1950. Patent rights were completely abolished. As for trademarks, a Trademark Governance Statute was promulgated, in which trademark legislation became a vehicle for supervising quality, not for granting exclusive rights. As to copyright, many writers became state workers receiving a salary from the state and creating works became their job. Therefore copyright was also abolished in practice as well.[18] By the mid-1960s, increasingly radical policies led to attacks on property rights and material incentives

---

[13]   Alford (*supra*, n 3).
[14]   Ibid.
[15]   Ibid 59.
[16]   王月辉, '中国对知识产权法律保护的理论与特点' (1996) 2 国际经贸研究, 15. (Wang Yuehui, 'The Theory and Features of IPR Legal Protection in China' (1996) 2 International Economic and Trade Studies, 15).
[17]   赵元果, 中国专利法的孕育与诞生 (第1版, 知识产权出版社 2003) 10 (Zhao Yuanguo, *The Preparation and Emergence of Chinese Patent Law* (IPR Press 2003) 10).
[18]   王月辉 (Wang Yuehui) (*supra*, n 16) 15.

in IP, as well as more general assaults on professionalism and the formal legal system itself.[19]

The traditional socialist ideology insisted that individuals who invented or created were engaged in social activities that utilized a repository of knowledge that belonged to all members of society.[20] Therefore any scientific and technological achievements were regarded as public goods, for public use, free of charge. This was reflected in Article 23 of the Invention Reward Statute in 1963, which stated that:

> Any inventions belong to the state, any individual or entities shall not have monopoly on them, any entities throughout nation shall be entitled to exploit inventions needed.

The third element that contributed to the resistance to IPRs was the economic condition at that time. At the end of the 1970s China still relied heavily on agriculture. Most industrial output was generated by state-owned enterprises for the purposes of a planned economy. The income of people was also very low. The data shows that in 1979, in Beijing city, the average spending of the municipal residents was 408.72 yuan, of which 368.4 yuan was spent on tangible goods. Only less than 10 per cent was devoted to non-commodity spending. Spending on foods and clothes took over 72 per cent.[21] Cultural products such as movies and books used to be provided by entities either free of charge or at extremely low prices. It would not be strange if IP was found useless in such a context. The real challenge was how these unfavourable conditions could possibly accommodate a modern IP regime.

2.3 Transplanting IP Norms through Legislation

Transplantation through legislation was employed as the first step towards establishing IP norms in China. The making of the current IP regime was initiated in the late 1970s when China opened relations with the outside world. This was the seminal event leading to the introduction of radical reforms in the Chinese legal system. Although the proposal to establish a patent system gave rise to severe criticism within the government, the Patent Act was passed in 1984 after five years of debates. On 1 April 1985,

---

[19]   Alford (*supra*, n 3) 57, 65.
[20]   Ibid 56.
[21]   北京市统计局, 北京统计年鉴 (北京: 中国统计出版社1980 E13) 210, 211, 215, 216 (Beijing Municipal Statistic Bureau, *Beijing Statistic Yearbook* (China Statistic Press 1980, E13) 210, 211, 215, 216).

the State Patent Office started to accept patent applications, and on that day 3,455 patent applications from both domestic and foreign applicants were filed. The Chinese Trademark Act was passed in 1982 and came into effect on 1 March 1983. The General Principles of Civil Law in which very basic rules regarding copyrights, trademarks and patents were set up, was passed in 1985. In 1990, the Chinese Copyright Act was passed and came into effect on 1 June 1991.

When transplanting Western IP rules, the legislator had to face some dilemmas. First, it had to deal with the conflict of ideologies. Second, it also had to tackle the question of how the transplantation of the foreign model would fit into the concrete Chinese condition, serving the state interest rather than harming the state's economic development. Herein the transplantation of patent law was taken as an example to demonstrate how the transplant of IP in China could overcome these problems.

When China first tried to introduce patent law, there was a controversial debate over whether China should establish a patent system. The first concern was that the patent system might not be compatible with the socialist system. In the traditional socialist view, intellectual invention and technological improvements should belong to the state representing the people, which could in turn be exploited by all state-owned enterprises. The fact that patents grant private ownership of inventions to the individual was an ideal that conflicted with the traditional ideals of many policy makers. They raised the question whether a socialist country could have a patent system. Instead, an alternative was proposed that the state should award the inventor, but that the technology should belong to the state.[22] The second concern was that the patent system would only protect foreign companies' monopoly interests in China and therefore could restrict domestic technological development because foreign companies would own most of the patents. In such a situation it would become difficult for domestic enterprises to imitate foreign technologies. In addition, the patent system could block the distribution and implementation of new technology.[23] Therefore there would be a disadvantage for China in having a patent system. The third concern on the part of industry was that the patent was not necessary for China because even without a patent system, it was still viable to import technology from foreign countries.[24] Those advocating a patent system responded to these concerns and defended their arguments and

---

[22] 赵元果 (Zhao Yuanguo) (*supra*, n 17) 61.
[23] Ibid 57–58.
[24] Ibid 79.

insisted that China needed a patent system. But the debate ended in a deadlock. The arguments of both sides were submitted to higher-level policy makers for consideration.[25] In the end, it was decided to establish a patent system, but the question was raised again as to what kind of system this should be.

In March 1979, a patent act-drafting team, composed of eight experts, was established to prepare the draft of the Patent Act. The draft of the Patent Act was revised over 20 times before it was finally passed in the National People's Congress in 1984. A lot of questions were sent to universities, governmental departments and industry for consultation, such as: terminology, technical problems, terms of protection, procedures and the structure of the organizations.

The next challenge, once it had been decided to establish a patent system in China, was how to maintain the socialist character of patent law while granting a private monopoly to inventions. To make the patent system compatible with the socialist ideology, scholars had to introduce a theory of the essence of a patent in order to justify patent rights. According to this theory, a patent was a means to protect the interests resulting from labour. It emphasized that the knowledge should belong to society, and protection of IPRs first should serve the state and public interest. The protection of IPRs is only a means to promote the dissemination of creation, invention and arts.[26] In the end, the socialist characteristics were justified based on the ownership of a patent. According to Article 6 of the Patent Act of 1984, in a state-owned entity or a collective-owned entity, the ownership of a patent for an employee invention should belong to the state in the case of state-owned entities. Accordingly the state entities were entitled to hold (rather than own) and exploit the patent. In the case of a collective-owned entity, the collective-owned entities were also entitled to own and exploit the patent. Because the state-owned enterprises and collective-owned enterprises were absolutely dominant in Chinese industry at that time, most patents filed by domestic applicants would belong to publicly-owned enterprises, either the state-owned or collective-owned entities. Therefore, the socialist essence of the Patent Act was maintained. Individuals could make some inventions and own patents but the private ownership of patents would only be complementary to the socialist public ownership.[27]

---

[25]   Ibid 79–80.
[26]   王月辉 (Wang Yuehui) (*supra*, n 16) 16.
[27]   汤宗舜, '论我国专利法的六个主要原则' (1984) 中国法学 25, 27 (Tang Zongshu, 'The Six Main Principles in Chinese Patent Law' (1984) China Legal Science 25, 27).

One concern was that the patent system, which originated from capitalism and by which patentees could extract monopoly profit, could not be compatible with the socialist principle of distribution according to labour. In dealing with this concern, the 1984 Patent Act established several restrictions on granting and exploiting patents. First, the Patent Act imposed restrictions on ownership; that is patents granted to state-owned entities would belong to the state although the state-owned entities retained the right to use the patent. Second, the law might impose a compulsory licence on those patents that were not exploited.[28] Article 51 of the 1984 Patent Act stipulated that patentees were obliged to make patented products or utilize their patented processes to make products in China, or license others to do so in China. Since the planned economy held a very significant position in China, the Patent Act also provided for the exploitation of patents by government orders. Article 14 of the 1984 Patent Act stipulated that the competent department of the State Council and a provincial government had the power to decide that the patents owned by state-owned entities should be exploited by designated entities; the designated entity should pay a royalty to the patent holder. The government could also grant a compulsory licence to use the patents owned by collective-owned entities or individuals in cases involving significant state or public interest.

The settlement of some other questions has shaped the future trajectory of Chinese patent law, such as whether to establish a single patent system or to establish dual systems including a patent and inventor reward system, and whether to grant a patent to utility models and designs. The first Chinese patent system largely adopted the German model of patent law with a number of adaptations. As industrial and technological development levels remained very low in China, the law did not provide protection for foodstuff, drugs and materials obtained through chemical methods. Although the 1984 Patent Act tried to strike a balance between the international norms and the economic and technical conditions of the country, many provisions in the Patent Act were not compatible with international standards, especially the Paris Convention.

---

[28] 吕润程，'试论我国专利法中的取舍问题' (1983) 社会科学 57, 57 (Lü Runcheng, 'Acceptance and Rejection in Chinese Patent Law' (1983) Social Science 57, 57).

3. THE ROLE OF COURTS AND ADMINISTRATIVE AUTHORITIES IN FORMING IP NORMS

3.1 Judicial Decision Making in Forming IP Norms in China

As in the continental legal system, Chinese courts are supposed to be merely law-applying institutions rather than forums for making law. Nonetheless, courts play a very important role in the transplantation of IP law and forming IP norms in China. The IP laws in the early days in China were usually very general and simple and many provisions were lacking in detail. Moreover, in the IP field many more new legal problems are continuing to emerge with the rapid evolution of technology. When a court has to deal with a case that cannot be solved by the direct interpretation of existing law, it is natural for the court to look at how the same or similar issues have been solved in other countries. Then the court uses the thinking and principles that it considers appropriate to interpret and apply the IP law to a specific case. For example, the doctrine of equivalence in patent infringement cases, which has been employed in Germany and the US, was first introduced in *Zhou Lin v. Aomei & Huaao* by the Beijing Intermediate People's Court.[29] Later, in 2001, this principle was incorporated into a judicial interpretation issued by the Supreme People's Court (SPC).[30]

Courts have created precedents in which IP rights are extended to cover a broader subject or grant stronger protection that could not be read into the formal IP rules. This is especially the case when the interpretation involves complicated technological problems. In *TV guidance*,[31] the question was raised whether an unauthorized publication of a TV guide

---

[29] 周林诉北京奥美光机电联合开发公司、北京华奥电子医疗仪器有限公司侵犯专利权纠纷案，北京市中级人民法院(1993)中经知初字第704号民事判决书。(Beijing Municipal Intermediate Court Decision 1993 Zhongjingzhichuzi No. 704, Zhoulin v. Beijing Aomei Mechanic and Electronic Joint Development Ltd, Beijing Huaao Electronic Medical Equipment Ltd. on Infringement of Patent).

[30] 《最高人民法院关于审理专利纠纷案件适用法律问题的若干规定》第17条，法释[2001]21号。(Article 17 of SPC's Regulations on the Application of Laws in Trials of Patent Infringement cases, Fashi [2001] No. 21). The Supreme Court is entitled to issue judicial interpretations, which are more like statutes, in order to elaborate and interpret the provisions of the law, with a view to facilitating the application of IP law. Many of those judicial interpretations are very broad and, already beyond the interpretation of law as such, are more like legislation.

[31] 广西广播电视报社诉广西煤矿工人报社电视节目预告表使用权纠纷案《中华人民共和国最高人民法院公报》1996 年 01 期 (Guangxi Broadcasting Newspaper Office v. Guanxi Coal Mine Worker's Newspaper Office on TV List Right Dispute, Supreme People's Court Gazette, 1996.1).

constituted infringement as TV guides were not in the category of subject matter protected by the Copyright Act. The first instance court held that the TV guide did not fall into the category of the subject matter protected by copyright law, therefore no infringement was found. The plaintiff appealed. The second instance court held that the plaintiff had a legitimate right to the TV guide, so that the unauthorized publishing of the TV guide constituted an infringement.[32] So the judge extended the subject matter for IP protection. Furthermore, courts have been at the forefront in solving many legal problems that could not be settled by direct interpretation of the existing IP law. In the case *Ownership of the Patent Pile Formation by Drilling Hole and Pressurizing Mortar*, the Beijing High People's Court clarified and established the rules on how to determine an employee invention.[33] In *HongKong Meiyi v. Patent Re-examination Board*, the Beijing High People's Court established the principle on how to examine the standards of inventive steps for an invention.[34] In *DuPont v. Guowang Domain Name*, the Beijing High People's Court held that the court should have the power to rule on whether a trademark was a well-known mark, a power which was exclusively exercised by the State Administration for Industry and Commerce. The Court also established the applicable rules in determining conflicts between trademarks and domain names.[35] Many such decisions were later incorporated into legislation by amendments to the law, or into judicial interpretations issued by the SPC.

Courts' discretion also has shaped IP norms from several perspectives. Due to the fact that IP laws in China have been made without their own cultural and historical roots in society, and do not match entirely the demands of industrial development, one concrete problem is how the court manages the possible tension and interaction between the formal IP rules and individualized justice in the context of local cultures, customs

---

[32]   Ibid.

[33]   '陶义诉北京市地铁地基工程公司发明专利权属纠纷案' 中华人民共和国最高人民法院公报1992.3 (Taoyi v. Beijing Municipal Subway Foundation Engineering Company on Patent Ownership Dispute, Supreme People's Court Gazette, 1992.1).

[34]   '香港美艺金属制品厂诉中国专利局专利复审委员会确认 "惰钳式门" 发明专利权纠纷上诉案' 中华人民共和国最高人民法院公报1992.2 (Hong Kong Meiyi Metal Products Factory v. Board of Patent Appeals of Patent Office on 'Idler Clamp Door' invention Patent Dispute Appeal, Supreme People's Court Gazette, 1992.2).

[35]   '美国杜邦公司诉北京国网信息有限公司计算机网络域名侵权纠纷案', 中华人民共和国最高人民法院公报 2002.3 (DuPont v. Beijing Guowang Information Co., Ltd. on Domain Name Infringement Dispute in Computer Network, Supreme People's Court Gazette, 2002.3).

and economic interests. As a matter of fact, China's IP laws in the early stages were very basic and simple and therefore left a lot of room for a court to interpret the law in order to apply it to concrete cases. Especially in the IP field, technology evolves quickly and creates many challenges for the IP rules.

The discretion of courts and judges has led to divergent local application of IP rules. First, the level of economic development in different regions of China can vary greatly. So it is reasonable that each region has different preferences regarding the protection of IPRs. Many provincial high courts have issued guidelines or opinions for interpreting and applying IP law to guide the lower-level courts in the provincial territory in interpreting and applying the law in IPR cases. The content of these guidelines or opinions on the same issue could be different from region to region. For example, the Patent Act, Trademark Act and Copyright Act provide for statutory damages. As to the base unit for calculating damages, the Beijing High People's Court's guideline provides that damages shall be calculated based on each work in terms of copyright infringement,[36] while the Jiangsu High People's Court's guideline provides that damages shall be calculated based on each right infringed.[37] There are also many other discrepancies in the Court guidelines. When it comes to practice, many discrepancies could even be magnified. In addition to differentiated regional policy, another factor is, as Liu Sida has indicated, that the operation of Chinese courts is influenced by hierarchical administrative systems. In China, the court system is not independent and is a bureaucratic organ with a clear administrative hierarchy, which is similar or identical to corresponding administrative bodies.[38] It is hard for the court and judge to resist the influence of administrative bodies. The officials within the court with different levels of hierarchy and power may exert influence in a specific case. And the political party, local administrative bodies and other entities may exert influence as well.[39] Judges are typically selected by the local CCP authority and appointed by local congress. The CCP officials may exercise

---

[36] See Article 10 of Beijing Municipal Higher People's Court Guidance on the Determination of Copyright Infringement Liability for Damages (北京市高级人民法院关于确定著作权侵权损害赔偿责任的指导意见).
[37] See Article 15 of Jiangsu Provincial Higher People's Court's Guidance on the Determination of Fixed Amount of Damage for Intellectual Property Infringement (江苏省高级人民法院关于知识产权侵权损害适用定额赔偿办法若干问题的指导意见).
[38] 刘思达, '法律移植与合法性冲突' (2005) 3 社会学研究, 36 (Liu Sida, 'Legal Transplants and the Conflicts of Legitimacy: Chinese Grassroots Judicial Practice in the Context of Modernity' (2005) 3 Sociological Research, 36).
[39] Ibid 38.

direct or indirect influence in individual cases, through the Political-Legal Committees at each level of government. The budget for each court is determined and allocated by the local government where the court sits. Local governments are able to exert influence on judges in judicial decisions in order to protect local industries or litigants. Hence, a judge may rule in favour of local litigants by either intentionally taking jurisdiction over such cases and issuing rulings favourable to local litigants or impeding enforcement of decisions detrimental to local litigants.[40] This has led to variable levels of service from region to region.

Moreover, not only IP laws, but also general policy considerations have a significant influence on judges' and courts' discretion. When a judge makes a judicial decision, he usually faces a complicated situation in which he does not only apply law as a benchmark, but is also guided by political and judicial policies.[41] Applying IP laws while also considering the political elements to achieve results consistent with a particular public policy or ideology was referred to by some commentators as ideological discretion.[42] One example is that the SPC issued a document titled 'Opinions of the Supreme People's Court on trials of IPR shall serve the overall interests under the current economic situation' on 21 April 2009.[43] In this document, the SPC requires all the lower courts to follow this document's guidance in IP trials. The purpose of the document is

> fully implementing the main ideas of the 'two Congresses,' and carrying out national IPR strategy, to make the IPR trials serve the overall interest of an effective response to the international financial crisis and promoting steady and rapid economic development, to make a more positive contribution to maintaining growth, people's livelihood and stability.[44]

The document requires the courts to strike a subtle balance between conforming to legal requirements and following state policies. For example, Section 14 of this document provides guidelines for the granting of a

---

[40]   Margaret YK Woo, 'Law and Discretion in the Contemporary Chinese Courts' (1999) 8 Pacific Rim Law & Policy Journal 581, 591.

[41]   孔祥俊, '裁判中的法律、政策与政治——以知识产权审判为例' (2008) 人民司法 24, 26 (Kong Xiangjun, 'The Law, Policy and Politics in Judicial Decisions – IP Trials as an Example' (2008) People's Judicature 24, 26).

[42]   Woo (*supra*, n 40) 586.

[43]   最高人民法院关于当前经济形势下知识产权审判服务大局若干问题的意见 (2009年4月21日印发, 法发2009〕23号) (Opinions of the Supreme People's Court on Trials of IPR Shall Serve the Overall Interests under the Current Economic Situation, 21 April 2009, FaFa 2009 No. 23).

[44]   Ibid.

preliminary injunction before the plaintiff files a suit. The section requires that the preliminary injunction should be granted with caution and the court should strike a balance between effectively enjoining infringement and maintaining the normal operation of an alleged infringing enterprise.[45]

Another example demonstrates how a judicial policy may direct judges to apply law in determining the burden of proof and the amount of damages, therefore functioning as a tool to enhance the level of protection. With respect to the damages awarded to IPR holders in infringement cases, where IP law provides for damages for infringement, judicial policies may guide the method of calculating damages.[46]

3.2 Administrative Activities in Forming and Applying IP Norms in China

Administrative authorities usually are not considered to play any essential role in legal norm making. Nonetheless in China administrative authorities actually have played an essential role in the transplantation and formation of IP norms in China.

In China, the driving force of legal transplantation through legislation has been the administrative authorities. The respective IP departments of the State Council may initiate and draft IP legislation. At the end of the 1970s, the government realized the importance of intellectuals in the modernization of the state and therefore decided to establish rules to provide protection for and to reward intellectual creations. In 1977, the State Publication Authority issued 'The Notice on the Provisional Measures for Implementation of the Remuneration and Subsidy for A Publication', which provided for remuneration for authors or translators based on a calculation of the numbers of words of their works. Later the administrative authority undertook efforts to make and revise relevant rules in order to implement the treaties between China and the US. In 1982, the Ministry of Broadcasting and TV issued 'The Provisional Statute on Governance of Audio and Video Recordings'. The department of publication in the Ministry of Culture revised old rules and issued 'The Provisional Regulations on Remuneration for Books', 'The Implementation Rules on the Provisional Regulation on Protection for Books and Journals' and 'The Criterion for Remuneration for Artist Publications'. In 1984, 'The Provisional Regulation on Protection for Copyrights of Books and Journals' was issued. The content of all these administrative regulations constituted the basis for future copyright law.

---

[45]   Ibid.
[46]   孔祥俊 (Kong Xiangjun) (*supra*, n 41) 26.

Administrative authorities also play a crucial role in transplanting patent norms in China. In 1978, several ministries, including the Ministry of Foreign Affairs and the Ministry of Foreign Trade, suggested the establishment of a patent system.[47] The State Technology Committee under the State Council at that time was a leading administration in charge of making patent law. The State Technology Committee collected many countries' patent laws and also visited over 10 countries to study different patent laws. In 1979, the Committee submitted a proposal to request establishing a patent system in China to the State Council, which listed and analysed the rationales for establishing a patent system in China. Then the State Council approved the proposal and decided to establish a patent office. The newly established patent office started to debate with the opposition, and prepared the draft of the Patent Act, which was finally passed in 1984.[48]

Administrative bodies have been affecting the formation of IP norms through making IP implementing regulations and the administrative enforcement of IP law. Because the texts of Chinese IP legislation are usually simple and not very detailed, it has been a general practice, when an IP law is passed at the Congress, that the law usually authorizes the State Council to make implementing regulations to elaborate the provisions in the law and to stipulate some matters that should be, but have not been, stipulated in the law. Those implementing regulations have binding effect, and when a court decides relevant IP cases, it may refer to such administrative regulations. For example, in the 1984 Patent Act, Article 68 authorizes the State Patent Office to make an implementing regulation. Therefore in 1985, the State Patent Office issued the 'Implementing Regulation of Patent Act'. The Implementing Regulation regulated very broad matters. Article 6 of the 1984 Patent Act defined the ownership of an employee invention, but it failed to define what an employee invention was. The Implementing Regulation further clarified how to determine an employee invention. It also applied in the case of copyright law and trademark law as well as other IP laws. This practice has given administrative bodies great power in creating administrative IP rules.

Moreover, Chinese IP laws granted administrative bodies wide powers in enforcing the laws and the administrative authorities have great discretion in the enforcement. Chinese IP laws grant the respective IP department in the government the power to prevent infringement of IPRs and the power to impose administrative penalties on infringers. When an IPR

---

[47]   赵元果 (Zhao Yuanguo) (*supra*, n 17) 41.
[48]   Ibid 49–55.

owner finds infringement of its IPR, he may petition the relevant department at the provincial or a lower level to stop the infringement and fine the infringer. This provides an alternative to bringing a lawsuit to a court in order to stop the infringement. This could be effective to crack down on infringements of IPRs and to reduce the cost for IP owners of preventing infringements. In the 1984 Patent Act, the patent administrative authority was granted the power to issue an injunction in patent infringement cases, and it also had the power to determine infringements. With regard to the trademark and copyright laws, the administrative powers are even stronger and a competent administrative authority has the power to investigate infringements, and the power to punish the infringer.[49] Since the amendment of IP laws is usually initiated and the draft of amendment is produced by the relevant administrative departments, the power of administrative bodies tends to be strengthened and secured. The strong position of administrative bodies in implementing law makes the Chinese IP regime unique compared with many Western countries from which the Chinese IP legislation was borrowed. Granting strong powers to administrative bodies may push forward the implementation of IP laws in China more smoothly where there is still strong resistance to the new system. The administrative bodies can also help the IP owner who may not fully understand how the IP system works to protect their IP, at least at the early stage. Nonetheless, the administrative power in implementing IP law has provoked some criticisms, such as lack of transparency, inconsistency between different levels and regions of government in implementing laws, insufficient training and financial resources, conflicts of interest, tedious procedures in the government bodies and lack of efficient cooperation between different government bodies.

4. THE DISSONANCE AND CONGRUENCE OF IP LAW AND IP NORMS IN CHINA

4.1 The Dissonance Between IP Law and IP Norms in China

The transplantation of an IP law does not necessarily lead to the establishment of the same or similar IP norms in comparison to the norm in the originating country. Comparative law scholar Mousourakis has indicated that '[l]aw is more than simply a body of rules or institutions;

---

[49] Article 48 of the China Copyright Act 1990 amended in 2010, Articles 60, 62 of the China Trademark Act 1982 amended in 2013.

it is also a social practice within a legal community. It is this social practice that shapes the actual meaning of the rules and institutions, their relative weight, and the way they are implemented and operate in society.'[50]

A norm is 'a model or standard accepted (voluntarily or involuntarily) by society or other large group, against which society judges someone or something. An example of a norm is the standards for right or wrong behavior.'[51] In China, IP legislation represents the status of 'ought'; the IP norms represent the status of 'is'. IP norms and laws are alternative mechanisms for regulating IPR activities in Chinese society. Moreover, their role and efficacy have varied at different levels of society and in different regions. At the local level, norms are far more dominant. At the national level, laws rather than norms are more important. Usually small players and individuals would prefer to follow norms. In the business community, both norms and laws, including 'soft' laws, are at work in shaping the behaviour of different classes of players. In the economically prosperous coastal areas of China, law is more respected. In the less-developed inland areas of China, norms are more prevalent. The most effective form of behaviour regulation is the complete convergence between laws and norms. Conversely, the most problematic is that the laws and norms are considerably disconnected. In reality, there must be a degree of congruence between the formal laws and the norms. Otherwise, the IP legal system would become meaningless.

There is a clear dissonance between formal IP law 'in books' and actual IP norms in practice in China. After transplanting Western IP law, one problem is how the Western norms can survive well in an environment where there are solid historic and cultural differences, on which the actual IP norms are based. There is no indigenous counterpart to the Western conception of IP in Chinese legal tradition. A monopoly on knowledge is difficult to justify in Chinese culture. It is natural that transplantation will lead to the adoption of legal solutions which are either undesirable on their merits or in tension with the existing system. The criticism of the introduction of IP law in China has never stopped. The doubt and resistance on the part of the public and the business community in China have made the enforcement of IPRs lack public recognition. In this context, the enforcement of IP law may not be

---

[50] George Mousourakis, 'Transplanting Legal Models across Culturally Diverse Societies: A Comparative Law Perspective' (2010) Osaka University Law Review 87, 90.

[51] Bryan A Garner, *Black's Law Dictionary* (9th edn, West 2009) 1159.

effective and strict. This conflict has led to the dissonance between IP law and IP norms in practice in China. According to research by Xu Chunming and Shan Xiaoguang, the intensity of enforcement of IPRs has been much lower than the intensity of the legislation in relation to IPRs in China.[52]

4.2   The Congruence of IP Law and IP Norms in China

In the early stages of industrialization, imitation is a common means to catch up with advanced countries. To some extent, counterfeiting, piracy and IP infringement could be tolerated by the policy makers. However, with increasing achievements in innovation by domestic innovators and the creation of some concrete results in the market, the policy makers may realize that the strict enforcement of IPR may serve national interests rather than just the interests of foreign companies. The dynamic of domestic innovation may motivate the policy makers to undertake efforts to narrow the gap between the IP law and IP norms. Figure 3.1 shows where China ranks among 20 national patent offices and shows that the Chinese office had the most patent applications in 2012. Among these patent applications to the Chinese patent office, domestic applicants took about 82 per cent as shown in Figure 3.2. Many domestic stakeholders – scientists, engineers, entrepreneurs, creative artists, designers and political leaders – have come to associate a stronger IP regime with their personal and national interests, and are pushing the government to change its attitude to IPRs.

In June 2008, China's State Council published the Outline of the National Intellectual Property Strategy, which provided a roadmap to how China plans to become one of the world's most innovative countries by 2020. It showed that the policy maker has now considered IP strategic significance for state competitiveness and economic development. The IP Strategy committed the government to take measures to improve its IP regime in accordance with its ambitious industrial and technology policies. It put its focus on the protection, utilization and management of IP as well as IP creation. The 2008 State IPR strategy represented an intention from the top political entity to narrow the gap between IP law and IP norms. The government has put the improvement of the judicial system as a key

---

[52]   许春明, 单晓光, '中国知识产权保护强度指标体系的构建及验证' (2008) 26 科学学研究 715, 719 (Xu Chunming, Shan Xiaoguang, 'Constructing of the Index System and Verification for the Intensity of Intellectual Property Protection in China' (2008) 26 Studies in Science of Science 715, 719).

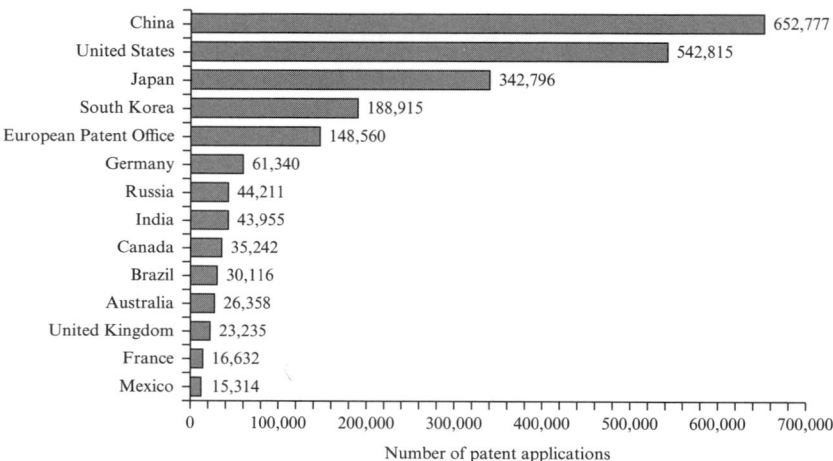

Source: WIPO, 2013 World Intellectual Property Indicators, p. 53.

Figure 3.1   Ranking of the 20 national patent offices with the most patent applications in 2012

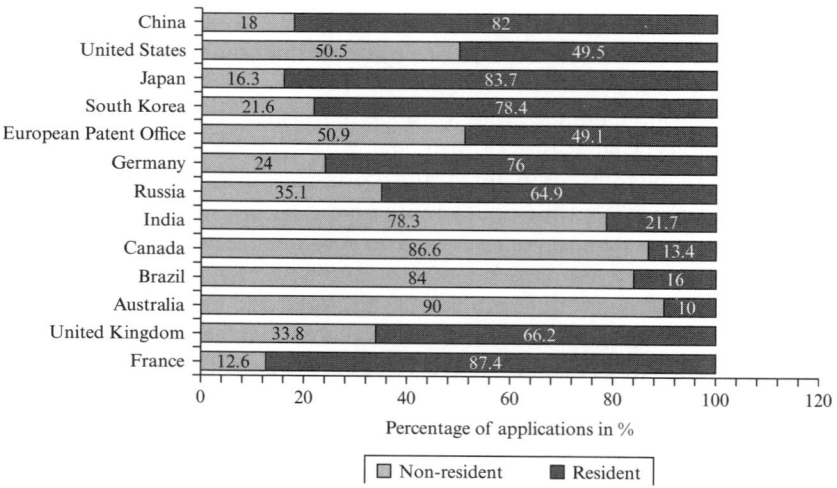

Source: WIPO, 2013 World Intellectual Property Indicators, p. 53.

Figure 3.2   Non-resident share of patent applications of the top 20 national patent offices in 2012

reform goal. One concrete step is that three specialized IP courts were established in 2014. The national IPR strategy and actions may push the country in the direction of harmonization of IP rules with the norms of the international IPR system.[53]

5.   CONCLUSION

The experience of China in transplanting IP law shows that the establishment of IP norms in China is a complicated process. After 30 years of transplanting IPRs in China, even though the IP legislation has become similar to and compatible with that of the West, the content of the norms in terms of IP is still quite different. The IP norms in China are being shaped by the convergence of political, economic, cultural and legal elements that may differ from those in other countries. The process of China transplanting foreign rules is also a process of creating its own legal norms which is diverted from its original source of transplantation and also may be diverted from the expectation of the legislators.

Legal transplant of IPRs in China in such a short period has led to a contradiction of indigenization and internationalization of IP rules.[54] The indigenization of IP rules means that the scope and standards of protection of IPRs should match the situation of technology, economy and culture of the state. Therefore the foreign rules need to be adapted to fit the concrete condition of the state. The internationalization of IP rules means that IP legislation in a state should be compatible with international standards. The internationalization of IP rules in China actually came at the price of providing protection for IPRs beyond the national technological and economic development level in the initial stages. As Teubner has indicated, in order for law to be successfully enforced within the social fields it aims to regulate, it must be adjusted to the logic of the social environment it tries to regulate.[55] As a result, the legal

---

[53]   Richard Suttmeier and Xiangkui Yao, 'China's IP Transition: Rethinking Intellectual Property Rights in a Rising China' (2011) NBR Special Report, 6.

[54]   万霞, '论知识产权法律制度的本土化与国际化 – 以中欧知识产权问题为视角' (2007) 外交评论 93, 94 (Wan Xia, 'Internationalization and Localization of IPR – From the Perspective of IPR in the EU and China' (2007) Foreign Affairs Review 93, 94).

[55]   Gunther Teubner, *Juridification of Social Spheres: A Comparative Analysis in the Areas of Labor, Corporate, Antitrust and Social Welfare Law* (Walter de Gruyter 1987) 25.

transplantation has resulted in the dissonance between the IP rules and IP norms in practice. This can partially explain why the enforcement of IPRs was so ineffective in China especially in the 1990s. Legislation needs to be constructed into appropriate norms in the light of the demands resulting from the concrete practical situation.

4. Intellectual property law revision in China: transplantation and transformation

Mingde Li

1. INTRODUCTION

The modern Chinese intellectual property system is founded upon the enactment of a series of related laws. China enacted its Trademark Law in August 1982, Patent Law in March 1984, Copyright Law in September 1990, and Unfair Competition Law in December 1993.[1] Subsequently, China has amended its intellectual property laws in three rounds. The first-round revision, between 1992 and 1993, was based upon the first Memorandum of Understanding between China and the United States.[2] The second-round revision, between 2000 and 2001, was necessitated by Chinese membership of the World Trade Organization (WTO), and since 2003, China has experienced the third-round revision of its intellectual property laws.

From a comparative legal analysis, China is an importer of international legal norms on the protection of intellectual property. This importation of norms is reflected in the enactment and revision of its intellectual property laws. In other words, China has based most of its legal norms on the protection of intellectual property on norms and practices from other countries and therefore Chinese laws can be considered to be in accordance with international standards and practices. However, the importation of norms into the Chinese intellectual property system has not always functioned well. When China launched its third-round revision

---

[1]   All of the laws and regulations can be found on the website of the Intellectual Property Office of China at <http://www.sipo.gov.cn/>.

[2]   See Memorandum of Understanding between the government of China and the government of the United States on the Protection of Intellectual Property (17 January 1992) available at <http://tcc.export.gov/trade_agreements/all_trade_agreements/exp_005362.asp> last accessed 10 April 2015.

of its intellectual property laws, it served as an opportunity to review the impact of the varied imported norms, and an opportunity to correct any misunderstandings as a result. In this sense, China is attempting to reinterpret some of the adopted intellectual property norms on the basis of its own social and economic development. Furthermore and in addition to being a norm importer, China may conceive some new norms if necessary for the country's social and economic cohesion.

This chapter will review some of the proposals for amending the Chinese Copyright Law, Trademark Law and Patent Law. The purpose of this review is to illustrate how the adopted norms on the protection of intellectual property have been transformed or understood in China.

2.   PROPOSALS FOR THE AMENDMENT OF THE COPYRIGHT LAW

The Copyright Law of China was enacted in September 1990 and came into effect in June 1991. In October 2001, the Copyright Law was amended for the first time as was necessitated by the obligations stipulated in the Agreement on Trade-Related Aspects of Intellectual Property Rights (TRIPS) Agreement. In February 2010, China amended the Copyright Law for a second time and this was a response to a panel decision of the dispute settlement body of the WTO.[3] This change resulted in the deletion of former article 4.1, and added another provision concerning the registration of copyright mortgage.[4] As is apparent, these changes to Chinese law were a result of external pressures.

In July 2011, the National Copyright Administration of China (NCAC) announced the start of the third revision of the Copyright Law, and entrusted three academic institutions – the Intellectual Property Center of China Academy of Social Sciences, the Intellectual Property

---

[3]   WTO, China – Measures Affecting the Protection and Enforcement of Intellectual Property Rights, WT/DS362/R, Report of the Panel, 26 January 2009. According to the panel report, art. 4.1 of the Copyright Law was not in accordance with the Berne Convention and the TRIPS Agreement, since that article provided that the works that were prohibited to be published by laws and regulations should not be protected by this Law. Because this provision violated the principle of automatic protection by the Berne Convention and the TRIPS Agreement, the report proposed that China amend the provision.

[4]   The Standing Committee of the National People's Congress, A Decision to Amend the Copyright Law (February 2010).

Research Center of Zhongnan University of Economics and Law and the Intellectual Property School of Renmin University – to draft their proposals for amending the law.[5] On the basis of these three expert proposals, the NCAC formed its first draft and published it for public consultation on 31 March 2012.[6] Surprisingly, the draft gave rise to huge numbers of opinions, discussions and debates among the public. On 6 July 2012, the NCAC published its second draft on the amendment of the Copyright Law for public consultation.[7] On the basis of the public consultation, the NCAC formed its third draft and submitted it to the State Council on 24 December 2012.[8] At the time of writing, this draft is still under consideration in the Legal Affairs Office under the State Council.

2.1 The Copyright Protection System in China

Initially, some scholars suggested combining the Copyright Law and related regulations, and drafting an overall copyright law, similar to the French, German, Japanese or US copyright systems. In China, the Copyright Law is a basic law, and there are five regulations under this law – the Implementing Regulations of the Copyright Law, the Regulations for the Protection of Software, the Regulations for the Copyright Management Society, the Regulations for the Protection of Network Rights, and the proposed Regulations for the Protection of Folklore – this is the so-called 'one law, five regulations'. Additionally, there are two branches of sub-regulations. The first branch of sub-regulations is promulgated by the administrative agencies,[9] and the second branch of sub-regulations is issued by the Supreme Court of China,[10] the High Court at the provincial

---

5   See the preface in Mingde Li, Yuying Guan and Guangliang Tang, *Experts Proposals for the Amendments of the Copyright Law and Explanations* (Law Press of China 2012) [李明德, 管育鹰, 唐广良: 《著作权法专家建议稿说明》, 法律出版社, 2012年].

6   NCAC, the Drafting Amendments of the Copyright Law (31 March 2012).

7   NCAC, the Drafting Amendments of the Copyright Law (6 July 2012).

8   NCAC, the Drafting Amendments of the Copyright Law to the State Council (24 December 2012).

9   For example, the Ordinance on the Copyright Administrative Penalty by NCAC (2003) and the Ordinance on the Administrative Protection of Copyright in the Internet by NCAC and the Administration of Industry and Information (2005).

10   For example, the Judicial Interpretation on Some Issues Concerning the Application of Law and Trial of Copyright Civil Cases by Supreme Court of China (2002).

level,[11] and some model cases.[12] So the copyright protection system in China is composed of one basic law, five regulations, some administrative regulations and ordinances, judicial guidance or opinions, and model cases. If one is going to talk about copyright protection in China, one should refer not only to the Copyright Law, but also to other regulations and sub-regulations.

The suggestion to draft an overall copyright law was rejected on the basis of limited legislative resources. Generally speaking, it would take about ten years or more to amend a law such as the Copyright Law, Patent Law or Trademark Law. If China were to draft an overall copyright law, it would be difficult for the country to respond in a timely manner to fast social and economic developments. Under the current copyright protection system, although it is difficult to amend the Copyright Law, it is easier for China to amend the Regulations, or issue administrative regulations or ordinances, or to issue judicial interpretations and guidance. Generally speaking, since most of the international copyright norms are imported into the Chinese Copyright Law and related regulations, China has utilized sub-regulations to respond to the challenges resulting from social and economic development, or has implemented the international norms in a mode suitable for China.[13] If China drafted an overall copyright law, it would lose the flexibility and speed that it currently possesses to respond effectively to social and economic developments.

Outlining the current copyright protection system in China is necessary in order to understand the most effective way to amend the Copyright Law. In this sense, the Copyright Law is a basic law providing the basic principles and most important values regarding the protection of original works. Accordingly, any amendment should outline and focus on these principles and values. Any outstanding issues, however, should be resolved by regulations, administrative rules, judicial interpretations and guidance, or even some cases.[14]

---

[11]   For example, the Guidance on the Determination of Damage Concerning Copyright Infringement by the High Court of Beijing (2005).

[12]   In China, the Supreme Court and the Provincial High Courts may publish some model cases annually to be studied by judges. Although these model cases have no binding power, the judges can learn how to decide a similar case.

[13]   In addition to the copyright system, the patent system, the trademark system and the unfair competition system in China are all composed of the basic laws, regulations, administrative regulations or ordinances, and judicial interpretations, guidance, and model cases, and function in a similar way.

[14]   For example, a model case can illustrate how to decide similar cases.

2.2 Repealing the Regulations for the Protection of Computer Software

The draft presented by the Chinese Academy of Social Sciences (CASS draft) proposed the repeal of the Regulations for the Protection of Computer Software.[15] In light of the TRIPS Agreement and the World Intellectual Property Organization Competition Treaty (WCT), computer programs shall be protected as literary works.[16] Therefore, in many countries computer programs are protected directly as literary works under their respective copyright laws. China, however, promulgated a special law in October 1991 – the Regulations for the Protection of Computer Software. Subsequently, these regulations were amended in January 2002.[17] The author has conducted research on the Copyright Law and the Regulations, and found out that most of the provisions in the Regulations are duplications of the texts of the Copyright Act.

The promulgation of the Regulations for the Protection of Computer Software by China is yet another example of Chinese conformity with international norms in its copyright regime. Specifically, between 1988 and 1993, there was an administrative body under the State Council (Administration of Mechanical and Electronic Industry) that was responsible for issues related to the computer software industry. According to the 1991 Regulations the owner of computer software could file a lawsuit only after their computer software was registered.[18] The body responsible for registering the software was the Administration of Mechanical and Electronic Industry, and this body issued the Ordinance on the Registration of Computer Software Copyright in 1991. This ordinance detailed the registration procedure for computer software, such as the application process, examination process, approval process and fees.[19]

However, after the promulgation of the 1991 Regulation, two important events occurred. First, China acceded to the Berne Convention in October 1992, a convention that stipulates that the enjoyment and the exercise of copyright shall vest immediately and without the formalities of registration. Appropriately, the Chinese Supreme Court issued an announcement to the effect that registration was not a requirement for

---

[15] See Mingde Li, Yuying Guan and Guangliang Tang (*supra*, n 5).
[16] See art. 10 TRIPS Agreement and art. 4 WCT.
[17] State Council, Regulations for the Protection of Computer Software, 1991 and 2002.
[18] See art. 24 of the Regulations for the Protection of Computer Software, 1991.
[19] See the Administration of Mechanical and Electronic Industry, Ordinance on the Registration of Computer Software Copyright, 1991.

a court to adjudicate on any computer software cases.[20] Furthermore, in 2002, the registration requirement was removed from the Regulation for the Protection of Computer Software. Secondly, the Administration of Mechanical and Electronic Industry was divided into two separate administrations in 1993, which were both disbanded in 1998 due to the reorganization of the State Council.[21]

On the basis of these two changes, and the adherence to the international practice that computer programs are protected as literary works, it is thought that it is not necessary for China to have a distinct regulation for the protection of computer software. In this respect, the CASS draft referred to the United States' amendment to its Copyright Law in 1980. This amendment provided for the protection of computer programs merely by adding a definition of computer program, and providing two limitations on copyright's exclusivity. These limitations included the permission to make an additional copy of the program and an adaptation of the program by the owner of the copy of the original computer program.[22] The CASS draft therefore proposes to add a similar definition of computer program in the Copyright Law, and to remove the exceptions provided for in the Regulations for the Protection of Computer Software, by including them in the Copyright Law, thus repealing these regulations. In addition, the CASS draft uses the term 'computer program' rather than 'software'. This proposal has already been accepted in the three versions of the drafts submitted to the NCAC and it is therefore strongly assumed that it would be accepted by the State Council and the Standing Committee of the National People's Congress.

2.3 Removing 'Video Recordings'

In the Chinese actions of adapting to international copyright norms, the country has tried to modify some of the norms on its own initiative. One example of this is the protection afforded to video recordings under Chinese law. According to the Rome Convention, the TRIPS Agreement and continental European copyright traditions, copyright's related rights extend to performances, sound recordings and broadcasts. However, when China enacted its Copyright Law, it added the term 'video recordings' to

---

[20]   Supreme Court of China, A Notice on Several Issues of Further Carrying out the Copyright Law of China: art. 4 (December 1993) [最高人民法院关于深入贯彻执行《中华人民共和国著作权)几个问题的通知》].
[21]   See the website of the State Council (www.gov.cn/guowuyuan).
[22]   See section 101 of the US Copyright Act on the definition of software, and section 117 on the limitations of software protection.

sound recordings.[23] However, what is a video recording, what is the difference between a cinematographic work and a video recording? This was not clear for a long time.[24]

During 2004 and 2005, Chinese intellectual property experts, including academics, judges, administrative officials and lawyers, discussed the nature of MTVs (Music Televisions)[25] and whether these were the same as a cinematographic work. The outcome was that most MTVs are cinematographic works, not video recordings. Specifically, cinematographic works and video recordings are no different in a technical sense because they are both motion pictures with or without accompanying sounds. The only difference between them is originality. If it has enough originality, it is a cinematographic work; if it does not have enough originality, it is a video recording. The originality here refers to the standard of author's right system, meaning a certain level of the author's personality, spirit and feelings is embedded in the work.

Moreover, because video recordings are not protected as a specific class of work by any international treaty the CASS draft proposes to eliminate the protection of video recordings as a specific class. Accordingly, China should not protect something that is not protected or defined by any international treaty. This CASS proposal has been accepted in three versions of the draft submitted to the NCAC,[26] and it is again assumed that it will be accepted by the State Council and the Standing Committee of the National People's Congress.

2.4   The Division of Moral Rights and Economic Rights

Although many continental European civil law countries and the Berne Convention signatories separate author's rights into moral rights and economic rights,[27] the current Copyright Law of China has adopted the

---

23   See arts 39–41 of the current Copyright Law of China (on video recordings).

24   The author believes that during the 1980s and early 1990s music performances and cinematographic works were recorded on magnetic tapes and sold in the market. However, what was recorded on the magnetic tapes that could be viewed is a cinematographic work. Because of the misunderstanding, the Copyright Law of China protects both cinematographic works (art. 10) and video recordings.

25   An MTV is composed of a series of moving pictures, accompanied by music and lyrics. One can watch the motion picture or sing the lyrics following the music, which is a fashion in East Asian countries.

26   See the Drafting Amendments of the Copyright Law to the State Council (24 December 2012).

27   See especially arts 121 and 122 of the French Copyright Law and art. *6bis* Berne Convention.

terminology of 'personal rights' and 'property rights'.[28] According to the continental European system, author's rights are property rights, and include both moral rights and economic rights. However, under the Copyright Law of China the term 'property rights' only refers to economic rights, and not to moral rights. Again this is an example of how China has adapted foreign copyright norms in its own way. Although the CASS draft proposes to use the terms 'author's moral rights' and 'economic rights' rather than 'personal rights' and 'property rights', it has not been accepted by the NCAC.

According to the Chinese Copyright Law, the author's property (economic) right consists of 12 exclusivities, namely reproduction, distribution, rental, display, performance, projecting, broadcasting, network communication, cinematographic adaptation and production, adaptation, translation and compilation.[29] Because these 12 exclusivities are interrelated, it is difficult for a right owner and an adjudicating court to determine which specific economic right was infringed.

This practice also related to the adaptation of international copyright norms into China. At the beginning of the establishment of the Chinese intellectual property system, China followed a principle of connecting with international norms. Since the Berne Convention, concluded originally over 100 years ago, provides for the exclusive rights of translation, reproduction, public performance, broadcasting, public recitation, adaptation, and cinematographic adaptation and reproduction,[30] the Copyright Law of China provided for all of these, save for the right of recitation. However, the nature of the exclusive rights, as originally provided for in the Berne Convention, has changed with the development of media technology, and other socio-economic factors. In this respect, the French Copyright Law only provides two economic rights, reproduction and performance, and the US Copyright Law provides five economic rights: reproduction, distribution, derivation, performance and display.[31] It is only after 30 years of this experience, that is the adaptation of international norms into Chinese law, that China has its own sense and awareness as to how best to provide for the rights enjoyed by authors. Thus, the CASS draft proposes that the author's economic rights shall consist of six copyright exclusivities, namely the rights of reproduction, distribution, derivation, performance, display and rental. Among these, the right of display shall only apply to works of

---

[28]   See art. 10 of the Copyright Law of China. The author believes that this was influenced by civil law scholars.
[29]   See art. 10 of the Copyright Law of China.
[30]   See arts 8–14 Berne Convention.
[31]   See arts 14 and 122 of the French Copyright Law and 17 U.S.C. § 106.

fine art and photographs, while the rental right shall only apply to audio-video works, computer programs and sound recordings. This proposal has been accepted by the NCAC to a certain degree. For example, the NCAC draft submitted to the State Council provides that an author should have nine economic rights – the three additional exclusivities are broadcasting, network communication and translation.[32] It is suggested that 'broadcasting' and 'network communication' could be merged into the performance right, while 'translation' could be merged into the derivation right.

2.5 Accommodating the Doctrine of Fair Use and Other Exceptions

According to the continental European system, a copyright is a private right. Therefore, any exceptions or limitations to this private right shall be provided for expressly. If there is no express provision, there is no exception or limitation. Similarly, the EU Information Society Copyright Directive[33] (the 'InfoSoc Directive') provides for a catalogue of exceptions and limitations. In light of the Directive, EU Member States can provide for exceptions and limitations within the scope of the Directive.[34] Adopting a similar approach, the Copyright Law of China provides an exhaustive list of 12 exceptions and limitations.[35] However, the US Copyright Law provides for a limitation on copyright by virtue of the doctrine of fair use. The doctrine is a common law doctrine but has now been codified in the US Copyright Law.[36] Other specific exceptions and limitations to copyright are provided for through sections 108 to 122.[37]

The *Kelly* case is an example of the doctrine of fair use in operation.[38] In *Kelly*, the defendant, a visual-image search engine company, displayed visual images as a result of a search query without permission. The court analysed the defendant's behaviour under fair use, and concluded that their use of the visual images was a fair use.[39] In Germany, a case concerning a similar use of visual images of this kind was initially held to be

---

[32] See the Drafting Amendments of the Copyright Law to the State Council (24 December 2012).

[33] Directive 2001/29/EC of the European Parliament and of the Council of 22 May 2001 on the harmonisation of certain aspects of copyright and related rights in the information society.

[34] See art. 5 InfoSoc Directive, and related recitals.

[35] See art. 22 of the Copyright Law of China.

[36] See 17 U.S.C. § 107.

[37] 17 U.S.C. §§ 108–122.

[38] *Kelly v. Arriba Soft Corp.*, 77 F. Supp. 2d 1116 (D. C. Cal. 1999).

[39] Ibid.

an infringement. Finally, the Federal Court of Justice of Germany held that such use was not an infringement under the provision of implied licence.[40]

On the basis of the reasoning above, the CASS draft proposes to add a fair use clause to the exceptions and limitations clause in the Copyright Law. Specifically, in addition to the 12 exceptions and limitations, the CASS draft adds a clause covering 'some other situations that belong to fair use'. According to the proposal, although the Copyright Law of China originated from the continental European system, China can introduce a fair use defence which is distinctively of US origin, to accommodate the requirements from practice. In this respect, the Copyright Law of course originated from the continental system, but in order to resolve the problems resulting from intellectual property protection, China should accept some norms from the Anglo-American system, and even create some new norms. It is not necessary for China to strictly adhere to the continental European system.

The CASS proposal has been accepted by the NCAC to a certain extent, and the NCAC draft provides for the terminology of 'some other situation' in addition to the exhaustive list of exceptions and limitations. Although it does not use the term 'fair use', it is an opening clause that can accommodate the practical requirements.[41] The NCAC draft's exceptions and limitations would be subject to the 'three-step test' as provided for under the Berne Convention, the TRIPS Agreement and the WCT.[42] The three-step test ensures that any limitation and exception is (i) confined to certain special cases, (ii) does not conflict with the normal exploitation of a work, and (iii) does not unreasonably prejudice the legitimate interests of the author. This means that a court will apply the 'some other situation' clause rarely and subject to the three-step test in order to comply with China's international treaty obligations.

3.   TRADEMARK LAW AMENDMENTS

The Trademark Law of China was enacted in 1982, and amended in 1993 and 2001. Since 2003, the Trademark Office, organized under the State Administration of Industry and Commerce, has initiated a review of the

---

[40]   BGH, IZR 69/08 of 29 April 2010 – *Vorschaubilder I.*
[41]   See art. 42(13) NCAC Draft, which includes the terminology 'some other situation' (其他情形).
[42]   See art. 9 Berne Convention, art. 13 TRIPS Agreement and art. 10 WCT.

Trademark Law and drafted several proposals.[43] After several years of preparation, the State Administration of Industry and Commerce submitted a draft to the State Council in November 2009.[44] In October 2012, the State Council submitted its proposal to the Standing Committee of the National People's Congress. The draft was first reviewed in December 2012 by the Standing Committee of the National People's Congress.[45] On 31 August 2012, the Standing Committee of the National People's Congress passed the amendments of the Trademark Law, which came into effect in May 2014.[46]

To amend an intellectual property law in China, such as the Trademark Law, the first step is for a competent administration under the State Council to draft a proposal. In the case of a trademark-related issue, the responsible body is the State Administration of Industry and Commerce (SAIC), and its subordinate branch, the Trademark Office. This process can last several years. The second step is for the proposal to undergo a review by the State Council and its Legal Affairs Office, and this may last two or three years. The third step is that the draft will be reviewed three times by the Standing Committee of the National People's Congress, a process that will last at least six months.[47] Therefore, generally, it takes between five and ten years to amend a law like the Trademark Law. Similarly, the process to amend the Copyright Law, the Patent Law and the Unfair Competition Law undergoes the same respective steps and also takes the same lengthy period of time.[48]

Due to the fact that the proposal to amend a law is first drafted by the competent administration, the interests or the requirements of the administration are well reflected in the draft. For example, the draft to amend

---

43   The author participated in the discussions on some of the proposals, such as in July 2006 and May 2008.

44   State Administration of Industry and Commerce, The Proposed Amendments of the Trademark Law of China (19 November 2009).

45   An Explanation of the Amendments Draft of the Trademark Law of China (24 December 2012), in the Standing Committee of the National People's Congress.

46   The Standing Committee of the National People's Congress, The Decision to Amend the Trademark Law of China (31 August 2013).

47   If the amendments are concerned with the basic laws, such as the Constitution, that shall be reviewed and passed by the National People's Congress. And the Standing Committee conducts its plenary meeting every other month, six times a year.

48   It should be noted that the proposals to amend the Copyright Law and the Patent Law are now under consideration in the Legal Affairs Office under the State Council, and the proposal to amend the Unfair Competition Law is still in its first stage. So in China there is a saying that the legislature is a rare resource.

the Trademark Law by the SAIC showed a strong tendency to expand the administrative power to regulate the registration and use of trademarks. At the State Council level, however, this administrative tendency will be mitigated on the basis of the opinions of other administrative agencies, the judiciary, private sector stakeholders and academics. In fact, this was exactly what happened to the draft to amend the Trademark Law. As part of the final step in the amendment process, the Standing Committee of the National People's Congress will hear more comprehensive opinions, mitigate against administrative tendencies, and pass the law or amendments.

It should be noted that the Chinese government changed its term in March 2013, and the newly inaugurated National People's Congress and its Standing Committee changed their working style. For example, in the past a law or the amendments of a law submitted by the State Council would be passed by the Standing Committee with some minor changes. However, with the proposal to amend the Trademark Law submitted by the State Council, the Standing Committee of the National People's Congress accepted many proposals from private sector stakeholders, the judiciary and academics to amend the draft submitted by the State Council. It is clear that in the future the Standing Committee of the National People's Congress will play a more important role in producing amendments of the Copyright Law, Patent Law and Unfair Competition Law of China.

3.1   Emphasizing the Use of Registered Trademarks

A trademark is a unique kind of intellectual property right. An intellectual property right is a right over the results of intellectual activities.[49] A trademark right is not a right to own the mark itself, but a right for the use of the mark in business, in that consumers can be confident about the origin of goods as indicated by the mark. As such, the essential function of the trademark is to guarantee the identity of the origin of the marked goods or service to the consumer or end user by enabling them, without any possibility of confusion, to distinguish the goods or service from others. The origin function is indicative of the goodwill or reputation associated with a particular mark and these are therefore enhanced through advertising or increased quality in the related products or services. For example, a trademark owner may use patented and unpatented technology to increase

---

[49]   For example, art. 2 of the Convention Establishing the World Intellectual Property Organization says that intellectual property shall include the rights 'resulting from intellectual activities'.

the quality of the trademarked products, or advertise its trademarked products or services and persuade the consumers to choose its products or services. Only from these or other commercial activities may the goodwill or reputation of a trademark and the claims to a right to a trademark be generated. In other words, if there is no commercial use of a mark, then there can be no goodwill associated with a mark, and accordingly, no trademark right can be claimed.

As the above made clear, a trademark right, as a property right, cannot purely be the result of an administrative registration. However, in China, due to the government and administrative agencies emphasizing the need to register a trademark, a misunderstanding about the concept of registration means that many people believe that the registration of a trademark is an automatic grant of property. Therefore, many enterprises and individuals in China have registered many marks but have never actually used the mark in commerce. In the last several years, trademark registration applications have amounted to more than one million every year, with the number of applications for 2013 being 1,881,500.[50] The total number of valid registrations for trademarks was in the region of 6,090,000 in 2012,[51] and it is estimated that there will be about ten million valid registrations by the end of 2014.

As a result of the large number of trademark grants and applications, China has become the world's number one country, in volume, for registered trademarks. However, a serious question needs to be asked – how many marks that are the subject of applications for registration are going to be used in commerce, and how many registered trademarks have actually been used in commerce? If a registered trademark has never been used in commerce, can we call it a registered trademark? Just as the term suggests, a trademark means a mark is used in trade. If a mark has never been used in trade or commerce, even it is registered by an administrative agency, it should not be a valid trademark. Perhaps it is proper that we refer to such marks as 'registered marks', but not as registered trademarks. It is the view of this author that two kinds of right subsist in a registered trademark that has been used in commerce: a substantive property right that results from the use of the mark in the course of trade, and a sort of 'procedural' right that results from registration. The 'procedural' right

---

[50] State Intellectual Property Office of China, White Paper on the Protection of Intellectual Property for 2013 (April 2014), available at <www.sipo.gov.cn>.

[51] State Administration of Industry and Commerce, *An Explanation on the Amendments of the Trademark Law of China to the Standing Committee of the National People's Congress* (December 2012).

should then be connected with the property right of a trademark, and may exist for at most three years if the mark has not been used.[52]

Under the reasoning above, the new Trademark Law emphasizes the requirement of use for trademarks in many articles. For example, article 4 provides that any trademark that is used in connection with goods or services can be registered. Article 8 provides that any sign that can distinguish one's goods or services from another's goods or services can be registered as a trademark. Article 48 defines use as meaning to use the trademark in connection with goods or services, the packaging of goods, advertising, exhibiting or other commercial activities where the mark is demonstrated to distinguish the origin of goods or services. Furthermore, article 64 provides that if the owner of a registered trademark seeks damages, evidence must demonstrate that the trademark has been used in commerce in the preceding three years.[53] It is apparent that the damage must be connected to the goodwill or reputation represented by a registered trademark.

The need to emphasize the concept of use for registered trademarks must be understood against the background of the Chinese culture, a culture where administrative powers have played an important role in regulating society. In light of this culture, most people have placed a lot of trust, often too much, in governmental agencies. Therefore, on the one hand, the administrative agencies overemphasize the need for the registration of a trademark, while on the other hand many private actors believe that their trademark rights arise solely from the act of registration. Generally, the concept of a trademark is new to Chinese culture and we are only in the initial stages of understanding, in fact, what a trademark is and what purpose administrative registration of a trademark serves.

3.2   Rectifying the Practice for Well-known Trademarks

In light of the Paris Convention and TRIPS Agreement, a well-known trademark is protected either under the doctrine of likelihood of confusion or likelihood of dilution.[54] It is important to highlight that the purpose of identifying a trademark as a well-known mark is to resolve disputes surrounding the use of the trademark and to determine the scope of protection granted to the mark. Once a particular dispute has been resolved, the fact that the specific mark was deemed to be well known is not formally

---

[52]   According to art. 49 of the Trademark Law of China, if a registered trademark has not been used for three years in succession, the registration shall be cancelled. See art. 19 TRIPS Agreement.

[53]   See arts 4, 8, 48 and 64 of the 2013 Trademark Law.

[54]   See art. 6*bis* Paris Convention and art. 16 TRIPS Agreement.

attached to that mark, that is the case-specific consideration should not give additional property value to the mark.

However, in China, according to the proposal by the SAIC, the well-known status of a mark would be maintained from the reputation associated with a trademark over many years. In other words, if a trademark was declared a well-known mark, it would enjoy stronger protection than a common trademark beyond the dispute. A trademark could be designated as well known either in an administrative procedure or a judicial procedure. The administrative system has created three layers of well-known trademarks: the national well-known trademarks, which could be identified by the Trademark Office and the Trademark Review Board and judicial system; the provincial well-known trademarks (*zhu ming* trademarks), which could be identified by the provincial administration of industry and commerce; and the well-known trademarks at the municipality level (*zhi ming* trademarks), which could be identified by the municipality administration of industry and commerce.

Again this formal and administrative recognition of well-known marks is an astonishing example of how a rule of intellectual property protection has been transformed upon adaptation in China. Since 1996, the SAIC, including its local subordinates, strongly advocated such a well-known trademark system to keep its administrative power in managing the use of trademarks and regulating the market.[55] Consequently, many trademark owners, in order to get a formal administrative title of a well-known trademark, have litigated with one another, and even pleaded some false cases. Many experts have criticized that there were a great number of formal titles of national well-known trademarks, but few of these are recognized as international and national brands in the market.

During the amendment of the Trademark Law, academics had strongly opposed such practices, proposing that if the trademark owner is prohibited from using the formal well-known status, for example in the advertisement of the goods or services, the bad practice may be corrected.[56] The SAIC, on the basis of its interests, has rejected the academics' proposal again and again. However, the State Council accepted the proposal to a certain degree and suggested a provision that the identification of a trademark as a well-known mark shall be regarded as a factual consideration in trademark disputes. This means that the effect of a well-known trademark shall be limited to each disputed case, and the owner shall not advertise

---

[55] In 1996, the State Administration of Industry and Commerce published its first list of well-known trademarks.

[56] The author had advocated this opinion for many years.

his or her trademark as a well-known mark after the dispute has been resolved. In this respect, the Standing Committee of the National People's Congress provides clearly that the trademark owner shall not advertise his or her products in the name of a 'well-known trademark'. If a trademark owner violates this provision, he or she shall be fined 100,000 CNY by a local administration of industry and commerce.[57]

Under the newly amended Trademark Law, it seems that the rule for the protection of well-known trademarks has returned to its correct point. However, it is not clear how to end the practices of provincial well-known trademarks and the well-known trademarks at the municipality level, which operate under the local authority.

3.3   The Standard for Trademark Infringement

In many countries, the likelihood of confusion is the objective standard for trademark infringement, and is closely related to the goodwill or reputation represented by a trademark. This standard means that any competitor shall not act as a free-rider on another's trademark. However, in China, the Trademark Law had provided for many years that if the same or a similar mark had been used with the same or similar goods, there could be a trademark infringement.[58] Naturally, in many cases, there is a likelihood of confusion when the same or a similar trademark is used with the same or similar goods. However, in some situations there may be no likelihood of confusion.

During the amendment process of the Trademark Law, academic circles, the judicial system and even the private sector in China advocated for the law to clearly stipulate that the standard for trademark infringement is the likelihood of confusion. The likelihood of confusion is directly related to the fact that the Trademark Law (including the Unfair Competition Law), is a law regulating market relationships. However, this idea was rejected again by the SAIC on the basis that it was not easy for the administrative officers to decide whether there was a likelihood of confusion. The State Council did not accept the standard either, on the grounds that they were not convinced by the related reasoning.[59]

The Standing Committee of the National People's Congress, however, accepted the proposal on the basis of comprehensive hearings. According to the amended law, when the same mark is used with similar goods

---

[57]   See arts 14 and 53 of the 2013 Trademark Law.
[58]   See art. 52 of the 2001 Trademark Law.
[59]   One of the officials from the Legal Affairs Office told the author that they were not convinced by the proposal.

or services, or a similar mark is used with the same or similar goods or services, the court shall decide whether there is a likelihood of confusion.[60] This is a major achievement, as after 30 years from the law's initial enactment it is the first time that the Trademark Law has a clause concerning the likelihood of confusion. The newly amended law, however, provides that if the same mark is used with the same goods or services, it is an infringement of the trademark, and there is no need for a court to consider likelihood of confusion. According to the TRIPS Agreement, where an identical mark is used for identical goods or services, there is a presumption in favour of the likelihood of confusion.[61] The wording 'presumption' means that the possibility also exists that there is no likelihood of confusion, that is the presumption can be rebutted. Accordingly, this issue may be resolved in the next amendment to the law, or by the judiciary.

3.4 Punitive Damages

In recent years, intellectual property owners in China have complained about the fact that they have won many cases but lost money. Specifically they spend a lot of money in acquiring evidence and hiring lawyers and experts, but only receive a limited amount of damages under the principle of compensation. In addition to this, many experts suggest that the amount of damages awarded against an infringer, under the principle of compensation, does not effectively deter future infringements of intellectual property rights.

During the third revision of the Trademark Law, Copyright Law and Patent Law, it was advocated strongly that China should introduce punitive damages akin to those under the Patent Law of the United States.[62] However, this proposal has been opposed by Chinese civil law experts, who argue that the civil laws of China originate from the European continental system and accordingly the principle for an award of damages should be compensatory and not punitive. They have further suggested that it would be unfair for a plaintiff to receive an amount of damages that is twice or three times what he or she would get in compensatory terms.

Although there are still some debates on the punitive damages issue, the amendment to the Trademark Law accepted the inclusion of punitive damages under article 63. According to the new Trademark Law, with

---

[60] See art. 57 of the 2013 Trademark Law.
[61] See art. 16 TRIPS Agreement.
[62] According to art. 284 of the Patent Law of the United States, a court can award damages twice or three times the amount of the plaintiff's loss or the infringer's profits.

respect to the repeated or malicious infringement of a trademark, a court can award damages that are twice or three times the plaintiff's actual loss or the infringer's profits or a reasonable royalty.[63] This article serves as an example for other intellectual property laws, and means that amendments to the Copyright Law and the Patent Law should follow this example. In fact, the drafting amendments of the Copyright Law and Patent Law do include punitive damages measures for serious copyright or patent infringement.

This again serves as an example of China being confronted with the challenge of integrating different legal traditions and norms into its system. In the author's view, the issue here is not about legal tradition and fairness, but rather how best to curb serious trademark, copyright and patent infringements. Although Chinese intellectual property law originates from the continental European system, if there is a need to resolve a practical problem, China is willing to adopt doctrines from the Anglo-American system. In fact, if it is necessary to resolve some new problems, China may even create some new norms.

3.5   Amending Unfair Competition Law

Unfair competition law is closely related to trademark law. From the perspective of the Anglo-American system, trademark law originated from unfair competition law and should be considered a branch of unfair competition law.[64] According to the Paris Convention, any competitive behaviour contrary to honest practices in industrial or commercial matters constitutes an act of unfair competition. On the basis of honest practices, the Paris Convention lists three specific acts as unfair competition: passing off, commercial disparagement and false advertising. The TRIPS Agreement adds another act to this list, namely the misappropriation of another's trade secrets.[65] This means that every signatory to these agreements, in order to fulfil its treaty obligations, shall pass laws to provide for the basic principle of honest practice and the prohibition of the four aforementioned acts.

China enacted its Unfair Competition Law in December 1993. This law does provide for the principle of honest practice and prohibits the four aforementioned acts. However, there are some additional provisions in the law, relating to topics such as antitrust, commercial

---

[63]   See 2013 Trademark Law, art. 63.
[64]   For example, the US Lanham Act originated from unfair competition law.
[65]   See art. 10*bis* Paris Convention and art. 39 TRIPS Agreement.

bribery, dumping and illegal tender. The Chinese law is a mixed law as such, and concerns itself with unfair competition, antitrust and some other commercial acts, which are often regulated under separate regulations. This is another example demonstrating how international practices and norms have been adapted and transformed in China. What one can say about the Unfair Competition Law of China is that it is not a copied law from a particular country and it corresponds to the requirements of the Paris Convention and TRIPS Agreement, but goes further.

In recent years, some Chinese scholars have confused the terms 'competition law' and 'unfair competition law', believing that they are both the same laws regulating market order. It is true that competition law and unfair competition law are laws regulating competitors' behaviour in the market. However, competition law, or antitrust law or antimonopoly law, is public law, authorizing government agencies to intervene in the competitive order of the market, in order to prevent monopolies or conglomerates that damage the competitive nature of markets. On the other hand, unfair competition law is private law, authorizing a competitor to prohibit another's unfair competitive practices, such as passing off, false advertising, commercial disparagement and the misappropriation of trade secrets.

In 2008, the SAIC started to amend the Unfair Competition Law. However, most of the experts who were invited and have participated in the related drafting activities are experts on competition law or antitrust law and only a few experts on intellectual property law were invited and have participated in the related activities. It is the author's view that the Unfair Competition Law should be a part of intellectual property law, prohibiting the four aforementioned behaviours under the Paris Convention and the TRIPS Agreement. The provisions relating to other topics, such as antitrust, commercial bribery, dumping and illegal tender, should be excluded from the scope of this law and should be regulated separately.

4. PATENT LAW AMENDMENTS

The Patent Law of China was enacted in March 1984, and subsequently amended three times, in 1991, 2000 and 2008. In November 2011, the State Council issued a document entitled 'Some Opinions on Further Actions to Curb Counterfeiting and Piracy Goods'. This document proposed that the administrations involved should set up a long-term mechanism to amend the laws and related regulations. Against this background, the

State Intellectual Property Office (SIPO) launched a new amendment of the Patent Law and submitted a draft to the State Council in January 2013.[66]

Since the new amendment was drafted in accordance with the Opinion by the State Council, it focused on enforcement and was not an overall amendment to the Patent Law. In this respect, SIPO outlined the problems of patent enforcement. These problems included the difficulty in obtaining evidence for patent infringements, the long delays in actions to invalidate a patent, the high costs involved in enforcing a patent right, low damages awarded, and the ineffectiveness of the available means to discourage patent infringement.[67] To resolve these problems, the draft proposed some measures.

To resolve the problems of the high costs involved with patent enforcement and the low amount of damages awarded the draft provides for a measure concerning punitive damages. In the case of an intentional infringer, a court may award an amount of damages that is twice or three times the amount of the plaintiff's loss, the infringer's profits or reasonable royalties.[68] To resolve the difficulties in obtaining evidence of infringement, the draft provides that if a patent infringement has occurred, the plaintiff may claim a certain amount of damages awarded on the basis of their own evidence. Then the defendant shall demonstrate their evidence and if the defendant refuses to show their evidence, the court can decide the amount of damages on the basis of the plaintiff's claims.[69] In fact, these two solutions have been provided in the new Trademark Law and also in the proposal to amend the Copyright Law.

The most prominent feature of the draft is the ability of the patent administration to investigate cases of suspected patent infringement. For example, the draft provides that if the patent administration suspects, on the basis of some evidence, that a party has infringed another's patent, the administration can interview the related parties, examine premises, copy contracts, invoices and accounts related to the products, and even seal up or seize the products. Furthermore, the draft provides that if the patent administration suspects that there are mass infringements or repeated infringements of patents, the administration may intervene on the basis of its own authority. If an intentional infringement is ascertained, the

---

[66]   SIPO, The Drafting Amendments of the Parent Law to the State Council (18 January 2013).

[67]   See ibid.

[68]   See ibid.

[69]   See ibid.

administration could issue an injunction, and confiscate and destroy the related products or equipment.[70]

To understand this amendment, we must refer to the unique intellectual property administrative system in China. Most countries in the world only have one patent, trademark and copyright office, each of which takes charge of related matters. However, in China, not only are there central state-level patent, trademark and copyright offices, but also local intellectual property offices, trademark administrations and copyright administrations at the provincial level, municipality level and even at the county level. It is fair to say that China is the only country in the world to establish such a complex administrative system for intellectual property.

In light of this intellectual property administrative system, one can understand that government agencies have played an important role in the creation, utilization and protection of intellectual property in China. First, they may promote patent, trademark and copyright applications and registrations. For example, it took about 15 years for China to reach its first million patent applications. Four years on, China reached its second million in patent applications and about two and a half years later, its third million in patent applications. In recent years, the number of patent applications received has amounted to more than one million every year, and in 2013, the number of patent applications amounted to 2,370,000.[71] Similarly, this exponential growth is also noticed in the registration of trademarks and copyrights. Secondly, the administrative system undertakes the task of dealing with disputes or infringements of intellectual property rights. Under the current Patent Law, Copyright Law, Trademark Law and Unfair Competition Law, if there is an infringement or dispute, the rights owner can either put forward a lawsuit to a competent court, or ask an administrative agency to investigate and stop the infringement. This represents a dual approach in China to deal with intellectual property disputes.

For the reasons outlined above, the administrative agencies have always tried to expand their executive powers and regulate more affairs in the protection of intellectual property rights. In this respect, they even have a sound argument that this dual approach in resolving intellectual property disputes is particularly Chinese and has developed well. However, if we say there are some positive elements for the administrative system, there

---

[70] See ibid.
[71] SIPO, White Paper on the Protection of Intellectual Property for 2013 (April 2014), available at <www.sipo.gov.cn>. It should be noted that there are three kinds of patents in China: invention patents, utility model patents and design patents.

are some negative effects on the protection of intellectual property arising from this system. Here we may emphasize that a patent (or a trademark or a copyright) is a private right. Inevitably, when there is an invention, the decision to apply for a patent, maintain a patent or enforce a patent over that invention will be that of the inventor/right holder. A government agency should not interfere too much in the application and enforcement of a patent. Many experts have criticized the fact that a government agency can go to a company in order to investigate a suspected patent infringement and even pursue coercive measures contained in the amendment as being detrimental to businesses in China.

5.   CONCLUDING REMARKS

In 1978 China enacted its modern Trademark Law, Patent Law, Copyright Law and Unfair Competition Law, and amended these laws thereafter. In this respect, China has been an importer of international legal norms, and has adapted and integrated many of these norms and practices into the Chinese intellectual property system. However, China is not a rigid importer of international legal norms in the protection of intellectual property. Wherever possible, China has tried to localize some of the norms of intellectual property protection on the basis of its own special political, economic and social situations. Thus there are particularly Chinese transformations based on the adaptation of international norms.

The transformations can be roughly divided into two kinds. The first kind of transformation is concerned with the special political situation of China. For example, China has established a legal system for the protection of intellectual property rights, which is composed of the basic law, the implementing regulations, special regulations, administrative rules and ordinances, judicial interpretations, judicial guidance and model cases. As another example, China has established its patent administration, copyright administration, trademark administration and unfair competition administration not only in the central government, but also at provincial, municipality and county levels. On the basis of this administrative system, China has adopted a dual approach to deal with infringement of patent, trademark, copyright and unfair competition cases.

The second kind of transformation resulted from the misunderstanding of some international norms. For example, the Copyright Law of China provides for the protection of video recordings, uses the terms personal right and property right, rather than moral right and economic right, and provides almost all of the economic rights from the Berne Convention. With the Trademark Law of China, it places too much emphasis on the registration of trademarks and the protection of the registered trademarks, and this results in many Chinese private actors believing, even today, that the registration of a trademark is a grant of a property right as such, even without use. Furthermore, the Trademark Law did not provide likelihood of confusion as a standard for trademark infringement until 2013, and this neglected the fact that the Trademark Law is a law to regulate market competition. In addition, with promotion by the trademark administrations, the well-known trademark was distorted as a special formal title attached to some trademarks, and as a result, there have been created three layers of well-known trademarks, namely national well-known trademarks, provincial well-known trademarks (*zhu ming* trademarks), and the well-known trademarks at the municipality level (*zhi ming* trademarks).

On the one hand, because some of the transformations are based on a misunderstanding of the international intellectual property norms, they have also distorted the doctrines of intellectual property protection and the market competition order in China. Therefore one of the tasks in the third-round revision of the Trademark Law, Copyright Law and Patent Law is to correct some of these doctrinal misunderstandings, for instance by removing the protection for video recordings, emphasizing the use of registered trademarks, and providing the likelihood of confusion as the objective standard for trademark infringement. Many of these misunderstandings, however, will exist in the future, such as the terms 'personal right' and 'property right' in the Copyright Law,[72] the emphasis on the registration of trademarks, and confusion as to the differences between the terms competition law and unfair competition law.

On the other hand, the transformation of some international norms is good news for China. It means that in the course of integrating international intellectual property norms, China has always tried to accommodate the international norms within its own political, economic and social structures. In other words, China is not a simple and rigid importer of international norms. On the basis of the Chinese experience of transformation, it is not so difficult for China to accept some intellectual property norms from the Anglo-American system, in spite of the fact that the Chinese intellectual property system is based primarily on the continental European system. In this respect, China has accepted a provision about punitive damages in the Trademark Law, and will provide for punitive damages in the Copyright Law and Patent Law. Again, China is now

---

[72] The NCAC draft does not accept the terms moral right and economic right. See the discussion about the copyright law amendments in this chapter.

going to accept the doctrine of fair use from the US Copyright Law and combine different legal doctrines in the Copyright Law of China.

It should be noted that the second kind of transformation is a result of practical requirements. In other words, to effectively curb serious infringements of trademarks, copyrights and patents, China has accepted the provision of punitive damages from the Anglo-American system. In order to respond to demands from practice in copyright protection, China should accept the doctrine of fair use proposed in a Chinese way. If we push this reasoning further, we can say that if it is necessary to resolve some practical challenges, China may create some new norms for the protection of intellectual property with unique Chinese traits, and in turn give something back to international society.

PART II

Comparing concepts and norms in Chinese and European IP law

5. The concept of originality in copyright law in China and Europe

Kan He

1. INTRODUCTION

In most countries, the term 'original' is used to describe a substantive requirement necessary to gain protection for a work under the respective copyright regime.[1] It functions as a filter or criterion to determine what deserves protection[2] and it determines the breadth of scope of copyright protection.[3]

The concept was initially introduced in Europe[4] and the 'originality' requirement has now spread across the world through the exportation of copyright law via colonialism or international treaties such as TRIPs.[5] It can definitively be stated that 'originality' is a norm in copyright law. However, the concept of originality is not uniform and varies in each jurisdiction. This is often due to cultural and/or socio-economic conditions in a given country. Generally, the concept is always determined by the courts, who decide on a case-by-case basis the tests or standards to achieve originality in civil cases.[6]

---

[1] Despite the fact that different countries name the requirement for the protection differently in their national legislation, it is common in the academic field to use 'original' in English to describe the threshold for whether a work is protected or not.

[2] See Elizabeth F Judge and Daniel Gervais, 'Of Silos and Constellations: Comparing Notions of Originality in Copyright Law' (2009) 27 Cardozo Arts & Entertainment 375, 378.

[3] Eleonora Rosati, *Originality in EU Copyright: Full Harmonization through Case Law* (Edward Elgar Publishing 2013) 59.

[4] More accurately, the UK is the first country that uses the term 'original' to set up a threshold for copyright protection. It then becomes a norm through using the term in most of the international treaties.

[5] Sike von Lewinski, *International Copyright Law and Policy* (OUP 2008) 32.

[6] It is rare to see a provision in copyright law that explicitly states the threshold for originality. Even in statute-law countries such as Germany, one cannot find such an article.

In Europe, different philosophical foundations on copyright shape the concept of originality. These differences in the concept of originality may become a barrier to establishing a true internal market and thus efforts have been made to harmonize copyright law in the EU through secondary legislation[7] or uniform interpretations made by the Court of Justice of the European Union (CJEU).[8]

China has transplanted the Western traditions of copyright law through the implementation of its obligations under various international treaties, bilateral agreements and free trade agreements. The early transplantation of copyright law in China resulted in a diverse understanding among scholars and judges on all aspects of copyright law, and originality, as a fundamental concept, is interpreted differently among scholars and courts.

This chapter will comment on the emergence of a harmonized understanding of the originality requirement in the EU and the emergence of a consensus of this concept in China. Furthermore, these two perspectives will be utilized for comparative purposes. However, this chapter will commence in Section 2 with an analysis of European policy makers' efforts to harmonize the definition and standard of originality. It is fair to conclude

---

[7]   There are three legal instruments used for harmonization of national laws in the EU: regulations, directives and recommendations. In the field of copyright, the EU has published eight directives to harmonize different aspects of copyright. They are Directive 2009/24/EC of the European Parliament and of the Council of 23 April 2009 on the legal protection of computer programs (Computer Directive); Directive 2006/115/EC of the European Parliament and of the Council of 23 April 2009 on rental rights and lending rights and on certain rights related to copyright; Directive 93/83/EEC of 27 September 1993 on the coordination of certain rules concerning copyright and rights related to copyright applicable to satellite broadcasting and cable retransmission; Directive 96/9/EC of the European Parliament and of the Council of 11 March 1996 on the legal protection of data-bases (Database Directive); Directive 2006/116/EC of the European Parliament and of the Council of 12 December 2006 on the term of protection of copyright and certain related rights (codified version); Directive 2001/84/EC of the European Parliament and of the Council of 27 September 2001 on the resale right for the benefit of the author of an original work of art; Directive 2001/29/EC of the European Parliament and of the Council of 22 May 2001 on the harmonization of certain aspects of copyright and related rights in the information society; Directive 2011/77/EU of the European Parliament and of the Council of 27 September 2011 amending Directive 2006/116/EC on the term of protection of copyright and certain related rights.

[8]   Since the *Infopaq* case, the CJEU (formerly ECJ) has caught its opportunities to establish a certain uniform standard for originality in different kinds of works such as photographic works (*Painer*), graphic display (*BSA*), football broadcasting (*Football Association Premier League*), etc. These cases will be discussed below.

that a uniform concept of originality, namely 'author's own intellectual creation' was established by an interpretation of the CJEU. Section 3 then presents the concept of originality as defined in China. In Section 4, a comparison between the EU's concept of originality and China's will be discussed from the perspective of norm giver or norm taker. The chapter concludes with an argument that each country may perform both the role of norm giver and norm taker in any future determinations concerning the concept of originality.

2. ORIGINALITY IN THE EU: ESTABLISHING A UNIFORM CONCEPT

2.1 'Author's Personal Creation' vs. 'Skill, Labour, and Judgement': Two Typical Standards for Originality in Europe

In Europe, there are two broad standards for originality; namely, an 'author's personal creation' or 'skill, labour, and judgement'. The former standard dominates most of the continental European countries. Under this standard, a work is considered original if it reflects the personality of the author or achieves a certain degree of creativity, such as *Gestaltungshöhe* ('level of creativity') in German law. The latter standard is the product of an authoritative UK court judgment, which provides that a 'work must not be copied from another work – that it should *originate from* author'.[9] Subsequently, this standard was developed further and would be determined by whether there has been 'the expenditure of a substantial amount of [an author's] own *skill, knowledge, mental labour, taste or judgment'*.[10]

It is often difficult to determine the exact degree of skill, labour and knowledge, or the level of creativity or personality to reach each originality requirement set by different jurisdictions. It is argued that the threshold in some cases may not be so divergent when these different standards are applied, as the level or scale will largely depend on the specific facts of the case.[11] However, it is commonly accepted that the standard of originality in author's right countries is higher than that in copyright countries.

---

[9] *University of London Press, Ltd v. University Tutorial Press Ltd* [1916] 2 Ch 601, 608–9 (emphasis added).

[10] *Ladbroke (Football) Ltd v. William Hill (Football) Ltd* [1964] 1 WLR 273 (emphasis added); Hugh Laddie, Peter Prescott, Mary Victoria and others, *The Modern Law of Copyright and Designs* (4th edn, LexisNexis 2011) Vol I, 80.

[11] *Macmillan & Co Ltd v. Cooper* (1923) 93 LJPC 113 [121] (Atkinson J).

2.2 'Author's Own Intellectual Creation': a Harmonized Concept in the EU

2.2.1 The originality in the Directives

Since differences in the copyright law of member states may impair the free movement of goods and services and the functioning of the EU's internal market, the EU has attempted to harmonize national laws in this field by issuing a number of directives. Among the directives, the Computer Directive, Database Directive and Term Directive clarify one substantive requirement for a computer program, a database as well as a photographic work: such works are in principle protected if they are 'original' in the sense that they are the author's own intellectual creation.[12]

In the preambles of these Directives, it is confirmed that this is the only test on originality concerning these three categories of works. The preambles state that the member states should not apply any qualitative or aesthetic test for computer programs and databases,[13] while no other criteria such as merit or purpose should be applied for photographic works.[14] In the view of one of the authoritative commentaries on EU copyright, the standard for originality established in these Directives is lower than that in the author's right system and higher than that in countries following copyright tradition.[15] However, with these abstract wordings and interpretations in the Directives, it is still not clear what the actual standard would be and what test is reasonable to examine originality for these three kinds of works. The national courts have a substantial degree of discretion in the application of these definitions but are restricted by any uniform interpretation made by the CJEU.

---

[12]   Art. 1(3) Computer Directive; art. 3(1) Database Directive; art. 6 Directive 2006/116/EC of the European Parliament and of the Council of 12 December 2006 on the term of term of protection of copyright and certain related rights, amended by Directive 2011/77/EU of the European Parliament and of the Council of 27 September 2011 (Term Directive).

[13]   Recital 8 in the preamble to the Computer Directive; recital 16 in the preamble to the Database Directive.

[14]   Recital 16 in the preamble to the Term Directive.

[15]   It is commonly accepted that this standard is a compromise between the two systems since the official memorandum on the proposals for the Computer Directive clearly rejected the low standard in the UK and the high standard in Germany. See Michel M Walter and Silke von Lewinski (eds), *European Copyright: A Commentary* (OUP 2012) sec. 5.1.17.

2.2.2 Harmonization through the jurisprudence of the CJEU

After harmonizing the originality requirement in these three Directives, the European Commission has no intention to further harmonize copyright law in the member states. In respect of originality, the Commission Staff Working Paper of 19 July 2004[16] concluded that there is no need to extend 'author's own intellectual creation' to other categories of works. However, it is said that this horizontal extension would be an appropriate measure of harmonization because 'the divergent requirements for the level of originality by Member States have the potential of posing barriers to intra-Community trade'.[17]

Since 2009, an expansionist CJEU has begun to harmonize by interpretation the concept of originality to other categories of works by interpreting the meaning or criteria for examining an 'author's own intellectual creation' in a number of referral cases.

2.2.2.1   Extending 'author's own intellectual creation' to all categories of works   In the *Infopaq* case,[18] the ECJ[19] showed its intent to create a uniform concept of originality. In addition to software, database and photographic originality as defined by the aforementioned Directives, the ECJ extended the definition of an 'author's own intellectual creation' to other categories of works. The ECJ based its argument on the fact that the InfoSoc Directive[20] was rooted in similar principles as other directives. Accordingly, the ECJ held that copyright within the meaning of Article 2(a) of the InfoSoc Directive applies only in relation to subject matter which is original in the sense that it is its author's own

---

[16]   European Commission, *Commission Staff Working Paper on the review of the EC legal framework in the field of copyright and related rights* (Brussels, 19 July 2004, SEC (2004) 995) 11.

[17]   Ibid 14; Walter and Von Lewinski (*supra*, n 15) sec. 16.0.8.

[18]   Case C-5/08 *Infopaq International A/S v. Danske Dagblades Forening* ECLI:EU:C:2009:465. The defendant in the case used an automated process consisting of the scanning and conversion into digital files to excerpt 11 words from an article in a Danish newspaper. The Danish Supreme Court referred several questions to the ECJ. In respect of originality, the first question is mostly relevant. It asks whether reproduction in art. 2 of the InfoSoc Directive (*infra*, n 20) is interpreted as meaning that it encompasses the storing and subsequent printing out of a newspaper text extract consisting of 11 words.

[19]   ECJ stands for European Court of Justice. It was the former body of the Court of Justice of the European Union.

[20]   Directive 2001/29/EC of the European Parliament and of the Council of 22 May 2001 on the harmonisation of certain aspects of copyright and related rights in the information society (InfoSoc Directive).

intellectual creation in order to establish a harmonized legal framework for copyright.[21]

Subsequently, in the *BSA* case,[22] the ECJ affirmed its ruling in the *Infopaq* case. It held that a graphic user interface could be protected in accordance with the InfoSoc Directive if it is author's own intellectual creation,[23] although it does not constitute a form of expression of a computer program within the meaning of Article 1(2) of the Computer Directive.[24]

Reflecting upon these two cases, it could be concluded that the ECJ extended 'author's own intellectual creation' to other categories of works, in addition to computer programs, databases and photographic works. By interpreting Article 2(a) of the InfoSoc Directive in this manner, debate has arisen as to whether the ECJ was allowed to act in such a manner. It is fair to say now that 'everything in the literary, scientific or artistic domain can be protected if it is original in the sense that it is author's intellectual creation regardless of categories of works stipulated in national laws'.[25]

2.2.2.2 Further harmonization on the meaning of originality After extending 'author's intellectual creation' to other categories of works, the ECJ further attempted to explain what an 'author's intellectual creation' means.

In the *Murphy* Case,[26] the Court ruled out sporting events *per se* as a

---

[21] Case C-5/08 *Infopaq International A/S v. Danske Dagblades Forening* ECLI:EU:C:2009:465, paras 36–37.

[22] Case C-393/09 *Bezpecnostni softwarova asociace v. Ministerstvo kultury* ECLI:EU:C:2010:816. In the national proceedings in the Czech Republic, the Ministry of Culture refused to allow BSA to collectively administer copyright in computer programs because the ministry held that graphic user interfaces cannot be protected in copyright law because it is a result of the display of the program on the screen, not a computer program. On appeal, the Supreme Administrative Court of the Czech Republic (Nejvyšší správní soud) referred two questions to the ECJ, the first of which is relevant to the discussion here. It asks whether the phrase 'the expression in any form of a computer program' in art. 1(2) of the Computer Directive includes the graphic user interface of the computer program or a part thereof.

[23] Ibid para 46.

[24] Ibid para 42.

[25] Rosati (*supra*, n 3) 100.

[26] Joined Cases C-403/08 and C-429/08 *Football Association Premier League Ltd, NetMed Hellas SA, Multichoice Hellas SA v. QC Leisure, David Richardson, AV station plc, Malcolm Chamberlain, Michael Madden, SR Leisure Ltd, Philip George Charles Houghton, Derek Owen and Karen Murphy v. Media Protection Service Ltd* ECLI:EU:C:2011:631. In the national proceedings in the UK, Football

protectable copyright work[27] by reasoning that sports events, in particular football matches, cannot be regarded as 'intellectual creations' classifiable as works within the meaning of the InfoSoc Directive because they are 'subjected to the rules of the game, leaving no room for creative freedom for the purpose of copyright'.[28]

Later in the *Painer* case,[29] the ECJ had an opportunity to interpret Article 6 of the Term Directive concerning the copyrightability of photographic works, especially whether works based on reality, such as portrait photographs could enjoy copyright protection. It held that a work is original if it reflects the author's personality.[30] And this is 'the case if the author was able to express his creative abilities in the protection of a work by making free and creative choices'.[31] Further, the court argued that a 'photographer can make free and creative choices in several ways and at various points in the production of a portrait photograph'.[32] Furthermore, the court noted that '[b]y making those various choices, the author of

---

Association Premier League Ltd and others (FAPL) claimed to be owners of recordings of football matches and concluded territory-restricted licences with different broadcasting organizations in different member states. They sued the suppliers of equipment and satellite decoder cards that enabled the reception of programmes of foreign broadcasters as well as licensees or operators of public houses who had screened live Premier League matches by using a foreign decoding device. In deciding the case, the High Court of Justice of England and Wales referred eight questions to the ECJ. In the case of Ms Murphy, Media Protection Service Ltd, representing the FAPL, sued Ms Murphy for receiving in her public house broadcasts of Premier League matches transmitted by NOVA, which was not allowed to license its broadcast in the UK. The Portsmouth Crown Court supported the plaintiff and the case was appealed to High Court of Justice of England and Wales. This Court stayed the proceedings and referred ten questions to the ECJ.

[27] Ibid para 96.
[28] Ibid para 98.
[29] Case C-145/10 *Eva-Maria Painer v. Standard Verlages GmbH and Others* ECLI:EU:C:2011:798. In this case, Painer had taken a photo of a girl named Natascha Kampusch. After this girl was abducted and escaped, the defendants, mostly news agencies, published the photo taken by Painer and released a portrait representing the supposed image of Kampusch created by computer from the contested photos. Painer sued these news agencies for injunctions and damages. The Austrian Courts decided to stay the proceedings and referred four questions to the ECJ. Here the relevant one is whether photographic works and/or photographs, particularly portrait photos, are afforded 'weak' copyright protection or no copyright protection at all against adaptations because, in view of their 'realistic image', the degree of formative freedom is too minor.
[30] Ibid para 88.
[31] Ibid para 89.
[32] Ibid para 90.

a portrait photograph can stamp the work created with his "personal touch"'.[33] In conclusion, it ruled that a photograph, even a portrait photograph, 'can be protected by copyright if, which it is for the national court to determine in each case, such photograph is an intellectual creation of the author reflecting his personality and expressing his free and creative choices in the production of that photograph'.[34]

In the *Football Dataco* case,[35] the ECJ clearly stated that the copyright protection for a database lies in the structure of the database and not its content or the elements constituting the database. Then it examined whether a database was 'the author's own intellectual creation' and found that this concept refers to the criterion of originality. It held that the 'criterion is satisfied when, through the selection or arrangement of the data which it contains, its author expresses his creative ability in an original manner by making free and creative choices and thus stamps his "personal touch"'.[36] 'It is not satisfied when the setting up of a database is dictated by technical considerations, rules or constraints which leaves no room for creative freedom.'[37] Further, it rejected the UK's criteria 'judgement, skill and labour'. It held that the 'setting up of the database required significant labour and skill of its author . . . [and] cannot as such justify the protection of it by copyright under the database directive if that skill and that labour do not express any originality in the selection or arrangement of that data'.[38] Additionally, it requires that national legislation does not set different conditions for the copyright protection of a database that are contrary to Article 3(1).[39]

It could be summarized from these cases that 'author's own intellectual

---

[33]   Ibid para 92.
[34]   Ibid para 99.
[35]   Case C-604/10 *Football Dataco Ltd et al v. Yahoo! and Others* ECLI:EU:C:2012:115. In this case, Football Dataco claimed to be the right owner of copyright in football fixture lists. It sued Yahoo! for its using these schedules to provide news and information and to organize betting activities. At first instance, the judge confirmed that these fixture lists were original and thus could be protected by copyright while ruling that they were not eligible for the *sui generis* right (*Football Dataco Ltd and Others v. Brittens Pools Ltd and others* [2010] EWHC 841 (Ch)). The defendant appealed the case and the appeal court confirmed that no *sui generis* right can be enjoyed by fixture lists. As far as copyright, the court had some doubt. Thus, it decided to stay the case and refer to the ECJ the question of what is meant by 'databases which, by reason of selection or arrangement of their contents, constitute the author's intellectual creations' (art. 3(1) Database Directive).
[36]   Ibid para 38.
[37]   Ibid para 39.
[38]   Ibid para 42.
[39]   Ibid para 52.

creation', in the eyes of the ECJ, means that an author stamps his 'personal touch' or that the work reflects his personality in the sense that he expresses his creative abilities in an original manner by making free and creative choices. However, it is arguable whether this interpretation applies to all categories of works. Given the capabilities of the CJEU, it can only interpret the relevant articles in directives in the context of questions referred to it by member states. Since the meaning of 'author's own intellectual creation' was decided in each case concerning a specific category of works, it is reasonable to say that this interpretation can only apply to those kinds of works. However, as the CJEU has extended 'author's own intellectual creation' to other categories of works, the meaning of that shall be applied to all categories of work in order to achieve a uniform understanding. It remains to be seen whether the CJEU may make a more explicit interpretation on this matter in the future.

3. ORIGINALITY IN CHINA

3.1 The Definition of a Work in the Copyright Law

Originality is not explicitly incorporated into the Copyright Law of China. The law itself only defines what qualifies as a work by listing forms of works. Article 3 of the Copyright Law states that 'works . . . are *created* in any of the following forms[40]. . .'.[41] The word 'created' mentioned here is defined as 'intellectual activities from which literary, artistic and scientific works are directly derived',[42] and 'the provision of administrative support, consultations, material means or other supporting services for others in their creative activities shall not be deemed as acts of creation'.[43]

The Implementing Regulations elaborate upon the definition of the term 'a work': 'A work is an *original intellectual creation* in the literary,

---

[40]   The forms includes written works; oral works; musical, dramatic, *quyi*, choreographic and acrobatic works; works of the fine arts and architecture; photographic works; cinematographic works and works created by a process analogous to cinematography; graphic works such as drawings of engineering designs and product designs, maps and sketches, and model works; computer software; and other works as provided for in laws and administrative regulations.

[41]   Art. 3, Copyright Law of the People's Republic of China <http://www.wipo.int/wipolex/en/text.jsp?file_id=186569> accessed 3 June 2015.

[42]   Art. 3, Implementing Regulations of 2 August 2002 of Copyright Law of PRC, amended in 2011 and 2013 <http://www.wipo.int/wipolex/en/text.jsp?file_id=125981> accessed 3 June 2015.

[43]   Ibid.

artistic and scientific domain, which is capable of reproduction in a certain physical way.'[44]

3.2   The Meaning of 'Originality'(独创性)

Neither the Copyright Law nor the Implementing Regulations offer a clear and explicit meaning for 'originality'. Most copyright scholars and judges in China admit that 'originality' involves two important meanings.[45] First, it means that an author creates the work independently (this is referred to as '独'). Second, originality also reflects the creativity of the authors since it is the fruit of their intellectual creative activities (this is referred to as '创').

3.2.1   Independent creation (独)
There is no dispute as to what 'independent creation' means. A work shall be created independently if it is not copied or plagiarized from others' works.

3.2.2   Creativity (创)
It is this concept that gives rise to different opinions from the courts. In some cases, the judges require no creativity in testing originality. In so far

---

[44]   Art. 2, Implementing Regulations of 2 August 2002 of Copyright Law of PRC, amended in 2011 and 2013.

[45]   Art. 15 of the 'Interpretation concerning Several Issues on Application of Law in Hearing Correctly the Civil Copyright of the Supreme People's Court of 12 October 2002' states that 'For the works created on the same theme by different authors, *the expressions* of which are *creative* and *independently completed*, the authors enjoy independent copyrights of their corresponding works'. Inferred from this article, 'originality' includes creative expression and independent completion. See also Wang, Qian, *Courses on Intellectual property Law* (3rd edn, Renmin University Press 2011) 25, 31; Li, Mingde and Xu, Chao, *Copyright Law* (2nd edn, Law Press 2009) 28–29; Song, Shenhai, 'On Originality of Works' (1993) 4 Law Science 26–27. Dong, Binghe, 'Preliminary Research on Originality of Work' (1996) 3 Journal of Yantai University (Philosophy and Social Science Edition) 30–35, 31; Jia, Youcheng, 'On Judicial Standard for the Originality of Work' (2013) 1 Chuanbo Yu Banquan 60–62, 60. However, a minority of scholars argue that originality only means creativity. It does not include the meaning of creating independently. See Qiao, Chunli, 'To Prove the Argument that "Independent Creation" as a Meaning of "Originality" Is Wrong' (2011) 7 Intellectual Property 35–38 (argues that 'create independently' describes the relationship between work and author and links to the ownership of the work. It shall function as a method to determine author, as evidence to a judge on reproduction and a defence for infringement, not as a meaning for originality).

as the author creates a work independently, it is protected. For instance, in the *Teaching Plan* case,[46] the court held that 'originality' is different from 'creativity'. It refers to the author's independent creation. It held that the plaintiff created the content in the column named 'teaching process' independently. The defendant did not offer any evidence to prove that the content was plagiarized. Thus, the content was original. In other cases, the courts require a work to reflect an author's personality or to reach a certain height of creativity. For instance, in the *Product Manual* case,[47] the court held that creativity requires a work to contain a certain level of creativity while another court had the opinion that originality shall reflect judgement and choice of the authors with their personality.[48]

It is certainly the case that the creativity element of the examination of the originality requirement is still under dispute among scholars and the courts in China. However, in most cases, this element is checked through examining the difference between the work in contention and prior ones. How big the difference needed is depends on what category of work the disputed work falls under and it is rare to find a work that does not pass the requirement of creativity.

3.3   Some Cases

3.3.1   Xue Huake v. Yan Yaya[49]

These are two cases between a plaintiff who was a photographer who took photos in the Xinjiang and Tibet regions and a defendant, who was an oil painter. The plaintiff, Xue Huake, sued the defendant for copyright

---

[46]   In this case, the plaintiff, a Chinese teacher in the elementary school, wrote 48 teaching plans and submitted them to the defendant in accordance with the rules of teaching. The defendant sold or destroyed 44 of the plans. The plaintiff claimed that the defendant deprived of her copyright right for the plans because the defendant destroyed her original manuscripts. *Gao Liya v. Four Kilometer Elementary School* in Nanan District, Chongqing (2005) First Instance Civil Case No. 603 of No. 1 Intermediate Court in Chongqing (高丽娅诉重庆市南岸区四公里小学校著作权纠纷案 (2005) 渝一中民初字第603号民事判决书).

[47]   In this case, the defendant, a former employee of the plaintiff, reproduced the plaintiff's product manual to sell the product. *Xin Xian Co. Ltd v. Qi Ang Co. Ltd*, cited in Jia, Youcheng (*supra*, n 45) 60.

[48]   *Shanxi Jinyu Pumping Co., Ltd v. Shanxi Linglong Pumping Co., Ltd* (2011) Final Trial of Civil Case No. 70, People's High Court in Shanxi Province (山西金玉泵业有限公司与山西临龙泵业有限公司侵害著作权纠纷上诉案 (2011) 晋民终字第70号民事判决书).

[49]   *Huake Xue v. Yaya Yan* (2011) First Trial of Civil Case No. 7231, People's Court of Chaoyang District; *Huake Xue v. Yaya Yan* (2011) First Trial of Civil Case No. 20681, People's Court of Chaoyang District. (薛华克诉燕娅娅侵犯著

infringement in that the defendant created three oil paintings deriving from photos taken by him that portrayed an old lady and a young student in Xinjiang. The defendant argued that these paintings were created independently by herself and were not copied or derived from the photos. In the 'old lady' case, the court rejected the claim of the plaintiff. It first held that both the photo and the oil painting are works that are created from the same source, that is the old lady, independently. Then it compared the photo with the oil painting and found that these two works involve different creative skills, different media and different representation skills. While similarities may lie in the images, the look and position of the old lady are neither imagined by the plaintiff nor created in the process of shooting. Based on this finding, the court held that it could not be proved that the defendant used the original expression in the plaintiff's photo because both of the works were created independently based on the image of the old lady.[50]

In the 'young student' case, the same court however supported the plaintiff's claims. The court first held that the plaintiff used the photo as a reference. As explained by the court, although there is a likelihood that the theme and content of these two works are similar since they represent the same subject, it is not possible that these two works are almost identical if they are created independently because the creation of the photo and the painting involve different creative processes and skills. Based on this holding, the court then examined whether the defendant uses the original expression in the plaintiff's photo. It held that the originality of photos lies in the choices of subject, the control of timing, as well as the angles of the shooting, the use of shooting skills and the editing at a later stage. This whole creating process reflects the personal judgement and choice of the author. As a realistic work, it is the graphic image not the subject that is the original expression protected in copyright law. By comparison, the graphic image of the oil painting and the photo is basically identical. Thus, the defendant used the original expression of the photos. The court finally admitted that the oil painting is a derivative work since the creation of the painting reflects the judgement and choice of the defendant in the way that she observed the subject and used her skills.[51] The plaintiff appealed the decision but the case was settled out of court.

作权纠纷案 (2011) 朝民初字第7231号，薛华克诉燕娅娅、北京瀚海拍卖有限公司侵害著作权纠纷案 (2011) 朝民初字第20681号，(2012) 二中民终字第11682号).

[50]   *Huake Xue v. Yaya Yan* (2011) First Trial of Civil Case No.7231 (薛华克诉燕娅娅侵犯著作权纠纷案 (2011) 朝民初字第7231号).

[51]   *Huake Xue v. Yaya Yan* (2011) First Trial of Civil Case No. 20681, People's Court of Chaoyang District (薛华克诉燕娅娅、北京瀚海拍卖有限公司侵害著作权纠纷案 (2011) 朝民初字第20681号).

3.3.2   Jiu Qi Software Co., Ltd v. Tian Cheng Software Co., Ltd[52]

The plaintiff, Jiu Qi Software Co., Ltd, the developer of the accounting software named 'Accounting Report of Ministry of Finance' sued the defendant for copyright infringement for the reason that the defendant copied the graphic user interface of the software and asked for compensation of 1.5 million CNY and an injunction. The defendant argued that the graphic user interface is not copyrightable because it is neither a computer program nor a work.[53] The first instance court held that the graphic user interface is a communication platform between the users and computers and thus is highly functional. Whether it is protected as a work shall be determined case by case based on the constituent facts. In this case, the elements of the interface involve the titles of the menu command buttons; the titles of the information column; the elements consisting of the graphic user's interface such as menu bar, dialogue boxes, etc; instruction on function of buttons; icons representing specific reports and layout of the interface. The court then analysed each element. First, the names of menu commands and buttons cannot be protected since they are an operating method, which is not the subject matter of copyright. Second, the names of information columns and the elements comprising the graphic user's interface cannot be protected in that they are commonly used by designers. Third, since the instruction can only be expressed in limited ways, the icons of specific reports are too simple and the layout of the display is just a simple combination of all the constituents that lacks originality, none of them can be protected. Therefore, the graphic user interface in this case could not be protected since it does not meet the requirement of originality despite the developer attributing his labour to the interface. The appeal court finally upheld the decision of the first instance court.

---

[52]   *Jiu Qi Software (Beijing) Co., Ltd v. Tian Cheng Software (Shanghai) Co., Ltd* (2004) First Trial of IP Case No. 100, No. 2 Intermediate People's Court in Shanghai; (2005) Final Trial of IP Case No. 38, High People's Court in Shanghai (北京久其软件股份有限公司诉上海天臣计算机软件有限公司著作权纠纷案 (2004) 沪二中民五知初字第100号, (2005) 沪高民三知终字第38号).

[53]   The computer program is protected under the 'Regulations on Protection of Computer Programs' in China. In this regulation, the computer program is protected within copyright when it is created independently. This requirement is lower than other categories of works.

3.3.3   Wang Tongyi et al v. Fang Shiming et al[54]

The plaintiffs sued the defendant for copyright infringement for the reason that the dictionary edited by the defendant copied the *Annals on Chinese History* and the *Fact Sheet on Scatter of Ethnic Minorities in China* that were annexed to the *Cihai*, the most authoritative Chinese dictionary, edited and published by the plaintiffs. The first instance court admitted that the contents of those works are factual and most of them come from historical records and thus they are not copyrightable. However, the expression or representation of the *Annals* can be different depending on the starting points of the author or the function of the *Annals*. The originality of this category of work is shown in how these objective facts are verified, selected and expressed so that the readers can use them in a scientific and reasonable manner. In respect of the fact sheets, the facts can be arranged in a variety of ways. They can show the difference in accordance with the author's purpose. In this case, both the *Annals* and *Fact Sheet* are original since they are arranged in a unique way. The defendant appealed. The appeal court confirmed the judgment of first instance. It held that the originality of these kinds of tables is reflected in the author's judgement, selection and arrangement of relevant facts following specific requirements. In this case, both of the works are copyrightable because they reflect the originality. The *Annals* is copyrightable because the author selected specific facts from the perspective of the function of the table and represented the selected facts by using the unique table. And the *Fact Sheet* is also copyrightable since regions of ethnic minorities are selected and these minorities as well as the regions are listed and ordered in certain rules.

4.   ANALYSIS

European countries, especially France, Germany and the UK, are traditionally considered as a norm giver in most cases and have exported their copyright traditions through colonization, bilateral agreements and international treaties. This can be illustrated by the fact that almost all countries in the world accept originality as a substantive requirement for a work to be protected in copyright law and the international treaties in the field of copyright were promoted and dominated by these countries.

---

[54]   *Wang Tong yi et al v. Fang Shiming et al* (1997) Final Civil Case No. 21 of Bejing High Court (王同亿等与方诗铭等 著作权侵权纠纷案 (1997) 高知终字第 21号).

Since the establishment of the EU, it is the governmental organs of the EU that have become a new form of norm giver to its member states and the process of harmonization of the concept of originality is illustrative of this.

At the first round of substantive harmonization, the European Commission first chose the area that was new to most of the member states, that is the Computer and Database Directives. It was in these two Directives that 'author's intellectual creation' was used to define 'originality'. It is also clear from the legislative history that the standard for originality, especially for computer programs, is a compromise between the UK's low standard and Germany's relatively high standard. In this sense, a new norm has been established. Then, in order to further harmonize the protection of terms, the EU had to distinguish certain photographic works from others to give them copyright protection.[55] By using the same term as in the Computer Software and Database Directives, the EU attempted to show its approach toward a uniform definition and by implementing these Directives, the member states became norm takers.

Then, the CJEU stepped in and tried to guide member states on the understanding of originality. It first extended 'author's own intellectual creation' to all categories of works and then tried to offer criteria to test the works. It interpreted 'author's own intellectual creation' as the author stamping his 'personal touch' in the sense that he expresses his creative abilities in an original manner by making free and creative choices. This reading first binds the referral court and then transplants into member states.

China, as a norm taker, introduced the concept of originality into its copyright law. Because of the abstract and foreign nature of the concept, scholars and judges give different definitions and apply different tests in cases. This diverse understanding leads to legal uncertainty and inefficiency, especially considering the automatic protection of copyright. The influence of legal education on scholars and judges also contributes to this diverse understanding of the concept. For instance, a judge studying in the US may be more likely to apply US standards in cases. This may actually cause some unfairness for the parties to the suits.

However, some consensus among scholars and judges can be identified, although it is difficult to summarize a uniform standard of originality by reading cases decided by courts. For instance, most of the courts recognize

---

[55] Before this Directive, photographs were protected either by copyright law or by neighbouring right laws or were not protected at all in member states. Since the Term Directive intended to offer a harmonized term for all kinds of works, including photographic works, it is necessary to identify what photographs can be protected by copyright law which protects works 70 years *post mortem auctoris*.

creativity as a necessary component of originality. It requires the expression of the work to differentiate itself from other expressions of work or those expressions in the public domain. Compared to the concept in the EU, it is not surprising to find that some common or similar interpretation of originality can be found.

It is true that the concept of originality is always related to the cultural or socio-economic situation in a country. Whether a norm giver or a norm taker, a reasonable standard of originality is formulated based on specific policy considerations such as public attitudes toward works or the particular market situation of a category of works. This determines the unique features of a particular country. However, this does not exclude the possibility that countries share or learn some common understandings from each other because the works objectively contain some features in common. For instance, by examining the *Painer* case and *Xue Huake* case, it can be found that both the ECJ and Chinese courts require that a portrait photo reflects the choices and personal judgements of an author.

When considering the future impact of technological changes on the creation of works, it can be expected that the experience in countries that have encountered a new technology may be shared and learnt by those countries encountering the same problem later. Although the later country may not accept the rulings in the earlier country, the experience of the earlier country can at least offer a positive or negative example on shaping standards for new categories of work. This may cause each country to have a role as a norm taker or a norm giver based on who created certain rules first. Thus, it is fair to say that each country may be a norm giver or norm taker in the future.

5.   CONCLUSION

Originality is one of the most basic and abstract concepts in copyright law. Both the EU and China are seeking to find reasonable standards to test originality. It is also a concept that relates to the specific social, economic and political situation in a particular country. Although certain countries, like China, can be considered norm takers that transplant the standard of originality, it is also possible that they may become future norm givers where new challenges are tackled in the country first. Therefore, a learning process for making policies concerning originality may continue and each country may have a dual role as norm giver and norm taker.

6. Orphan works in China and Europe

Yuying Guan

1. INTRODUCTION

The term 'orphan work' refers to a copyrighted work whose owner cannot be identified and located by a party who wishes to make use of such a work in a manner that requires the authorization of the copyright owner. In 2006, the US Copyright Office issued a detailed report on orphan works[1] and subsequently the term 'orphan work' was introduced into China. The US orphan work proposal is described by some commentators as resolving the 'market failure' in connecting copyright owners with potential users.[2] The debate surrounding orphan works is controversial and reform looks unlikely – the Orphan Work Act 2008[3] initially passed in the US Senate but subsequently died after failing to pass in the House of Representatives.[4] Nevertheless, in China, lobbyists keep pushing the National Copyright Administration (NCAC) to establish an orphan works system for commercial users. According to article 51 of the latest draft of the Third Amendment of Chinese Copyright Law[5] (hereinafter NCAC Draft), a user who seeks to digitize copyrighted works already published may do so upon meeting certain requirements. First, it must be established that the copyright owner cannot be identified or that the copyright owner cannot be contacted. Upon satisfying either of these conditions, the user who wants to digitize them may apply and deposit a fee at a designated institute assigned by the copyright administrative authority under the State

---

[1] US Copyright Office, *Report on Orphan Works* (April 2006) <http://www.copyright.gov/orphan/orphan-report-full.pdf> accessed 1 April 2015.

[2] David R Hansen, *Orphan Works: Definitional Issues* (19 December 2011) <http://ssrn.com/abstract=1974614> accessed 1 April 2015.

[3] The Library of Congress, Bill Summary & Status 112th Congress (2011–2012) H.R.5889.

[4] <https://www.govtrack.us/congress/bills/110/s2913> accessed 1 April 2015.

[5] Chinese Copyright Law (NCAC's latest revised draft, 6 June 2014) <http://www.chinalaw.gov.cn/article/cazjgg/201406/20140600396188.shtml> accessed 1 April 2015.

Council. Thus, we can see that China's proposal on orphan works aims to resolve the problem by issuing compulsory licences on orphan works for any potential users.

The European Union's (EU) approach takes the public interest in cultural preservation into account.[6] According to the 'Orphan Works Directive'[7] (hereinafter the Directive) the measure is concerned with the use of orphan works by public cultural institutions rather than all users,[8] which makes the passing of the EU Directive much less controversial than the US 2008 Act. The EU Directive leaves to the individual Member States the difficult task of adopting implementing legislation, and the truth is that each EU Member State might have a different interest regarding the use of orphan works in practice. It is therefore interesting to observe the different approaches applied by the Member States. Furthermore, the Directive required Member States to bring into force the necessary measures to comply with the Directive by 29 October 2014.

Both the NCAC Draft and the Directive follow the same core conceptual solution – if the user has performed a 'reasonably diligent search' for the copyright owner, but is unable to locate that owner, then that user enjoys a limitation in the scope of copyright infringement if the copyright owner of the material is established at a later date and attempts to sue for copyright infringement. However, the background and the details are different for the EU and Chinese orphan works proposals. This chapter will address the orphan works issue based on a comparative analysis of the EU and Chinese approaches to the orphan works problem.

2.   THE EU APPROACH

The Directive deliberately delimits the subject matter and scope of its application. According to its article 1, the Directive only concerns 'certain uses made of orphan works by publicly accessible libraries, educational establishments and museums, as well as by archives, film or audio heritage institutions and public-service broadcasting organizations, established in the Member States'. The aim of the Directive is to eradicate the fears of

---

[6]   European Commission, i2010: Digital Libraries High Level Expert Group, *Report on Digital Preservation, Orphan Works, and Out-of-Print Works, Selected Implementation Issues* (18 April 2007) <http://ec.europa.eu/information_society/newsroom/cf/itemlongdetail.cfm?item_id=3366> accessed 1 April 2015.

[7]   Directive 2012/28/EU of the European Parliament and of the Council of 25 October 2012 on certain permitted uses of orphan works.

[8]   Article 1(1) of the Directive.

copyright infringement accruing to public cultural organizations engaged in the large-scale digitization of collections or archives needed to create the European Digital Library. This library will contribute to the preservation and dissemination of European cultural heritage. Though these organizations might be allowed to conclude agreements with commercial partners for the digitization and making available to the public of orphan works, such agreements should not grant the commercial partner any exclusive rights to use or control the use of the orphan works.[9] Besides delimiting the scope of use, article 2(1) of the Directive gives the following definition of orphan works:

> A work or a phonogram shall be considered an orphan work if none of the right holders in that work or phonogram is identified or, even if one or more of them is identified, none is located despite a diligent search for the right holders having been carried out and recorded . . .

Article 3 demands that

> a diligent search is carried out in good faith in respect of each work or other protected subject-matter, by consulting the appropriate sources for the category of works and other protected subject-matter in question. The diligent search shall be carried out prior to the use of the work or phonogram.

The orphan status can be reversed, should a copyright owner subsequently appear and assert their rights. Accordingly, fair compensation will be granted to the copyright owner.[10]

We can see that the legal framework of the Directive covers digitization and dissemination of orphan works, but only for use in the public interest and by organizations acting in the public interest. In the opinion of the author, the Directive emphasizes the public interest of preservation and dissemination of European cultural heritage, mainly because large-scale digitization and online dissemination (even executed by public cultural organizations) has been beyond the scope of the exceptions and limitations stipulated in the InfoSoc Directive.[11] The dissemination of these

---

[9] See recitals 1, 18 and 22 in the preamble to the Directive.

[10] Article 6(5) of the Directive. See also recital 18 in the preamble to the Directive.

[11] Directive 2001/29/EC of the European Parliament and of the Council of 22 May 2001 on the harmonisation of certain aspects of copyright and related rights in the information society. According to recital 40 in its preamble and article 5(2)(c) of Directive 2001/29/EC, exceptions and limitations are allowed for publicly accessible libraries, educational establishments, museums, or archives only in

library resources to the outside world is crucial for maintaining European cultural influence and enhancing EU competitiveness. Yet, the present EU copyright regime does not seem to leave room for flexible expansion in the scope of exceptions and limitations, even for the mission of constructing the European Digital Library. Thus a new scheme for the utilization of orphan works must be agreed in the EU and implemented by the Member States. Since the Directive was formally approved by the EU Parliament and the Council of Ministers in late 2012, Member States had to transpose the Directive into national law by 29 October 2014.

3.   EU MEMBER STATES

Most Member States in the EU strongly adhere to the author's right tradition in their copyright regimes. Therefore, the interest of the public is taken into account in the EU only by explicitly and narrowly construed limitations and exceptions. One could question the compatibility of a general fair use principle, similar to that in US copyright law, or a compulsory licence scheme for orphan works discussed in the US with the continental European legal tradition. However, being the source of the Anglo-American legal system, it is more natural for the United Kingdom (UK) to follow the perspective of the US 2008 Orphan Work Act, which empowers commercial users.

Specifically, the UK Parliament enacted the Enterprise and Regulatory Reform Act 2013 (ERRA), which sets out a plan for letting people buy and use orphan works with an escrow fund for absentee rights holders. This is a fundamental change to UK copyright legislation, since the objective behind ERRA is to enable the commercial exploitation of copyrighted works without fear of being held liable for infringement should the copyright owner ever come to light and make a claim at some point in the future. In early 2014, the UK government introduced a Bill transposing into English law the Directive on certain permitted uses of orphan works, as well as another Bill to allow the obtaining of statutory licences to use orphan works commercially. In response to public consultation, the UK government clarified that the licensing scheme for orphan works is for both commercial and non-commercial

---

respect of 'specific acts of reproduction', mainly for non-commercial preservation purposes; and reproduction or making available of works in the collections of these cultural institutions must be within their premises for the purpose of research or private study.

uses but the commercial licences could be granted in the UK only.[12] The Copyright and Rights in Performances (Certain Permitted Uses of Orphan Works) Regulations, together with the Copyright and Rights in Performances (Licensing of Orphan Works) Regulations came into force on 29 October 2014, although they are both not uncontroversial, and the UK Intellectual Property Office (IPO) released relevant guidance at the same time for their implementation. However, the passing of the licensing scheme Bill was so rushed, that the diligent search tool, provided by the UK Orphan Work Register System, proved to be unworkable at the time of the coming into force of the Acts.[13] In January 2015, the UK IPO introduced an updated application procedure for applying for a licence to use an orphan work.[14] It is interesting to observe how the UK orphan work expropriation, which is based on a compulsory system with strict requirements of diligent search and domestic use, will be developed and executed in the future.

Comparatively, the transposition of the EU Orphan Works Directive into national law is more complicated in continental European countries. France seems to accept the US perspective to the extent that its orphan works proposal does not differentiate commercial or non-commercial uses deliberately, yet the subject matter is limited to out-of-commerce books.[15] The French Act n°2012-287, namely the Law on Digital Exploitation of Unavailable Books, was issued on 1 March 2012, even earlier than

---

[12] UK Intellectual Property Office, *Government response to the technical consultation on orphan works* (May 2014) <https://www.gov.uk/government/uploads/system/uploads/attachment_data/file/315078/Orphan_Works_Government_Response.pdf> accessed 1 April 2015.

[13] Andrew Orlowski, 'UK.gov rushes out broken "Orphan Works" system as EU Directive comes in' (*The Register*, 29 October 2014) <http://www.thereg ister.co.uk/2014/10/29/govts_orphan_scheme_plops_out_broken_on_arrival/> accessed 1 April 2015.

[14] See <https://www.gov.uk/apply-for-a-licence-to-use-an-orphan-work# orphan-works-register> accessed 1 April 2015.

[15] Out-of-commerce works are works that are still protected by copyright but are no longer commercially available because the authors and publishers have decided neither to publish new editions nor to sell copies through the customary channels of commerce. In the past, works such as books were referred to as being either 'in-print' or 'out-of-print'. Today, with the advent of electronic channels of commerce, the term 'out-of-commerce' is used (with electronic publishing a book will be 'in-commerce' even if only available in electronic form); See European Commission, 'Memorandum of Understanding (MoU) on Key Principles on the Digitisation and Making Available of Out-of-Commerce Works – Frequently Asked Questions' (MEMO/11/619, Brussels, 20 September 2011) <http://europa.eu/rapid/press-release_MEMO-11-619_en.htm> accessed 1 April 2015.

the Directive, introducing a new chapter (Chapter IV) to the French Intellectual Property Code. This Act creates a database managed by the French National Library, where the status on the availability of books (including orphan works) can be registered. A compulsory licence can be issued for the books registered in the database, provided that remuneration is paid to the rights owner. Additionally, authors can opt out of the system within six months of the inscription of a book in the register.[16] In contrast, the German legislature passed a new law on 27 June 2013 implementing the Directive by introducing article 61 into the German Copyright Law (UrhG). The new UrhG provisions enable libraries, museums and other cultural institutions to digitize and display their orphan works online after a diligent search for right holders. Concurrently, a new law for out-of-print-works was adopted, introducing article 13 d-e into the Copyright Administration Law (UrhWahrnG), allowing collecting societies to grant rights to third parties for public display. In both cases, only non-commercial use is permitted and later appearing right holders can prohibit the use.[17]

Meanwhile, the Dutch Ministries of Justice and of Culture are currently discussing the needs and possibilities of introducing Extended Collective Licensing (ECL) on orphan works as implementation of the Directive. In practice orphan works can be used through an ECL-like agreement in the Netherlands. For example, the EYE Film Institute has negotiated the use of orphan works through ECL for digital exploitation of audiovisual works with the relevant collecting societies, and an opt-out is offered to the right holders.[18] It should be without question for the Netherlands to empower the cultural heritage institutions to exploit orphan works under conditions set by the Directive. In Denmark where the ECL system has been in place for some time, the government considered that it was sufficiently efficient to cater for the rights of reappearing authors of

---

[16]   Lucie Guibault, 'France solves its XXe century book problem!' (Kluwer Copyright Blog, 13 April 2012) <http://kluwercopyrightblog.com/2012/04/13/france-solves-its-xxe-century-book-problem/> accessed 1 April 2015.

[17]   See <http://de.clarin.eu/de/component/content/article/80-schulungen-und-support/juristischer-support/272-legal-orphan-works.html> accessed 1 April 2015.

[18]   See the Netherlands' Progress Report 2011–2013 on the implementation of the Commission Recommendation on Digitization and Online Accessibility of Cultural Material and Digital Preservation <http://www.den.nl/art/uploads/files/OCW%20Progress%20report%202011-2013_Implementation%20of%20the%20commission%20recommendation%20on%20digitisation%20and%20online%20accesibility%20of%20cultural%20material%20an%20digital%20preservation.pdf> accessed 1 April 2015.

orphan works.[19] In Finland, the implementing legislation (Act on the Use of Orphan Works, 763/2013) was passed separately from its Copyright Act. According to the new law, public libraries and museums may make available to the public orphan works and copy them for the permitted purposes, such as preservation or restoration.[20] We can see that Nordic countries, including Finland, where ECL has been established and used, demonstrate a tendency to apply the ECL scheme to resolve the orphan works issue,[21] and the Finnish Act defines orphan works, eligible institutions, diligent search, and permitted uses in a manner that faithfully follows the Directive.

4. THE CHINESE APPROACH

In the NCAC Draft[22] a brief proposal for the exploitation of orphan works is set out at article 51. When the orphan works issue is discussed in a Chinese context and comments made on the orphan work proposal in the NCAC Draft, the following two aspects need special attention. First, section 13 of the Chinese Regulation on the Implementation of the Copyright Law (CRIC 2013) reads as follows:

> In the case of a work of unknown authorship, the copyright thereof shall be exercised by the holder of the original copy of the work except the right of attribution. After the authorship has been ascertained, the copyright shall be exercised by the author or the heirs thereof.

Noticeably, section 13 of the CRIC 2013 is proposed in the NCAC Draft as article 27. Secondly, section 7 of the Regulation on Protection of the Right to Network Dissemination of Information (RPRNDI 2006) establishes a fair use exception for publicly accessible libraries to digitize their holdings

---

[19] Marcella Favale et al., *Copyright, and the Regulation of Orphan Works. A Comparative Review of Seven Jurisdictions and a Rights Clearance Simulation* (Intellectual Property Office 2013) 24 <https://www.gov.uk/government/publications/copyright-and-the-regulation-of-orphan-works> accessed 1 April 2015.

[20] Foundation for Cultural Policy Research Cupore and the Finnish Ministry of Education and Culture, *Assessing Copyright and Related Rights Systems: Copyright Law. Report on Piloting in Finland* (2014) <http://www.cupore.fi/documents/170914_Publication_Pilotreport_DS5Copyrightlaw.pdf> accessed 1 April 2015.

[21] Favale et al. (*supra*, n 19) 66.

[22] See *supra*, n 5.

and make them available to their members within their premises.[23] Accordingly, in practice, public cultural institutions enjoy the freedom of executing large-scale digitization for almost all of their out-of-commerce holdings, including orphan works in a frangible tangible format for the purposes of preservation, and displaying them publically inside premises. This is a Chinese characteristic fair use exception to the right of reproduction, which is different from US fair use doctrine or European statutory licences for libraries based on article 5(2)(c) of the InfoSoc Directive.

We see that in the present Chinese Copyright Law regime the holder of an original copy of an unknown authorship work can exploit it (in accordance with section 13 CRIC 2013), and the public cultural institutions can digitize the out-of-commerce or destructible works for preservation purposes as a fair use limitation on the right of reproduction (in accordance with section 7 RPRNDI 2006). So why is there a new orphan work proposal added in the NCAC Draft as article 51? In this respect, this chapter explores the following three perspectives.

The first purpose may be separation of public cultural institutions that have become state-owned business entities, such as publishers, film studios and broadcasters, from other public cultural organizations. These state entities generally disregard concerns about copyright infringement. The disregard is a result of their reliance on a special policy consideration provided for by the Chinese government that helped these entities to deal with problems during the process of marketization. To counter any threat of copyright infringement, these state entities may invoke a specific clause[24] in the Chinese Copyright Law that exempts them from this threat when exploiting their 'copyrighted assets in stock'.[25] This exemption is a

---

[23]   Section 7 RPRNDI 2006: 'A library, archives, memorial, museum and art gallery may, in the absence of the copyright holder's permission, provide the relevant digital works as lawfully published and preserved by the aforesaid institutions as well as the works that shall, according to law, be subject to digital photocopying for display or and make them available to their members through the information network within their premises and without paying any remuneration. Whereas the aforesaid institutions may not directly or indirectly seek for any economic interest from such activities, unless it is otherwise stipulated by the parties concerned.'

[24]   Article 11 Chinese Copyright Law (2010): 'The author of a work is the citizen who has created the work. Where a work is created according to the intention and under the supervision and responsibility of a legal entity or another organization, such legal entity or organization shall be the author of the work. The citizen, legal entity or organization whose name is affixed to a work shall, without the contrary proof, be the author of the work.'

[25]   See the Bill introduced by Mr Chen Qinghua in 2012 from the Chinese People's Political Consultative Conference <http://www.cppcc.gov.cn/zxww/2013/02/28/ARTI1362050439265187.shtml> and its Reply from the

powerful alternative to the orphan works proposal in the NCAC Draft because, in the absence of contrary evidence, many of these copyrighted assets could be regarded as works for hire according to article 11 of the present Copyright Law. This is especially the case for those works created under the editorship of 'the editorial committee' (i.e. edited works) without specifying individual editors and authors of these entities, or audiovisual materials that could only be created by utilizing materials and technical capabilities of these entities. Under these exemptions, these entities could exploit these assets as if they were copyright owners. For historical reasons,[26] most of these assets have been kept by these entities without resolving any copyright issues related to the works. However, these materials prepared by the employees or other staff to complete the duties or tasks of the entities without any names can reasonably be presumed to be works for hire. For works of unknown authorship held by these state entities, the right of exhibition could be exercised by the holder (namely these entities) for the original copy of such work without making any modifications. Lastly, for a work of unknown authorship that embodies important historical value, these entities could donate it to a public cultural institution for digitalization and preservation.

Second, another reason stems from the position of other public cultural institutions, such as publicly accessible libraries, museums and archives. These institutions are supposed to be non-profit public units with fiscal allocation; as mentioned above, section 7 of the RPRNDI has empowered them to digitalize and preserve their holdings as a mission of public interest, and such digitalization and preservation should be financially supported by government. Yet, at present, financial support from the government is lacking and these public institutions have the ambition to make full use of their rich holdings by providing more attractive services. One of these services includes online access to this material – this service requires a new rule that goes beyond the exceptions provided for in the RPRNDI in order to legitimize the utilization of their holdings, including orphan works, based on a compulsory licence. This approach echoes the considerations expressed by the public cultural institutions in some EU countries, but there is an obvious difference also – the Chinese are calling for a compulsory licence to utilize all their holdings, whereas the EU

Ministry of Finance <http://www.mof.gov.cn/zhuantihuigu/2012lhtadf/2012zxw yta/201303/t20130301_741919.html> both accessed 1 April 2015.

[26] There has never been a clear record of copyright ownership in the state-owned cultural entities, see *Improving the Capital Management of Copyright in State-Owned Cultural Enterprises* <http://wzb.mof.gov.cn/pdlb/yjbg/201207/ t20120704_664017.html> accessed 1 April 2015.

approach requires consultation with the right holders or collective management organizations (CMOs) in order to make an agreement for using
the works that are not in orphan status.

Thirdly, the position of the commercial information service providers
in China could be considered another main factor for the Chinese orphan
work proposal expressed in article 51 of the NCAC Draft. This rising
industry is composed of the commercial information providers and uses
the confusing name 'Digital Library',[27] which might easily mislead people
about their role in copyright transactions. Section 7 of the RPRNDI
cannot be applied by these commercial information service providers. In
judicial practice, Chinese courts have given judgments that these digital
libraries were liable for unauthorized scanning of copyrighted works and
providing them online. It is not surprising that this industry is strongly
calling for the Chinese orphan work proposal, which may set a statutory
licence for their digitalizing these works as much as possible and providing
them online.

In brief, the Chinese orphan works proposal seeks to establish a lodg-
ment system, by which any user can apply and deposit a fee for using
orphan works. This fee will be assigned to the copyright owner upon
being identified or located in the future. This approach is similar to the
approaches in both the US or UK, in the sense that there is no prohibition
of commercial use, and the substance of such a system is to create a non-
exclusive statutory licence on orphan works by any users, limiting the right
of public transmission.

From this chapter's perspective, the commercial use of orphan works is
still controversial, especially if it just transplants the idea of compulsory
licences for orphan works but without elaborately designing a system as
executed in the UK. Comparatively, the Chinese orphan works proposal
provides only for a simple scheme. The last statement of article 51 of the
NCAC Draft states that '[t]he specific implementation measures shall be
formulated by the administrative department of copyright under the State
Council separately'. Accordingly, this implies that there is a long way to
go for China to reach a detailed licensing scheme similar to that of the UK
for instance.

Upon surveying the Chinese orphan works issue and the push to enact
the orphan works proposal, it is evident that the Internet industries play

---

[27]   Many commercial online databanks are using the confusing name Digital
Library (in Chinese), such as 中国法律数字图书馆 [China Digital Library of Laws]
<http://www.law.cnki.net>, 超星数字图书馆 [Chaoxing Digital Library] <www.
ssreader.com>, 书生之家数字图书馆 [Home of Scholars Digital Library]
<www.21dmedia.com>, all accessed 1 April 2015.

an important role. The rapid development of web technology and its extensive use are bringing about great changes to people's lives, and China faces serious challenges to enforce copyright protection, along with the EU and its Member States. According to the statistics, copyright cases in China have increased tremendously in recent years.[28] Copyright cases constitute almost half of all the intellectual property cases and Internet-related copyright cases constitute more than half of all copyright cases.[29] With the development of digital technology, there is a tension between copyright owners who increasingly seek to enlarge copyright protection, and booming Internet industries, whose business models often depend on the distribution of copyrighted material. The orphan works problem is only one contributory factor. The main reason is that the information service providers would prefer a statutory licence in order to simplify copyright matters, evade infringement risks and reduce transaction costs in exploiting copyrighted works.

It is important that Chinese lawmakers should consider the balance between copyright owners and the Internet industry, yet this balance, to some extent, should differ from that of the developed countries. The orphan works issue in these Western countries reflects assertions from the users against extending the duration of copyright protection. On the contrary, copyright protection in China has a much shorter history, and the copyright owners have been exhausted in fighting rampant piracy battles until now. There has never been a strong copyright industry in China, which means that copyright owners have always been at a disadvantage in negotiating with commercial users. Taking these elements into account, to impose any new restriction on the copyright right holders now, such as adding a statutory licence on orphan works for all users in the Copyright Law, might discourage the creation of original works in the long run.

If we must add an orphan work proposal in the Third Amendment of Chinese Copyright Law, the approach of the EU Directive, which applies only to non-commercial users, is preferred to the US or UK mode incorporating both commercial and non-commercial users. Again, given that many commercial databank service providers may also operate under the name of 'digital library', it is crucial to differentiate between libraries with public cultural purposes and those commercial databanks if China is to

---

[28]   The Supreme People's Court: *The Judicial Protection of Intellectual Property Rights in China (2012) & (2013)* <http://www.court.gov.cn/zscq/bhcg/> accessed 1 November 2014.

[29]   See Yang Weihan: *The Supreme People's Court Issued Judicial Interpretation Strengthening Copyright Protection on Internet* <http://news.xinhuanet.com/legal/2012-12/26/c_114170529.htm> accessed 1 November 2014.

introduce an EU type of orphan works proposal. Furthermore, a detailed scheme for the use of orphan works, including the process of registration, the criteria of diligent search, the application and grant of statutory licence, the rule for collecting fees and their distribution, the possibility of opt-out, etc., is now without any operating rules or detailed procedures. Without strict and detailed operational procedures for designating 'orphan' status to works, users may abuse the system. This is because users may consider a work an orphan work, and choose to deposit fees to use such works, which would be likely to be set at a lower level than the market-based royalty. Making a work 'orphaned' in this way would sacrifice the copyright owner's interest. Additionally, more research is needed to consider the introduction of other related mechanisms such as a statutory levy and extended collective management.

5.   CONCLUSION

In sum, the Chinese orphan work proposal in the NCAC Draft is far from sufficient and more research is needed as regards its rationality and feasibility.

Specifically, article 27 of the Draft could be revised as follows:

> In the case of a work of unknown authorship, the right of exhibition of the original copy thereof could be exercised by the holder, as far as the copyright status of the work is described in an appropriate way. The holder can make digital photocopying for the purpose of display or conservation to protect the original copy from destruction.

Furthermore, according to article 43(8) of the NCAC Draft, a fair use could be invoked upon the 'reproduction of a work in its collections by a library, archive, memorial hall, museum, art gallery or similar institution, for the purpose of the display or preservation of a copy of the work'. This fair use exception is enough for the public libraries, etc. to carry on their public mission of culture preservation.

If the Chinese legislature intend to encourage the public cultural institutions to provide orphan works through the information network beyond their premises, the EU Directive proposal could be introduced. The core is that Internet transmission of orphan works should be subject to a statutory licence clearly stipulated in the Copyright Law; consequently article 51 of NCAC Draft could be revised as:

> For those copyrighted works whose original copies are kept in a library, archives, memorial, museum and art gallery, these public institutions who

want to digitize and provide to their registered users through Internet may apply and deposit fee to an institute assigned by the copyright administrative authority under the State Council after a diligent search in vain, if any of the following conditions can be met: (i) The copyright owner cannot be identified; or (ii) The copyright owner can be identified yet cannot be contacted; (iii) The copyrighted work is out-of-commerce. The specific implementation measures shall be formulated by the administrative department of copyright under the State Council separately.

Thus the implementation measures such as the criteria of diligent search, the licence application, the fee deposit, and the payment of remuneration once the right holder is identified or located, etc. should be stipulated in details in a supporting regulation. Furthermore the aforesaid public institutions, such as libraries, museums and archives, applying this statutory licence may not directly or indirectly seek economic benefit from such activities, except that they may be reimbursed for the cost of digitalization and transmission.

As a final note, when the new Chinese Copyright Law introduces a statutory licence for the public cultural institutions to transmit orphan works through the Internet following the EU's norm, the experience in EU Member States of implementing the Directive deserves attention. We see that other closely associated mechanisms, such as effectively running copyright collecting societies, and especially the norm of extended collective management, are indispensable for the operation of the proposed orphan work scheme in the EU. So the legislature needs to consider the interaction among these relative mechanisms when conducting the copyright reform in China.

7. Art law and resale rights in Europe and China

Lin Zhou and Rosa Maria Ballardini

1. INTRODUCTION

In today's global economy, it is generally understood that countries fall into two broad categories as far as legal developments are concerned: 'norm maker' or 'norm taker' types of countries.[1] Developing countries like China are generally considered to be norm takers, rather than norm makers, especially when it comes to regulating intellectual property law.[2]

Droit de suite came into the copyright system in Europe nearly 100 years ago and, as a consequence of the harmonization reached via the EU Resale Right Directive,[3] such a right is currently contemplated in similar ways in each of the EU Member States. Chinese copyright legislation, however, does not provide for *droit de suite*, although Chinese lawmakers recently published draft legislation contemplating the resale right. If *droit de suite* is legislated for in China, it is yet another example of China's role as a norm taker. It is here contended that *droit de suite* provides a good case of a norm that could help China to reconsider its role as a norm taker, informing the country that priority should at times be given to China's cultural policy and its interaction with copyright law.

The resale right has been an ongoing argument of research and discussion among scholars for a long time. However, the fact that the costs and benefits involved with such a mechanism are difficult to measure and that, to date, empirical evidence on the matter is insufficient, has generated different opinions on the effects that the resale right produces on the art

---

[1]   See N. Bruun and L. Zhang, 'Legal Transplant of Intellectual Property Rights in China: Norm Taker or Norm Maker?', Chapter 3 of this volume.

[2]   See P.K. Yu, 'The Transplant and Transformation of Intellectual Property Laws in China', Chapter 2 of this volume.

[3]   Directive 2001/84/EC of the European Parliament and of the Council of 27 September 2001 on the resale right for the benefit of the author of an original work of art.

market in general. These divergences are also reflected in the sundry types of regulatory mechanisms that have been implemented in intellectual property laws worldwide.

This chapter will be set out as follows. It will first provide an introduction to the historical developments in regulating the art market in general. Subsequently, it will provide an insight into the solution adopted by the European Union for tackling the issue of visual arts via resale royalties; in this context, the chapter argues that the resale right represents a *hybrid* product within the copyright regime and, as such, distorts the general common understanding of the copyright rules. This analysis will aid the discussion on whether China should act as a 'norm taker' and adopt similar solutions to the EU or whether it should instead act as a 'norm maker' and follow its own path with respect to the problem of visual arts and resale rights.

2. THE CHINESE PERSPECTIVE

2.1 The New Policy and the Art Market Since 1978

The development of the resale right discourse has followed a very peculiar path in China. Indeed, in order to understand the roots of the discussions on *droit de suite* in China it is essential to take a few steps back and look at the history and origins of Chinese art law.

For quite a long time in China's contemporary art history[4] artistic creation was carried out mainly as a 'political task' or as a 'tool for propaganda', guided by the slogan 'literature and art should be subordinated to politics',[5] and, therefore, no free art market was in place. In the early 1980s, works of art were gradually changing in nature from mere political tools to art commodities. Accordingly, this transition raised the issue of art commercialization. There were few issues related to art law, because most artworks at that time were traded either privately or in stores with the characteristics of a planned economy.

For example, research on contemporary art history shows that art galleries were relatively rare during the last century, while in 2012 the number of art galleries was 3,106 nationally.[6] According to a report by

---

[4]   This chapter takes the year 1949 as the starting point of contemporary Chinese art history. See W. Hongjian and Y. Baolin, *An Introduction to Fine Arts* (Higher Education Publishing House 1994) 520–521.

[5]   Ibid., 520–545.

[6]   See *2013 Asian Art Market Report* (Hunan Art Publishing House 2014) 6.

the European Fine Art Foundation,[7] in 2011 China's share of the world art market was 30 per cent, up from 23 per cent in 2010, surpassing the US as the world's leading source of art and antique buyers. Statistics show that the scale of the whole cultural industry in China in 2011 was 677.8 billion yuan (around 78 billion euro).[8] Of this, the art market's share was 210.8 billion yuan (around 24 billion euro), performing better than several other markets, such as books, magazines, newspapers, films, digital publications, web music, animation and network games.[9]

With the development of the art market the issue of art law arose. A few keen artists, critics and legal workers,[10] driven by their professional needs and a strong interest in art, began to study and analyse this new phenomenon, that is the marriage between art and law. They wrote books and gave lectures, providing legal advice to operators in the art market, as well as serving as consultants to the Department of Cultural Administration. The era of Chinese art law was born.

2.2   The Art Market Needs Art Law

In China, art law concerns legal problems related to creation, exploration, production, auction, sale, movement, collection and exhibition, as well as issues relating to cultural heritage and the administration of art. These legal problems and issues consist of several measures, such as the importation, exportation, auction and authentication of artworks, insurance, tax, freedom of speech, and the protection of intellectual property. Indeed, these problems should be solved and regulated by several different bodies of laws and regulations, not via a single unified rule.[11]

The protection of artists' rights is one of the main aspects of art law. Even though China's Constitution has guaranteed its citizens 'freedom of

---

[7]   See C.M.C. Andrew, *The International Art Market in 2011. Observations on the Art Trade over 25 Years* (The European Fine Art Foundation 2012) <https://www.tefaf.com/media/tefafmedia/TEFAF%20AMR%202012%20DEF_LR.pdf> accessed 18 May 2015.

[8]   See Department of Art Market of China Cultural Ministry, *2011 China Art Market Annual Report* (People's Art Publishing House 2012).

[9]   See *2013 Asian Art Market Report* (*supra*, n 6) at 6.

[10]   For instance, see Zuoren Wu (Chairman of Chinese Artists' Association), 'Strengthen legal consciousness and protecting legal interests of artists' *Legal Daily* (3 October 1990) 3; Guo Shoukang (Professor of Renmin University), 'On the Resale Right of the Artists' (1991) 3 Art; Lin Zhou, *Copyright Protection for Artists* (Publishing House of Beijing University of Technology April 1992).

[11]   The term 'art law' has been used in China for quite a long time, but it has never been given a proper definition.

artistic creation' since 1954,[12] the first law to protect artists' intellectual property rights was not passed until 1990, when the Copyright Law of the People's Republic of China[13] was promulgated.

It should be pointed out that, from the very beginning, China's Copyright Law provided a broad scope of protection for artists. For instance, the law places photographic works and works of fine art under the same provision, equally protecting these two categories as 'works'. This means that the term of protection for both photographic works and works of fine art is set at 50 years after the author's death.[14] Both Chinese and foreign artists enjoy the same protection according to the Copyright Law.

Auction is perhaps the best way of trading art works with unique cultural values, but for a long time auction was forbidden in China. In 1986 the first state-owned auction house in China was established,[15] while the Chinese Association of Auctioneers was founded in 1995.[16] Currently, there are hundreds of auction houses in China. The Auction Law of the People's Republic of China was adopted at the 20th meeting of the Standing Committee of the 8th National People's Congress on 5 July 1996 and entered into force on 1 January 1997. This law defines an auction as a type of 'trading in which a certain article or property right is transferred to one who offers the highest price in an open competitive bidding'.[17]

Concerning the business of works of fine art, the Chinese Ministry of Culture promulgated the 'Measures for the Administration of the Business of Works of Fine Art' in 2004, which makes clear in article 1 that 'these measures are formulated with a view to strengthening the administration of the business of works of fine art, protecting the lawful rights and interests of creators, operators and consumers, and promoting the healthy

---

[12]   See arts 87 and 95 of the Constitution of the People's Republic of China (1954).

[13]   Art. 1 of the Copyright Law of the People's Republic of China states: 'This Law is enacted in accordance with the Constitution for the purposes of protecting the copyright of authors in their literary, artistic and scientific works and rights related to copyright for encouraging the creation and dissemination of works which would contribute to the construction of socialist spiritual and material civilization and for promoting the development and flourishing of socialist culture and sciences.'

[14]   See arts 3 and 21 of the Copyright Law of the People's Republic of China.

[15]   The Guangzhou Huanan Auction Company was the first auction house, established in 1996.

[16]   See   <http://www.caa123.org.cn/frontNcShowIntroAction.do?method= showNewsByID&ID=103> accessed 18 May 2015.

[17]   Art. 3 Auction Law of the People's Republic of China.

development of the art market'.[18] According to this measure, 'works of fine art' are defined as 'drawings, calligraphy and seal cuttings, sculpture carvings, artistic photography, art in instalments, applied arts' and the 'limited editions' of these works. Business-related activities concerning works of fine art comprise the 'purchase, sale, rent, framing and mounting of paintings, dealing, evaluation, consultation, as well as the activities in commercial exhibitions and competition of works of fine art'.[19]

Along with the development of the art market in China, several laws and regulations have been drafted by the policy makers, who believe the prosperity of the art market is good for the development of the Chinese economy and also promotes the ability of people to appreciate art and enjoy life.

2.3   Controversy on the Legislation of *Droit de Suite*

China used to be a country with rigorous limitations imposed on access to information. Indeed, the significant changes that have occurred in access to information in China since 1978 are cornerstone pillars that portray China moving from a 'dying' country towards a nation that is developing rapidly and is increasing in confidence. The key reasons behind all these changes and developments are a result of information freedom.

The Copyright Law in China was promulgated on 17 September 1990. Soon after that, in October 1990, Mr Wu Zuoren, the Chairman of the Chinese Artists' Association, proposed in a seminar, for the first time, to introduce *droit de suite* legislation. However, it was not until 2012 that this idea was turned into a draft proposal for a law, when policy makers suggested an amendment to the Copyright Law accordingly. The draft reads as follows:

> Article 14. After the first sale of the original copy of a work of fine art, a photography work or a manuscript of literature or musical composition, a creator, his heirs or legatees are entitled to have a share in the increased value of each resale of the original copy or manuscript through auction, this right is enjoyable only by the creator or his heirs or legatees exclusively. An implementing measure with respect to this right will be enacted by the State Council at some other time.

---

[18]   See Measures for the Administration of the Business of Works of Fine Art (2014). The Measures were renewed in 2004 by the Ministry of Culture, see   <http://www.chinaculture.org/gb/cn_law/2004-06/28/content_49608.htm> accessed 18 May 2015.

[19]   See art. 2 Measures for the Administration of the Business of Works of Fine Art (2014).

This draft caused hot debate in art circles and among legal professionals. At the request of the Chinese Copyright Society and the Chinese Association of Auctioneers, an investigation focused on the possibility of introducing *droit de suite* in China was launched in 2013.[20] The results of this investigation are analysed in section 4.1 below.

3. *DROIT DE SUITE*: A EUROPEAN ORIGIN

3.1 History and Objectives of *Droit de Suite* in Europe

France was the first country in the world to codify *droit de suite* into law in 1920.[21] In order to understand the purpose of introducing this right, one should remember the economic situation of that precise period of time in France. Artists returning from World War I, as well as their families, were often penniless and starving on the streets of Paris, while their works were often sold at auctions at high prices (much higher than the author's original compensation). On this basis, an argument was made in favour of a 'just' royalty for starving artists: the idea of *droit de suite* was born.[22]

The resale right gained increased popularity during the following years, especially after the inclusion of a provision in the Berne Convention to encourage the signatory Members to codify *droit de suite* in their own legal systems.[23] By the end of the 1990s, all EU countries, with the exception of the UK, Ireland, the Netherlands and Austria, had codified some kind of *droit de suite* into their legislation. Indeed, that the resale right was born in a civil law country where authors' moral rights have traditionally been highly

---

[20] Z. Lin, 'Report on A Survey About Legislation and Implementation of Resale Rights in China' (2014) 85 China Intellectual Property 50.

[21] See Loi de 20 mai 1920 (1921) Recueil Dalloz périodique et critique (D.P. IV) 335, (1920) Duvergier & Bocquet 539, amended by Loi de 11 mars 1957 (Copyright Act of 1957), art. 42 [1957] J.O. 2723.2726-27 (1957) B.L.D. 197. 202.

[22] See M. Reddy, 'The Droit de Suite: Why American Fine Artists Should have the Right to a Release Royalty' (1995) 15 Loyola of Los Angeles Entertainment Law Review 509, 520–521. See also J. Pfeffer, 'The Costs and Legal Impracticalities Facing Implementation of the European Union's Droit de Suite Directive in the United Kingdom' (2004) 24(2) Northwestern Journal of International Law & Business 533–562.

[23] See Berne Convention for the Protection of Literary and Artistic Works, art. 14*ter*, §1 (9 September 1986), revised 24 July 1971, 828 U.N.T.S. 221. It should be noted that this right is an exception to Berne's general principle of national treatment; see WIPO's *Guide to the Berne Convention for the Protection of Literary and Artistic Works (Paris Act, 1971)* (WIPO 1978).

important does not come as a surprise, nor is it a surprise that common law countries like the UK and Ireland did not contemplate such a right.

Notwithstanding partial harmonization, the European landscape on authors' resale rights was very heterogeneous; even if all the laws of those countries generally provided royalties for artists when their works were sold in the secondary market, such provisions differed in many instances, especially in respect to the application of the right (e.g. only to public auctions, or also to private sales), the amount of the royalty, and to what sum the royalty should apply (to the total sales price or only to the profit).[24] This un-harmonized situation, it was believed, had created distortions of competition, as well as displacement of sales within the EU, especially because operators tended to avoid conducting transactions in Member States with resale rights protection for not paying royalties.[25] On this basis, the Commission thought that harmonizing this instrument would not only strengthen the importance of the resale right globally, but also would have a significant impact on the competitive environment within the internal market in the field of visual arts, giving the EU a competitive advantage over the US and China.

The solution was pursued via one of the traditional EU harmonization instruments, namely the passing of a directive. Certainly, the Directive on the resale right for the benefit of the author of an original work of art, passed down in 2001, represents but one piece of the puzzle towards the harmonization of European copyright and neighbouring rights law, a project that began in 1991 and is still continuing.[26] According to the Directive, in order for the resale right to apply, the artist, the work and the sale must all qualify.

First, the artist must be a citizen of one of the EU Member States or of another country that protects resale rights (artists who have their habitual residence in one of the EU countries can be considered as nationals of such countries at the discretion of the respective Member State).[27]

---

[24]   For more details on the specific differences see L. De Pierredon-Fawcett, *The Droit de Suite in Literary and Artistic Property: A Comparative Law Study* (Columbia University Law School 1992).

[25]   See M. Gaber, 'The Resale Right Directive: a Comparative Analysis of its Implementation in Germany and the United Kingdom' in V. Vadi and H. Schneider (eds), *Art, Cultural Heritage and the Market. Ethical and Legal Issues* (Springer 2014) 297.

[26]   See B. Hugenholtz, 'Copyright in Europe: Twenty Years Ago, Today and What the Future Holds' (2013) Fordham Intellectual Property, Media & Entertainment Law Journal 503.

[27]   Art. 7 Directive 2001/84/EC. For issues related to *droit de suite* and territoriality before the introduction of the Directive, see, for example, *Folgerechtt bei*

Second, the resale right only covers 'original works' of the artists or 'one of a limited number' (that is copies that have been numbered, signed, or otherwise duly authorized copies) including 'works of graphic or plastic art' (the Directive includes a specific list of works covered).[28] The Commission hoped that this limited scope would 'redress the balance between the economic situation of authors of graphic and plastic works of art and that of other creators who benefit from successive exploitation of their works'.[29]

Third, 'resales' are specifically defined as transactions where at least one party involved is acting 'in the course of a business of dealing in works of art'. In other words, the right only applies when there is the presence of a professional party or intermediary, while direct sales between private individuals or sales by private individuals to public museums are not caught by *droit de suite*. Furthermore, if the seller acquired the work of art less than three years earlier directly from the artist and the resale price is less than 10,000 euro, there is no resale right.[30]

The resale right is inalienable, not assignable (except via succession) and cannot be waived, either in advance or by way of contract (and no agreement to repay the royalty can be made).[31] Member States may also provide for compulsory or optional collective management of the royalty. For instance, in some Member States, such as the UK, the resale right cannot be collected by the artists themselves, but the right may only be exercised by a collecting society.[32]

Finally, because four EU countries (the UK, Ireland, the Netherlands and Austria) did not contemplate *droit de suite* prior to the passing of the Directive, a transitional period until 2010 (which was then further postponed by two years) was contemplated. As a consequence, the Directive was fully implemented by all the Member States on 1 January 2012.

3.2   Evaluating the Directive: Pros and Cons of *Droit de Suite*

The Directive itself requires that the Commission should conduct a study on its implementation 'paying particular attention to the competitiveness

---

Auslandsbezug ('Droit de suite with Respect to Sales Abroad'), German Federal Supreme Court, 16 June 1994, Case No. I ZR 24/92, 26 IIC 573 (1995).

28   Art. 2 Directive 2001/84/EC.

29   Recital 3 in the preamble to Directive 2001/84/EC.

30   See also Case C-41/14 *Christie's France SNC v. Syndicat National des Antiquaires*, 26 February 2015.

31   Art. 1 Directive 2001/84/EC.

32   Artist's Resale Right Regulations 2006 (S.I. 2006/346).

of the market in modern and contemporary art in the Community, especially . . . in relation to relevant markets that do not apply the resale right'.[33] In response to this task, the Commission published a report on 14 December 2011[34] based on a broad public consultation, which received over 500 answers from a wide range of experts (including artists, deceased artists' successors, art market professionals, collecting societies, artists' trade associations and various public authorities). This report focused especially on the impact and the effect of introducing the resale right in countries that previously had not contemplated it, such as the UK. Indeed, in the UK several organizations, as well as art dealers and individuals, have expressed resistance and scepticism towards the harmonization of resale rights ever since the first discussions over a possible introduction of a directive. Several of the often identified negative aspects of *droit de suite* were used to support the UK position. For instance, among the negative general aspects it has been pointed out that the resale right might reduce an artist's first selling price, shift most of the risks onto artists, and create transaction costs.[35] Not only did critics contend that the right harms the artists (especially unknown artists), sellers and the art market in general, but also that such a right is seldom enforced.[36] Moreover, it has been stressed that it takes more than the artist to increase the value of art works, particularly because the pieces of art themselves typically have no inherent value; in addition to the artists, collectors, dealers, gallery owners, and museums all play an important role once the work is created. Along these lines, it has been pointed out that artists might benefit much more from a 'successful sale' (which increases artists' reputations and future sales of their works) than from a resale royalty. Finally, another traditional argument against *droit de suite* is the fear of location shopping for art sales: art-related transactions might be moved to jurisdictions without resale royalty laws to avoid paying this 'tax'. Indeed, this was the main argument behind the resistance of the UK to implementing the resale right law.

---

[33]   See art. 11 Directive 2001/84/EC.

[34]   European Commission, *Report on the Implementation and Effect of the Resale Right Directive (2001/84/EC)*, Brussels 14 December 2011) COM(2011) 878 final <http://ec.europa.eu/internal_market/copyright/resale-right/index_en.htm> accessed 18 May 2015.

[35]   C. Banterghansa and K. Graddy, 'The Impact of Droit the Suite in the UK: an Empirical Analysis' (2011) 35(2) Journal of Cultural Economics 81–100; V. Ginsburgh, 'The Economic Consequences of Droit de Suite in the European Union' (2006) 35(1–2) Economic Analysis and Policy 61–71.

[36]   See, for instance, H. Hanssman and M. Santilli, 'Royalties for Artists versus Royalties for Authors and Composers' (2001) 25 Journal of Cultural Economics 259, 260.

On the positive side, the strongest argument in support of the resale right is that such a right equates artists with other creative persons, compensating them for their contribution and reputation.[37] Furthermore, benefits might come from the fact that the royalty right might increase artists' future revenue and might allow the sharing of risks between market participants (even though the artist's risks are increased).[38]

Indeed, from an economic perspective, if the benefits outweigh the costs, this net benefit should be compared to the transaction costs in order to draw conclusions on whether the resale right is good or bad for European artists. However, the variables mentioned are very difficult to measure and, therefore, it is very challenging (if not impossible) to argue from an economic point of view clearly for or against the effectiveness of the resale right mechanism. This perspective came out also from the above-mentioned Commission Report on the EU Directive.[39] The Commission's study, in fact, produced mixed results, which overall failed to demonstrate that the Directive had been especially detrimental and that the EU art market had been damaged by the harmonization of the resale rights. Indeed, the study pointed out that the EU lost share in the global market for modern and contemporary art after the harmonization of the resale right law (achieving aggregate sales of €15.6 billion in 2011, down 2 per cent on 2010 and representing 34 per cent of the global art market). At the same time, however, as the Commission stresses, there are several different variables (e.g. taxation systems, changes in taste, changes in the global distribution of wealth, economic crises, etc.) that can affect internal art markets; the introduction of *droit de suite* is but one of these variables. On the other hand, instead, the Report points towards one factor that undoubtedly needed improvement, namely the management of the resale right. To this end, the Report highlighted that even though most Member States have implemented some kind of collective management system for the collection of royalties, there are significant divergences between Member States and, as such, this is a problematic area that requires action at Union level.[40]

---

[37]   See, for example T. Goetzl, 'In Support of the Resale Royalty' (1988) 7 Cardozo Arts & Entertainment Law Journal 249, 255.
[38]   J. Solow, 'An Economic Analysis of the Droit de Suite' (1998) 22 Journal of Cultural Economics 209–226.
[39]   See M. Gallo, *Report on the Report on the Implementation and Effect of the Resale Right Directive (2001/84.EC)* (2012/2038(INI)), prepared for the Committee on Legal Affairs of the European Parliament.
[40]   See also 'Key Principles and Recommendations on the Management of the Author Resale Right' (17 February 2014) <http://ec.europa.eu/internal_market/copyright/docs/resale/140214-resale-right-key-principles-and-recommendations_en.pdf> accessed 18 May 2015.

Finally, it should be noted that because the scope of the Directive was significantly expanded in 2012 (as previously mentioned the Directive was fully implemented only in 2012) the effects of the Directive should be furthered monitored and reported.

3.3 *Droit de Suite* Distorts the General Understanding of European Copyright Law

Several observations can be made when discussing the issue of the resale right within the context of the overall body of IP laws. For many years, when discussing the resale right, scholars have focused on the question related to the traditional 'delicate balance' between public and private rights. Is the conferring of a temporary monopoly to an artist (via granting a resale right) justified from the perspective of the benefit that such mechanisms will bring to the whole of society from an economic and/or cultural perspective?

To answer these questions scholars have used several economic variables, especially in order to try to show whether the *droit de suite* is good or bad for the art market (and, by analogy, for cultural development). As explained, also the EU Commission Report to evaluate the effects of the Directive was merely based on this kind of analysis. Even though the economic analysis has provided some insights into the problem, it is well recognized that these studies have also shown how difficult it is to quantify and draw conclusions. Furthermore, and most importantly, the economic analysis does not suffice to provide any sound explanation of the nature and function of the resale right mechanism *per se*. At the same time, however, precisely this kind of information is of vital importance for any nation, such as China, that might want to engage in discussing possible future implementation of the *droit the suite* tool. Therefore, while considering whether or not to implement *droit de suite*, a nation should primarily analyse these fundamental objectives, rather than only concentrating on the economic effects of implementing such a right into the art market. The resale right has two premises: one is that works of visual art (whose value typically lies in the original or in a limited edition) are not equally rewarded in comparison to other copyrighted works whose economics are driven by the prospect of mass distribution; the second one is that artists should be granted a share in their work's increased resale value.[41] Precisely these are the premises that should form

---

[41] P. Goldstein and B. Hugenholtz, *International Copyright. Principles, Law, and Practice* (OUP 2013).

the basis for a discussion on the possible introduction of the resale right mechanism.

Arguably, the resale right represents a *hybrid* product within the copyright regime and, as such, distorts the general common understanding of copyright rules. As a starting point, it is important to point out some basic concepts of copyright law in order to shed light on the way such principles have been implemented in a very peculiar manner regarding the resale right mechanism. Certainly, it should be stressed that even though several universal rules and principles have been developed, copyright law still remains, nowadays, to a large extent a matter of national law. As such, these types of questions should be addressed on the basis of each nation's legal traditions and principles. At the same time, however, the many globally acknowledged axioms of copyright law, together with some level of harmonization of copyright law in the EU and the intrinsic nature of the resale right mechanism *per se*, allow us to conduct some analysis also on a European level.

Among the universally acknowledged rules is, for example, that copyright protects 'original' 'literary and artistic works'. Furthermore, it is commonly accepted that copyright attaches both economic and (at least to some extent) moral rights. Generally speaking, civil law countries ground their copyright systems deeply in the author's natural right/*droit d'auteur* defence and, as such, are commonly thought to provide more rigorous moral rights protection than common law countries, which, instead, root their copyright laws in utilitarian theories.

Among the economic rights, most copyright laws contemplate the right holder's rights to control the reproduction, distribution, public performance, broadcasting and other communication of a work to the public.[42] On the other hand, moral rights, such as the rights of paternity and integrity, protect the author's reputational interests. Indeed, in most countries authors' moral rights are doctrinally separated from economic rights.[43] Economic rights are concerned with a work's exploitation and, as such, they result in some monetary reward and they last for a limited period of time. On the other hand, moral rights are concerned with the author's reputation; even though it is commonly believed that moral rights are 'absolute', this approach is followed only by a few pieces of legislation in the EU, France being the most striking example of such an extreme. On the contrary, in fact, most EU jurisdictions contemplate some possibilities for the waiving of moral rights.[44]

---

[42] Ibid.
[43] See also art. 6*bis*(1) Berne Convention, 1971, Paris Text.
[44] Within the EU see, for example, Germany and the UK.

Several points arise from the general copyright framework portrayed above in relation to the nature of the resale right enshrined in the EU Directive and the premises on which it was based. As mentioned, the first premise was to equalize all copyright holders. This way, the *droit de suite* addresses the very specific moral issue of a 'fair' and 'non-discriminative' way to reward artists. At the same time, however (and here lies the unpredictable nature of the *droit*), it creates a specific *ad hoc* right that applies only to visual artists, thus discriminating against all the other categories of copyright holders. For instance, contemporary artists that do not use conservative materials like canvas, oil, acrylics or stone are discriminated against.[45] Furthermore, because there is only a small margin of profit when selling unrecognized artists, galleries might well turn to already established artists for their sales materials. Overall, this creates 'unfairness' (both external, that is among copyright holders, and internal, that is among 'artists') rather than 'fairness'.

The second premise for the *droit de suite* was that artists who sell their works at very low prices should be allowed to share in the work's increased resale value. The resale right as regulated under the EU Directive, however, applies not only when the value of the work of art has increased (with respect to the original selling price from the artist), but rather indiscriminately to any transactions concluded after the second resale of the piece. This indicates that the second cornerstone principle of the *droit* has also not been met by the Directive.

Finally, another peculiarity of the *droit de suite* is doubts over its legitimacy. Under the EU Directive, the moral concerns embedded in the resale right tool have been met via the creation of an economic incentive. Officially, the resale right is categorized as an economic right, especially as a sub-category of the distribution right of copyright. Accordingly, it provides for monetary rewards to artists and it lasts for 70 years *post mortem auctoris*. At the same time, however, it relates neither to the exploitation of the work nor to the use (in order to exclude or receive compensation) of such work (as traditional economic rights do).[46] Additionally, the resale right is not only a moral right (according to such a definition in copyright law), as it embeds elements from the most rigorous approaches of civil law countries towards moral rights: it is inalienable, not assignable (except via succession), and cannot be waived by way of contract. In other words,

---

[45]   J. Wuenschel, 'Article 95 EC Revisited: Is the Artist's Resale Right Directive a Community Act beyond EC Competence?' (2009) 4(2) Journal of Intellectual Property Law & Practice 130–136.

[46]   See also D. Vaver, 'The National Treatment Requirements of the Berne and Universal Copyright Conventions' (1986) 17 IIC 557–607, 715–33.

the resale right instrument appears to be a *hybrid* product that takes some elements from both economic and moral rights of copyright law, but does not clearly belong to one of the two. On this basis, it can be argued that the resale right mechanism distorts the general understanding of European copyright law by granting artists an inalienable economic right.[47]

Overall, the above analysis shows that, although some arguments could be made from an EU perspective in favour of harmonizing of resale right to remove barriers to the internal market, the instrument contemplated in the EU Directive appears unjustified and ineffective at the least. Certainly, at this point it appears to be difficult, if not impossible, for the EU to step back from this legislative move. Even repealing the Directive, for instance, would not automatically repeal the national laws on the resale right of the Member States. Arguably, this is also a matter that should be taken into account in the framework of the ongoing projects aimed at reforming EU copyright law.[48] As law reforms are, by definition, very slow, it would seem that the most efficient tool is for the EU national courts and the Court of Justice of the European Union to interpret the resale right in such a restrictive manner as to radically limit its scope and applicability.

4. THE RESALE RIGHT IN CHINA: A 'NORM MAKER' OR A 'NORM TAKER' CASE?

As reported above, the resale right tool implemented in the EU embeds many problematic elements. Some directly relate to the specific rules that the EU legislator decided to implement when harmonizing the resale right (e.g. that the right applies indiscriminately to any transactions even if the sale is at a loss or does not include any profit); some others, instead, are associated with the nature of the resale right *per se* (e.g. the fact that it is a hybrid type of right). Indeed, the European example represents an interesting starting point for discussing *droit de suite* in China. On this note, this chapter argues that the current Chinese legal environment is not ready for the introduction of a resale right mechanism.

---

[47] See Wuenschel (*supra*, n 45).

[48] For instance, see Directorate General Internal Market and Services/ Directorate D – Intellectual Property/D1 – Copyright, *Report on the Responses to the Public Consultations on the Review of the EU Copyright Rules* (July 2014) <http://ec.europa.eu/internal_market/consultations/2013/copyright-rules/docs/co ntributions/consultation-report_en.pdf> accessed 18 May 2015.

4.1   Investigating the Application of the *Droit de Suite* Mechanisms in China

In 2013, a suggestion for amending the Copyright Law by adding a clause related to the *droit de suite* was presented and put out for consultation to the public. In order to enhance knowledge of the Chinese art market and the possible repercussions on the market from the introduction of the resale right, a research project was launched. The study was based on theoretical comparative analysis and on an empirical study conducted via interviews and questionnaires among five categories of interested parties, namely artists, heirs, art galleries, auction houses, and private collectors located in Beijing. The study concluded that China is currently not a suitable place for introducing the resale right. The results of this project[49] can be summarized as follows.

On a theoretical level, the study relied heavily upon 'Western-type' arguments (with strong comparisons with and reference to the European system). Among those, for instance, it points out some of the arguments according to which the *droit de suite* does not bring many advantages to European artists and that the share of the EU in the global art market has been reduced after the harmonization of the resale right.[50] Furthermore, the study highlights that having *droit de suite* puts the EU at a competitive disadvantage with the rest of the world and, thus, the only way for the EU to survive is to 'drag everyone down to this level'; accordingly, *droit de suite* appears often as a requirement for bilateral treaties between the EU and third countries.[51] Unfortunately, though, none of the intrinsic characteristic of the *droit de suite* (discussed in Section 3.3 above) were mentioned.

Indeed, the most original and valuable contribution of the Report lies in having highlighted and empirically investigated some China-specific relevant types of arguments to show whether the *droit de suite* mechanism would be suitable or not for implementation in the current Chinese

---

[49]   Z. Lin, 'Report on a Survey about Legislation and Implementation of Resale Rights in China' (2014) 85 China Intellectual Property 50.

[50]   Gallo (n 39).

[51]   See, for instance, the treaties between the EU and India, art. 7.6 Negotiating Text, EU/India FTA (BTIA) <http://keionline.org/node/1691> accessed 18 May 2015; Kyu-Bin Lim and Alice Young-Ran Choi: 'Korea-EU Free Trade Agreement Regarding Intellectual Property Rights' Kim & Chang IP Newsletter 2009/10, 1 <http://www.kimchang.com/UserFiles/files/IPNewsletter_0201.pdf> accessed 18 May 2015: 'Under the Korea-EU FTA, both Korea and EU promised to discuss the appropriateness and feasibility of introducing artists' resale right into Korea within 2 years from the effective date of the Korea-EU FTA.'

environment. In this context, among the theoretical arguments, the Report highlights that the mechanism of *droit de suite* could not tally with the theory of Chinese copyright law. Chinese copyright is understood as a monopoly granted to creators to control the 'use' of an 'original work'. The 'use' mainly refers to making one or more copies of the work with the aid of duplication technology. According to the copyright rule, if there is no creation, there is no copyright. Likewise, if there is no duplication, there is no copyright infringement. It is in this sense, we could say, that the increasing market value of a piece of art work after its first sale bears no relationship to the art work and the copyright owned by the artist. Accordingly, *droit de suite* could not find its justification in the theory of copyright law in China. Moreover, the Report highlights how the overall regulatory framework of artworks in China, such as in respect of auction law, tax law and property inheritance law, is not yet sufficiently complete and, as such, is not suitable for the introduction of *droit de suite* under current rules.

Furthermore, based on the empirical study the following results (all pointing towards a negative answer in respect to introducing *droit de suite* in China) were highlighted in the Report:

- At present, the living conditions of Chinese artists are totally different from the time when the *droit de suite* was born in France. According to an investigation, in fact, around two-thirds of artists' yearly income surpassed 100,000 yuan (around 11,300 euro), which is above the entire social average income.
- More than half of the artists selling their paintings for the first time were young artists between 20 and 29 years old (57 per cent). The vast majority of artists sold their works through their own studios and their own galleries: 41 per cent of the artists had their own studio; 27 per cent ran their own galleries, 13 per cent cooperated with galleries, while only 8 per cent signed contracts. Furthermore, artists were more concerned with 'selling their works' than with 'reselling' them in the secondary market. Because the introduction of *droit de suite* might reduce the desire to purchase art works, especially affecting first sales, this might indicate that introducing such mechanisms might affect especially young artists negatively.
- Most of the artists did not pay taxes when selling their art works and no records of first sales of the works were usually kept. Each year, only 3 per cent of the artists paid taxes, while 67 per cent never paid any tax; occasional tax payers accounted for 30 per cent. Furthermore, 46 per cent of the artists generally did not provide any

bills and vouchers, while 23 per cent admitted to providing vouchers occasionally. In such an environment, calculating the royalties for applying *droit de suite* might often be impossible.

- Most of the Chinese art collectors are hobbyists not investors in art works who expect the value of their paintings to increase over time. Concerning the suppliers, most of the art galleries are very young: 80 per cent of the galleries have run for more than three years, while only 30 per cent for more than 10 years. The two main businesses of the galleries are sale on a 'commission basis' (51 per cent) and 'resale' (48 per cent). The former refers to the selling of the art works on behalf of the artists, while resale is defined as selling the work after purchasing it from the artists. Art galleries prefer sale on a commission basis. Most of the galleries resell their art works within a period of five years, one-third of the galleries resell their works when there are profits, while less than 10 per cent resell work after more than 10 years. Indeed, that such a large share of artworks are resold within a short period of time indicated that the market is not sufficiently stable; for instance, in the European art market, resale takes place within a longer period of time in order to recoup investments in a more profitable way. Moreover, in China, the resale of the works is more concentrated in contemporary works (91 per cent contemporary works, 6 per cent modern works, while only 3 per cent ancient works). Overall, this indicates that the Chinese art market and the collectors' community are unstable and extremely sensitive to any changes in the market. The implementation of *droit de suite* would add costs to the transactions with a negative effect on the collectors' community as a whole.

- The knowledge of *droit de suite* among Chinese art market operators was heterogeneous in the categories investigated. Artists were generally not aware of the *droit de suite*: 34 per cent had heard about it, 66 per cent were not aware of it. Artists with high-level income were more keen on implementing a resale right mechanism in China than those with lower-level incomes. Most galleries (53 per cent) knew hardly anything about the *droit de suite*, 35 per cent had simply heard of it, while only 12 per cent had more detailed knowledge of the right. Among the auction companies, however, the level of knowledge was higher: 72 per cent had heard about it, 14 per cent were very familiar with the mechanism, while 14 per cent were not aware of it. Most artists believed that the art works were constantly resold in the secondary markets, but that artists themselves should not influence the resale prices, as the art market has its own rules, which galleries, art dealers, critics and curators follow. Forty-one per cent of the art galleries did not worry about a possible introduction of the *droit de suite* mechanism, while 35 per cent expressed concern. More than half of the galleries (53 per cent) believed that *droit de suite* legislation could have a negative impact on the art market, 29 per cent that it might have a positive effect, while 18 per cent were indifferent. Among the auction companies, 71.3 per cent expressed concern and were very worried about the negative effects of a possible introduction of the *droit de suite* in China, while 28.57 per cent expressed no concern. Furthermore, 52.38 per cent of the auction companies believed that the implementation of the *droit de suite* would have negative impacts on the Chinese art market.

● The traditional Chinese 'ink and wash' paintings are very different from Western oil paintings. The quantity of these works is immense; on the one hand, they are very easily copied and counterfeited, while, on the other, the authentication process is extremely difficult. Counterfeited paintings and works are prevalent in the Chinese art market. Artists and their heirs may be reluctant to accept royalties from the resale right since they cannot be confident whether the resold work is an authentic one that comes from the artist.

5.   CONCLUDING REMARKS

Innovation and creativity are the key factors for a country to achieve prosperity and modernization. Generally speaking, all inventions and creations are just different forms of information shared among various societies. We say that intellectual property as a mechanism to protect creators and innovators is a cost that society needs to bear in order to enhance certain activities and encourage more innovation and creation.

Chinese artists do not lack the skills and creativeness of famous masters like Picasso, but they do lack several basic conditions, especially, for example, a well-regulated art market and an effective legal environment, in order to be able to achieve the status of a 'Chinese Picasso'. Indeed, the art market needs art law and, in return, art law sets the rules and guarantees a smooth and healthy development for the art market. Although the process towards a well-regulated and prosperous Chinese art market has begun, it is still very undeveloped and several further steps need to be taken in this direction. Certainly, as the analysis presented here has explained, the Chinese legal environment is not suitable soil for receiving and properly enforcing the *droit de suite* mechanism under current rules. As such, it is here contended that in discussing matters about resale rights, China should prioritize its own cultural policy, as well as its interaction with the copyright system, and act as a 'norm-maker' disregarding the *droit de suite* mechanism accordingly.

8. Parallel trademark law reforms in China and Europe – an informal convergence?

Liguo Zhang and Max Oker-Blom

1. INTRODUCTION

Trademark laws in China and Europe are currently going through major reforms. In China, the current Trademark Law was first introduced in 1982 and came into effect from 1 March 1983. Due to the fact that the law was instituted as a result of US–China trade negotiations, contemporary Chinese trademark law is rooted in norms of foreign origin because there was no local trademark law at the time.[1] The 1982 Trademark Law was very basic and simple, and many important issues were not covered. To fulfil the requirements laid down in international treaties[2] and deal with some practical problems arising from the implementation, the Trademark Law was amended twice, in 1993 and in 2001, a period when China was preparing to join the World Trade Organization (WTO). In 2008, the Chinese State Council published the Outline of State IP Strategy, which set a roadmap to improve the intellectual property (IP) regime and IP protection. In this context, the Trademark Law was amended again in 2013 on China's own initiative. Overall, the 2013 Amendment focuses on three aspects. First, the application and opposition procedure were improved to increase efficiency. Second, the Amendment added rules to prevent trademark abuse, such as in the case of well-known marks or conflicts with prior rights. Third, the Amendment strengthens the protection and

---

[1]   See Niklas Bruun and Liguo Zhang, 'Legal Transplant of Intellectual Property Rights in China: Norm Taker or Norm Maker?', Chapter 3 in this volume.

[2]   The 1993 and 2001 Amendment to the Trademark Act took measures to be in compliance with the requirement laid down in the Paris Convention for the Protection of Industrial Property, the 2001 Amendment aimed to be in compliance with the WTO TRIPs Agreement.

enforcement of trademarks by raising the damages available and reducing the burden of proof for trademark holders.

EU trademark law is also going through a reform for both procedural and substantive reasons. The European trademark system currently operates on a dual level, whereby national trademark systems in the EU coexist with Community trademarks. The Community Trade Mark Regulation (CTMR or Regulation) was enacted in 1994, and became operational from 1 April 1996.[3] While the Trade Mark Directive[4] (TMD or Directive) strives towards harmonizing the laws of the Member States for the purposes of the smooth operation of the free movement of goods and services, the CTMR establishes a unitary right extending throughout the whole territory of the EU.[5] This means, among other things, that it has equal effect in the whole of the Community and that the rights, being, for example, revoked or declared invalid, also concern the total territory of the Union. As noted in a Max Planck Study: 'User organizations agree that the coexistence of CTMs and national trade mark rights is fundamental and necessary for the efficient functioning of a trade mark system capable of meeting the needs of companies of different sizes, markets and geographical needs, and that it should therefore be maintained.'[6] This was also the starting point for the renewed efforts to create a Community-wide trademark system in the 1970s.[7] It is interesting to note, however, that a statement contained in the Memorandum on the Creation of an

---

[3]   Council Regulation (EC) No 40/94 of December 1993 on the Community trade mark. The regulation was later codified as 207/2009/EC (the Regulation). As known, it was possible to file applications from the beginning of 1996, but the Office for Harmonization in the Internal Market (OHIM) became operational on 1 April of the same year. The work on creating a unified trademark system had already started in the late 1950s and early 1960s. See e.g. David Tatham and William Richards, *ECTA Guide to E.U. Trade Mark Legislation* (Sweet and Maxwell 1998) 3.

[4]   Codified as Directive 2008/95/EC of the European Parliament and of the Council of 22 October 2008 to approximate the laws of the Member States relating to trade marks.

[5]   See recitals 2 and 3 in the preamble to the CTMR and on the unitary character Art. 1(2) CTMR.

[6]   The Max Planck Institute for Intellectual Property and Competition Law, *Study on the Overall Functioning of the European Trade Mark System* (Munich, 15 February 2011) 31–32 <http://ec.europa.eu/internal_market/indprop/docs/tm/20110308_allensbach-study_en.pdf> accessed 8 June 2015 (the Max Planck Study).

[7]   See Max Oker-Blom, 'EU-varumärket: en framgångshistoria' (2007) 143(2) Tidskrift utgiven av Juridiska föreningen i Finland106–107. Today this principle of coexistence is expressed in recital 6 of the preamble to the CTMR.

EEC Trade Mark in 1976 noted that the only way to solve a conflict between the free movement of goods and national trademark systems was to abolish the latter, and apparently triggered demands for reform.

As early as 2006, approximately ten years after the Community Trade Mark (CTM) was introduced, the discussion started regarding a review of the functioning of the CTM and the trademark system in the EU as a whole. These discussions were, at least partly, triggered by the user survey performed on behalf of OHIM in 2005.[8] The CTM has clearly been a success. Paradoxically this success, as well as the time lapsed, also caused an urge to revise the system. An early Commission proposal included a 'legal package' comprising three legal instruments, including proposals for a new directive[9] and a new regulation[10] (hereinafter referred to collectively as the Proposal, and individually as the Proposed New Directive and the Proposed New Regulation).[11] On 21 April 2015, a trialogue, that is discussions between the Commission, Parliament and the Council, led to a provisional agreement concerning two legal instruments:[12] a recast of the 1989 Directive (codified as 2008/95/EC) approximating the laws of the Member States relating to trade marks, and the revision of the 1994 Regulation (codified as 207/2009/EC) on the Community trade mark. The proposal of the final compromised texts was published on 8 June 2015 (hereinafter Directive Compromise Text and Regulation Compromise Text, respectively).[13]

---

[8]   The study was undertaken by GFK Emer Ad Hoc Research in cooperation with the User Satisfaction Task Force, which was headed by Ingrid Desrois. It was published on OHIM's website on 27 March 2006. OHIM published its response on the result of the survey on 19 June 2006.

[9]   Commission Proposal for a Directive of the European Parliament and of the Council to approximate the laws of the Member States relating to trade marks (Recast) COM(2013) 162 final.

[10]   Commission Proposal for a Regulation of the European Parliament and of the Council amending Council Regulation (EC) No 207/2009 on the Community trade mark, COM(2013) 161 final.

[11]   See for example, <http://www.ecta.org/IMG/pdf/ecta_opinion_on_legislative_package_summary.pdf> accessed 11 June 2013.

[12]   <http://europa.eu/rapid/press-release_MEMO-15-4824_en.htm> accessed 11 June 2015.

[13]   Revision of the European Trade Mark system Proposal for a Regulation of the European Parliament and of the Council amending Council Regulation (EC) No 207/2009 on the Community Trade Mark and Proposal for a Directive of the European Parliament and of the Council to approximate the laws of the Member States relating to trade marks (Recast) – Analysis of the final compromise texts with a view to agreement, Revision of the European Trade Mark system, <http://data.consilium.europa.eu/doc/document/ST-9547-2015-ADD-2/en/pdf> accessed

Just as in Europe, the Trademark Act of 2001 required a sign to be visible in order to be registered.[14] The conditions are spelt out in Article 8, which was amended in 2013. Trademarks capable of registration in the amended Trademark Act include all kinds of signs capable of distinguishing goods or services of one undertaking or individual from those of another. These signs include traditional marks such as words, characters, figurative marks, letter of the alphabet and numerals, but also three-dimensional shapes and colour combinations, and even non-visible signs such as sound, as well as a combination thereof. To be registered, those signs have to be distinctive and recognizable and should not be in conflict with any earlier-obtained rights of another.[15] A profound change in the 2013 Amendment is that sound marks can be registered as long as they are capable of distinguishing the goods or services of one undertaking or individual from those of others. However, the 2013 Amendment still does not permit a smell mark and a single colour to be registered as a trademark.[16]

This chapter documents parallel ongoing trademark law reforms in China and in the EU.[17] The reforms are substantive as well as procedural, including broad institutional reforms on the institutional governance of OHIM in the EU,[18] as well as procedural efficiencies of the Trademark Office (TMO) and the Trademark Review and Adjudication Board in

---

11 June 2015 (Directive Compromise Text); Proposal for a Regulation of the European Parliament and of the Council amending Council Regulation (EC) No 207/2009 on the Community Trade Mark and Proposal for a Directive of the European Parliament and of the Council to approximate the laws of the Member States relating to trade marks (Recast) – Analysis of the final compromise texts with a view to agreement <http://data.consilium.europa.eu/doc/document/ST-9547-2015-ADD-1/en/pdf> accessed 11 June 2015 (Regulation Compromise Text).

[14]   Art. 8 of the 2001 Trademark Act provided that any visible signs that are capable of distinguishing a natural person, legal person or other organization's goods from others, including scripts, graphics, letters, numbers, three-dimensional marks and combination of colours, as well as combinations of these elements, can be the subject of an application for registration as a trademark.

[15]   See Art. 8 of the 2013 Trademark Act.

[16]   See Art. 8 of the 2013 Trademark Act.

[17]   Despite the EU trademark reform comprising, as said, both the Directive and the Regulation, i.e. national and EU law, this chapter focuses on the latter. This chapter will, however, if necessary and for the sake of clarity, refer to the Directive when discussing the proposed changes and amendments.

[18]   At first OHIM's position as an administratively and financially autonomous body was questioned by the Commission, although being supervised by the latter. The Commission would prefer to change its status and equalize it with all the other EU agencies. This is to some extent reflected in the Commission proposal to rename OHIM as the EU Trade Marks and Designs Agency. This was later changed by the Parliament to the European Union Intellectual Property Agency,

China.[19] The motivation and reasons are not the same because China, as a nation state, cannot be compared substantively with EU-wide trademark protection, such as the CTMR. However, focusing on the similarities observed in the reform proposals which focus on trademark use, this chapter observes that the reforms in China seem to be converging with the European system to a certain extent. The chapter concludes by noting that despite the absence of formal legal instruments between China and the EU, commonly faced problems may informally direct the attention of Chinese legislation towards the solutions used and adopted elsewhere, in this case Europe.

2. THE USE OF TRADEMARKS IN ACQUISITION OF TRADEMARK RIGHTS IN EUROPE AND CHINA

2.1 Trademark Use in the Requirement for Protection in Europe

The exclusive right provided for by a CTM is always based on registration.[20] Protection cannot be obtained by establishment, even less by starting to use a trademark.[21] According to Article 25(1)(a) and (b) of the CTMR an application for a CTM shall, at the choice of the applicant, either be filed at the Office, that is OHIM, or at the central industrial property office of a Member State. The Member States are not, however, according to the Directive Compromise Text,[22] deprived of the right to continue to protect trademarks acquired through use. As for the application for registration,

---

while the Council, representing the Members States, has opted for status quo, i.e. no change.

[19] The 2013 Amendment has made several changes in terms of filing procedure which aims to improve efficiency and convenience for applicants. The Amendment allows applicants to file an application for registration of same trademark for goods in different classes within an application, which used to need to file separately in 2001 Amendment. The 2013 Amendment also provides that applications can be filed through electronic mean of data transmission. The 2013 Amendment set a nine months' time cap for the State TMO to complete the examination of an application for registration. In the examination procedure, the Amendment adds that during the examination, the TMO may request applicants to clarify or correct application if it considers necessary. But if applicant fails to do so, it does not affect the decision by the TMO. These provisions are newly added in the 2013 Amendment.

[20] Art. 6 CTMR.

[21] See e.g. Pirkko-Liisa Haarmann, *Immateriaalioikeus* (Talentum 2014) 349.

[22] Recital 11 in the preamble.

it is now suggested in Article 25 of the Regulation Compromise Text that an application for an EU trademark shall be filed exclusively at the Office. This suggestion is supported by noting that there has been a gradual decline of filings of CTMs at the intellectual property offices of the Member States. With the introduction of electronic filing it is of course no surprise that the number of CTM applications at the local offices today is insignificant.

One important change proposed relates to the graphical representation. Non-traditional trademarks such as sensorial signs (smell, sound, touch, movement, single colour) have always been problematic in the contemporary trademark law system. In a registration-based system, there is a need to establish an objective register that identifies the subject of property protection and to notify the public and the relevant authorities.[23] On the other hand, when these signs are used, they are often subjectively experienced and may well be devoid of objectivity. The graphical representation requirement in the law, in this context, has functioned as a proxy to give the register a sense of objectivity, and thus has been used as a criterion for the trademark offices to refuse registration of signs that are devoid of objectivity. At the same time, the requirement has been criticized for being an inflexible filter, preventing the trademark system from fully reflecting economic and business reality of branding including sounds, lights and movements, as well as smells as tools of marketing a brand.[24]

According to Article 4 CTMR, a CTM may consist of any sign capable of being represented graphically, particularly words, including personal names, designs, letters, numerals and the shape of goods or of their packaging, provided that such signs are capable of distinguishing the goods or services of one undertaking from those of other undertakings. In Article 4(b) of the Regulation Compromise Text the requirement of graphical representation is abolished. Instead the wording 'in a manner which enables the competent authorities and the public to determine the precise subject of the protection afforded to its proprietor' is used. Recital 9 indicates that this change is motivated by allowing more flexibility while ensuring greater legal certainty. A sign can thus be represented in any appropriate form using generally available technology as long as the representation is clear, precise, self-contained, easily accessible, intelligible, durable and objective. This suggestion is welcomed due to an assumption

---

[23]   See Case C-273/00 *Ralf Sieckmann v. Deutsches Patent- und Markenamt* ECLI:EU:C:2002:748, paras 44–53.

[24]   See Graeme B. Dinwoodie, 'The Death of Ontology: A Teleological Approach to Trademark Law' (1999), 84 Iowa Law Review 611–752.

that this will lead to more comprehensive protection of different kinds of trademarks. At the same time, however, a wish has been expressed that the *Sieckmann* criteria,[25] first adopted in the Proposal and now in the Regulation and Directive Proposed Texts, be elaborated in order to avoid the public being confronted with uncertainty.[26]

In addition a CTM cannot, or shall not as is stated in Article 7, be registered if it is, among other things, devoid of any distinctive character (b), if it consists exclusively of a shape which results from the nature of the goods themselves (e)(i), the shape of goods which is necessary to obtain a technical result (e)(ii) or the shape which gives substantial value to the goods (e)(iii). The Office considers these so-called absolute grounds *ex officio*, but it considers the relative grounds, such as risk of confusion with an earlier mark, upon opposition of the proprietor of the earlier mark only.[27] In quite a few Member States the local offices do also consider relative grounds of refusal *ex officio*.[28] The Commission proposed to abolish this practice by prohibiting it. In the Directive Compromise Text it has been reintroduced by allowing Member States to decide for themselves.[29]

2.2 Actual Use for Trademark Registration in China

Chinese trademark law had long been centred on trademark registration, and the protection of a mark was strictly based on registration. The underlying reason was that a trademark right is an exclusive right, and therefore it would be difficult to approve the acquisition of such a right solely based on use. Therefore the previous version of the Trademark Act strictly adhered to the first-to-file principle. A mark without registration even having been used in trade, hardly gained protection. This has resulted in several problems, such as pre-empting registration of a mark with no intention to use, known as trademark ambush. One well-known example is the 'iPad' trademark. When Apple introduced the iPad successfully, a Taiwanese company Proview Technology claimed that it owned the iPad trademark in China and its Shenzhen subsidiary filed a trademark

---

[25] *Ralf Sieckmann v. Deutsches Patent- und Markenamt (supra*, n 23).

[26] See e.g. the opinion of ECTA (Brussels, 21 June 2013) p. 3 with regard to the (similar) proposed text by the Commission <http://www.ecta.org/IMG/pdf/ecta_opinion_on_legislative_package_summary.pdf> accessed 11 June 2015.

[27] Art. 8 CTMR on relative grounds for refusal.

[28] Twelve countries, according to the Max Planck Study (*supra*, n 6) 18.

[29] See with regard to this recital 16 in the preamble to the Directive Compromise Text, where it is stated that this 'should be a matter for national procedural rules which should not be prejudiced by this Directive'.

infringement case against Apple in court. Finally Apple settled the lawsuit by agreeing to pay $60 million for the legal rights to use the iPad trademark in China.[30] To overcome such problems, the 2013 Amendment has given more weight to the actual use of a mark regarding protection of trademarks.

In practice, it was essential to take account of trademark use in the acquisition of a mark, maintenance of a trademark and enforcement of a trademark. However, the Trademark Act had not defined the meaning of trademark use until 2013. Article 48 of the 2013 Trademark Act incorporated the definition of 'use of trademarks' as: 'any activities using a trademark on goods, package or container of goods and transaction paperwork of goods, using trademark in advertising, exhibition, and other commercial activities, for identifying the origin of goods'. In the 2013 Trademark Act, the use of a mark plays a primary role in the acquisition of a trademark, maintenance of a trademark, and enforcement of a trademark. This represents a move from a focus on registration to the use of marks in trade. However, the 2013 Amendment fails to provide a clear answer as to what amounts to the use of a mark within the meaning of trademark law. In many complicated circumstances the courts have been forced to interpret the concept in many contexts.

The actual use of a mark plays a role in several circumstances in acquiring a trademark right. Article 4 of the Trademark Act provides that 'any natural person, legal person, and other organizations that need to acquire exclusive trademark rights for its product or service shall apply for registration of the mark with the Trademark Office'. It indicates that registration is the means to acquire a trademark right in China. However, this does not mean trademark use is meaningless in the process of acquiring trademark protection. In special circumstances, an unregistered mark can gain protection. Such protection does not result from the creativeness or novelty of the mark, but from the use of the mark to identify the origin of goods or services.

The 2013 Amendment tries to strike a balance between protection based on registration and the exception based on having gained reputation through use while restricting pre-emption of a mark through bad-faith registration. First, a mark that has been in prior use has an advantage in the process of application for registration of a trademark in a situation

---

[30]   Keith Bradsher, 'Apple Settles an iPad Trademark Dispute in China' *The New York Times* (Hong Kong, 2 July 2012) <http://www.nytimes.com/2012/07/02/business/global/apple-settles-an-ipad-trademark-dispute-in-china.html> accessed 8 June 2015.

where there are two or more identical or similar trademark applications for the identical or similar goods on the same day. According to Article 31 of the 2013 Trademark Act:

> where two or more applicants file application to register identical or similar trademarks for the same or similar goods, the Trademark Office shall first examine and approve for publication of the mark with the earliest application date. Where the applications are filed on the same date, the Trademark Office shall first examine and approve for publication the mark with the earliest date of use.

Secondly, a well-known mark has privilege even though it has not been registered. According to Article 13 of the Trademark Act, where a mark is a reproduction, imitation, or translation of another's well-known mark which has not been registered in China, and where the goods are identical or similar, which may cause public confusion and be detrimental to the interests of the well-known mark holder, no registration will be granted and the use of the mark is prohibited. In such a case, even though the goods are not identical or dissimilar, but are liable to mislead the public and be detrimental to the interests of the well-known mark holder, no registration is granted and the use of the mark is prohibited as well. If a mark becomes well known, it must have been in use for a while because it can only gain reputation through use. This special protection for an unregistered well-known mark results from the use of the mark.

Thirdly, the actual use of a mark may be used to exclude others from attaining registration of an identical or similar mark for identical or similar goods where the registration applicant has acted in bad faith. If actual use of a mark could be employed to exclude any others from attaining registration of a mark, then the first-to-file principle would be made meaningless; hence it must be combined with the applicant's bad faith to justify the function of trademark use. Article 15 prohibits registering a trademark that is identical or similar to an earlier used unregistered trademark for identical or similar goods on the condition that the applicant has a prior contractual relationship or business relationship with the prior trademark user and therefore knows of the existence of the trademark, and the prior user opposes the registration. Where the applicant takes advantage of its knowledge of another's unregistered trademark in a contractual relationship or business relationship, apparently the applicant behaves in bad faith when it files an application to take over the trademarks. In addition, Article 32 of the 2013 Trademark Act also prohibits registration of another's mark by an unjust means.

The 2013 Trademark Act sets an opposition procedure before a mark is officially registered. In the opposition procedure, a trademark user can file an opposition to exclude another from registering and using an identical or similar mark for one of the legitimate reasons mentioned above. If it fails to file opposition against an applicant in the period provided by law, it cannot exclude the registration anymore. Furthermore, according to Article 59 of the 2013 Trademark Act, if a prior user's mark has already gained a certain level of influence, the registered trademark holder has no right to prevent the prior user from using the mark. Nonetheless, the prior user's right is very limited; it cannot license the use of the mark and it may not sue others for infringement of its mark.

3. THE REQUIREMENT OF TRADEMARK USE IN MAINTAINING A TRADEMARK IN EUROPE AND CHINA

3.1 Actual Use to Maintain Protection in Europe

Where trademark rights are obtained through registration, as is the case with respect to the CTM, they cease either by a declaration of the relevant office, that is OHIM, or by a failure to renew the registration, which is in force for ten years from the date of filing the application.[31]

The CTM may also be cancelled, that is the protection lost, due to the mark being revoked or declared invalid. A CTM is liable to be revoked if it has not been put to genuine use in the Community, if the trademark has become generic or if the mark is misleading the public.[32]

These provisions have basically stood the test of time and little has been said about changing or altering them. There is one exception, however, and that is the concept of genuine use and its territorial extension or geographical scope.[33] Instead of leaving the issue to be decided case by case, it has been argued that the establishment of some legislative criteria in this respect would result in clarification and a greater degree of predictability.[34] It is worth noting, however, that the Max Planck Study proposes to leave Article 15 in the CTMR unchanged, while the test for territorial extent of use should be developed by the courts. According to the Study it should be clarified in the Preamble of the CTMR that political boundaries do not constitute valid criteria in

---

[31] CTMR, Art. 50 and Art. 46, respectively.
[32] CTMR, Art. 51(1)(a), Art. 51(1)(b), and Art 51(1)(c), respectively.
[33] Art. 15 CTMR.
[34] See e.g. the opinion of ECTA (*supra*, n 26) pp. 9–10.

determining genuine use. This does not mean, according to the Study, that the dimensions of the EU should be excluded by the courts when making the assessment.[35]

3.2 Trademark Use to Maintain Protection in China

Due to the fact that the 2001 Trademark Act adhered strictly to the first-to-file principle and registration was essential for attaining protection, this led to the extensive pre-emptive registration of another's business names as a trademark and another's marks that have been in use but not registered. The 2013 Trademark Act gives more weight to the use of a trademark in good faith and prevents registration of trademarks in bad faith.[36] Where a mark is registered but not in use, the mark cannot identify the origin of goods or services. However, due to the exclusivity of a registered trademark, no one else is allowed to use this mark for identical or similar goods. This may lead to a waste of resources. Accordingly, Article 49 of the Trademark Act provides for the revocation of a trademark that has not been in use continually for three years. It stipulates that, without legitimate justification, a trademark that has not been in use continually for three years can be revoked, and anyone is entitled to apply to the TMO for the registered trademark to be revoked. The continuous use of a trademark is necessary to maintain the validity of a trademark. However, the Trademark Act provides no detailed answer about what constitutes use within the meaning of Article 48. Many questions concerning the meaning of use are unsettled. For example, does the use of a mark on goods, other than those that the trademark has been registered against, amount to use within the meaning of Article 48? Does an illegal use of a mark amount to use within the meaning of the Trademark Act? The courts have provided an interpretation of the meaning of trademark in specific cases.

In *Tiansi v. Trademark Review and Adjudication Board and Wei Tingjian*, the Supreme People's Court (SPC) pointed out that where actual use and the intention to use a mark are present, the standard of proof for use could be low. However, in a case of maintaining the mark there may be a conflict with public and consumer interest and the standard, accordingly, could be high.[37] In *JianKang Diyi v. Trademark Review and Adjudication*

---

[35] The Max Planck Study (*supra*, n 6) 139.
[36] See Arts 7, 15 and 59 of the 2013 Trademark Act.
[37] 天丝医药保健有限公司与国家工商行政管理总局商标评审委员会第三人韦廷建第 800816 号"红牛及图"商标撤销复审行政纠纷案，中华人民共和国最高人民法院 (2011) 知行字第 28 号行政裁定书 (*Tiansi Pharmaceutical and Health Ltd.*

Board, the Beijing First Intermediate People's Court held that trademark licensing and use in publicity materials, in light of the circumstances, were sufficient in proving actual use. However, the Beijing High People's Court overturned the decision and held that trademark licensing is a transaction between the licensor and licensee, and therefore did not present the mark to consumers in a way representing the identification function of a trademark. Hence the Court concluded that the licensing or assigning of a mark was not use within the meaning of the Trademark Act. The Court also found that the publicity materials bearing the mark were designed for goods other than the class of goods the mark was registered for, therefore it did not amount to use of a mark within the meaning of the Trademark Act.[38]

In *Shantou Kangwang v. Trademark Review and Adjudication Board*, the Beijing First Intermediate People's Court held that the use of a mark should comply with law; and use within the meaning of the Trademark Act referred only to legitimate use. However, in 2010, the SPC made a decision which was in conflict with this interpretation. In *Castel Freres SAS v. Trademark Review and Adjudication Board and Li Daozhi*, the SPC pointed out that the purpose of Article 49 was to encourage trademark use and clear up idle trademarks.[39] The SPC also indicated that as long as a mark was publicly and actually used in commercial activities, and the activities as such did not violate trademark law, the mark holder had fulfilled its obligation of use, regardless of whether the activities had violated other laws.[40]

---

v. Trademark Review and Adjudication Board and Wei Tingjian, No 800816 'Red Bull and its graphic' case on trademark revocation review administrative dispute, SPC Administrative Ruling, 2011 Zhixingzi No. 28).

[38]   健康第一有限公司与中华人民共和国国家工商行政管理总局商标评审委员会商标行政纠纷案，北京市高级人民法院　(2006)　高行终字第　78　号行政判决书　(*JianKang Diyi Ltd. v. Trademark Review and Adjudication Board* on the matter of trademark administrative dispute, Beijing First Intermediate People's Court administrative decision, 2006 Gaoxingzhong No. 78).

[39]   最高人民法院 (2010) 知行字第55号行政裁定书 (SPC administrative ruling, 2010 Zhixingzi No. 55).

[40]   Ibid.

4. THE USE OF A MARK IN ENFORCEMENT OF TRADEMARKS

4.1 Trademark Use in the Scope of Protection in the EU

4.1.1 Scope of protection and trademark use

The registration of a trademark, under the CTMR, gives the proprietor a right to prevent unauthorized registration or use in the course of trade of: (i) an identical mark for identical goods or services (the so-called double identity cases), (ii) an identical or similar mark for identical or similar goods, if this entails the likelihood of confusion (including association), and (iii) an identical or similar mark for goods or services which are not similar to those for which the mark is protected, if the mark has a reputation and if the use made of it takes unfair advantage of, or is detrimental to, the reputation or the distinctive character of the mark. This is stated in Article 9(1) of the CTMR. This is also regulated by Article 5 of the Trademark Directive (TMD). The expression 'in the course of trade' also has certain territorial implications, and it is here where the so-called goods-in-transit issue enters the scene. Transit goods are not, in a strict sense, using the trademark in the course of trade, as the marks or signs are affixed before the goods are exported. The marks are not used in the course of trade either, as these products may not necessarily enter the market of the transit countries. This issue has clearly been one of the most topical subjects of debate throughout the reform process. The possibility of enforcing trademark rights effectively in relation to goods in transit is limited to counterfeit goods intended to enter the internal market at the moment.

Case law in the EU has been somewhat ambiguous. It seems as though the Court of Justice of the European Union (CJEU) at first supported the proposition that EU customs could stop counterfeit goods in transit, but in a second set of rulings concluded that goods in transit did not constitute an infringement of trademark rights.[41]

According to the decision in *Polo/Lauren Company v. PT Dwidua Langgeng Pratama Intl Freight Forwarders* and *Montres Rolex & Ors*,[42] it was stated that goods entering the EU territory are subject to customs

---

[41] See e.g. Barbara Diaz Alaminos and Max Oker-Blom, 'Stopping Fakes in their Tracks', Intellectual Property Magazine, May 2014, 34–53, on which this section is partly based.

[42] Case C-383/98 *The Polo/Lauren Company v. PT Dwidua Langgeng Pratama Intl Freight Forwarders* [2000] ECR I-2519 and Case C-60/02 *Criminal proceedings against X* [2004] ECR I-651.

control regardless of whether or not they are destined for a third country. In these two instances, EU customs detained consignments suspected of infringing IP rights which originated from and were destined for a non-EU Member State. The CJEU was asked whether, based on the Community Customs Code[43] and the Border Measures Regulation,[44] the goods in question could be prevented from continuing their transit to the market of destination. The answer in the *Polo/Lauren Company* case was that such goods can be stopped because these goods could be brought into the single market. In *Rolex*, the CJEU went a step further by stating that Member States should have legislation allowing them to stop counterfeit goods and, if this was not the case, the legislation of the relevant Member State would not be applied.

In both *Class Intl BV v. Colgate Palmolive Co* and *Montex Holding Ltd v. Diesel SpA*[45] the CJEU, on the other hand, concluded that transit, as such, does not constitute an infringement and that for a trademark owner to stop goods in transit, there has to be a risk that these goods may enter the internal market. The preliminary question referred to the Court concerned the interpretation of the CTMR and the TMD, in particular the rights conferred on the owner of a trademark to prevent the transit of suspected counterfeit goods through EU territory.

In order to solve this conflict related to the use in the course of trade, the so-called 'manufacturing fiction' doctrine was created. The determination as to whether or not goods infringe an IP right is thus to be made on the premise that the underlying goods are manufactured in the country through which the goods transit. This fiction was, however, overruled by the *Philips/Nokia* judgment.[46] In this judgment the previous rulings in *Class Intl* and *Montex* were confirmed. In other words, in order for customs to be able to stop the goods infringing IP rights, there has to be evidence that the goods are intended to enter the internal market. The CJEU lowered the standard of proof, however, by stating, among other things, that the burden of proof would be satisfied

---

[43]   Council Regulation No 528/2013 establishing the Community Customs Code (2013) OJ L 165/62.

[44]   Council Regulation No 608/2013 concerning customs enforcement of intellectual property rights and repealing Council Regulation No 1383/2003 (2013) OJ L 181/15.

[45]   Case C-405/03 *Class Intl BV v. Colgate Palmolive CO* [2005] ECR I-8735 and Case C-281/05 *Montex Holdings Ltd v. Diesel SpA* [2006] ECR I-10881.

[46]   Joined cases C-446/09 and C-495/09 *Koninklijke Philips Electronics NV v. Lucheng Meijing Industrial Company Ltd* and *Nokia Corporation v. Commission of Revenue and Customs* [2011] ECR I-12435.

if the destination of goods is undeclared, there is a lack of precise or reliable information as to the identity or address of the manufacturer or consignor of the goods or a lack of cooperation with customs authorities.

The EU Commission's Proposal was a response to the existing, somewhat uncertain, situation concerning the possibility of stopping infringing goods in transit right away, without proving that they might enter the internal market.[47] The Commission proposed a modification in recital 18 and Article 9(5) in the Proposed New Regulation. The same modification can be found in recital 22 and Article 10(5) of the Proposed New Directive. Accordingly, EU customs would be able to stop counterfeit goods in transit through the EU territory even if they were not destined for an EU country, allowing EU trademark owners to 'prevent third parties from bringing goods into the customs territory of the Union without being released for free circulation there'.[48]

This proposal was criticized, however, by those concerned about the validity of the regulation in relation to the Agreement on Trade Related Aspects of Intellectual Property Rights (TRIPS)[49] and the General Agreement on Tariffs and Trade (GATT). Both the TRIPS and GATT agreements are aimed at eliminating barriers to international trade.[50] This concern is also believed to be reflected in the *Phillips/Nokia* decision, according to which, as indicated above, only goods in transit intended for an EU country could be detained by EU customs. In the first reading by the European Parliament, which was concluded on 25 February 2014, this line of thought was thus combined with the Commission proposal by adding the text 'without prejudice to WTO rules, in particular Article V

---

[47] In the explanatory memorandum to the Proposal it is stated, among other things, that '[t]he implications of the Phillips/Nokia judgment have met with strong criticism from stakeholders as placing an inappropriately high burden of proof on right holders, and hindering the fight against counterfeiting'. The memorandum continues: 'It is therefore proposed to fill the existing gap by entitling right holders to prevent third parties from bringing goods, from third countries, bearing without authorization a trade mark which is essentially identical to the trade mark registered in respect of those goods, into the customs territory of the Union, regardless of whether they are released for free circulation' <http://eur-lex.europa.eu/legal-content/EN/TXT/?uri=CELEX:52013PC0161> accessed 8 June 2015.

[48] Recital 18 of the Proposed New Regulation and recital 22 of the Proposed New Directive.

[49] See Annette Kur and Thomas Dreier, *European Intellectual Property Law: Text, Cases and Materials* (Edward Elgar Publishing 2013) 24–31.

[50] See Diaz Alaminos and Oker-Blom (*supra*, n 41) 35, particularly footnote 14.

of the GATT on freedom of transit' and 'without prejudice to the smooth transit of generic medicines'.[51]

According to the Regulation Compromise Text the right to stop goods in transit without the existence of evidence that the goods might enter the internal market might lapse

> during the proceedings to determine whether the registered trade mark has been infringed, initiated in accordance with the provisions of the Regulation (EU) No 608/2013 concerning customs enforcement of intellectual property rights, evidence is provided by the declarant or the holder of the goods that the proprietor of the registered trade mark is not entitled to prohibit the placing of the goods on the market in the country of final destination.[52]

The reference to WTO rules and GATT has been restricted to the recitals.[53]

There is thus an effort to accommodate the concerns voiced in the EU Parliament with the Commission's aim of taking into account the proprietor's interest. The proposal for the new regulation and directive is no doubt a balancing act between a measure to stop illegitimate trade and promoting legitimate international trade[54] – clearly not an easy exercise.

4.1.2 Limitation and trademark use

Article 12 in the CTMR allows for certain actions to be taken by third parties in the course of trade, even if they concern use of a protected sign.

---

[51] European Parliament, *European Parliament legislative resolution of 25 February 2014 on the proposal for a directive of the European Parliament and of the Council to approximate the laws of the Member States relating to trade marks (recast) (COM(2013)0162 – C7-0088/2013 – 2013/0089(COD))* proposed amendments to recital 22 and article 10(5) <http://www.europarl.europa.eu/sides/getDoc.do?pubRef=-//EP//TEXT+TA+P7-TA-2014-0119+0+DOC+XML+V0//EN> accessed 11 June 2015; Id., *European Parliament legislative resolution of 25 February 2014 on the proposal for a regulation of the European Parliament and of the Council amending Council Regulation (EC) No 207/2009 on the Community trade mark (COM(2013)0161 – C7-0087/2013 – 2013/0088(COD))* proposed amendments to recital 18 and article 9(5) < http://www.europarl.europa.eu/sides/getDoc.do?pubRef=-//EP//TEXT+TA+P7-TA-2014-0118+0+DOC+XML+V0//EN&language=EN> accessed 11 June 2015. See also recital 19(a) in the Regulation Compromise Text and recital 22 in the Directive Compromise Text.

[52] Art. 9(5) of the Regulation Compromise Text. See also Art. 10(5) of the Directive Compromise Text.

[53] See recital 19(a) and 22 in the Regulation Compromise Text and the Directive Compromise Text, respectively.

[54] See the Max Planck Study (*supra*, n 6) 112, where the need for such a balance is explicated.

The limitations concern use of one's name or address, of signs or indications in a descriptive meaning and of a sign where it is necessary to indicate the purpose, provided that this is done in accordance with *bona fide* practices of industrial and commercial affairs.[55]

When the TMD was enacted the Commission and the Council issued a Joint Statement declaring that names meant only names of natural persons. In a decision made by the CJEU[56] regarding the question whether a trade name conflicting with a prior trademark could nevertheless be used in commerce, the Court declared that such a statement, meaning the one issued by the Commission and Council, is not legally binding and that the wording of Article 6(1)(a) in the TMD does not reflect any restriction in the meaning of 'name'.[57]

In the Proposal, the so-called own-name defence for companies is abolished and it is emphasized that it concerns one's own personal name only. The Proposal provides for the concept of a 'natural person'.[58] According to the Proposal, this puts trade names and trademarks on an equal footing.

4.2 Trademark Use in Enforcement in China

4.2.1 Scope of protection

The interpretation of use of a mark in the context of enforcement of trademarks could be different from that in maintaining a trademark. In a trademark maintenance case, the questions focus on what types of use fall within the scope of use within the meaning of trademark law. In contrast, an infringement case focuses on what kinds of use fall outside the scope of use within the meaning of trademark law. According to Article 57 of the Trademark Act, two categories of trademark use fall into the scope of infringement of a trademark: first, using a trademark that is identical with a registered trademark for identical goods without the authorization of a trademark holder; and second, using a trademark that is similar to a registered trademark for identical goods, or that is identical with or similar to a registered trademark for identical or similar goods, without the authorization of a trademark holder, which may cause likelihood of confusion.

Article 48 of the 2013 Trademark Act defines the meaning of use of a mark but not all trademark use that falls within the scope of Article 48 constitutes infringement of a trademark. The Trademark Act also defines

---

[55]   See Art. 6(1) in the TMD.
[56]   Case C-245/02 *Anheuser-Bush v. Budejovicky Budvar* [2004] ECR I-10989.
[57]   See Kur and Dreier (*supra*, n 49) 220.
[58]   Art. 12(1)(a) in the Proposed New Regulation, see also Art. 12(1)(a) of the Regulation Compromise Text.

several situations where use of a mark is exempted from infringement and involves three situations. First, where a registered mark covers the general name, figure, model of the goods, or indicates the quality, main ingredients, function, purpose, weight, amount or other characteristics of the goods, the mark holder has no right to prevent others from using the mark. Second, where a three-dimensional mark covers the shape resulting from the nature of the goods, or which is indispensable to obtain a technical effect or to give the goods substantive value, the mark holder has no right to prevent others from using the mark. Third, before filing the application for registration of a mark, if another party has already used an identical or similar mark for identical or similar goods prior to the use by the applicant and has already gained a certain level of influence, the registered trademark holder has no right to prevent the prior user from using the mark for the original extent of the prior user's activities.

In terms of use of a trademark in the course of trade, the widespread use of the Internet has raised many questions and controversies. Use of a trademark in an online environment is a new challenge for the interpretation of the meaning of use of a mark. In *Puma v. taobao.com*, taobao.com was an e-commerce company, providing consumer-to-consumer and business-to-consumer sales services via the Internet.[59] The plaintiff, right owner of the mark 'Puma', sued taobao.com and an individual who ran an online store on taobao.com selling fake 'Puma' shoes. The Guangzhou Intermediate People's Court held that an online platform could avoid liability only if it had examined its users' identification before permitting their operation on the platform. However, the online platform's activities would lead to a finding of contributory liability where the online platform knew of the infringement, and failed to remove the infringing information or item.[60]

With respect to search engine keywords and trademark infringement, this issue was addressed in *Dazhong Banchang v. Baidu.com*. In this case the defendant, Baidu.com, was a leading search engine operator in the Chinese market.[61] The plaintiffs found that when they typed their

---

59   鲁道夫·达斯勒体育用品波马股份公司与浙江淘宝网络有限公司、陈仰蓉销售假冒注册商标的商品纠纷案，广东省广州市中级人民法院(2006)穗中法民三初字第179号 民事判决书 (*Puma Aktiengesellschaft Rudolf Dassler Sport v. Zhejiang Taobao Network Ltd., Chen Yangrong* on the dispute of sale of good counterfeiting registered trademark, Guangzhou Intermediate People's Court civil decision, 2006 Suizhongfa Minsanchu No. 179).

60   Ibid.

61   大众交通（集团）股份有限公司、上海大众搬场物流有限公司诉北京百度网讯科技有限公司、百度在线网络技术（北京）有限公司、百度在线网络技

trademark 'Dazhong Banchang' into baidu.com, the queried results that were top ranked linked to websites containing counterfeited goods and information relating to the plaintiff. The advertisers had paid baidu. com for the keywords in question. The plaintiff alleged the search engine infringed its trademark. The Shanghai Second Intermediate People's Court found that the advertisers that paid baidu.com for buying the keywords had used the plaintiff's trademark without authorization on their own websites. The advertisers' websites advertised identical or similar services to the plaintiff's, therefore these websites had infringed the plaintiff's trademark. The Court also held that the search engine had an obligation to scrutinize the keywords and its clients' qualifications to use such keywords. Accordingly, the search engine had not fulfilled its scrutiny obligation in its keywords bid ranking service, and the search engine's actions constituted a contributory infringement of a trademark.[62]

The conflict between trademarks and domain names is obvious because a registered trademark may be used as a domain name by another. The Chinese SPC issued a judicial interpretation in 2002. This interpretation stated that where a trademark is registered by another as a domain name and used to conduct e-commerce for the relevant goods that is likely to cause confusion, then this would constitute a trademark infringement.[63] In *Lingzhi v. Cui Huansuo, Du Xinghua*, the plaintiffs had possessed the 'Jack & Jones' trademark in China since 2006. One of the defendants registered the domain name 'www.jackjonescn.net' in 2007.[64] The two defendants used the domain name to operate a website. The advertisement and the products sold on the website used logos that were identical or similar to the plaintiff's trademark without authorization. The Court found that the defendants had infringed the plaintiff's trademark.

术（北京）有限公司上海软件技术分公司侵犯商标专用权与不正当竞争纠纷一案，上海市第二中级人民法院(2007)沪二中民五(知)初字第147号民事判决书 (*Dazhong Transportation Ltd., Shanghai Dazhong Banchang Logistic Ltd. v. Beijing Baidu Wangxun Technology Ltd., Baidu Online Network Technology Ltd (Beijing), Shanghai Software Technology Branch of Baidu Online Network Technology Ltd (Beijing)* on infringement of trademark right and unfair competition, Shanghai Second People's Intermediate Court civil decision, 2007 Huerzhong Minwu (zhi) Chuzi No. 147).

[62]   Ibid.

[63]   《最高人民法院关于审理商标民事纠纷案件适用法律若干问题的解释》第一条，法释[2002]32号，2002年10月12日 (Article 1 of SPC's Interpretations on the Application of law in the trial of Trademark Civil Disputes, Fashi [2002] No. 32, 12 October 2002).

[64]   北京市海淀区人民法院（2010）海民初字第1438号民事判决书   (Haidian District People's Court in Beijing civil decision, 2010 Haiminchuzi No. 1438).

In China, there are also cross-border issues regarding trademark infringement. An OEM (Original Equipment Manufacturer) model in China is very successful and popular. Under this model, a foreign trademark holder may authorize a manufacturer located in China to assemble a product by employing low-cost labour in China and then export all those products into third countries rather than selling them in the Chinese market. If the trademark borne on the assembled products is registered by another in China for the identical or similar products, this raises a question whether the Chinese trademark holder is entitled to have the goods seized. In *UGG*, the defendant exported boots bearing the mark 'UGG Grand Australia', which were seized by the customs authorities. The plaintiff, who owned the trademark 'UGG' registered in China, claimed the defendant had infringed its 'UGG' trademark. The defendant argued that its use of 'UGG' on the boots did not amount to use of the mark within the meaning of trademark law because the goods were not for the Chinese market and would not go into circulation in the Chinese market. Accordingly, there would be no confusion and mistake regarding the relevant consumers. The Qingdao Intermediate People's Court held that the defendant had used the mark, which was identical to the plaintiff's, on identical goods without authorization, therefore it constituted infringement of the plaintiff's trademark.[65] The defendant appealed to the Shandong Provincial High People's Court and the Court rejected the appeal and upheld the decision in October 2011. However, the SPC made a contradictory decision in another case. In 2012 the SPC ruled that where one party authorized a manufacturer in a Chinese territory to manufacture a product only for exportation, and the advertising and reporting of the products took place abroad, it did not constitute use of the mark in China.[66]

4.2.2   Limitations

In addition to the limitations to trademark exclusivity stipulated in the Trademark Act, courts have also developed some principles defining the boundary of use in infringement cases. Several decisions have indicated

---

[65]   叶身铭,"'UGG 案'引发的商标使用与侵权的思考," 中华商标, no. 11 (2013): 83–85 (Ye Shenming, 'The Reflection on the use of a trademark in the "UGG" case' (2013) 11 Chinese Trademark 83–85.

[66]   株式会社良品计画与国家工商行政管理总局商标评审委员会、京棉田纺织品有限公司商标异议复审行政纠纷案，最高人民法院（2012）行提字第2号行政判决书 (*Kabushiki-gaisha Ryōhin Keikaku v. the Trademark Review and Adjudication Board, Jingmian Textile Ltd.* on trademark objection review administrative dispute, the SPC administrative decision, 2012 Xingtizi No. 2).

that the use of a mark should represent the function of a mark by indicating the origin of the goods or service; otherwise it does not amount to use within the meaning of the Trademark Act. In *Owen*, the plaintiff owned the 'Owen' mark for clothes and the defendant manufactured shirts, the front of which bore the trademark 'UMBRO' and the back of which bore the mark 'Owen 10'. The advertisement for the shirts used the image of the English football player Michael Owen wearing the number 10 shirt. The plaintiff claimed the defendant had infringed its trademark. The Court confirmed that the defendant had used the mark of the plaintiff in the course of trade but the Court also pointed out that it was general practice in the sport industry to use an athlete's image or name and his shirt number on sport shirts; consumers certainly would connect 'Owen' with the famous English football player Owen in this case. The function of the Owen mark in the shirts here was to use Owen's image for advertising, rather than indicating the origin of the goods. The trademark in the shirt for indication of its origin was the mark 'UMBRO'. Therefore the Court found no infringement.[67] In *Pfizer v. Jiangsu Lianhuan, Jiankang Xingainian, Guangzhou Weierman*, Pfizer owned the three-dimensional, blue, diamond-shaped mark in China. The SPC held that because the diamond-shaped, blue-colour tablet appeared on a non-transparent package, the colour and the shape of the tablet could not function as indicating the origin and producer of the goods, therefore it did not amount to the use of a mark within the meaning of the Trademark Act.[68]

Some trademark uses may constitute infringement but are exempted from damages. The Trademark Act provides for an exemption from damages as a defence in civil proceedings. An alleged infringer may raise a counterplea in a civil proceeding that the trademark owner has never used the trademark in question. If the trademark owner fails to provide evidence proving actual use within three years and any loss resulting from the infringement, the alleged infringer is not liable for any damages. The underlying reason is that where a mark is not in actual use, it does not function as identifying the origin of goods or services; as a consequence the infringing mark does not cause any likelihood of confusion among consumers. Furthermore, an unused mark does not bear reputation, and an infringer cannot be said to benefit from the trademark holder's

---

[67] 安徽省合肥市中级人民法院（2002）合民三初字第 94 号民事判决书 (Hefei Municipal Intermediate People's Court civil decision 2002 Heminsanchuzi No. 94). In this case, the plaintiff appealed, but in the second instance, the parties settled the dispute, and the defendant paid a small amount to the plaintiff.

[68] 最高人民法院 (2009) 民申字第 268 号民事判决书 (The SPC civil decision, 2009 Minshenzi No. 268).

reputation. Accordingly, an infringement does not cause injury to the trademark holder either. This provision originated from the *Honghe* decision of the SPC in 2009. At first instance, the Court found that the defendants had infringed the plaintiff's trademark and granted an injunction and damages of Rmb 10,000,000 yuan. The second-instance Court upheld the decision. In 2009, the SPC heard the case and confirmed the infringement but pointed out that although the defendants had infringed the trademark and should incur liability, it should take into account the fact that the trademark had not been in actual use. The damages were reduced to Rmb20,000 yuan.[69] The principle established in this decision was incorporated into the 2013 Amendment.

5.   CONCLUSION

Trademark reforms in the EU and China seem to share some common points of convergence despite differences in the purposes and contexts for reform. The Chinese Amendment was driven by the need to localize the trademark system, while the EU reform initiative stems from the need to update and modernize the EU trademark system, which has been in place for some time.

Streamlining procedures to apply for and register a trademark is one of the purposes of trademark law reform both in the EU and China. Substantively, there seem to be some common points as well. The European Commission's proposal suggested that the graphical representation should be abolished. It will give the green light to many non-traditional marks, such as sound marks. The Chinese 2013 Amendment added sound into the list of signs that can be registered as a trademark. Regarding trademark uses, the prevention of abuse from registration-based protection seems to be highlighted in the trademark law reforms as well. For example, bad-faith registration, either as a ground for opposition (relative ground for refusal) or revocation, is found in the EU trademark reform proposal, as well as in the 2013 Amendment in China.

One significant diverging point seems to be on the trademark uses as seen in the enforcement against transit goods. According to the decision of *Philips/Nokia*, non-Community goods in transit through the EU territory do not constitute infringement of intellectual property applicable in the EU, if there is no evidence that those goods will actually be placed on the

---

[69]   中华人民共和国最高人民法院(2008)民提字第52号民事判决书 (The SPC civil decision 2008 Mintizi No. 52).

EU market.[70] This decision raised controversial concern in the EU because stakeholders consider this may place an inappropriately high burden of proof on right holders to enjoin infringement. The proposal aims at diminishing these concerns and suggests that a trademark holder should be entitled to prevent third parties from bringing infringement goods from third countries into the customs territory of the EU regardless of whether they are put on the EU market.[71]

Regarding transit goods, in 2012 the SPC ruled that where a manufacturer in a Chinese territory is authorized to produce a product only for exportation, and the promotion of the products takes place abroad, it does not constitute use of the mark in China.[72] The SPC's approach is quite opposite to the European proposal but the 2013 Amendment has not clarified this issue.

The scope and meaning of use of a mark is becoming essential in Chinese trademark law, as has been reflected in the 2013 Amendment. However the 2013 Trademark Act provides only a very basic description of use of a mark and the courts have to interpret the use of a mark in a context based on their own discretion. As a result, there could be diverging interpretations on the use of a mark in different courts. This could lead to disparity and uncertainty in applying trademark law. Although the SPC has made several decisions on this issue, precedents in China are not legally binding and it is necessary for the competent authority to elaborate on Article 48 of the Trademark Act.

The Chinese trademark law reform is driven by the need to localize trademark law in accordance with local conditions. In contrast, the overall aim and direction of EU trademark reform, as the EU Commission stated in the Communication of May 2011, strives to simplify, streamline and modernize the system. This is reflected in its suggestion to rename OHIM, to handle the surplus, to decide itself, through delegated acts, on the size of fees, to abolish the requirement on graphical representation, to abolish *ex officio* examination of relative grounds in the Member States, and so on. It is believed that the Commission wants to make OHIM an agency among the other EU agencies, focusing on its main tasks, registering trademarks and designs, and to use the CTM procedures as a benchmark for the national systems. This would, the Commission believes, best serve the integration of the internal market and thus the EU economy. This is of course no surprise, taking into account the task of the Commission, that is to be

---

[70] See *supra*, n 46 and accompanying text.
[71] See *supra*, n 52.
[72] See *supra*, n 66 and accompanying text.

the 'guardian' of the internal market. The subsequent proposals, described above, by the Parliament and particularly the Council show, however, that the EU is not only the 'playing ground' for the Commission, but that it is a construction characterized by internal tensions between the Commission on the one hand, and the Council, that is Member States, on the other. Although having obtained extended powers, the Parliament is to be found somewhere in the middle, leaning on the expertise of the Commission and pressure from the Member States.

The comparison above shows that the efficiency and effectiveness of registration and fighting infringement are the key elements in the EU and Chinese trademark reform. It is necessary for both the EU and China to communicate sufficiently the relevant trademark issues, therefore effectively dealing with some common challenges and avoiding absurd bifurcation on trademark protection, which may result in obstacles to trade.

It has to be kept in mind that although there are increasing similarities between EU trademark law and Chinese trademark law, because of the different social environments, the operational norms in terms of trademarks can be very different. Therefore it is natural that protection and enforcement in China and the EU could diverge in the same or similar cases due to the difference between formal trademark rules and operational trademark norms.[73]

---

[73] See Bruun and Zhang (*supra*, n 1).

9. The glocalization of patent linkage in China

Benjamin Pi-Wei Liu*

1. INTRODUCTION

Patent linkage is a system of administrative intellectual property (IP) protection that links the marketing approval of generic drugs to the status of patents covering the underlying technology. It was invented in the United States within an updated pharmaceutical regulatory regime that attempts to balance the competing demands of R&D cost, business motives and medical welfare under the Drug Price Competition and Patent Restoration Act, also known as the Hatch-Waxman Act.[1] Now at its 30th anniversary, the Hatch-Waxman Act is 'by any measure and by every measure . . . one of our nation's most effective laws', according to the President of the Generic Pharmaceutical Association.[2]

---

* Editor's note. Benjamin Pi-Wei Liu was an assistant professor of intellectual property law at John Marshall Law School and was an important member of the extended research group of the research project TRANSIP. The editors as well as the project members are extremely grateful for his wonderful contribution to the research project. The manuscript was received on 26 November 2014. He passed away on 1 December 2014, after a sudden illness. We will miss him dearly.

[1] Drug Price Competition and Patent Term Restoration Act of 1984, Pub. L. No. 98-417, 98 Stat. 1585 (1984) (codified as amended at 21 U.S.C. §355 (2000 & Supp. III 2005)). Analysis of the Hatch-Waxman Act is legion. See generally Jeremy Bulow, 'The Gaming of Pharmaceutical Patents' (2004) 4 Innovation Pol'y & the Econ. 145, 147–51, available at <http://www.nber.org/chapters/c10802. pdf>; Rebecca S. Eisenberg, 'Patents, Product Exclusivity, and Information Dissemination: How Law Directs Biopharmaceutical Research and Development' (2003) 72 Fordham L. Rev. 477, 482–86; Gerald J. Mossinghoff, 'Overview of the Hatch-Waxman Act and Its Impact on the Drug Development Process' (1999) 54 Food & Drug L.J. 187, 189–92.

[2] *Examining Concerns Regarding FDA's Proposed Changes to Generic Drug Labeling*: Testimony before the House Energy and Commerce Comm. on Health Subcomm., 2 (3 March 2014) (statement of Ralph G. Neas), available at

The transplant of regulatory patent linkage presents a more controversial story. Patent linkage is not required to meet the international IP standards under the Agreement on Trade-Related Aspects of Intellectual Property Rights (TRIPS) and it is among the TRIPs-plus provisions that the US trade negotiators are working hard to transplant. Europe has steadfastly resisted patent linkage.[3] Likewise, developing countries such as India have rejected a bid to transplant patent linkage out of Indian concerns for medical access and its own generics pharmaceutical industry.[4] Nevertheless, the United States Trade Representatives (USTR) convinced many of its trading partners to adopt the patent linkage requirement through the carrot of free trade agreements and the stick of Special 301 retaliations.[5]

This chapter examines how China has dealt with patent linkage. Contrary to conventional wisdom, China in fact adopted an ambitious set of patent linkage regulations as early as 2002 and became the first country outside North America to do so. As written, Chinese linkage regulation conformed to the standard of patent linkage that US trade negotiators were then promoting in Chile and Australia and it was even more protective of the patentee than the US domestic patent linkage under the Hatch-Waxman Act. But the laws failed because its administrative apparatus was not up to the task of implementing the maximalist protection.

What happened in China ostensibly supports the view of a system theorist like Teubner who views the role of legal irritants to 'not automatically displace pre-existing legal meanings and practices but instead trigger a new set of unpredictable choices and outcomes'.[6] In this way system theory challenges the entire IP transplant project and the 'instrumental

---

<http://www.gphaonline.org/media/cms/RGN_Labeling_Testimony_HouseEC Health_3.3.14FINAL.pdf>.

[3] European Commission, *Pharmaceutical Sector Inquiry Report*, <http://ec.europa.eu/competition/sectors/pharmaceuticals/inquiry/communication_en. pdf> 23: 'The Commission will continue to strictly enforce the applicable Community law and, for instance, act against patent linkage, as according to Community legislation, marketing authorisation bodies cannot take the patent status of the originator medicine into account when deciding on marketing authorisations of generic medicines.'

[4] Cynthia Ho, *Access to Medicine in the Global Economy: International Agreements on Patents and Related Rights* (OUP 2011) 120: 'Indian courts have yet to hold that regulatory authorities must recognize patent linkage.'

[5] *See* Mohammed K El Saibid, *A Policy Guide for Negotiators and Implementers in the WHO Eastern Mediterranean Region* (World Health Organization 2010) 94.

[6] John Gillespie, 'Toward a Discursive Analysis of Legal Transfers into Developing East Asia' (2008) 40 International Law and Politics 657, 665.

notion that legal transfer can simply create new legal rules that will induce predetermined behavior among recipients'.[7] However, there is no denying that the transplantation of patent law to China is itself 'successful' by some measure – it now processes more patents than any country in the world. The contrast between the maturation of an imported patent system and the failure of regulatory patent linkage presents the theoretical question of when a transplanted legal regime is viable.[8]

Section 2 of this chapter summarizes the patent linkage scheme in three settings: its original US context in the Hatch-Waxman Act, its spread through bilateral free trade agreements and its implementation in China. Section 3 addresses implementation problems in China due to unbalanced transplant, agency constraints and aggressive enforcement. The reality is that even when the United States successfully persuades developing countries to adopt patent linkage, their frail administrative institutions may fail to deliver maximalist protection. Section 4 highlights the lesson Chinese patent linkage presents for the larger legal transplant project. If the promoters of IP protection truly desire to improve the IP rights in a middle-income country such as China, there is no greater champion for the cause than a programme of protection that is actually operational and beneficial to the host country.

2. REGULATORY PATENT LINKAGE: ORIGIN AND TRANSPLANTS

Patent linkage – the practice of conditioning the marketing approval of a drug when it infringes the patent of another – was created in the US and later spread through US-led bilateral and multilateral free trade agreements (FTA). Interestingly, China adopted patent linkage outside any FTA obligations and presumably absorbed patent linkage through mimesis.[9] This section describes the regulatory patent linkage under the

---

[7] John Gillespie, 'Developing a Decentred Analysis of Legal Transfers' in Penelope (Pip) Nicholson and Sarah Biddulph (eds), *Examining Practice, Interrogating Theory: Comparative Legal Studies in Asia* (Martinus Nijhoff Publishers 2008) 39.

[8] Otto Kahn-Freund, 'On the Use and Misuses of Comparative Law' (1974) 37 Mod. L. Rev. 1.

[9] Xavier Seuba, 'International Regulation of Pharmaceuticals: Codification by Means of Legal Transplantation' (ICTSD Programme on Innovation, Technology and Intellectual Property, July 2014) <http://www.ictsd.org/sites/default/files/research/International%20Regulation%20of%20Pharmaceuticals%20Codification%20by%20Means%20of%20Legal%20Transplantation_0.pdf>.

Hatch-Waxman Act in the US, its international spread through FTAs, and its operation in China.

2.1   Regulatory Patent Linkage under the Hatch-Waxman Act

Patent linkage emerged as part of the Hatch-Waxman Act, comprehensive legislation that balances the interests of generic drug makers against those of brand drug companies.[10] At the time, generic versions of patented drugs were often not available even after the patent expired because the cost of generating the required clinical data overshadowed the potential profit.[11] Under the Hatch-Waxman Act '[g]eneric drug companies are not required to conduct their own independent clinical trials to prove safety and efficacy, but can instead rely on the research of the pioneer pharmaceutical companies'.[12] In exchange, research companies received stronger IP protection including patent linkage.

To begin the process, 'a pioneering or brand name drug company seeking to manufacture a new drug must prepare, file, and have approved' a new drug application (NDA). During and after the NDA approval process, the brand name drug company can submit a list to the administrators (FDA) identifying its own patents claiming any composition that is a part of the approved drug and any approved use of the drug. This self-identified drug-patent association (feature 1) reasonably places the burden of identifying patents on the patent owners and their licensees who are the

---

[10]   See generally Rebecca S. Eisenberg, 'The Role of the FDA in Innovation Policy' (2007) 13 Mich. Telecomm. Tech. L. Rev. 345, 352, 356–58 (discussing the Hatch-Waxman Act); FTC, *Generic Drug Entry Prior to Patent Expiration: An FTC Study* (FTC, July 2002) 3–8 <http://www.ftc.gov/os/2002/07/genericdrugstudy. pdf> (reviewing the Hatch-Waxman Act and the FDA implementing regulations); *Abbott Labs. v. Young*, 920 F.2d 984, 991 (D.C. Cir. 1990) (Edwards, J., dissenting on other grounds): '[The Hatch-Waxman Act] emerged from Congress' efforts to balance two conflicting policy objectives: to induce name-brand pharmaceutical firms to make the investments necessary to research and develop new drug products, while simultaneously enabling competitors to bring cheaper, generic copies of those drugs to market.'
[11]   H. Rep. No. 98-857 (Part II), at 27–31 (1984), reprinted in 1984 U.S.C.C.A.N. 2686, 2711–13.
[12]   *Janssen Pharmaceutica, N.V. v. Apotex, Inc.*, 540 F.3d 1353 (Fed. Cir. 2008); 21 U.S.C. §355(j)(2)(A)(iv) (2000); Christopher M. Holman, 'Do Reverse Payment Settlements Violates the Antitrust Laws?' (2007) 23 Santa Clara Computer & High Tech. L.J. 489, 510: 'The ANDA route to pre-marketing approval essentially allows a generic company to free ride on much of the costs incurred by the branded drug company in obtaining approval of the original NDA.'

lowest-cost information providers.[13] Once the drug is approved, the FDA will publish information about the drug in the 'Orange Book': *Approved Drug Products with Therapeutic Equivalence Evaluations*, including the drug-patent association the patentees provided (feature 2).[14]

Before developing a generic drug, companies can examine the Orange Book to ascertain patents covering the drug product and its uses. The generics company can also examine the product packaging for patent number markings pursuant to 35 U.S.C. §287(a) or directly ask the brand company to disclose any patented manufacturing process pursuant to 35 U.S.C. §287(b). While Section 287(a) and (b) are general rules under patent law and not enacted under the Hatch-Waxman Act, it is an important tool to inform generics manufacturers of their patent risk (feature 3). In the meantime, a research safe harbour under 35 U.S.C. §271(e)(1) exempts potentially infringing conduct as long as it is 'reasonably related to the development and submission of information under a Federal law which regulates the manufacture, use or sale of drugs' (feature 4).[15]

A generics company will submit an abbreviated new drug application (ANDA) once its product is ready for approval. With respect to the patents contained in the Orange Book, ANDA applicants must assert one of four certifications to put the FDA on notice (feature 5) that:

- approval is possible because the drug has no associated patents in the Orange Book (Paragraph I Certification);
- approval is possible because the listed patent already expired (Paragraph II Certification);
- approval is possible at the expiration of the listed patent (Paragraph III Certification); or
- approval is possible because the listed patent is invalid, not infringed, or unenforceable (Paragraph IV Certification).[16]

In the special situation that the listed patents are directed to one approved use, but the ANDA applicants seek approval for a different medical use (as drugs are often approved for multiple indications), the applicant can avoid patent linkage by filing a 'Section VIII statement' that explicitly carves out the non-infringing use (feature 6).

A Paragraph IV Certification sets into motion cascading events. The

---

13   21 U.S.C. §355(b)(1)(G).
14   21 U.S.C. §355(b)(1)(G); 21 C.F.R. §314.3 (2014).
15   35 U.S.C. §271(e)(1).
16   21 U.S.C. §355(j)(2)(A)(vii)(I–IV).

ANDA applicant must immediately notify the brand name registrant of the factual and legal basis of the Paragraph IV Certification (feature 7).[17] Following that, the FDA will hold the ANDA application for 45 days (feature 8). Meanwhile, the brand name company decides whether to file a regular patent infringement law suit (feature 9). If an infringement law suit is not filed within this 45-day window, the FDA will grant market registration at the end of its health and safety approval, at which point the generic drug company may start sales and marketing immediately. If the brand drug company disagrees with the Paragraph IV Certification and chooses to file a patent infringement lawsuit, the FDA will stay the approval process pending the outcome of the patent lawsuit or for up to 30 months if the lawsuit is still ongoing (feature 10).

The Hatch-Waxman Act provides a reward to encourage patent challenges and the earlier availability of generic medicine. If an ANDA applicant prevailed in the Paragraph IV lawsuit or if the patentee failed to initiate the lawsuit within the 45-day window, the generic registrant will receive a 180-day exclusivity during which no other generics companies can launch the same product. The 180 days are measured from the time that the registrant is ready to market the drug such that the winner can enjoy the full benefit of the 180-day exclusive pricing period (feature 11).

To summarize, the US patent linkage regime comprises an array of coordinated features including: (1) drug-patent association; (2) public patent listing; (3) a process disclosure safe harbour; (4) a Bolar research exemption; (5) a non-infringing certification; (6) a carve-out exception for non-infringing medical indication; (7) a notice of generics application; (8) a 45-day holding period; (9) a patent infringement suit; (10) a 30-month marketing delay; and (11) a 180-day generics exclusivity period. To be sure, the division of the linkage regime into 11 features can be arbitrary. Each feature may be further subdivided and other subtle aspects of patent linkage may warrant discussion. Nonetheless, these 11 features provide a sufficiently fine-grained roadmap to navigate the evolution of patent linkage outside US borders, which is the subject of the next section.

2.2   Transplanting Regulatory Patent Linkage through the FTAs

USTR efforts to promote patent linkage overseas appeared in Special 301 reports and diplomatic cables at the turn of the Millennium. Subsequently patent linkage became a regular feature of US bilateral and multilateral

---

[17]   21 U.S.C. §355(j)(2)(B).

agreements beginning with the US Australia FTA (AUSFTA) in 2005.[18] This section traces its international adoption through bilateral free trade agreements and summarizes its shortcomings.

Past patent linkage clauses mandate two obligations that are variations of the original linkage provision in Article 17.10.4 of the AUSFTA.[19] First, when a generic drug applicant seeks government approval to market a drug and intends to rely on data developed by the patent owner, AUSFTA requires the government to 'provide for the patent owner to be notified of such request and the identity of [requestor]'.[20] The notice requirement parallels the Hatch-Waxman Act with two caveats. First, notwithstanding the ambiguous treaty text, the generics applicants carry out the actual notice in the US and Australia. In other words, the government does not need to provide the actual notice itself as long as the market approval process directs generics companies to notify the brand company. This distinction reduces the public burden of administering a linkage system. The second obligation requires the actual patent linkage – that is 'measures in its marketing approval process to prevent . . . marketing a product' – claimed in a patent unless by consent or acquiescence of the patent owner.[21] Moreover, these provisions do not explain how drug administrators determine when the product is indeed claimed in a patent. It appears to turn drug regulators into 'patent police' – a task they are ill-equipped to perform. The US FDA has repeatedly emphasized its own role in the linkage system as 'ministerial'.[22] Its public statement expressed concerns that it lacks authority, resources, and the capability to address patent issues.[23] All substantive

---

[18]   Sean M. Flynn, Margot Kaminski, Brook K. Baker and Jimmy Koo, 'Public Interest Analysis of the US TPP Proposal for an IP Chapter' (2012) 28 Am. U. Int'l L. Rev. 105, 177: 'Although patent/registration linkage is not mentioned in TRIPS and is not required in many countries, including most TPP negotiating countries, it has become a common and contested feature of U.S. free trade agreements.'

[19]   Australia–United States Free Trade Agreement art. 17.10.4 (effective 1 January 2005) [hereinafter AUSFTA]; see generally Kevin Outterson, 'Pharmaceutical Arbitrage: Balancing Access and Innovation in International Prescription Drug Markets' (2005) 5 Yale J. Health Pol'y L. & Ethics 193, 237–38: 'The recent Free Trade Agreement with Australia requires linkage between drug approval and patent status for the first time, exporting a portion of Hatch-Waxman to Australia.'

[20]   See AUSFTA (*supra*, n 19), art. 17.10.4(b).

[21]   Ibid., art. 17.10.4(a).

[22]   Applications for FDA Approval to Market a New Drug, 68 Fed. Reg. 36676 (Jun. 18, 2003), available at <http://www.gpo.gov/fdsys/pkg/FR-2003-06-18/pdf/03-15065.pdf> (repeatedly emphasizing that the FDA's role is merely ministerial and not related to substantive patent determination).

[23]   Ibid.

infringement issues are left to the courts, thereby eliminating the danger of conflicting infringement analysis.

Entire books have been written to criticize the effect of these and other TRIPs-plus provisions on access to medicine and the local generics industry in developing countries.[24] Xavier Seuba catalogued the criticisms against transplanting patent linkage.[25] First, patent linkage is complex and prone to abuse even for the expert regulators in the US. The US Congress has amended its patent linkage system, the Supreme Court continues to address disputes arising under the linkage system, and the Federal Trade Commission has issued several studies highlighting related shortcomings and abuses. Transplanting this complex body of law may be inherently difficult and conflict with local institutions.[26]

Second, the FTAs appear to mandate a stricter version of linkage that would not have passed muster in the US. For example, recall that patent linkage under the Hatch-Waxman Act only imposes a 30-month mandatory delay, not an outright prohibition of approval. However, the text of some FTAs prohibits the marketing of a product claimed in a patent unless by consent or acquiescence of the patent owner. Thus, generic drug makers occasionally market a product 'at risk' while an infringement lawsuit is still ongoing.

Third, the FTAs transplanted an incomplete version of the Hatch-Waxman Act.[27] Out of the 11 features identified in the US patent linkage regime, the AUSFTA only codified the notice of generics applications and a heightened marketing prohibition. Features on the pro-generics side of the balance are missing, including placing the burden of identifying drug-patents associations on the patent owner, disclosing the patent information to lower the search cost of the generic companies, a carve-out mechanism to expedite non-infringing uses, and a reward to

---

[24]   See e.g., Pedro Roffe, Geoff Tansey and David Vivas-Eugui (eds), *Negotiating Health: Intellectual Property and Access to Medicines* (Routledge 2005); Carlos M. Correa, 'Expanding Patent Rights in Pharmaceuticals: The Linkage between Patents and Drug Registration' in Neil Weinstock Netanel (ed.), *The Development Agenda: Global Intellectual Property and Developing Countries* (OUP 2009) 247; Judit Rius Sanjuan, *Patent-Registration Linkage* (Consumer Project on Technology 2006) 6 <http://www.cptech.org/publications/CPTechDPNo2Linkage.pdf>; Brook K. Baker, 'Ending Drug Registration Apartheid: Taming Data Exclusivity and Patent/Registration Linkage' (2008) 34 Am. J.L. & Med. 303.
[25]   See generally Seuba (*supra*, n 9).
[26]   Ibid at 11.
[27]   Ibid. at 12–13.

patent challengers.[28] Many of the ignored features are key to the administration of a patent linkage regime and their absence exacerbates the challenges of implementing a successful regime.

Fourth, linkage rules in the FTA may not match the social and economic conditions of the recipient state. A core thread of the legal transplant scholarship focuses on the development of 'national legal orders enshrining intellectual property rules ... that match the social and economic needs'.[29] Developing countries often accept stricter IP rules in exchange for market access. Consequently, the type of patent rules they adopt may not match the stage of development. For patent linkage, the predominant question is whether rules limiting generic drug makers are appropriate in light of the limited resources and healthcare needs confronting developing countries like China.

2.3 Regulatory Patent Linkage in China

The origin of regulatory patent linkage in China is traceable to the broader legal transplant project following China's economic reform led by Deng Xiaoping. As the scholar of Chinese law Chen Jianfu noted, the 1984 Chinese Patent Law exemplifies the first batch of economic legislation that '[was] distinctively Western in style, form, structure and language.'[30] When China embraced the market economic system in the last decade of the 20th century the pace accelerated for 'the direct call for "legal transplant", "assimilation", "harmonisation with international practice" and "internationalisation" of Chinese law'.[31] By 2002, China had joined the World Trade Organization and revised its IP law to comply with obligations under TRIPS.[32] It adopted patent linkage in the same year, becoming the only country to implement a regulatory patent linkage system absent a treaty obligation.[33]

The State Food and Drug Administration (SFDA) promulgated patent

---

[28] *Access to Medicines Issues in the US–Korea Free Trade Negotiations:* Testimony Before the House Comm. on Ways and Means Subcomm. on Trade, 7 (20 March 2007) (statement of Prof. Sean M. Flynn) <http://www.wcl.american.edu/pijip/documents/koreatestimony03202007.doc>.

[29] Seuba (*supra*, n 9) at 1.

[30] Jianfu Chen, 'The Transformation of Chinese Law' (2007) 37 Hong Kong L.J. 689, 707.

[31] Ibid. at 709.

[32] Ibid. at 712.

[33] Benjamin P. Liu, 'Fighting Poison with Poison? The Chinese Experience with Pharmaceutical Patent Linkage' (2012) 11 J. Marshall Rev. Intell. Prop. L. 623.

linkage in Articles 18 and 19 of the Provisions for Drug Registration.[34] It has been amended since and the 2007 revision contains the latest version.[35] Article 18 sets out the process for listing patent information, the requirement of a non-infringement statement, and stating a general reference to patent dispute resolution.[36] Article 19 sets out the actual prohibition against the premature approval of drugs until patent expiry and a two-year grace period permitting registration application before patent expiry.[37]

Chinese patent linkage shares several common features with the US original: both require the disclosure of drugs-patents associations, a public listing of such associations and a non-infringing declaration from generic drug applicants. On the other hand, it leaves out the notice to the patent owner and a number of ameliorating features including: the process disclosure safe harbour; the Bolar research exemption; the carve-out exception for non-infringing medical indication; and the 180-day exclusivity for patent challengers.

Apart from these additions and subtractions, Chinese patent linkage modified two important aspects of the US patent linkage rules. First, US drug regulators must grant approval after 30 months if the patent dispute remains undecided but Chinese regulators cannot grant approval until the patents no longer apply. This means that protracted litigation can keep generic drugs off the market. Second, the Hatch-Waxman Act explicitly allocates the power to adjudicate patent disputes with courts but Chinese linkage regulation does not limit dispute resolution to the courts. As a result, Chinese drug regulators began assessing the merit of infringement.

---

[34]   See ibid.

[35]   *Yaopin Zhuce Guanli Banfa* (药品注册管理办法) [Provisions for Drug Registration] (promulgated by the St. Food and Drug Admin., 28 February 2005, effective 1 October 2007) SFDA, 10 July 2007 (China) <http://eng.sfda.gov.cn/WS03/CL0768/61645.html>.

[36]   Drug Registration Provisions, art. 18 ('An applicant shall provide the information on patent and its ownership of the applicant or other parties in China, in respect of the drug applied for registration, its formula, manufacturing processes and/or uses, etc. Where another party owns the patent in China, the applicant shall provide a statement of non-infringement. The drug regulatory department shall publish the information or the statement submitted by the applicant on its official website. Where a patent dispute occurs in the process of drug registration, it shall be settled in accordance with relevant laws and regulations on patent.').

[37]   Ibid. art. 19 ('For a drug patented in China, applicants other than the patentee may submit the application for registration two years prior to the expiry date of the patent. The State Food and Drug Administration shall review the drug application in accordance with the Provisions, and after the expiry date of the patent, check and issue the drug approval number, Import Drug License or a Pharmaceutical Product License if the application conforms to the provisions.').

On paper, Chinese patent linkage offers very strong protection and illustrates the successful political mobilization of multinational pharmaceutical companies. It contains more onerous prohibitions but none of the pro-generic features in the Hatch-Waxman Act. In reality, however, the Chinese linkage regime operated poorly. Although the regulation remains on the books, the SFDA no longer enforces its linkage regulations.[38] In 2009 a Bolar exemption was inserted into Chinese patent law, which exempts from liability all infringing acts that generic drug applicants engaged in for the purpose of seeking marketing approval. This amendment placed pre-approval conduct outside the reach of patent law and defeated the entire purpose of providing legal certainty before regulatory approval. Although Article 18 of the Provisions for Drug Registration called for the resolution of any infringement disputes during the regulatory approval process, the Bolar exemption swallowed the rules of infringement, essentially gutting patent linkage since 2008 even though it remains on the Provisions for Drug Registration.

To remedy this contradiction between the national patent law and regulatory statute, China is currently in the process of revising the linkage provision of the Provisions for Drug Registration. On 12 November 2013, the China Food and Drug Administration (CFDA) (a reorganized SFDA) circulated a new version of the Provisions for Drug Registration deleting the linking provisions of Article 19 and amended Article 18 to call for the resolution of infringement disputes *after* the regulatory approval. This amendment would remove regulatory patent linkage altogether.[39] However, the CFDA changed its position a few months later, circulating a new draft amendment of the Provisions for Drug Registration that resurrected a modified Article 19.[40] Whereas the current Article 19 bars the application or issuance of approval before the expiration of the patents, the proposed amendment explicitly permits the CFDA to receive and issue market approval before patent expiry.[41] Instead, the approval would not take legal effect before patent expiry. Article 18 in the new proposal keeps the current regulation and allows patent disputes to resolve before regulatory approval.[42]

---

[38]   Ibid.
[39]   Drug Registration Provisions Amendment (Comment Draft), art. 18 (12 November 2013) <http://www.sfda.gov.cn/WS01/CL0778/94158.html>.
[40]   Drug Registration Provisions (Amendment Draft), arts. 18–19 (19 February 2014) <http://www.chinalaw.gov.cn/article/cazjgg/201402/20140200394953.shtml>.
[41]   Ibid.
[42]   Ibid.

3.   THE CHALLENGES OF TRANSPLANTING PATENT LINKAGE

Why did the transplanting of patent linkage fail in China? The problem appeared more pragmatic than ideological, rooted in the pursuit of maximalist protection and aggressive enforcement that exceeded the load of the frail regulatory arrangement. In other words, patent linkage in China failed because its promoters *succeeded spectacularly*.

3.1   Maximalist Protection

The regulatory patent linkage rule in China is the dream of strong IP proponents. It was maximalist in three senses: it protected drugs beyond what was required in other jurisdictions, it lacked pro-generic features that balanced the harshness of linkage in other jurisdictions, and it vests tremendous power in the hands of drug regulators to halt approval. What China sought to implement went beyond the level of protection *anywhere*. It is certainly a 'legal irritant' according to Gunther Teubner, but an errant irritant without a proven record, which ultimately stretched Chinese patent linkage beyond the limit of enforceability as detailed below.

3.1.1   Linkage exceeding its source
One reason why patent linkage failed in China is because it is unusually broad beyond what is mandated under the Hatch-Waxman Act. The Chinese version covered all drug applications without regard to whether it is a new drug or generic drug, whether it is a small molecule drug or biologics, whether it is a process patent or a method of use patent or a product patent, and whether they relate to previously filed applications.

   This is akin to the FTAs that the US concluded in the early part of the 2000s. For example, the US–Chile FTA requires that, '[w]ith respect to pharmaceutical products that are subject to a patent, each Party shall . . . not grant marketing approval to any third party prior to the expiration of the patent term, unless by consent or acquiescence of the patent owner'.[43] In contrast, the Hatch-Waxman Act limits the universe of patents capable of triggering linkage to those specifically connected to the original drug. Regulatory patent linkage commences only with the filing of a generic drug application that relies on the safety and efficacy data of a previously approved drug and for this reason the original drug is also known as the reference drug.

---

43   Chile–US Free Trade Agreement, art. 17.10.2.

There is some logical justification to this breadth because some Chinese drug companies file generic drugs as NDAs and these 'new' drugs may therefore infringe existing patents.[44] But this broad linkage scope proves unworkable in practice. Without references to a pre-existing drug to be copied (as in the case of generic drug applications), how does the SFDA ascertain whether a supposedly new drug infringes one of the hundreds of thousands of pharmaceutical patents? Conversely, when a patent does cover the drug submitted for approval, there is also no guarantee that the SFDA will identify the correct patent and apply it against the pending application. In both instances the imperfect information and the lack of certainty breed opportunity for corruption. There is no regular mechanism that enables the State Intellectual Property Office (SIPO) to lend its expertise during the approval process, although this author's conversation with SIPO examiners suggests that the SFDA had sought SIPO's input on occasion. Since all working linkage systems require reference, there are no proven solutions to the problems generated by a reference-less linkage system.

The reference-less linkage system incentivizes strategic behaviour: companies can either put up with climbing compliance costs or, more likely, provide superficial compliance knowing that the SFDA may not have the resources to verify. If companies find that the standard operation procedure in the industry is to satisfy patent linkage primarily through misrepresentation and blanket statements of non-infringement, it creates the impression that not all regulations needed to be complied with and undermines the credibility and legitimacy of the patent linkage framework.

3.1.2   Linkage unchecked by balancing features

Chinese patent linkage also illustrates a kind of partial transplantation. As mentioned earlier, it lacked the Bolar research exemption; the process disclosure safe harbour; the carve-out exception for non-infringing medical indication; and the 180-day exclusivity for patent challengers. Of these, the lack of Bolar exemption became the Achilles' heel of patent linkage and provides another example of how the commitment to a maximalist linkage can backfire.

A Bolar exemption allows pharmaceutical companies to conduct experiments and reverse-engineer innovative drugs without fear of patent infringement. Without it, generics companies cannot study and reproduce the original drug formula without infringing patents. A Bolar exemption

---

[44]   See Liu (*supra*, n 33) 649–51 (discussing the filing of a new drug application for what is really a generic drug).

is built into the Hatch-Waxman Act with an artificial infringement trigger that deems the filing of an ANDA an act of infringement.[45] Together, these two features ensure that generics companies can experiment to their hearts' content without concerning themselves with patent infringement until the moment they submit a drug application to the FDA, at which point patent owners and generics applicants are given the opportunity to litigate patent issues in court before the drug enters the market.

Bolar exemptions were not a default feature of earlier FTAs and the Chinese patent linkage began without a Bolar exemption.[46] It did not excuse any incidental patent infringement incurred during the research and development of generics drugs. The inability to reverse-engineer or experiment with existing drugs severely hampers the development of China's generics industry and the patent regime was forced to change over the years. Judicial decisions slowly moved from punishing generics exploration to creating a judicial exception permitting the generics company to experiment with patented drugs, until finally in 2009 a Bolar exemption was formally codified in the Third Amendment to Chinese patent law.

The story of Bolar also illustrates the path-dependency of a legal transplant project. Had China imported Bolar exemption and the corresponding artificial infringement trigger, it would have preserved a set of two mutually balancing mechanisms. Instead, Chinese linkage began with overly strong protection without a Bolar exemption. The subsequent importation of the Bolar exemption was driven by the need to fix a perceived defect of overly strong patent rights. Given the context, policymakers are unlikely to give corresponding thought to the artificial litigation trigger.

3.1.3   Patent linkage with strong administrative discretion

The third example of a maximal protection deals with the rise of a new discretionary power permitting drug regulators to resolve patent

---

[45]   35 U.S.C. §271(e)(1) (2010) ('It shall not be an act of infringement to make, use, offer to sell, or sell within the United States or import into the United States a patented invention . . . solely for uses reasonably related to the development and submission of information under a Federal law which regulates the manufacture, use, or sale of drugs or veterinary biological products'); *see also* ibid. §271(e)(2)(A) ('It shall be an act of infringement to submit . . . an application under section 505(j) of the Federal Food, Drug, and Cosmetic Act or described in section 505(b)(2) of such Act for a drug claimed in a patent or the use of which is claimed in a patent.').

[46]   35 U.S.C. §271 (e)(1) ('It shall not be an act of infringement to make, use, offer to sell, or sell within the United States or import into the United States a patented invention . . . solely for uses reasonably related to the development and submission of information under a Federal law which regulates the manufacture, use, or sale of drugs or veterinary biological products.').

infringement issues and deny drug approval absent corroborating judicial decisions. This new power shifted the relative turf between drug regulators and the courts and illustrates the type of rule that Otto Kahn-Freund finds difficult to transfer because it is 'designed to allocate power, rule making, decision making, and . . . policy making power', which are inextricable from the governance structure.

Chinese patent linkage law adopted a dual track system – both the SFDA and the courts may assess patent issues arising out of the approval process. Drug regulators play a limited role under the Hatch-Waxman Act. This departs from the practice in the US, where the FDA merely pauses the approval process for 30 months without passing judgment on whether the patent was in fact infringed, a role that it repeatedly termed 'ministerial'.[47] Its own public statement expressed concerns that it lacks authority, resources, and the capability to address patent issues.[48] All substantive infringement issues are left to the courts, thereby eliminating the danger of conflicting infringement analysis.

The administrative discretion was supported by the US industry. In 2002, the American Chamber of Commerce in Shanghai asked Chinese drug regulators to decide drug-patent infringement issues; otherwise 'the pioneer company must rely on China's underdeveloped court and legal system, impractical for halting even inadvertent infringement'.[49] To concerned patentees, having two gatekeepers may appear to better protect the patentee. In an earlier iteration of the patent linkage regulation, the SFDA was even empowered to revoke a previously granted SFDA approval upon a finding of infringement by the courts. Again, this expansive administrative enforcement power echoes an earlier generation of linkage rules in FTAs that require a country to 'implement measures in its marketing approval process to prevent [others] from marketing a product covered by a patent during the term of that patent, unless by consent or with the acquiescence of the patent owner'.[50]

---

[47] Applications for FDA Approval to Market a New Drug, 68 Fed. Reg. 36676 (18 June 2003) <http://www.gpo.gov/fdsys/pkg/FR-2003-06-18/pdf/03-15065.pdf> (repeatedly emphasizing that the FDA's role is merely ministerial and not related to substantive patent determination).

[48] Ibid.

[49] The American Chamber of Commerce of Shanghai, *2002 Position Papers*, p. 54 <http://www.amcham-shanghai.org/NR/rdonlyres/2E8F3E2A-8FEB-4958-9F3E-BFE6C61167F1/954/PHARMACEUTICAL.pdf> accessed 4 December 2012.

[50] See e.g., Chile–United States Free Trade Agreement, art. 16.10(4)(a) (effective 1 January 2004); Morocco–United States Free Trade Agreement, art. 15.10(4)(a) (effective 1 January 2006); Singapore–United States Free Trade Agreement, art. 16.8(4)(c) (effective 1 January 2004).

However, the power to approve created new rent-seeking opportunities, further feeding the spectre of corruption. It also created tension between the courts and the SFDA since the two forums may generate contradictory decisions and the SFDA does not wish to appear negligent or to open itself to litigation (especially since it is particularly susceptible to and has received bad press in the tainted food or corruption scandals). The dual-track system also creates uncertainty, as approved drugs may become unapproved or reapproved given the vagaries of a patent dispute.

Perhaps out of the realization that the administrative approach was not workable, the industry's old view that court enforcement in China was too weak and should be supplanted by administrative enforcement shifted by 180 degrees. P*h*RMA, the association of multinational pharmaceutical companies, stated in its 2012 Special 301 Submission to the USTR: 'China should enable patent holder companies to file patent infringement suits before marketing authorization is granted for follow-on products and afford sufficient time for such disputes to be resolved before marketing occurs.'[51]

Brand drug innovators now want Chinese courts to resolve infringement disputes before market approval and relegate the SFDA to the ministerial role of administering an automatic delay, much as it is done in the US. This flip-flip suggests their newfound realization of the administrative enforcement challenges and a desire to invest in the development of the judicial system.

3.2   Agency Constraints

Founded in 1998, the SFDA is a relatively young institution and lacks the deep regulatory experience acquired by the FDA during its 100-years-plus history.[52] And yet this fledgling agency must guard the medical safety of the third largest pharmaceutical market of 1.4 billion people. It faces chronic problems of capacity, corruption and coordination, which limit its ability to implement a complex regulatory linkage system.

---

[51]   Pharmaceutical Research and Manufacturers of America (P*h*RMA) Special 301 Submission 2012, P*h*RMA (21 February 2012) <http://keionline.org/sites/default/files/PhRMA_Special301_21feb2012_0900006480fb1bd5.pdf>.

[52]   Xinhua News, 'Yaopin Jianguan Ju Lishiyange yu Zhineng (药品监管局历史沿革与职能)' <http://news.xinhuanet.com/zhengfu/2003-04/01/content_809 228.htm> (dating the founding of the SFDA to 1998); 'Centennial of FDA' (page last updated 13 May 2009) <http://www.fda.gov/AboutFDA/WhatWeDo/History/CentennialofFDA/default.htm> (dating the beginning of the FDA to 1906).

3.2.1 Capacity

Numerical comparisons between the SFDA and FDA give an idea of the scale of the capacity problem. The SFDA division in charge of pharmaceutical approval lists a staff of 120, in contrast with the US FDA, which employs about 2889 regulators as of 2009.[53] Yet China's population is four times that of the US and there are about 8413 listed pharmaceutical companies operating in its territory.[54] The highly fragmented industry resulted in 3066 NDAs being submitted to the SFDA in 2010,[55] compared with the 157 drug applications submitted to the FDA in 2010.[56] The vast number of pharmaceutical-related outfits also masks unscrupulous operators and small actors where accountability is often lacking and creates a cut-throat market where the incentive to cheat is high. All of this increases the difficulty of monitoring and verifying information submitted by companies, including IP information.

Reports of adverse drug incidents reflect the consequence of its limited capacity. In 2006, counterfeit Armaillarisin A manufactured by Qiqihar No. 2 Pharmaceutical Co., Ltd. killed 14 patients due to the incorporation of toxic diglycol in place of propylene glycol.[57] In the same year, bacteria-infested clindamycin injections sold by Anhui Xinyuan Biopharmaceutical

---

[53] *See* Lin Chunxia (林春霞) 'Guojiaji Yaopin Shenpin Zhuanjia Shuliang Buji Meiguo 1/20 (国家级药品审评专家数量不及美国1/20)' *Zhongguo Jingji Shibao (中国经济时报)/China Economic Times* (4 March 2011) <http://finance. jrj.com.cn/2011/03/0403199355135.shtml>; 'How Many People are Employed by FDA and in What Areas do They Work?' <http://www.fda.gov/AboutFDA/ Transparency/Basics/ucm213161.htm> (reporting 2889 employees working for the Center of Drug Evaluation and Research).

[54] China Food and Drug Administration, 'Statistic Inquiry' <http://app1. sfda.gov.cn/datasearch/face3/dir.html> (listing 7,135 registered entries of pharmaceutical companies following "药品生产企业"); but see Zhongguo Yiyao Lianmeng (中国医药联盟), 'Zhongguo Yiyao Chanye Waiyouneihuan Tiaozheng Shi Biran (中国医药产业外忧内患调整是必然)' (14 December 2011) <http://www. chinamsr.com/2011/1214/42435.shtml> (estimating 6,000 pharmaceutical companies in China).

[55] Department of Health & Human Services Food & Drug Administration, *FY 2010. Performance Report to the President and Congress for the Prescription Drug User Fee Act* (2011) p. 11 <http://www.fda.gov/downloads/AboutFDA/ ReportsManualsForms/Reports/UserFeeReports/PerformanceReports/PDUFA/ UCM243358.pdf>.

[56] Guojia Shipin Yaopin Jiandu Guanli Ju Fabu (国家食品药品监督管理局 发布), '2010 Nian Yaopin Zhuce Shenpi Niandu Baogao (2010年药品注册审批年 度报告)' (9 October 2011) <http://www.sfda.gov.cn/WS01/CL0236/65856.html>.

[57] NSD Bio Group, LLC, *Potential Health & Safety Impacts from Pharmaceuticals and Supplements Containing Chinese-Sourced Raw Ingredients. Prepared for U.S. China Economic and Security Review Commission* (April

Co, Ltd. killed 11 and injured 400 due to substandard decontamination processes.[58] The next year, tainted Methotrexate and Cytarabine injections sold by Shanghai Hualian Pharmaceutical Factory disabled and sickened hundreds.[59] In 2012, the media revealed medical gel capsules containing high levels of carcinogenic chromium because the gelatin was extracted from industrial leather scrap.[60] This is not so much a criticism of the SFDA's operation as an acknowledgement of the reality dogging the agency. It is probably unrealistic to expect strong IP protection coming out of the SFDA until it can satisfy its basic health and safety mandate.

Turning to specific IP competence, the drug-patent registration list that the SFDA maintains contains numerous clerical errors and reveals weakness in the capacity to process IP data. Short-handed and lacking patent expertise, the SFDA notes: '[I]f the patent is for a "process," then SFDA feels it cannot and should not be put in the position of needing to make a determination, and will often approve the registration application if the generic (subsequent) applicant claims non-infringement and agrees to bear the legal liability of infringement.'[61] Its professed inability to resolve patent issues does not bode well for those who entrust drug administrators with an IP enforcement role.

3.2.2 Corruption

The World Health Organization warns that official corruption in the pharmaceutical sector is a worldwide problem.[62] Because they are the last gatekeeper between pharmaceutical companies and the promise of profit, drug regulators face intense extra-legal pressure and temptation. One of the largest scandals in the history of the US FDA erupted shortly after the

---

2010)   pp. 37–39   <http://www.uscc.gov/sites/default/files/Research/2010/NSD_BIO_Pharma_Report--Revised_FINAL_for_PDF--14_%20April_2010.pdf>.

[58]   Ibid. at 35–36.

[59]   Ibid. at 39.

[60]   Laurie Burkitt, 'China Halts Sale of Some Drugs' Wall Street Journal Online (Beijing, 17 April 2012) <http://online.wsj.com/article/SB100014240527023042993045773475634189360668.html>.

[61]   See the minutes of the Pharmaceutical Task Force Meeting of 30 August 2005 of the Medical Device and Pharmaceutical Subgroup of the US–China Joint Commission on Commerce and Trade, pp. 3–4 <http://ita.doc.gov/td/health/jcctpharma05_1.pdf>.

[62]   World Health Organization, *Measuring Transparency in Medicines Registration, Selection, and Procurement: Four Country Assessment Studies* (2006) p. iii <http://www.who.int/medicines/areas/policy/goodgovernance/Transparency4CountryStudy.pdf>: 'The pharmaceutical sector is particularly vulnerable to corruption, which manifests itself in various forms, including bribery, fraud, favouritism, collusion and embezzlement at different levels of the medicines chain.'

passage of the Hatch-Waxman Act, when generics companies submitted false data, swapped test samples and bribed drug regulators.[63]

Thus it is not surprising that the SFDA experienced waves of corruption and culminated in the execution of its former head commissioner on bribery charges in 2007 in connection with the approval of drug registrations. Even then, and after the administration had been reorganized as part of an anti-corruption campaign, a deputy commissioner who survived the earlier purge was arrested in 2010 for his own misconduct. The capacity constraint led to wholly insufficient double-checking and oversight, which creates an enabling environment for corruption, and rather predictably some regulators sold clinical data to generics applicants or otherwise granted certifications for the payment of money. During the investigation of the Qiqihar scandal mentioned in the previous section, the vice general manager of the company confessed that the company 'bought the GMP certificate for 100,000 RMB'.[64]

3.2.3 Coordination

The complex linkage regime requires collaboration between drug regulators, the patent office and the courts, which is lacking within the agency, between health regulators and patent agencies, and between administrative agencies and the courts. For example, pharmaceutical applicants are not permitted to submit their application until two years prior to the expiry of a patent covering the drug. However, the assessment of patent issues was reserved for the central approval agency, not the local SFDA agency in charge of application acceptance. The local agency may have an incentive to accept known infringing applications because it may feel beholden to powerful local business interests as opposed to the wishes of the central SFDA agency. The divergent interests and responsibilities of the local and central offices creates a classic principal–agent problem.

---

[63] 'The Generic Drug Scandal' *NY Times* (2 October 1989) <http://www.nytimes.com/1989/10/02/opinion/the-generic-drug-scandal.html>; James T. O'Reilly, 'Losing Deference in the FDA's Second Century: Judicial Review, Politics, and a Diminished Legacy of Expertise' (2008) 93 Cornell L. Rev. 939, 957: 'Second, in 1989, the FDA became engulfed in scandal when news broke that members of the Agency's generic drug approval staff had received bribes and gifts to expedite certain applications.'

[64] NSD Bio Group (*supra*, n 57) at 39; Yu Yalian and Cao Jingjing (余亚莲 曹晶晶), '"Qieryao" An: Changfang Hua 10 Wan Goumai Guojia Quanwei Zhiliang Renzheng Shu ("齐二药" 案:厂方花10万购买国家权威质量认证书) [Qiqihar No. 2 Pharma's GMP Certificate was purchased for 100,000 CNY]' *Xin Kuai Bao* (新快报) [News Express] (reprinted in NetEase, 9 August 2007) <http://news.163.com/07/0809/05/3LEC6JDI0001124J.html>.

For an example of inter-agency conflict, the error-prone drug-patent listing evidences a failure of coordination between the SFDA and SIPO. The SFDA drug-patent list depends entirely on data entered by the applicant, which often contains incorrect or incomplete information. Simple but critical errors such as incorrect expiration dates remain uncorrected.[65] In contrast, communications between the United States Patent and Trademark Office (USPTO) and the FDA ensure that patent expiration information is up to date.[66]

Tension also existed between courts and the SFDA as it exists in all linkage systems that require the drug regulators to assess substantive patent issues. Studies of the Canadian patent linkage system describe awkward situations where the Canadian drug regulators and Canadian courts may reach contrary decisions and a similar conflict might arise in China.[67] Even if courts have the final say, the status of a drug marketing application is still in limbo before parties exhaust the opportunity for reviews and appeals. The situation is arguably more complex in China, where SIPO is in charge of patent invalidation, the People's Courts are in charge of patent infringement determination and the SFDA conducts its own administrative assessment of patent issues during the approval process. The excessive fragmentation of substantive patent adjudication hinders, rather than promotes, the goal of patent linkage to promote the transparent and efficient resolution of pharmaceutical patent disputes such that patent owners and generic drug manufacturers can have greater certainty in the marketplace.

3.3   Aggressive Enforcement

High-profile pharmaceutical disputes arose under the new patent linkage law before the SFDA had time to consolidate and digest the patent linkage system. A closer look at the history of this relatively brief era highlights the problem of enforcing maximalist law through a frail agency. There,

---

[65]   Liu (*supra*, n 33) 633–36 (detailing the defects in the drug-patent registry).

[66]   See USPTO, *USPTO Image File Wrapper Petition Decisions 0001* (USPTO 2003) <http://books.google.com/books?ibid=uTMkMjNTVNQC&pg=PP42&lpg =PP42&dq=USPTO+and+FDA++patent+expiration+information&source=bl &ots=qvPm9KNF6W&sig=X1XXiM6wfhrZmDRwyz2Z0wIFa0A&hl=en&sa= X&ei=jlilUKazNqmcyQGht4HQCQ&ved=0CDwQ6AEwAzgK>.

[67]   Emir Aly Crowne and Cristina Mihalceanu, 'Innovators and Generics: Proposals for Balancing Pharmaceutical Patent Protection and Public Access to Cheaper Medicines in Canada (or Don't NOC the Players, Hate the Regulations)' (2011) 51 IDEA 693, 713–14 (discussing the potential for conflicting infringement determinations under the Canadian linkage system).

foreign patentees aggressively used the favourable linkage law against generics developers. Although it was initially successful in getting results for these patentees, the practical outcome was not compatible with China's situation. The law was eventually trimmed back, leaving a linkage system that was weaker than would have been the case if the Chinese government had adopted a more balanced approach.

The 2004 Viagra patent dispute is an example of patent linkage at work – a point often overlooked among the vast English scholarship analysing this dispute.[68] It involved the attempt by 13 generic drug companies to invalidate the Chinese Viagra patent. Although the patent was initially invalidated by SIPO for failing to support the invention with appropriate clinical data, courts later reversed SIPO. The Viagra case demonstrated the Chinese patent linkage in operation – the SFDA withheld the marketing approval under patent linkage, forcing the generics companies to invalidate the patent.[69] The trouble is that the Viagra example may be an example of patent linkage being abused for a defective patent.

There was a subtle but material translation error when the patent application was translated and filed in China, and it was appropriate for SIPO to invalidate the patent for a description defect. The patent claimed the use of sildenafil, the active ingredient in Viagra, for the manufacture of drugs to treat male erectile dysfunction. The patent described five groups of compound embodiments with increasing specificity where each group is a subset of the previous group. The fourth smallest group was the 'particularly preferred group of compounds' and disclosed over 100 compounds. Of these, nine were further selected for a smallest grouping of the 'especially preferred individual compounds'. The patent disclosure provided some data showing clinical activity but did not specifically identify the compound underlying the data.[70] Instead, it attributed the data to one of the nine especially preferred individual compounds according to the English language patent submitted in the US. Unfortunately, the distinction between 'particularly preferred group of compounds' (group 4) and 'especially preferred individual compounds' (group 5) was lost in

---

68   Peter K. Yu, 'From Pirates to Partners (Episode II): Protecting Intellectual Property in China in the Twenty-First Century' (2006) 55 Am. U. L. Rev. 901, 985; J. Andrews, 'Pfizer's Viagra Patent and the Promise of Patent Protection in China' (2006) 28 Loy. L.A. Int'l & Comp. L. Rev. 1, 9–19 (detailing the Viagra dispute).

69   'Guochan "Weige" Reng Weiyou Zhunshengzheng Tuiguang Bulü Jiannan (国产 "伟哥" 仍未有准生证 推广步履艰难)' *Xinxi Shibao (信息时报) [Info. Times]* (28 July 2004) <http://finance.sina.com.cn/b/20040728/1026907233.shtml>.

70   U.S. Patent No. 6,469,012 (filed 4 Mar. 1996).

the translation of the Chinese patent.[71] Thus the disclosed clinical data could have come from any one of over 100 compounds in the fourth smallest group according to the Chinese patent instead of the nine compounds in the fifth smallest group. Consequently, SIPO determined that a person of ordinary skill would not be able to tell which one of the over 100 compounds generated the efficacy data without undue experimentation. On appeal, the Beijing Intermediate People's Court reversed and rescued the patent, based on the reasoning that a person of ordinary skill reading this patent would naturally infer that the data must have come from one of the nine compounds that were identified in the fifth group because one can infer that the data inventor disclosed was drawn from one of the nine best molecules.[72]

Invalidating Viagra's patent due to the mistranslation of a single word seems severe, and yet the 13 generics companies rightly challenged the patent after putting their investment on the line. Regardless of the equity of the case, that the Viagra patent was eventually upheld possibly left a sour taste with SFDA and SIPO administrators who were attempting to perform their jobs, and it showcased the power of patent linkage to forestall cheaper generic alternatives even when the patent is suspect.

A more egregious instance of abused occurred with an injectable antibiotic patent owned by a Chinese company, Welman Pharmaceuticals, which was tied up in court for nine years before the Supreme People's Court of China invalidated it in December 2011. The patent owner was able to use procedural tools to tie up and stay the invalidation proceeding for several years.[73] In the meantime, the patent was used in courts, arbitration panels and the SFDA to stop competitors.[74] This is the type of abuse critics of patent linkage attribute to multinational pharmaceutical companies – the assertion of weak patents for the purpose of triggering a regulatory delay. That a Chinese company was able to carry out this abuse shortly after the inception of Chinese patent linkage system shows how easy it is for an aggressive patentee to abuse a maximalist regime within an underdeveloped regulatory regime.

---

[71]   China Patent App. No. 94,192,386, Pub. No. 1,124,926 (filed 13 May 1994).
[72]   Tony Chen, 'Beijing High Court Upholds Viagra Patent in China' (2008) *Jones Day* 30, 32, <http://www.jonesday.com/files/Publication/288b184e-c6ee-44b5-800f-30838f34da54/Presentation/PublicationAttachment/aa464b25-7839-4af9-be34-30d62faf4d56/Beijing_High_Court.pdf>.
[73]   See generally Liu (*supra*, n 33), 651–52 (discussing the Welman antibiotic patent dispute).
[74]   Ibid.

4. LESSONS FOR LEGAL TRANSFER THEORIES

The rise and fall of patent linkage in China poses interesting questions for the prevailing theories of legal transfer. This section considers the linkage history through the theoretical lens developed by Niklas Luhmann, Gunther Teubner and John Giuseppe, and identifies regulatory features that will improve or undermine transferability.

Niklas Luhmann argues that law is an 'autopoietic' system – a system that is self-contained and capable of perpetuating itself through self-referential discourses. Nonetheless, this system is capable of incorporating external social facts and norms much as a living cell is self-contained and perpetuates itself but is capable of interacting and absorbing its environment. The opposite of autopoietic law is allopoietic law, which is produced through its environmental context.[75] Gunther Teubner extends system theory to the phenomenon of legal transfer and argues that borrowed law amounts to a 'legal irritant' that perturbs and reshapes the internal logic of the recipient legal system.[76] Such irritant has the power to 'unleash an evolutionary dynamic in which the external rule's meaning will be reconstructed and the internal context will undergo fundamental change'.[77] In this way, law is both separate from and connected to society through channels of discourse, and legal transfer is a part of this discursive phenomenon. System theory invites middle-level principles to explain the ways law propagates through discursive channels, but it simultaneously undermines the usefulness of such explanations. A self-perpetuating autopoietic system is complex and unpredictable, and it calls into question 'the instrumental notion that legal transfer can simply create new legal rules that will induce predetermined behaviour among recipients'.[78] This indeterminacy challenges the prospect of transplanting patent linkage (or any patent rules) to reduce infringement.

Studies of specific legal transfer have taken up the challenge of developing middle principles for explaining the degrees of legal transfer. Susan Sell shows how a small group of elite multinational companies worked through international institutions and installed a global IP

---

[75]   Marcelo Neves, 'From Autopoiesis to the Allopoiesis of the Law' (2001) 28(1) J. Law & Soc. 242, 258.

[76]   Gunther Teubner, 'Legal Irritants: Good Faith in British Law or How Unifying Law Ends Up in New Divergences' (1998) 61 Modern L. Rev. 11, 12.

[77]   Gillespie, 'Developing a Decentred Analysis of Legal Transfers' (*supra*, n 7) 39.

[78]   Ibid.

standard through TRIPS. On the other hand, legal transfer falters in the presence of strong local resistance.[79] The predominant debate of global pharmaceutical IP protection follows this local resistance model, pitting the interests of the US and its pharmaceutical constituents at one end, and developing country and its generics' needs at the other.[80] The US pharmaceutical industry viewed the 'lack of action on ... patent linkage as [a] key concern' and asked the US government 'to urge SFDA to stop issuing licenses to Chinese companies who do not own patents for their pharmaceutical products'.[81] Implicit in this charge is the assumption that the SFDA is fully capable of blocking infringing generics but for a conscious desire to protect local generics companies to the detriment of exogenous patent rights. This tells a narrative of resistance pitting the profit of the transferor against the welfare of the transferee.

However, the showdown between global elites and local resistance does not explain the failure of patent linkage in China. The SFDA was a younger organization then and was eager to adopt regulatory practices from developed countries.[82] China also embraced IP provisions, building up its patent system to what it is today.[83] Patent linkage is but a part of this effort, no different from any other IP rights provisions embraced by China. Patent linkage failed, absent the resistance of local actors or access to medicine advocates.

Taking seriously the system theory notion of transfer as a discursive phenomenon, John Gillespie applied discursive analysis to the process and outcome of transferring corporate law to East Asia.[84] To Gillespie, resistance is part of the course of transfer because 'dialogue and discord are necessary for legal transfers to enter and influence local regulatory conversation and practices'.[85] Success or failure of a transfer is measured

---

[79]   Susan Sell, *Private Power, Public Law: The Globalization of Intellectual Property Rights* (Cambridge University Press 2003).

[80]   Correa (*supra*, n 24).

[81]   *2010 Shanghai IPR Roundtable – Candid Commentary From Industry*, leaked by Wikileaks, reprinted on Cablegatesearch.net, <http://www.cablegatesearch.net/cable.php?ibid=10SHANGHAI53> accessed 30 November 2012.

[82]   Dali Yang, 'Regulatory Learning and Its Discontents in China: Promise and Tragedy at the State Food and Drug Administration' in John Gillespie and Randall Peerenboom (eds), *Pushing Back Globalization* (Routledge 2009) 139.

[83]   Xuan-Thao Nguyen, 'The China We Hardly Know: Revealing the New China's Intellectual Property Regime' (2011) 55 St. Louis U. L.J. 773.

[84]   Gillespie, 'Toward a Discursive Analysis of Legal Transfers into Developing East Asia' (*supra*, n 6).

[85]   Ibid. at 714.

by the extent to which 'regulations acquire social force through preference convergence and consensus'.[86]

Patent linkage was a solution without an underlying problem. Multinational corporations relied on the instrumental notion that linkage regulations will induce behaviour favourable to its intellectual property in China without considering whether the regulation would generate consensual uptake by local actors. The linkage experience in China then becomes a list of what not to do when transferring law from one country to another.

First, transfer may succeed better if it avoids untested, *sui generis* implementation. While there is no guarantee that the laws for country A are fit for country B, it is even less likely that a maximalist regime untested anywhere will generate the local consensus and buy-in. Thus when the Chinese patent linkage regulations exceeded the protections offered in the US or ignored balancing features, Chinese regulators found themselves in untested terrain without experience and precedent. In contrast, when China implemented its patent system, it was on modelled existing systems and achieved success.

Second, transfer may better succeed if it addresses specific needs. As Gillespie notes, transferred law is more useful if it enables 'recipients to find new solutions to regulatory problems'.[87] Patent linkage was not directed to any clear need within the recipient country. Instead it serviced needs outside China. Without a clear local need, it is difficult to identify domestic beneficiaries of the law who are willing to support its ongoing viability. Without a clear local need, regulations that primarily benefit outsiders may come across as more abusive than useful. It also permits aggressive practices such as those employed by Welman, which further undermines consensus building within the recipient country.

Third, transfer may better succeed if it starts out gradually. Transferred regulations do not gain social force overnight. A new regulation must prove useful and credible over time in order to generate convergence and consensus. This is most easily done if the transferred regulation is allowed to prove itself within a controlled setting over time. Some mechanisms for managing this process include the transition period in TRIPS and the flexible enforcement rule that allows countries to devote no more resources to IP enforcement than to any other regulatory regimes.[88] The Chinese government is also known for its gradualism and practices such as testing out a new rule in certain experimental cities first. In the case of patent linkage,

---

[86]   Ibid. at 720.
[87]   Ibid.
[88]   TRIPs art. 41 paragraph 5.

China would have been better off testing the system for a more limited set of drugs or implementing the rules in pieces, setting up the patent-drug registry system before tying it with the market approval process.

These strategies make the same theoretical move – they shift the law from allopoiesis produced by others towards self-produced autopoiesis. These recommendations enhance the operability of the law, the credibility of its agents, and the compatibility with local legal structures. Thus they promote a pinching off of the transferred rule from the economy or politics of the donor country such that the continued vitality of transferred law depends on its concordance with the legal logic of the recipient country.

5.   CONCLUSION

The greatest value of exploring the intersection of patent linkage and China is to consider the finer ebbs and flows of the international IP regime and in particular the interaction between globalizing negotiation on the one hand, and the localization of foreign legal designs on the other. Currently, knowledge of patent linkage is limited to the countries more similar to the US such as Australia and Canada. China presents the challenges of implementing patent linkage in developing countries – the messy and nitty-gritty process of accounting for the vagaries of institutions and implementation.[89]

That patent linkage failed in China absent strong local resistance shows that the globalization of strong patent rules is about approaches as much it is about bargaining power. Promoters of pharmaceutical patent protection could have supported a stronger and more capable judiciary, shared administrative and anti-corruption expertise with the SFDA, advised regulators about patent linkage in a more limited setting, and openly discussed strengths and weaknesses of a linkage system based on the US experience. Each of these approaches would have strengthened China's legal system and enhanced patent protection. Instead, promoters of patent linkage mistook a grand promise for feasible policy and missed an opportunity for sustained improvement of China's IP system. The story suggests that, when transferring law for the benefit of the donor country, less is sometimes more.

---

[89]   Yu (*supra*, n 68) (identifying the various costs of enforcing IP rights).

10. Recent IP legal reforms in China and the EU in light of implementing IPR strategies

Liguo Zhang

1. INTRODUCTION

In June 2008, China's State Council released the 'Outline of the National Intellectual Property Strategy', which provided a roadmap to how China plans to become one of the world's most innovative countries by 2020.[1] Similarly, on 24 May 2011, the European Commission released a communication entitled 'A Single Market for Intellectual Property Rights Boosting Creativity and Innovation to Provide Economic Growth, High Quality Jobs and First Class Products and Services in Europe'.[2] In this communication, the European Commission clearly described its new intellectual property rights (IPR) strategy to address some challenges in the new knowledge-based economy. The strategy is focused on fostering innovation, furthering growth and competitiveness in the EU economy and also allowing cultural diversity. In the last few years, both the European Commission and the Chinese government have taken measures to implement their strategies respectively. One significant change brought about by the strategies is that both the EU and China have introduced legal reform to their intellectual property (IP) systems. Many complementary measures, other than legal measures, have also brought about changes to the environments for protection and exploitation of IP rights in both the EU and China.

This chapter reviews recent developments in implementing the respective

---

[1] State Council on the Issuance of the Outline of National Intellectual Property Strategy （国务院关于印发国家知识产权战略纲要的通知），国发〔2008〕18 号 (2008).

[2] European Commission, 'A Single Market for Intellectual Property Rights Boosting Creativity and Innovation to Provide Economic Growth, High Quality Jobs and First Class Products and Services in Europe' COM (2011) 287 final.

IPR strategies in China and the EU. The process shows significant differences and diverging perspectives regarding the implementation of the IPR strategies in China and the EU. First, the EU's approach is to realize its political purpose by a legal method, whereas China's approach is to improve its IP legal system and performance by political methods. Second, China's strategy is a progressive strategy, which steers China towards becoming a highly innovative economy like the EU. Furthermore, this chapter critically assesses the results of the IPR strategies' implementation in both China and the EU. In order to find out how the Chinese and EU IPR strategies have promoted legal reform in those respective jurisdictions, this chapter initially analyses IP legal reforms in China and the EU resulting from their respective IPR strategies. Accordingly, this chapter then analyses the achievements and deficiencies of these measures in the implementation of the IP strategies.

2.   CHINA'S NATIONAL IPR STRATEGY

China has long been accused of providing insufficient protection for IPRs. Whether or not this accusation is accurate, recent actions by the Chinese government in implementing the IPR Strategy are indicative of the trend of enhancing IPR protection in China. This has been reflected in the revision of relevant IP laws and the actions of governmental departments in stimulating the creation of more IP and cracking down on infringement of IPRs.

China's IPR Strategy clearly identified several deficiencies with respect to the current IP system: 'China's intellectual property regime still needs improvement. The quality and quantity of the indigenous created intellectual property still cannot meet the demands of economic and social development; . . . infringement of intellectual property is still a relatively serious problem.'[3] In dealing with these deficiencies, the Chinese IPR Strategy was particularly aimed towards: improving the IP regime; improving the creation, utilization, protection and management of IPRs; preventing abuses of IPRs; and fostering a culture of IPRs. It set up two stages of objectives. First, by 2013, a series of highly specific working targets was to be reached and included provision for more indigenous patents, world-renowned brands, high-value copyright related works, new plant varieties, geographic indications, and traditional knowledge.

---

[3]   State Council on the Issuance of the Outline of National Intellectual Property Strategy (*supra*, n 1).

Furthermore, the benefit of utilizing IPRs shall be increased significantly and the share of IPR-intensive products shall grow significantly. Piracy and counterfeiting should be significantly reduced and general awareness of IPRs should be greatly heightened and lead towards the shaping of a pro-IPR culture. Secondly, by 2020, China should be a country of high-level IP creation, utilization, protection and management.

In order to realize these targets, the Chinese strategy committed the government to introduce measures from these perspectives, such as enhancing Chinese IP innovative capacity, encouraging the transformation and exploitation of IP, accelerating IPR legal development, improving the implementation of IP laws, strengthening the management of IPRs, developing IPR intermediary services, reinforcing IPR professionals' development, boosting IPR cultural awareness, and extending IP international communications and cooperation.

In the last few years, China has amended its patent law and trademark law. Other IP laws still are in the process of being revised. Meanwhile, many governmental departments have taken actions in carrying out the tasks set in the IPR Strategy. On the one hand, the process of implementing the IPR Strategy shows the Chinese government's strong desire to improve IP protection and Chinese innovative capacity. On the other hand, it also shows that the government's interventions are playing a central role in IPR strategy.

2.1 The Revision of IP Laws in Implementing the IPR Strategy

In principle, IP is a property rule entitlement.[4] The function of the IP system is that property rights define a bundle of transferable rights, which allow resources to be allocated to their most highly valued use, and provide owners an opportunity to reap the fruits of their investments. A strong property rule for IPRs demands strong protection against infringement backed up by injunctions and the prospective award of high damages. A strong property rule for IPRs may also encourage the negotiation and exchange of such rights, thus effectively allocating technological resources among market players.[5] Recent revisions to the Patent Act and the Trademark Act, in the context of implementing the national

---

[4] Guido Calabresi and A Douglas Melamed, 'Property Rules, Liability Rules, and Inalienability: One View of the Cathedral' (1971) 85 Harvard Law Review 1089.

[5] F Scott Kieff, 'Coordination, Property, and Intellectual Property: An Unconventional Approach to Anticompetitive Effects and Downstream Access' (2006) 56 Emory Law Journal 327, 347.

IPR Strategy, have focused on enhancing the enforcement measures which strengthen the property rule for IPRs and improving efficiency in acquiring and exploiting IPRs.

2.1.1 Patent law

The Chinese Patent Act was amended in 2008. The 2008 Amendment made 36 changes with the intention of promoting national innovation, enhancing patent protection, and balancing the public interest. First of all, the 2008 Amendment introduced some measures to facilitate patent filing and improve patent quality. Secondly, it elaborated upon rules regarding the exploitation of patents. For example, it clarified the implementation of a joint patent and introduced the international patent exhaustion principle.[6] To implement the Doha Declaration on the TRIPS Agreement and Public Health, the Amendment provided for rules under which the State Intellectual Property Office (SIPO) may grant compulsory licences upon application to qualified applicants.[7] Moreover, the Amendment especially strengthened enforcement measures against infringement. It provided statutory damages whereby a court may order an infringer to pay statutory damages between RMB 10,000 and 1,000,000, even where no evidence is available to establish proof of damage. Furthermore, a patent holder may be awarded damages to cover reasonable expenses incurred by the patent holder to prevent infringement. Furthermore, the Amendment stipulated that the patentee or privies may apply to a competent court to preserve evidence prior to the commencement of legal proceedings where there is a risk of evidence being destroyed or being difficult to obtain later. In addition, the Amendment clarified some situations where the exploitation of a patent does not constitute infringement or does not result in liability for damages, which is expected to improve legal certainty in exploiting a patent.[8]

2.1.2 Trademark law

The current Trademark Act in China was first enacted in 1982 and came into effect on 1 March 1983. The 1982 Trademark Act was amended in 1993, 2001 and 2013. The 2013 Amendment was an action in implementing the national IP strategy. Overall, the 2013 Amendment focused on

---

[6]   Under the international exhaustion principle, a patent is not infringed when a patented product or a product directly obtained from a patented process, which has been sold by the patentee or by others authorized by the patentee anywhere in the world is imported.

[7]   Article 50 Patent Act 2008.

[8]   Articles 69, 70 Patent Act 2008.

three perspectives. First, the application and opposition procedure was improved to increase efficiency. For example, the 2013 Amendment set several time constraints for examining a trademark application and review. The opposition procedure is also simplified. Second, the Amendment added rules to prevent the abuse of trademarks. It stipulated that the principle of good faith should be complied with in the application, registration and use of a trademark. It even indicated several specific situations that may amount to bad faith. It prohibited a well-known mark holder from printing 'well-known mark' on the package of the product for the purpose of advertisement and a promotion, which has been regarded as deviating from the purpose of the well-known mark regime. In addition, it committed trademark agents to good faith practices. Third, the Amendment strengthened the protection and enforcement of trademarks by raising the amount of damages available and reducing the burden of proof placed on trademark holders. In addition, sound marks can be registered as a result of the 2013 Amendment.

2.1.3 Copyright law
The Copyright Act was amended in 2010 but this amendment only made a trivial change in order to be compliant with the World Trade Organization (WTO) Agreement on Trade-Related Aspects of Intellectual Property Rights (TRIPS Agreement). A significant revision of Chinese copyright law in order to deal with the challenges resulting from the Internet and digital technology is ongoing.

2.1.4 IP courts
The China IPR Strategy indicated the need to establish an IP appeal court but it did not clarify the functions and jurisdiction of the court. In August 2014, the Standing Committee of the National People's Congress passed the decision to establish IP courts in Beijing, Shanghai and Guangzhou cities.[9] But these IP courts are not appeal courts. The main jurisdiction for these courts is to hear the first instance IP cases only in those three regional jurisdictions. How the IP courts may improve the enforcement of IP still remains unclear.

2.2 The Role of Governments in Implementing the IPR Strategy

The initiation and implementation of the IPR Strategy is a result of strong governmental intervention. The effective implementation of the strategy

---

[9] See Chapter 16 in this volume.

requires complex inter-ministerial cooperation in the central government and intergovernmental cooperation between the central government, provinces and municipalities. The office of the Inter-Ministerial Joint Meeting for Implementation of the strategy was established in 2008, and was composed of 28 ministries and departments.[10] Each year the meeting assigns concrete tasks to each responsible ministry to fulfil. Then each ministry makes its own plan and policy to implement the specific task. For example, the 2011 Promotion Plan contained 176 concrete measures and 13 key measures.[11] The strong government intervention has made significant achievements. IPRs were traditionally not a focus of many governmental departments and were even largely overlooked. Thanks to the IPR Strategy, many relevant governmental departments have been activated to take measures to implement the IPR Strategy. In totality, the State Council and its ministries have issued over 300 documents, including industrial policies and guidelines to elaborate on the national IPR Strategy and to commit or guide the lower-level governments, entities and/ or undertakings to take measures to implement the strategy. For example, the Ministry of Industry and Information Technology has authored a guideline on the management of IPRs in industrial enterprises to promote it in approximately 1,000 enterprises, and to establish model enterprises in managing IPRs.[12] This guideline also urged the lower government departments to take more practical measures to implement it. In addition, the Ministry of Industry and Information Technology has made 'the twelfth five-year development plan for software and IT services industry' to plan and promote the development of hi-tech and new-tech to implement the IPR Strategy.[13] Relevant governmental departments have made national patent, trademark strategy, and copyright strategies, as well as IPR strategies in the fields of agriculture, forestry, national defence, industry and technology respectively.

At a local level, local governments were encouraged to promulgate local

---

[10]   'Official website of Chinese National Intellectual Property Strategy' <http://www.nipso.cn/aboutus.asp> accessed 3 December 2014.

[11]   See SIPO Official website,'2011 National Intellectual Property Strategy Promotion Plan (2011年国家知识产权战略实施推进计划)' <http://www.sipo.gov.cn/yw/2011/201104/t20110425_600965.html> accessed 3 December 2014.

[12]   'Office of the Ministry of Information Industry on the Fostering Project on the capacity of industrial Enterprises to exploit intellectual Property in 2014 (工业和信息化部办公厅关于做好2014年工业企业知识产权运用能力培育工程工作的通知)', 15 January 2014.

[13]   'Ministry of Industry and Information Technology on Software and IT Services Industry "Twelfth Five-Year Plan" (工业和信息化部软件和信息技术服务业 "十二五" 发展规划)', April 2012.

IP strategies following the instructions of the national IPR Strategy based on their practical situations. Twenty-eight provinces and 159 municipal governments had made official documents to guide the implementation of national IPR strategy in their respective administrative areas by 2012.[14] In implementing the strategy, several model provinces and model cities were recognized based on certain criteria, with the aim of shaping a model for other local governments to implement their own strategies.[15]

With respect to the enforcement of IP law, the relevant governmental departments have made plans and launched special campaigns to combat IPR infringements. The special campaigns aim to gather personnel and resources from all relevant departments to crack down on specific types of infringement activities in a short period. They cover a broad range of infringing activities, such as producing and distributing counterfeit goods, pirating audio-visual media, and trading in infringing goods. Those campaigns could be national or regional. One recent example was that the Leading Group for Cracking down on Counterfeit Goods and Infringing IPRs under the State Council issued a work plan for fighting the manufacturing and sale of fake and shoddy goods in the online environment on 18 June 2014. The plan involved a range of agencies, including Customs, General Administration of Quality Supervision, Inspection and Quarantine, General Administration of Press, Publication, Radio, Film and Television, State Administration for Industry & Commerce, Ministry of Agriculture, and the Chinese Food and Drug Administration taking joint action.[16] In addition, SIPO has set up over 70 'IP protection help centres' around the country, and provides consultancy, support and help directly to local firms. An IPR assistance hotline '12330' has been in operation.

In order to promote an IPR-favourable social environment, the authorities are trying to incorporate IPR knowledge into school textbooks. In 2008, the State Administration of Copyright launched an annual competition for essays on copyright for college students. In order to boost the

---

[14] '2012 National Local Intellectual Property Strategy Implementation Meeting (2012年度全国地方知识产权战略实施工作会议召开)' <http://www.gov.cn/gzdt/2012-11/28/content_2277407.htm> accessed 3 December 2014.

[15] Wu Hui and Xiao Xiao (吴　辉,肖潇), 'The First Model Cities on the Implementation of National IP Strategy (首批国家知识产权示范城市名单出炉)' *Chinese IPR Newspaper* (中国知识产权报) (27 April 2012).

[16] The Leading Group for Fighting IP Infringement and the Manufacturing and Sale of Fake and Shoddy Goods, *Notice on Issuing the Work Plan for Fighting IP Infringement and the Manufacturing and Sale of Fake and Shoddy Goods in the Internet Field* (18 June 2014).

training for qualified IPR personnel, SIPO provides funding to establish state-sponsored IPR training bases in some Chinese universities for training IP enforcement officials and company IP staff.[17]

3.   EU IPR STRATEGY

The EU IPR strategy in particular has three focuses: the functioning of the Common Market in terms of IPRs, the challenge from new technologies to IPRs, and the enforcement of IPRs within the EU and also at its borders.[18] The strategy planned an overhaul of IPR legislation with the intention to harmonize the IP regimes with respect to patents, copyright, trademarks, geographic indications and trade secrets, therefore reducing the complexity of costs and transactions and increasing legal certainty in particular for SMEs. The objective of the strategy is to enable Europe to be 'a world leader in innovative licensing solutions for the seamless exploitation of innovative technological products and of knowledge and cultural products'.[19] In the last few years, the European Commission has taken concrete steps to push forward the implementation of its strategy.

3.1   The Harmonization and Unification of the Trade Mark System in the EU

The harmonization and unification of the trademark system represents a successful model for further moves in other IP fields for the EU. The current EU trademark system includes the Trademark Directive harmonizing national laws, and the Trademark Regulation, which established the Community Trademark and the Office for Harmonization in the Internal Market (OHIM).[20] The EU IPR strategy further suggested revising the current trademark regime, in order to streamline and harmonize registration procedures and modernize the existing provisions and increase legal certainty. It committed to amending outdated provisions and removing ambiguities, clarifying trademark rights in terms of their scope and limitations and incorporating extensive case law precedents of the Court of

---

[17]   SIPO, *Management Measures for National Intellectual Property Training Base (tentative)*   (国家知识产权局, 国家知识产权培训基地管理办法(试行)), 15 January 2010.

[18]   European Commission (*supra*, n 2) 6.

[19]   Ibid.

[20]   Regulation 40/94 on the Community trade mark and Directive 89/104 to approximate the laws of the Member States relating to trade marks.

Justice of the EU. The strategy also included a plan to improve the means of fighting against counterfeit goods in transit through the EU[21] and to facilitate cooperation between the Member States' trademark offices and the OHIM in order to promote the convergence of their practices and the development of common tools. For this purpose, on 27 March 2013, the Commission adopted proposals for a revision of the Community Trademark Regulation 207/2009/EC, the Trademark Directive 2008/95/EC and Regulation 2869/95 on fees payable to the OHIM.[22]

3.2 Reform of the Patent System in Europe

Establishing a single European patent has been discussed for decades in the EU. The current European Patent Office, established according to the European Patent Convention in 1977, does not grant EU patents or even Europe-wide patents, but a bundle of national patents. Because of the lack of a patent regime at the EU level, the European patent system has been complex, fragmented and costly. Another problem pertaining to the patent system is lack of a patent dispute regime at the EU level. The national laws in the Member States with respect to patent infringement and revocation vary. Patent holders in the old patent system naturally end up with legal disputes resolved in different national courts. This has resulted in two specific problems. First, it is extremely expensive and time consuming for patent holders. Second, it causes legal uncertainty because the courts in different Member States could make different decisions with respect to the same patent. In dealing with these problems, the IPR strategy proposes a unitary patent and unified court system, and machine translation system.[23]

As a part of the plan implementing the strategy, two Regulations were approved by 25 EU Member States (all Member States except Italy and

---

[21] The proposal is based on the *IP Translator* decision by the Court of Justice (Case C-307/10 *Chartered Institute of Patent Attorneys v. Registrar of Trade Marks* ECLI:EU:C:2012:361), in which it considered not only that the representation of a trademark must be clear and precise, but the goods and services for which protection is sought must also be identified 'with sufficient clarity and precision to enable the competent authorities and economic operators, on that basis alone, to determine the extent of the protection conferred by the trade mark' (para 64).

[22] European Commission, *Proposal for a Regulation of the European Parliament and of the Council Amending Council Regulation (EC) No 207/2009 on the Community Trade Mark* (Brussels, 27 March 2013, COM/2013/0161 Final, 2013/0088 (COD)) <http://eur-lex.europa.eu/LexUriServ/LexUriServ.do?uri=CELEX:52013PC0161:EN:NOT> accessed 3 October 2014.

[23] European Commission (*supra*, n 2) 7–8.

Spain) and the European Parliament in 2012. These measures provided for the creation of a unitary patent in the EU.[24] In February 2013, the Agreement on a Unified Patent Court was signed by 24 Member States and is aimed at establishing a single and specialized patent court.[25]

The Regulation on the unitary patent (UPR) creates a European patent with unitary effect (unitary patent). The unitary patent provides uniform protection throughout the EU and has equal effect in all the participating Member States. The unitary patent provided by the UPR has three characteristics. First, a unitary patent has unitary character and can only be limited, transferred or revoked, or lapse, in respect of all the states in which it has taken effect.[26] A unitary patent can be licensed in respect of the whole or part of the territories of the participating Member States.[27] Second, the unitary patent is a European patent, granted by the European Patent Office (EPO) under the rules and procedures of the European Patent Convention upon request of patent applicants.[28] Third, the unitary patent will co-exist with national patents and with European bundle patents.[29]

The Agreement on a Unified Patent Court deals with significant variations between national court systems. The Agreement creates a specialized patent court with exclusive jurisdiction for litigation relating to European patents and unitary patents for the Member States that are parties to the Agreement.[30] The Member States confer on the Court exclusive competence for cases regarding infringement and revocation proceedings of European patents and European patents with unitary effect valid in the territories of the participating states.[31] The Unified Patent Court comprises a Court of First Instance, a Court of Appeal, an

---

[24]   Council Decision of 10 March 2011 authorising enhanced cooperation in the area of the creation of unitary patent protection (2011/167/EU); Regulation (EU) No 1257/2012 of the European Parliament and of the Council of 12 December 2012 implementing enhanced cooperation in the area of the creation of unitary patent protection; Council Regulation (EU) No 1260/2012 of 17 December 2012 implementing enhanced cooperation in the area of the creation of unitary patent protection with regard to the applicable translation arrangements.

[25]   Agreement on a Unified Patent Court (2013/C 175/01).

[26]   Regulation (EU) No 1257/2012 of the European Parliament and of the Council of 12 December 2012 implementing enhanced cooperation in the area of the creation of unitary patent protection.

[27]   Ibid recital 7 in the preamble.

[28]   Ibid Article 9.

[29]   Ibid recital 26 in the preamble.

[30]   Agreement on a Unified Patent Court (2013/C 175/01).

[31]   Ibid.

Arbitration and Mediation Centre and a common Registry. The Court of First Instance consists of a central division in Paris with sections in London and Munich along with several local and regional divisions, which may be set up in a Contracting Member State upon its request.[32] Cases will be distributed within the central division on the basis of the Sections of the International Patent Classification.[33] The seat of the Court of Appeal is Luxembourg.[34]

Regulation 1260/2012 stipulates the language issues.[35] A European patent application may be filed in any language. If it is not filed in one of the official languages of the EPO, that is English, French or German, a translation in one of these languages has to be filed.[36] In the event of an infringement dispute, a patent holder needs to provide the alleged infringer at his request and choice a full translation of the unitary patent in the language of the state of the alleged infringement taking place or the state of the alleged infringer's domicile. In addition, the competent court may require a full translation of the patent into the language used in the proceedings of that court.[37] The Regulation sets a 6–12-year transition period for high-quality machine translations of patent applications and specifications into all official languages of the Union.[38]

3.3 Creation of a Comprehensive Framework for Copyright in the Digital Single Market[39]

The conflict between the borderless Internet and the fragmented online markets in the EU Member States has caused a barrier to electronic access to copyright-protected works and services across a digital single market. The target of the IPR strategy is to achieve a well-functioning digital single market by 2015. The Commission has taken two parallel tracks of action:

---

[32] Ibid Articles 6 and 7.
[33] Ibid Article 7(2) and Annex II.
[34] Ibid Article 9.
[35] Council Regulation (EU) No 1260/2012 of 17 December 2012 implementing enhanced cooperation in the area of the creation of unitary patent protection with regard to the applicable translation arrangements.
[36] Ibid Articles 3 and 5.
[37] Ibid Article 4.
[38] Ibid Article 6.
[39] The latest commission communication on the digital single market is not discussed here
    (European Commission, A Digital Single Market Strategy for Europe (Brussels, 6 May 2015, COM (2015) 192 final) <http://ec.europa.eu/priorities/digital-single-market/docs/dsm-communication_en.pdf> accessed 1 June 2015.

one is to review and modernize the EU copyright legislative framework and another is to facilitate cross-border licensing under the name of 'Licensing Europe' to realize the target.[40]

The EU IPR strategy proposes a set of plans under the name 'Licensing Europe' which is aimed at delivering effective solutions to address practical barriers to the circulation of content in the digital environment. It is comprised of four parallel work strands.[41] First, the work strand of cross-border access and the portability of services aims to identify the main categories of restrictions on cross-border access and portability and the main reasons behind these restrictions. Then it may provide practical solutions to promote multi-territory access. Second, the work strand of user-generated content intends to find solutions to make the licensing term of user-generated content more transparent. Third, the work strand of the audio-visual sector and cultural heritage institutions aims to introduce smooth, easier and technologically neutral solutions for cross-border and pan-European licensing in the audio-visual sector. Fourth, the work strand of text and data mining (TDM) will assess the demand for TDM access at the EU level for text mining of scientific publications and data for research purposes, and suitable means to meet this demand. Particularly, the Commission will look at the licensing model and technological platform to facilitate TDM access.

In order to implement 'Licensing Europe', the European Commission has already taken a number of actions. Since 2011, the Commission has submitted several proposals to make or revise relevant Directives. These Directives include the so-called Orphan Works Directive[42] and the Collective Management Directive.[43] The Orphan Works Directive is a necessary step in creating a legal framework to facilitate the digitization and dissemination of works and other subject-matter which are protected by copyright or related rights and for which no rights holder is identified or can be located.[44] The Directive intends to provide a common approach

---

[40]   European Commission, *Communication from the Commission on Content in the Digital Single Market* (Brussels, 18 December 2012, COM (2012) 0789 final) <http://eur-lex.europa.eu/legal-content/EN/TXT/HTML/?uri=CELEX:52012DC 0789&from=EN> accessed 1 December 2014.

[41]   Ibid.

[42]   Directive 2012/28/EU of the European Parliament and of the Council of 25 October 2012 on certain permitted uses of orphan works.

[43]   Directive 2014/26/EU of the European Parliament and of the Council of 26 February 2014 on collective management of copyright and related rights and multi-territorial licensing of rights in musical works for online use in the internal market.

[44]   Recital 3 in the preamble to the Orphan Works Directive.

in determining the orphan work status of a work and for permitted uses of orphan works. The Collective Management Directive intends to deal with the variation in the national laws concerning the governance and supervisory framework of collective management organizations (CMOs), in order to ensure a high standard of governance, financial management, transparency and reporting.[45] Rights holders will have the right to choose a CMO to manage their rights or categories of rights or types of works regardless of the territory of establishment of the CMO or the territory of the rights holder's residence.[46] The Directive set rules for multi-territorial licensing of online rights in musical works by CMOs.[47] Moreover, the Directive sets out a number of key measures to improve the governance of CMOs, such as the general assembly of members and supervision of CMOs,[48] rules on improvement of transparency and rules on the collection, use and distribution of rights revenue.[49]

In addition to these legal measures, the Commission also took action to promote a contractually based solution in the form of a Memorandum of Understanding on out-of-print books, access to works by visually impaired people, and support for the development of technological solutions.[50] Moreover, the Commission is developing solutions for author resale rights by contractual measures. In December 2011, the Commission proposed to establish a stakeholder dialogue in order to make recommendations to improve the system of resale right collection and distribution in the EU. On 17 February 2014, representatives of CMOs, authors and art market professionals signed up to 'Key Principles and Recommendations on the management of the Author Resale Right' as part of the plan to improve the administration of the author resale right.[51]

The Commission has carried out a review of the EU copyright framework, which is a part of the strategy with respect to the modernization of EU copyright law. The review specifically addressed 'territoriality in the Internal Market; harmonisation, limitations and exceptions to

---

[45]   Recitals 5, 8 and 9 in the preamble to the Collective Management Directive.
[46]   Ibid Article 5(2).
[47]   Ibid Articles 23–32.
[48]   Ibid Articles 18–21.
[49]   Ibid Articles 9 and 10.
[50]   European Commission, *Green Paper on the Online Distribution of Audiovisual Works in the European Union: Opportunities and Challenges towards a Digital Single Market* (Brussels, 13 July 2011, COM (2011) 427 final) <http://ec.europa.eu/internal_market/consultations/2011/audiovisual_en.htm> accessed 1 December 2014.
[51]   See EC Official website, 'Resale Right – European Commission' <http://ec.europa.eu/internal_market/copyright/resale-right/index_en.htm> accessed 6 December 2014.

copyright in the digital age; fragmentation of the EU copyright market; and how to improve the effectiveness and efficiency of enforcement while underpinning its legitimacy in the wider context of copyright reform'.[52]

3.4 Complementary Protection of IPRs and Enforcement of IPRs

The divergence in protection of trade secrets in Member States inevitably leads to different levels of protection. In November 2013 the European Commission proposed Directives on the protection of undisclosed know-how and business information (trade secrets) against their unlawful acquisition, use and disclosure with the intention to harmonize protection for trade secrets in the Member States. In addition, the Commission has launched a feasibility study that will consider EU-wide protection of geo-graphical indications for non-agricultural products.

In order to improve the fight against counterfeiting and piracy, the European Observatory on Counterfeiting and Piracy was restructured as the European Observatory on Infringements of Intellectual Property Rights under the OHIM.[53] The OHIM is assigned more responsibility on the enforcement of IP. The strategy suggested that the OHIM will also improve day-to-day cooperation between enforcement authorities and cooperation with private stakeholders, *inter alia* by building a new electronic information exchange and an early warning system on counterfeit and pirated products.

With the aim of enhancing enforcement and streamlining procedures, the new Regulation 5129/2013/EC replacing the Counterfeiting Goods Regulation 1383/2003 was passed and came into effect in the EU on 1 January 2014. It extends customs measures to cover a larger number of IP rights than under Regulation 1383/2003 and facilitates the destruction of small consignments of goods. In addition, the Commission intends to review the IPR Enforcement Directive 2004/48/EC to identify ways to

---

[52]   European Commission (*supra*, n 40) 5. The Commission had conducted a public consultation on the review of the EU copyright during December 2013 and February 2014. See European Commission, Report on the responses to the Public Consultation on the Review of the EU Copyright Rules (July 2014) <http://ec.europa.eu/internal_market/consultations/2013/copyright-rules/docs/contribu tions/consultation-report_en.pdf> accessed 1 June 2015).

[53]   In September 2008 the Council adopted a Resolution on a comprehensive EU anti-counterfeiting and anti-piracy plan. This Resolution endorsed the need to step up the fight against fake goods and called for the creation of a European Observatory on Counterfeiting and Piracy.

create a framework allowing, in particular, more effective combating of infringements of IPR via the Internet.

4. THE ACHIEVEMENTS AND DEFICIENCIES IN IMPLEMENTING THE IPR STRATEGIES

4.1 Chinese Perspective

The most important achievement of the China IPR Strategy is the fact that it has changed the perception of IPRs in China, especially in the government. The current IP system in China was transplanted largely from Europe at the beginning of the 1980s under foreign pressures. IPRs used to be considered as detrimental to its technological development in some governmental departments and among the public. Nonetheless, the publishing and implementing of the national IPR Strategy reached a milestone in the development of the IPR system in China. The process of developing IP law under external pressures is now transforming into a process based on internal demand and planning. IPRs are viewed to have a positive impact on the nation's development. The change of perception of IPRs has led to a change of policy, which is essential to improving IP protection in China.

Economic growth has been the top priority in China's national policy. The governments at all levels have aimed largely at economic growth. The making and implementing of China's IPR Strategy imply that the policy on IPRs is being changed and it has been emphasized that economic development should be driven by innovation. Thus, this policy change may imply that more resources will be allocated to the protection of IPRs. Consequently it enables other measures promoting IP protection to be implemented more smoothly. For example, the establishment of an IP court was discussed for many years and such a court was only established successfully in the context of the implementation of the IPR Strategy. The revision of IP law also became a priority on the agenda of the National People's Congress, in order to ensure that the Patent Amendment and Trademark Amendment, which introduced enhanced enforcement measures, could be passed very quickly.

The implementation of China's IPR Strategy also comes with deficiencies. First, administrative interventions rather than IP legal mechanisms have played a central role in promoting the number of IPRs and cracking down on counterfeiting and piracy. With respect to the method of implementing the IPR Strategy, the government has been playing a central role. However, many measures taken by Chinese authorities do create some positive effects. For example, by 2013, four patents were granted per 10,000 inhabitants, a figure which is beyond the pre-set target of 3.3 patents per 10,000 inhabitants.[54] Trademark applications reached 1.88 million in 2013. Average processing time for a trademark application has dropped to ten months. Geographical indications (GIs) showed increases as well, with 2,190 GIs registered by 2013 in total in China. China also has made steps towards its goal of increasing the reach of Chinese companies abroad. In 2013, China was the sixth biggest filer under the Madrid Protocol, with 2273 applications filed internationally.[55] To a certain extent, government intervention is even necessary for such a country where there is no IPR tradition historically to provide effective protection for IPRs. However, these achievements are largely a result of governmental stimulus measures and direct financial input, and have little to do with the improvement of the IP legal system. Several ministries jointly undertook special stimulus measures to help to achieve the targets in the IPR Strategy. For example, the Ministry of Finance made 'Management Measures for Special Funds to Subsidize Patent Applications Abroad' to subsidize Chinese applicants to file patent application through the Patent Cooperation Treaty (PCT) and Paris Convention.[56] SIPO put forward 'Opinions about IPR Support the Development of Small and Micro Enterprises'.[57] In 2009, RMB 52.85 million funding was allocated to SMEs, public institutions and research institutes to support their 1146 PCT applications. The government provides great support for the export of patent products and use of the country's tax and financial policies to encourage patent filing and commercialization.

Government intervention usually comes with many numerical targets as a benchmark to assess the performance of the measures.[58]

---

[54]   'Scientific Management: Establishing Foundation and Ensuring Development (科学管理：奠定基础　保障发展)' <http://www.nipso.cn/onews.asp?id=21513> accessed 11 December 2014.

[55]   'Interpretation to 2014 National Intellectual Property Strategy Promotion Plan (2) (2014年国家知识产权战略实施推进计划》解读（二）)' <http://www.nipso.cn/onews.asp?id=21208> accessed 11 December 2014.

[56]   Ministry of Finance, *Management Measures for Special Funds to Subsidize Patent Applications Abroad* (财政部关于印发《资助向国外申请专利专项资金管理办法》的通知，财建[2012]147号) 14 April 2012.

[57]   SIPO, *Opinions about IPR Support the Development of Small and Micro Enterprises* (国家知识产权局关于知识产权支持小微企业发展的若干意见，国知发管字〔2014〕57号) 11 October 2014.

[58]   'Legal protection: Take Measures to Provide Support (依法保护：多措并举提供支撑)' <http://www.nipso.cn/onews.asp?id=21514> accessed 11 December 2014.

Correspondingly, the lower government departments provide numerical results when they are reporting their achievements in implementing the IPR Strategy. SIPO, the Trademark Office and other departments that are in charge of a specific IPR always demonstrate the number of IPRs and how the volume of them has increased based on the previous year as an achievement. Even improvements in the enforcement of IPRs are also demonstrated by numbers. For example, the State Administration for Industry and Commerce (SAIC) demonstrated that it had investigated infringement cases and counterfeiting cases totalling 83,100 at an amount of RMB 1.121 billion.[59] It is still concerned that these stimulus measures may only contribute to an increase in the volume of numbers of patents and trademarks rather than to stimulating innovation and exploration of technology.

The strong governmental intervention model has also led to another problem. The implementation of the strategy through a hierarchal governmental system comes with a weakening effect. Namely, the strength and effect of many measures taken or proposed by the central government may decline as the level of government intervention decreases. At the lower level of governments, many measures may not have been implemented as were proposed and many measures may end up with only some beautiful slogans. China's IPR Strategy is a national strategy. The governments at all levels have been active in promoting innovation and IPR protection. However, the developmental level in different regions varies significantly. The IPR Strategy may not fit the economic and social conditions of many regions. The law and policy in promoting IPR protection may be applied and implemented differently. This may cause some difficulty in enforcing IP law and IP policies. It even may leave more space for the counterfeiting and pirating industry to survive.

Another deficiency concerns the enforcement of IP law. To facilitate the protection of IPRs, by revising IP law, the burden of proof for IPR holders has been reduced and the damages in IPR infringement cases have been raised. However, the difficulty in enforcing IP law in China results from complicated factors. By revising IP law alone, the effect will be very limited. If China cannot successfully improve its entire environment of legal operation, revising IP law alone will not do much to help solve the counterfeiting and piracy problems. The governmental departments have

---

[59]   Xiaomao Wei, Di Zhang and Shimeng Zhao, *Interpretation: 2014 National Strategic Plan to promote the implementation of intellectual property rights* (1) (魏小毛, 张娣, 赵世猛, '解读: 2014年国家知识产权战略实施推进计划(一)') <http://www.sipo.gov.cn/zcfg/zcjd/201405/t20140507_945993.html> accessed 5 January 2015.

jointly launched an annual campaign against infringement of IPRs. As to the effect of this special campaign against infringement, it is doubtful whether the campaign will offer concrete solutions and solve IPR protection problems in the long term, or whether it will only provide short-term results. IP law and the market should create a sustainable and reliable mechanism to stimulate the acquisition and exploration of IPRs and accordingly this shows that the current Chinese IP legal reform has been insufficient in providing such mechanisms so far.

4.2   EU Perspective

The main focus of the EU IPR strategy is to reduce the disparity in Member States' national IP law. The long-term goal is to create a unitary IP regime for the whole EU. The EU IPR strategy is only one step in achieving such a target. The harmonization and unification in trademark laws has been regarded as a successful model. Directive 89/104 was passed in 1989, with the attention of approximating the trademark laws, which has most directly affected the functioning of the Common Market. In the field of patents, the Commission proposed a Directive to harmonize the legislation of the Member States as regards the utility models at the Community level. The Commission also put forward a proposal for a Directive on the patentability of computer-implemented inventions to harmonize and clarify national patent law in this field. However, these efforts in the patent field were unsuccessful. In the field of designs, rights in registered designs have been harmonized Community wide from 1998, when Directive 98/71 was adopted. In the field of copyright, the first major step was to apply a common standard for the copyright protection of computer programs, enacted in the Computer Programs Directive in 1991. After that, several Directives have been adopted that cover the subject matter, scope, limitations, CMOs, term and enforcement of copyright and related rights.

Through a steady expansion of the harmonization of trademark law, copyright law and design law, the disparity in these fields has been reduced in the Member States. Although much progress has been made, Directives do not provide an adequate basis for completing the single market. Due to the territoriality of IPRs, the scope of protection of an IPR is limited to the territory of the state where the right is granted and the EU IP system cannot be established merely by the harmonization of national legislation. Even if complete harmonization were achieved, the realization of the Common Market would not be possible without a substantial unification of national laws.

The unification of trademark laws was another successful model again. Council Regulation 40/90 on the Community Trademark, which was adopted in 1993, created a Community Trademark with a single filing for a registration covering the whole EU. It enables a Community Trademark holder to benefit from a single set of rules of protection across the EU territory. The substantive provisions are almost the same as those in the Trademark Directive. The Community design was introduced with Regulation 6/2002. In 1992, Regulation 2081/92 on the protection of geographical indications and designations of origin for agricultural products and foodstuffs was adopted and in 1994 the Community adopted Regulation 2100/94 on Community plant variety rights. In August 2000, a Proposal for a Council Regulation on the Community Patent was introduced. However the Council meeting in March 2004 failed to reach an agreement on the proposed Community Patent. After decades of efforts in the patent field, the unitary patent system is one crucial step closer to its goal. The unitary patent and unified patent court system are a very significant step in the unification of IP law in the EU.

Even though copyright does not require registration to attain protection, the territoriality of copyright has been a main obstacle to the creation of a single digital market.[60] The measures on the harmonization of copyright law have not done enough to realize its original plan set in the IPR strategy. The Orphan Works Directive only applies to 'publicly accessible libraries, educational establishments and museums, as well as by archives, film or audio heritage institutions and public-service broadcasting organisations'.[61] The Collective Management Directive is a big step towards good governance of the CMOs and facilitates cross-border licensing in the EU. However, it is also concerning that the Directive may not simplify multi-territorial licensing because it may not be able to avoid the fragmentation of repertoires and lacks incentive for major rights holders to refrain from removing repertoires from CMOs.

The IPR strategy does not solve all the problems it highlighted and could create a lot more new problems. The harmonization of copyrights sometimes may even make Member States' copyright regimes more complex. One example is the new orphan works regulation in Hungary where there has been a pre-existing regulation to settle orphan works issues. To transfer the Orphan Works Directives into Hungary, the country has to introduce a dual model: the licensing model (for the benefit of every user), and the limitation model (for the benefit of specific

---

[60]   P Bernt Hugenholtz, 'Harmonisation or Unification of European Union Copyright Law' (2012) 38 Monash University Law Review 4, 8–9.
[61]   The Orphan Works Directive (*supra*, n 2).

institutions).[62] The unitary patent and unified patent court system have raised concerns with many stakeholders. Most alarmingly, the unitary patent would be a third layer to the current European and national patents. This three-layer patent system may create an opportunity for yet more abusive legal behaviour practised by some firms. For instance, a firm could file for a national patent on minor improvements to an invention, made by itself or by another firm, that has already been granted a unitary patent. Moreover, the extra layer could lead to a greater amount of litigation in parallel, which would hold back small technology firms and universities even more. Another concern is that the unified patent litigation system may facilitate the operation of patent 'trolls' in Europe because the system could make it too easy for patent 'trolls' to threaten pan-European injunctions or extract unreasonable royalties from a European firm. The IP strategy should not only consider how to push forward the harmonization and unification of IP law, but also take measures to handle the unforeseen effects that have come with the harmonization and unification process so far.

5. BRIEF REMARKS

There are significant differences between the strategies and legal reforms of the EU and China. The EU's approach is to realize its political purpose through legal means, but China's approach is to improve its IP legal system and performance through political means. The operation of a common market is the priority of the European Commission. The implementation of the EU IPR strategy is carried out through legislation, agreements and consultation. Based on Articles 118 and 288 of the Treaty on the Functioning of the European Union, making Regulations and Directives to promote the harmonization and unification of IP law in Member States has been an effective way to improve the common market. In China, for historical and cultural reasons, the development of the IP legal system and the implementation of IP rules often encounter difficulties. By political methods implemented through the hierarchal administrative system, the central government may motivate more resources and push the lower-level bodies to improve the protection of IPRs.

The focuses of the EU and China IPR strategies are quite different as well. China and the EU are at different stages in their development in

---

[62]   Peter Mezei, 'The New Orphan Works Regulation of Hungary' (2014) 45 IIC-International Review of Intellectual Property and Competition Law 940, 941.

terms of their IP systems. Since IPR is a driver for innovation and creativity in the EU, many of Europe's industries and sectors rely on the effective protection of IPRs. The fragmentation of the IPRs landscape in the EU has implications for Europe's growth, job creation and competitiveness. Against this background, the EU strategy is to remove the obstacles to the common market to release potential in terms of innovation and creation, therefore keeping the lead in the IP economy in the world. In this context, the EU's IPR strategy aims to promote the operation of a common market while dealing with some issues brought about by the development of new technology, especially digital technology. The scenario in China is quite different from that in the EU. First, IPR is playing a marginal role in the Chinese economy. China's rapid development has been relying on the high consumption of energy, low labour costs, and low-end assembly or manufacturing. Although this is necessary at a specific stage to support development, such a development pattern cannot be sustained with increasing labour costs and competition from other emerging economies whose development also takes advantage of labour supplies. The Chinese IPR Strategy was made based on the acknowledgement that IPR is becoming a strategic resource for state development. IP and innovation are the core element of international competiveness. Obviously, the China IPR Strategy is aimed at progressing the development and the exploitation of IPR in China to the level in the EU and other innovative countries. There is a growing expectation that IPR will play increasing importance in China's future economy. To make this happen is one of the main targets of the Chinese strategy. The China IPR Strategy has stimulated the revision of IP laws creating rules in dealing with its own practical problems and fulfilling the demands of domestic innovation. This may raise a new concern as to whether China will be developing its IP norms in divergence from international standards.

The implementation of the IPR strategies has also highlighted the direction for China and the EU to cooperate on IPR in the future. The EU IPR strategy suggested promoting protection and enforcement of IPR in the context of the World Intellectual Property Organization, the WTO and the International Union for the Protection of New Varieties of Plants (UPOV) aimed at a global level. The EU IP strategy also proposed active customs cooperation with both source countries and other consuming countries by means of specific initiatives such as the EU-China Action Plan on customs cooperation on IPR enforcement. The enforcement of IPR will become the focus of China and the EU. In addition, in dealing with many new problems emerging with new technologies, such as copyright protection in the digital environment and software patents, it is very important to learn from other countries' practice and experiences.

PART III

Governance of practices and IP enforcement

11. China's CMC system and its problems from the Copyright Law of 1990 to its third amendment

Weiguang Wu

1. INTRODUCTION

Since the coming into effect of the Regulation on the Collective Administration of Copyright (RCAC) in 2005, a system of collective management for copyright and related rights (CMC) has been formally established and implemented in China. Subsequently, several collective rights management organizations (CMOs) have been set up and collect levies according to the RCAC and their own by-laws. However, China's CMC system has seriously concerned academics and industries in recent years.[1] These concerns have mainly focused on the following four issues: first, whether a CMC system is indispensable to China, especially in the information society; second, whether non-profit organizations should be the only permitted CMOs in China; third, whether the statutory monopoly on blanket licences by CMOs has ruined the ability of copyright holders to differentiate the price of their works, which results in the loss of bargaining power as holders of private rights; and fourth, whether, in the era of globalization and the information society, China's CMC system should be reformed in accordance with international developments and the requirements of modern, innovative business models.

This chapter observes that China's statutory monopoly and non-profit CMC system has been heavily influenced by Western developed countries. It argues that this kind of CMC system has jeopardized the essence of copyright as a private right, impairing the fundamental rules of a market economy and stifling innovative business models. It is expected that the Chinese CMC system will be reformed in the third amendment of the Copyright Law that is

---

[1] 'Draft copyright law enrages China's music industry' (China Daily, 12 April 2012) <http://www.chinadaily.com.cn/china/2012-04/12/content_15027035.htm> accessed 5 June 2015.

underway now and a more competitive and open system for both non-profit and for-profit organizations is expected to be adopted.

This chapter consists of four sections (in addition to this introduction). In Section 2, I discuss the definitions and different types and functions of CMC organizations. In Section 3, I give a brief overview of China's CMC system and its process of development. In Section 4, I analyse the defects of China's CMC system and its possible changes in the forthcoming third amendment of the Copyright Law. Finally, in Section 5, I conclude that a competitive and market-oriented CMC system in China should be adopted.

2. CMC AND CMOs IN CHINA

2.1 Definitions and Features

The RCAC defines a CMC system as consisting of the following activities carried out by CMOs

> in their respective own names upon authorization by the obligees, so as to exercise the obligees' relevant rights in a centralized way: (1) Concluding license contracts concerning copyright or a copyright-related right with users (herein-after referred to as the license contract); (2) Charging royalties from the user; (3) Transferring royalties to the obligee; and (4) Participating in litigation or arbitration, etc. involving copyright or a copyright-related right.[2]

In many developed countries, CMOs may be either for-profit or not-for-profit. In China, however, CMOs are mandatorily not-for-profit. Similar to the concept of CMOs, there are some other types of organizations that help copyright holders to deal with licensing, collection of and/or calculation of royalties, such as collecting societies or rights clearance organizations. However, as American scholar Glynn Lunney points out:

> With a copyright collective, the pricing and licensing terms for the portfolio of copyrights licensed to the collective are set by the collective to maximize the revenue of the portfolio as whole . . . In contrast, under the collecting society model, pricing and licensing terms are set by the individual copyright owners. The collecting society does not set those terms itself; it merely enforces, and collects the licensing fees due, given the licensing terms set by the individual copyright owners for the use as issue.[3]

---

[2]   Regulation on the Collective Administration of Copyright, art. 2.
[3]   Glynn Lunney, 'Copyright Collectives and Collecting Societies: The United States Experience' in Daniel Gervais (ed), *Collective Management of Copyright and Related Rights* (Kluwer Law International 2006) 311.

Under the RCAC, China's CMOs have four features that distinguish them from collecting societies:

(1) *Non-profit organizations.* According to the RCAC, China's CMOs shall be non-profit organizations that are structured and registered in the Ministry of Civil Affairs instead of with the Administrations for Industry and Commerce.[4] The requirement of non-profit organizations not only excludes enterprises from the CMC business but also subjects the CMOs to the approval and supervision of the National Copyright Office.[5]

(2) *Statutory monopoly.* According to the RCAC, China's CMOs have a statutory monopoly over specific types of works or specific uses of types of works.[6] Whether the statutory monopoly requirement is reasonable for a market of China's scale is a question among academic circles, as well as within the industry; especially, with the assistance of digital technology, some similar CMOs have emerged and challenged the monopoly of legitimate CMOs, such as various collecting societies.

(3) *Trust.* China's CMOs are trust organizations for copyright holders. Therefore, as trustees, CMOs can exercise the rights to the works included in the trust in their own name.[7] According to the organization of trusts, CMOs have quite a degree of independence and discretion in managing their business. This independence and discretion results in a tension regarding the supervision between CMOs, as trustees, and copyright holders, as beneficiaries.

(4) *The widespread adoption of blanket licences.* Neither the Copyright Law, nor the RCAC mandates the use of blanket licences in China. Nonetheless, they are widely adopted by CMOs because they are more efficient due to low bargaining and administration costs. Blanket licences have given rise to a number of problems resulting from the development of digital technology, such as the fact that an increasing share of copyright holders now ask for pricing transparency. As with the technological possibility to differentiate pricing based on individual usages of works, there are also concerns about fairness surrounding the use of blanket licences.

---

[4] Regulation on the Collective Administration of Copyright of China, art. 3.
[5] Regulation on Registration and Administration of Social Organizations, art. 3.
[6] Regulation on the Collective Administration of Copyright of China, arts. 6–7.
[7] Regulation on the Collective Administration of Copyright of China, art. 2.

2.2 Functions of CMOs

What are the main functions of CMOs? The answer seems quite clear: to reduce the transaction costs of copyright licensing that may hinder market efficacy between copyright holders and users. Therefore, whenever copyrighted works cannot be marketed directly and efficiently by copyright holders, they may be better managed by CMOs.[8]

The CMC system functions to reduce transaction costs in three different ways. First, the CMC system can reduce the cost of searching for information through the concentration of works and copyrights. As opposed to tangible goods, whose physical possessors are presumed to be the owners, the rights associated with copyrighted works are legally created without a physical nexus between the right holders and their works. Therefore, it is sometimes quite difficult to search for and contact copyright holders of individual works, such as a musical composition or a sound recording. As rights are managed collectively and traded as a portfolio, the CMO model increases the ability to distribute the profits accruing from the utilisation of copyrighted works among the right holders.

Second, for small works, such as musical or literary works, the cost of bargaining is quite high if one licenses the works individually. Therefore, blanket licences for collective works as a portfolio are widely used by CMOs. This was illustrated by the United States Supreme Court in *BMI v. CBS*:

> As we have already indicated, ASCAP [the CMO] and the blanket license developed together out of the practical situation in the marketplace: thousands of users, thousands of copyright owners, and millions of compositions. . . . Individual sales transactions in this industry are quite expensive, as would be individual monitoring and enforcement, especially in light of the resources of single composers.[9]

Third, CMC systems can reduce the costs of enforcement and management of licences sharply. Collective management and licensing of a large amount of works by professional staff reduces the cost of managing an individual work and is also beneficial for non-experienced copyright holders. For instance, in China it is almost impossible for individual copyright holders to collect royalties from karaoke entertainment enterprises (KOEEs) directly one by one, because of the high cost and the difficulty of bargaining with the thousands of KOEEs in China.

---

[8]   Regulation on the Collective Administration of Copyright of China, art. 4.
[9]   *Broadcast Music, Inc. v. CBS, Inc.*, 441 U.S. 1 (1979).

The advantages of the CMC system seem quite obvious, and justify the adoption of a CMC system that legitimizes the existence of CMOs. However, the question is why non-profit CMOs with a statutory monopoly, excluding (for-profit) enterprises, are the only option in China because, according to Coase's theory, transaction costs exist within all business transactions no matter what products are involved, and the function of enterprises is to reduce those transaction costs.[10]

In China, because the concept of CMOs does not include collecting societies, it appears that the enterprises in the market are not prohibited from running a business as a collecting society. The question is, however, whether enterprises acting as collecting societies have to initially acquire licences from an upstream CMO, or whether a collecting society can obtain licences directly from the copyright holders and compete with CMOs to some extent. If the answer is the former, it seems that collecting societies have no need and space to exist in the market because their function and advantages could be substituted by collecting societies. But if the answer is the latter, then the statutory monopoly privilege of CMOs would be ruined because collecting societies compete with them. In practice, the National Copyright Office has issued an administrative order to prohibit businesses similar to collecting societies in Nan Jing.[11] Therefore, the concerns and debate around the CMC in China are not only theoretical, but also practical. Before discussing these questions, one needs to be aware of the history of CMC in China. As economist Douglass North stated:

> History matters. It matters not just because we can learn from the past, but because the present and the future are connected to the past by the continuity of a society's institutions. Today's and tomorrow's choices are shaped by the past. And the past can only be made intelligible as a story of institutional evolution.[12]

---

[10]   See R.H. Coase, *The Firm, the Market and the Law* (University of Chicago Press 1988).

[11]   Guo Quan Ban, 'Notice of prohibition of CMC Activities Without Permission of National Copyright Office' (2005, no. 49) <http://www.ncac.gov.cn/chinacopyright/contents/483/17636.html> accessed 7 November 2014: 'Recently, National Copyright Office got information through public media that Beijing YinDeLi International Music Limited Company is collecting copyright royalties from KARA OK enterprises by the authorization of overseas music copyright holders. According to CMCR, YinDeLi's business is kind of CMC, which can only be operated by permitted organizations. Therefore, YinDeLi's business is illegal and shall be prohibited.'

[12]   Douglass C. North, *Institutions, Institutional Change and Economic Performance* vii (Cambridge University Press 1990).

3.   THE DEVELOPMENT OF CHINA'S CMC SYSTEM

3.1   The History and Status Quo of China's CMC System

The first copyright law of the People's Republic of China was promulgated in 1990, 41 years after the foundation of the state and 11 years after the reform and open policy. At that moment, China was not yet a contracting party to the Berne Convention. The Copyright Law of 1990 was considered quite a speculative legislative instrument for the attraction of foreign technologies and investments. Therefore, the law was quite preliminary and basic, without any specific provisions relating to a CMC system. In addition to the Copyright Law of 1990, the State Council issued the Regulation for the Implementation of the Copyright Law of 1991. This regulation clarified that copyrights could be collectively managed.[13] However, the provisions on CMC were very general and ambiguous, without any detailed requirements on what kind of CMC system should be set up and how to operate CMOs. During the following ten years, only one CMO was established, which was the Music Copyright Society of China, established in 1992.

The Copyright Law of China of 2001 was considered a huge improvement for China's copyright system because the purpose of the amendment was to achieve membership of the World Trade Organization (WTO). Shaped by the Agreement on Trade-Related Aspects of Intellectual Property Rights (TRIPs), the Copyright Law of 2001 ensured that international standards and requirements were met in China. The speculative objective of the Copyright Law 2001, to facilitate accession to the WTO, was quite obvious. For instance, the proposal submitted by the Copyright Office to the State Council, for a vote in the People's Congress, did not contain any article that touched on copyright issues concerning the Internet because TRIPs did not contain anything related to the Internet. The State Council, however, returned the proposal to the Copyright Office and requested the inclusion of specific articles on copyright issues related to the Internet. The new proposal containing Internet-related articles was hastily drafted by the State Copyright Office and eventually was enacted as the Copyright Law of 2001.

The Copyright Law of 2001 formally made provision for a CMC system to form part of copyright law in China. The establishment of a CMC system and its supervision became the statutory obligation of the National

---

[13]   Regulations for the Implementation of the Copyright Law of 1991, art. 54.

Copyright Office.[14] Subsequently, in 2004, the RCAC was promulgated by the State Council according to the requirements of the Copyright Law of 2001 and came into effect in 2005. In addition to the Copyright Law of 2001, the RCAC is the primary legal source governing the regulation of the CMC system. As a result of a WTO panel decision, China was required to review the implications of Article 4 of the Copyright Law of 2001 and subsequently, in 2010, an amendment to the Copyright Law was passed. The amendment resulted in article 4 being replaced and the result of these changes being implemented by the current Copyright Law of 2010.[15] The RCAC was also slightly adjusted in order to reflect changes to article numbering from the Copyright Law of 2001.

Since the RCAC has come into effect, the CMC system and CMOs have developed quickly in China. In addition to the legislative underpinnings of the RCAC, this development can also be attributed as a response to the needs of the copyright market. At this point in time five CMOs have been established in China. They are the Music Copyright Society of China (MCSC), established in 1992;[16] the China Audio-Video Copyright Association (CAVCA), founded in 2005;[17] the China Written Works Copyright Society (CWWCS), founded in 2008;[18] the Images Copyright

---

[14]   Copyright Law of 2001, art. 8.
[15]   Copyright Law of 2001, art. 4: 'Works whose publication or dissemination is prohibited by law shall not be protected by this law. Copyright owners, in exercising their copyright, shall not violate the Constitution or laws or infringe upon the public interests.' Copyright Law of 2010, art. 4: 'Copyright owners, in exercising their copyright, shall not violate the Constitution or laws or infringe upon the public interests. The state shall supervise and administer the publication and circulation of works in accordance with the law.'
[16]   MCSC, which was established in 17 December 1992, is a non-profit social organization with the status of a legal person in whose name the Chinese music copyright owners exercise their rights by way of collective administration (<http://www.mcsc.com.cn/Introduction.php?partid=28> accessed 7 November 2014).
[17]   As the only collective management organization in the field of audio-visual works in China, which was approved by the National Copyright Administration of China and was registered with the Ministry of Civil Affairs, China Audio-Video Copyright Association collectively manages the copyright and related rights of audio-visual programs according to the law (<http://www.cavca.org/enindex. php> accessed 7 November 2014).
[18]   China Written Works Copyright Society (CWWCS), which was founded on 24 October 2008, is the sole copyright collective management organization in the field of written works. It is a non-profit organization approved by the National Copyright Administration of the People's Republic of China (NCAC) and Ministry of Civil Affairs of the People's Republic of China (MCA). The NCAC has awarded the 'Collective Management of Copyright License' to CWWCS already

Society of China (ICSC), established in 2008;[19] and the China Film Copyright Association (CFCA), founded in 2009.[20] It may be noted that most of the CMOs were founded in the initial ten-year period following Chinese accession to the WTO in 2001. As opposed to CMOs in European and other Western countries, which were created and structured in the early period of the last century, China's CMOs have emerged in the era of the information society and globalization of the 21st century. It is apparent that China should take advantage of this temporal deviation in order to adapt socio-economic and technological advances into its CMC system.

Evidently, China's CMC system is almost an imitation of the European CMC systems that emerged more than half a century ago. However, due to history, European countries are now having problems in adapting their traditional CMC systems to meet the requirements of the information society. As scholar Jorg Reinbothe observes:

> In countries without a particular history and tradition of collective rights management, these issues may raise no particular problems. They do so, however, in most Member States of the European Union, including and in particular Germany, with a long and successful tradition of collective rights management and its comprehensive legal framework, the LACNR.[21]

3.2   The Debates on the CMC System in China

Since the establishment of a CMC system and CMOs in China, the debates surrounding them have continued. Hot issues include the mandatory requirement of non-profit organizations, the statutory monopoly of CMOs, the rate of levies charged by CMOs, the legal authority of CMOs to manage copyrights and whether to adopt extended collective licensing. Among these, two very prominent debates occurred in the last decade. The first concerned the collection of levies by CMOs from KOEEs. The second debate focused on the effort to adopt measures for extended collective licensing in the third amendment to the Copyright Law.

(<http://www.prccopyright.org.cn/staticnews/2010-03-31/100331104501923/1.html> accessed 7 November 2014).

[19]   <http://www.cpanet.cn/templets/default/zhuzuoquan/about.html> accessed 7 November 2014.

[20]   <http://www.cfca-c.org> accessed 7 November 2014.

[21]   Jorg Reinbothe, 'Collective Rights Management in Germany' in Daniel Gervais (ed), *Collective Management of Copyright and Related Rights* (Kluwer Law International 2006) 225.

3.2.1 The CMC system and KOEEs

In 2006, the National Copyright Office authorized the relevant CMOs to undertake the collection of levies from KOEEs.[22] This event triggered a heated argument among CMOs and KOEEs about whether the CMOs had full legal authority to collect levies. Arguments and debates similar to those that occurred between the KOEEs and CMOs are quite rare in China's copyright law history because China is still a rather rigid and controlled society: both enterprises and citizens have strongly obedient characteristics. Superficially, it seems that the debates of the KOEEs and the CMOs occurred between two legally equal entities in the market, since one side consisted of enterprises that used copyright-protected works and the other side was made up of the MCSC and CAVCA non-profit organizations.[23] However, substantively it was a conflict between the KOEEs and the National Copyright Office because the levy collection and CMOs were supported and supervised by the National Copyright Office

The arguments between the KOEEs and the CMOs focused on the following controversial issues:

(1) whether the rate of levies imposed by the National Copyright Office was reasonable; how the rate was calculated;

(2) whether MCSC and especially CAVCA, since their establishment had not yet been finalized, had legitimate authority to collect levies from KOEEs;

(3) whether MCSC and CAVCA should show KOEEs the licences they had obtained from authors before collecting levies for these authors' works from KOEEs;

(4) whether KOEEs could directly get licences from authors and (other) right holders such as the four big music labels, circumventing MCSC and CAVCA;

---

[22] National Copyright Office No.1 Announcement of 2006: 'The reference point of Levy shall be paid by Karaoke entertainment enterprises to MCSC and CAVAC (on the establishment) is CNY 12 Yuan per box per day (including levies for music works and MTV works). The rate can be reduced according to the different developing levels of regions in the nation or different scales and levels of Kara Ok entertainment enterprises in the same regions.' (<http://www.ncac.gov.cn/chinacopyright/contents/483/17678.html> accessed 7 November 2014.)

[23] Works used by KOEEs relate to two copyrights, one is the right of performance for music works, collectively managed by MCSC; the other is the right of projection for cinematographic works and works created in a way similar to cinematography (MTV), collectively managed by CAVCA.

(5) whether KOEEs could be immunized from infringement allegations from authors who had not yet joined MCSC or CAVCA if they had submitted levies;
(6) whether the levies collected by MCSC and CAVCA if KOEEs consent to submit were fairly distributed to authors and how; and
(7) whether CAVCA could cooperate with a for-profit state-related enterprise that shares a portion of the levies from CAVCA in collecting levies from KOEEs.

The first question was quite difficult to answer because the appropriate price of commercial goods can only be discovered through the process of bargaining in the market. How the rate of levies should be determined by CMOs is a hard question everywhere. Even though, according to the National Copyright Office, CNY 12 Yuan per room per day was just a reference point,[24] MCSC and CAVCA simply took CNY 12 Yuan as the rate of levies to collect from the KOEEs in Beijing and Guangdong. During the argument between the KOEEs, MCSC and CAVCA, some KOEEs argued that the reasonable rate should be CNY 1 Yuan per room per day because CNY 12 Yuan was irrational and baseless. The argument forwarded by the CMOs and the National Copyright Office was that, in comparison to Japan, Hong Kong and Taiwan, CNY 12 Yuan was reasonable even though they could not give an exact basis of calculation for it. The result was that the territory of China was roughly categorized into several regions according to their economic development levels, and that the rate of levies was adjusted accordingly for the different regions, ranging from CNY 8 to CNY 11 Yuan.[25]

As regards the second to the fifth questions, the KOEEs argued that MCSC and CAVCA should show legal documents that they were trusted by the copyright holders to collect levies from them.[26] But because getting authorizations from copyright holders took a long time, CAVCA had not yet finished its registration as a civil organization at that moment and many copyright holders were still hesitant to join CMOs. CAVCA therefore could not show authorizations from a considerable number of copyright holders to the KOEEs during its first two years. However, in order to solve this problem and collect levies from KOEEs, CAVCA promised the KOEEs that if they paid levies, they would be immunized from

---

[24] See supra n. 22.
[25] The rates for Karaoke industry levies on different provinces are available at <http://www.cavca.org/syzzq.php>.
[26] Since January 2007 MCSC has delegated its right to collect levies from KOEEs to CAVCA.

infringement allegations from non-CAVCA member copyright holders through the negotiation of CAVCA.[27] Due to both pressure asserted and promises made, most of the KOEEs gave in to CAVCA and began to submit levies.[28] Today, CAVCA claims that it has been authorized by 90 per cent of the copyright holders within its domain of activities.[29] Obviously, the difficulties CMOs met when they sought authorization by copyright holders while collecting levies from the KOEEs stimulated their lobbying efforts for the inclusion of extended collective licensing to be included in the third amendment of the Copyright Law.[30]

Finally, with regard to questions six and seven, a very controversial issue is whether CAVCA can cooperate with a commercial company to collect levies from KOEEs because the commercial company will reserve more than a quarter of the levy amount collected from the KOEEs as compensation for its cost and effort in collecting. Perhaps this is due to the fact that CAVCA, as a new CMO and non-profit entity, experiences a lack of resources that hinders its ability to collect levies directly from all KOEEs in a country as large as China. From the beginning, CAVCA has cooperated with a company named Tian He Culture Corporation Ltd to collect levies from KOEEs.[31] Tian He took over many tasks that CAVCA could not do, such as contacting, negotiating and collecting levies from the KOEEs. The payment to Tian He is 27 per cent of the amount of levies it collects for CAVCA. The cooperation triggered serious concerns and debates within the industry and academic circles. The debate around this cooperation is whether it is legal or not for CAVCA, as a non-profit organization, to cooperate with a for-profit corporation to collect levies, and whether it is fair for both the copyright holders and KOEEs that Tian He and CAVCA take 50 per cent of the levies together. If CAVCA is allowed to cooperate with a corporation to

---

[27] Some courts have refused to award damages to non-membership copyright holders when suing KOEEs for copyright infringement on the ground that the KOEEs in question had paid levies to CAVCA, and it could not be forced to pay twice. The courts suggested non-membership copyright holders claim compensation from CAVCA.

[28] CAVCA does not reveal the amount of levies collected from KOEEs every year, but media reported that between 2007 and 2010, CAVCA collected CNY 170,000,000 Yuan in total (<http://www.infzm.com/content/40747> accessed 7 November 2014).

[29] <http://www.cavca.org/news.php?un=syz_qa&up=24>accessed 7 November 2014.

[30] Infra, Section 3.2.2.

[31] <http://www.cavca.org/news_show.php?un=xhgg&id=609> accessed 7 November 2014.

collect levies, why are CMOs themselves required to be non-profit civil organizations?

The collection of levies from KOEEs has entered its eighth year since it started in 2007. The debate surrounding it is not likely to stop any time soon and one must wait and see what direction the debate will take in the future.

3.2.2   Extended collective licensing and the third amendment of the Copyright Law

Since 2012, China has been undergoing the process of amending its copyright law for the third time. This amendment is considered to be, for the first time in Chinese copyright law history, necessitated by internal domestic demands instead of external international pressure, such as was the case for the Copyright Laws of 1990 and 2001. The articles on extended collective licensing were added into the first proposal for the third amendment. This proposal, once again, stirred an intense debate around the CMC system as a whole in China.[32] In contrast to the karaoke levy debate, the debate this time is between the authors and producers of musical works on one side, and MCSC and the National Copyright Office, the drafter of the proposal, on the other. Under the extended collective licensing system, the National Copyright Office may authorize CMOs that already represent a large number of right holders to also conduct collective copyright management on behalf of non-members.[33] This regime has been strongly criticized by academic scholars in China because it not only upholds, but reinforces, the statutory monopoly of CMOs, which was already unsatisfactory to many scholars.[34]

---

[32]   The former legal counsel of KODA, the Danish music performing rights CMC organization, explained it as follows: 'The extended collective license is a solution . . . for rights clearance in certain cases of mass uses of protected works, in particular photocopying. It has existed in the Nordic copyright laws since the early 1960s, first in the field of broadcasting.' Quoted in Daniel Gervais, 'Application of an Extended Collective Licensing Regime in Canada: Principles and Issues related to Implementation' (Department of Canadian Heritage 2003) 14 <http://works. bepress.com/daniel_gervais/29> accessed 7 November 2014.

[33]   The first proposal for the third amendment of the Copyright Law of China (March 2012), art. 60: 'Collective rights management organizations, after getting authorizations from copyright holders and representing their interest nationwide, may ask for an authorization of great representativeness from the administrative copyright department of the State Council for all copyrights and related rights holders, except for deny in written by right holders.'

[34]   Fuxiao Jiang and Daniel J. Gervais, 'Collective Management Organizations in China: Practice, Problems and Possible Solutions' (2012) 15(3) Journal of World

The proposed extended collective licensing system is clearly the result of lobbying by CMOs distressed by the number of copyright holders who disassociated themselves from CMOs and who sometimes challenge their monopoly position by directly licensing to users. The National Copyright Office proposed the introduction of extended collective licensing on the grounds that the extended collective licensing has proven itself a mature and successful system in the Nordic countries. The doubt within academic circles focuses on the argument that what is mature and successful in the Nordic countries will not necessarily be so in China because of the huge differences in market size and the state of socio-economic development. Therefore, extended collective licensing may not lead to fair and legitimate results in China.

Some preconditions need to be met for extended collective licensing to work well. As Finnish scholar Tarja Koskinen-Olsson points out:

> [The] system presupposes that there exists a well developed system of organizations and that such organizations represent a substantial number of rights holders in the field concerned. It presupposes in other words that 'copyright market' is well organized and disciplined. If such is the case, the system is likely to function very well and experience in the Nordic countries has proven that.[35]

As we have discussed, some key controversies are still unresolved in China. How can we be confident that these preconditions have been met here?

Another strong voice against the articles of extended collective licensing came from the music industry because the use of extended collective licensing plus the statutory licensing for musical works that was included in the first proposal meant that the music industry was nearly entirely excluded from direct contact with end users.[36] The authors of musical

---

Intellectual Property, 221–237 <http://ssrn.com/abstract=2171190> accessed 5 June 2015.

[35] Tarja Koskinen-Olsson, 'Collective Management in the Nordic Countries' in Daniel Gervais (ed), *Collective Management of Copyright and Related Rights* (Kluwer Law International 2006) 281.

[36] The first proposal for the third amendment of the Copyright Law of China (March 2012), art. 46: 'After 3 months of first publication of a musical recording, other producers of musical record may make musical recordings by using the musical works included in the musical recording first mentioned without permission of the copyright holders of the musical works if the conditions specified in article 48 are met.'

Art. 48: 'In accordance with the provisions of article 44, 45, 46 and 47, the following conditions shall be met using the disclosed works without prior permission of its authors: 1) the user shall apply for use of the record to the copyright administrative organs before use; 2) the user shall specify the names of the authors,

works claimed that if extended collective licensing were included in the law, their situation would become worse and they would not be able to survive in the information society. The combination of extended collective licensing, to be included in article 60, and the statutory licensing, included in articles 46 and 48, means that nearly all musical works would be automatically collectively managed by the authorized CMO; and phonogram producers could use the musical works and pay levies to the CMO with statutory licences without necessarily licensing the musical works from authors. The result would be that music works authors are almost entirely excluded from the market. They would lose the ability to deny others the use of their works, to negotiate the rate of royalties with users and to set up new business models for the licensing of their works.[37] The reason forwarded by the National Copyright Office, as the drafter of the proposal, was that this system would dramatically reduce transaction costs and barriers for musical works in the Chinese market and that it would legalize China's market for musical works which has been plagued by copyright infringement for quite a long time. Obviously, such arrangements would alleviate the administrative burdens of copyright administration organs and increase China's international reputation with respect to copyright protection.[38]

Neither the music industry nor academic scholars in China bought the arguments of the CMOs and the National Copyright Office. They suspected that these proposals were a kind of conspiracy of CMOs and the National Copyright Office to interfere with the market economy by using their administrative powers. Under the proposed arrangement, both the copyright holders and the users of works were to be exploited by CMOs secretly and mandatorily without any negotiation with authors. The authors of musical works warned that if the proposed statutory texts were to be passed, they would quit their membership from the CMOs

---

the title and source of the works before use; and 3) the user shall pay levies to the collective rights management organizations according to the standard rate which was ratified by the copyright administrative organs in the month after the use; as well as submit the names of the authors, the titles of the works and their source.

If users notify the use of a statutory license to a copyright administration organ, the organs shall publish such notification on its website.

The collective rights management organizations shall distribute the levies collected to their members in time and shall set up a free search system for their members concerning information about the use of works and the levies charged.'

[37] 'Draft copyright law enrages China's music industry' <http://english.sina.com/china/2012/0411/457224.html> accessed 7 November 2014.

[38] 'Musicians Sound Off at Copyright Changes' <http://english.sipo.gov.cn/news/iprspecial/201204/t20120428_682524.html> accessed 7 November 2014.

collectively.[39] As a preliminary victory for authors of musical works and academics in this battle surrounding the amendment, the proposed article 46 for the third amendment was deleted in the second proposal and the scope of extended collective licensing was narrowed to some specific uses of works.[40] It seems that the victory is continuing. In the second proposal for the third amendment published in 2014 for public consultation, the scope of extended collective licensing is narrowed down to only one situation; namely, on-demand music performances used in KOEEs.[41]

To summarize, during the third amendment of China's Copyright Law, the battle concerning extended collective licensing ended with a compromise. Extended collective licensing will not be adopted in a general way, but only with regard to one specific use of works within karaoke industries, that is on-demand music performance systems which are widely used within that industry. Therefore, the predominance of the use of the CMC system in KOEEs is further expanded under the third amendment of the Copyright Law. If the article on extended collective licensing finally enters into effect, it is beyond doubt that the CMOs will have clear legal authority to collect levies from all the KOEEs for all authors of musical and audio-visual works.

---

[39] Ren Zhongyuan and Lan Fang, 'China music industry's copyright swan song' <http://www.marketwatch.com/story/china-music-industrys-copyright-swan song-2012-05-01> accessed 7 November 2014.

[40] The second proposal for the third amendment of the Copyright Law of China (March 2012), art. 60: 'Collective rights management organizations, after getting authorizations from copyright holders and representing the interest of copyright holders in national wide, may have great representativeness for all copyrights and related rights holders for the following situations, except for deny in written by right holders. 1) Broadcasting organizations publicly display literal, music, paint or photographic works that have been disclosed before. 2) Self-demand music service providers publicly perform music or audio-video works that have been disclosed before, through self-demand music systems. Collective rights management organizations shall fairly treat all of its members when distributing levies.'

[41] Proposal of the third amendment of the Copyright Law for the State Council Legal Office's review, art. 63: 'Collective rights management organizations, after getting authorizations from copyright holders and representing the interest of copyright holders in national wide, may have great representativeness for all copyrights and related rights holders for self-demand music service providers publicly perform music or audio-video works that have been disclosed before, through self-demand music systems. Collective rights management organizations shall fairly treat all of its members when distributing levies.'

4. THE FUTURE OF CHINA'S CMC SYSTEM AND ITS CONCERNS

4.1 The Statutory Monopoly, Non-profit Organizations and the Market Economy

The content in both the Copyright Law of 2001 and the Copyright Law of 2010 that CMOs should be not-for-profit has been maintained in the third proposal for the third amendment of the Copyright Law for State Council Legal Office review, despite the fact that this requirement has been seriously and continuously criticized since 2001.[42] Because the Chinese government has strict regulations and restrictions concerning the establishment and operation of non-profit organizations, the requirement practically means CMOs will still have a statutory monopoly in the future. This indicates that China's policy on the CMC system is not yet fundamentally different from the traditional European continental ideology that originated in France and Germany in the middle of the last century.

However, the adoption of the market economy and the arrival of the information society seriously challenge the fairness and legitimacy of the not-for-profit requirement and the statutory monopoly of CMOs in China. If non-profit organizations can collectively manage copyrights, why are for-profit enterprises not allowed to do so? Since nearly all the tangible goods can be sold online with very low transaction costs, why can works not be licensed one by one instead of through blanket licences used by CMOs?[43]

A small degree of progress has been made in resolving this tension in the proposal for the third amendment of the Copyright Law for the State Council Legal Office review through two particular articles that have been inserted into the proposal.

The first article, that is article 61 in the proposal, provides that only the rights that are difficult to exercise or control effectively by the right holders can be collectively managed by CMOs,[44] which has already been

---

[42] Proposal for the third amendment of the Copyright Law for the State Council Legal Office's review, art. 61.

[43] Shira Perlmutter, 'Convergence and the Future of Copyright' (2001) 24 Colum.-VLA J.L. & Arts 163, quoted in Peter Yu, 'Five Disharmonizing Trends in the International Intellectual Property Regime' (2006) MSU Legal Studies Research Paper No. 03-28, 23 <http://ssrn.com/abstract=923177> accessed 7 November 2014 (also published in Peter Yu (ed), *Intellectual Property and Information Wealth. Vol. 4* (Praeger Publishers 2007)).

[44] Proposal for the third amendment of the Copyright Law for the State Council Legal Office's review, art. 61.

specified in the RCAC and has now been included and emphasized in the proposal as law.[45] By this restriction, only copyright and related rights that cannot be effectively exercised or controlled can be managed by CMOs. This provision will probably shrink the scope of CMOs. Moreover, considering the further developments of market and technology, fewer and fewer rights can be controlled or exercised effectively and it seems the scope of CMOs will be reduced even further. The second article, that is article 62, aims to alleviate the tension between the copyright holders, users and CMOs concerning the rate of levies.[46]

The foregoing indicates that the CMC system in the proposal for the third amendment of the Copyright Law for the State Council Legal Office's review is generally still old wine in a new bottle. After several rounds of debates and amendments, the current proposal is most likely the last one and the articles in the proposal will be the law after an affirmative vote in the National People's Congress in the near future.

4.2 The Statutory Monopoly, Non-profit Organizations and International Trends

It appears that another reason for China to stubbornly maintain the statutory monopoly and not-for-profit requirement may be based on the tradition of the European continental law system. Since China started its institutional transformation from an authoritarian political regime to a more democratic one at the beginning of the 20th century, China has taken the European continental law system, especially the German legal system, as a model. The main reason was that, compared with the common law system, the system based on statutory law of the European continent was easier to learn and transfer. Another reason was that China hoped to follow the road of German political reform at the end of the 19th century, when Germany transformed from an ancient feudalist country to a modern capitalistic country. Nowadays, China's legal society still considers that it belongs to the continental legal family generally. Because a CMC system with non-profit, social organizations and a statutory monopoly was the standard model used in both Germany and France, China automatically introduced this system and its rationale in 2004.

A more pragmatic reason underlying the academic explanation may be that the Chinese government favours these kinds of organizations because

---

[45] Regulation on the Collective Administration of Copyright, art. 4.
[46] See the proposal for the third amendment of the Copyright Law for the State Council Legal Office's review, art. 62.

the government still regulates the market heavily, despite the gradual transformation from a centrally planned economy to a market economy. It may also be the case that the Chinese legislative department for copyright law seem to have deliberately closed its eyes when the European Union, including Germany, began the transformation from a monopolized and not-for-profit model to a more competitive, market-oriented model for CMOs. In 2005, the European Commission concluded in a study that 'the present structures for cross-border collective management of legitimate online music services . . . are based on models developed for the analogue environment need to be improved for music to fulfil its unique potential as a driver for online services'.[47]

The Directive on Collective Management of Copyright and Related Rights clearly specifies that:

> This Directive does not require collective management organisations to adopt a specific legal form. In practice, those organisations operate in various legal forms such as associations, cooperatives or limited liability companies, which are controlled or owned by holders of copyright and related rights or by entities representing such right holders.[48]

Furthermore, it provides that 'right holders should be free to entrust the management of their rights to independent management entities'.[49]

For instance, CMOs in Germany were traditionally organized as economic non-profit associations, such as GEMA and VG WORT. But more commercial CMOs have the status of a limited company.[50] Even Japan, which is a follower of the European continental law system as well, abandoned the system characterized by statutory monopolies and non-profit organizations and adopted a mixed and competitive model in 2000. In the past, the 1939 Japanese law concerning copyright intermediary businesses prohibited any person or organization from conducting the

---

[47]   European Commission, *Commission Staff Working Document. Study on a Community Initiative on the Cross-Border Collective Management of Copyright* (Brussels, 7 July 2005) 5 <http://ec.europa.eu/internal_market/copyright/docs/management/study-collectivemgmt_en.pdf> accessed 7 November 2014.

[48]   Recital 14 in the preamble to Directive 2014/26/EU of the European Parliament and of the Council of 26 February 2014 on collective management of copyright and related rights and multi-territorial licensing of rights in musical works for online use in the internal market.

[49]   Ibid recital 15 in the preamble.

[50]   Jorg Reinbothe, 'Collective Rights Management in Germany' in Daniel Gervais (ed), *Collective Management of Copyright and Related Rights* (Kluwer Law International 2006) 201.

business of an intermediary without authorization from the Commissioner of the Agency for Cultural Affairs. Although there was no written policy, it was the practice that the Commissioner authorized only one person or organization per type of copyrighted work. However, the 2000 Law of Management Business of Copyright and Neighbouring Rights allows not only public-interest corporations, but also commercial corporations to register as conducting the management operations of copyright and neighbouring rights and this has substantially increased the number of competitive CMC organizations in Japan.[51]

5.   CONCLUSION

The CMC system in China is quite new compared with those in Western developed countries. In comparison with their experience of more than a hundred years, theory and practice of CMC have not yet fully developed in China, whose CMC system is a simple institutional transplantation of the system used in European continental countries. Because China is currently still constructing its CMC system, it should take the opportunity to adapt it to the recent development of the information society. However, it seems that this has not received specific consideration during the development of China's CMC system over the past ten years, including during discussions regarding the third amendment of the Copyright Law. When and how China's CMC system will substantially meet the requirements of the Chinese market and match the features of the information society is still in question.

---

[51]   Koji Okumura, 'Collective Management of Copyright and Neighbouring Rights in Japan' in Daniel Gervais (ed), *Collective Management of Copyright and Related Rights* (Kluwer Law International 2006) 349–354.

12. Collective rights management in China and Europe: between market and authority

Nari Lee and Yang Li

1. INTRODUCTION

There are several intellectual property (IP) institutions that make relevant governance decisions related to national systems of creation innovation and competition, namely the legislature, the judiciary, the administration and the market. The law, the court, governmental agencies and the administration, as well as market participants, are crucial decision makers in the governance of IP.[1] These institutions interact with each other, and a reform at one level would likely lead to change in other institution or at least change the dynamics among these institutions. As noted in the preceding chapters of this volume, after the initial wave of legal transplant of IP norms and system, China is currently going through a third wave of system reforms. The introduction of IP law and decisions on how to govern innovation and creation may be made through the operation of the market, as IP rights allow governance decision to be made in the market by the right holders The rights themselves not only provide nec-

---

[1] N. Lee, *Exclusion and Coordination of Fragmentation: Five Essays toward a Pluralistic Theory of Patent Right*. Publications of the University of Eastern Finland. Dissertations in Social Sciences and Business Studies, Itä-Suomen yliopisto, Joensuu, at 28–34 <http://urn.fi/URN:ISBN:978-952-61-0123-1> accessed 10 December 2014. See also, Yoshiyuki Tamura, 'Towards the New Paradigm of Intellectual Property Law. The Law and Policy of Intellectual Property: Building a New Framework' (2008) 20 Intellectual Property Law and Policy Journal 1. Similar institutions' focused research perspectives may be found in Antonina Bakardjieva-Engelbrekt, 'Copyright from an Institutional Perspective: Actors, Interests, Stakes and the Logic of Participation' (2007) 4 Review of Economic Research on Copyright Issues 65; Arti Rai, 'Engaging Facts and Policy: a Multi-Institutional Approach to Patent System Reform' (2003) 103 Columbia Law Review 1035, at 1039, highlighting the need to engage in comparative institutional analysis.

essary exclusivity to govern intangible resources that are at the core of the IP rights, but also coordinate and manage how they may be used in innovation and creation.

Among the four IP institutions, the perspective of legal transplant may highlight the role and function of the legislature and therefore the governance decisions made by the law and legislation. As explored in the previous chapters of this volume, the rounds of IP law reforms have been an important initial step in China to accommodate the transplanted system and norms of IP. The transplanted norms have provided a framework in which the other three important institutions operate and new institutional arrangements are to be made. The state and administration participate in the law and policy making through administrative decision making, and the court participates by judicial interpretation of the law. Additionally, various entrepreneurial and individual governance decisions are now made possible through the assertion of private IP rights in the market.

In a society with the rule of law, the four institutions serve different functions and are limited by the competences that are mandated to them through the democratic process. As all of these institutions are socially constructed, in any given society, they may be rearranged in ways that are most suitable for that particular society. As such, it is possible for society to arrange them in such ways that some are given more competence than others. Inevitably, such selection is closely connected to the overall governance decision made in society, as well as its polity. There are ongoing IP system reform initiatives that are taking place both in Europe and in China, through legislative, administrative and judicial reforms.[2] In other words, as these institutions are closely connected, when they change, they seem to change together and any reform proposals at one level need to take into account their impacts at another level and how the roles of each institution are affected by such reform. Change may be introduced in various ways. One example has been the influence of the change in the foreign systems from which the initial norms originate, in response to particular problems. This was seen in the European discussion of orphan works and the resale right has sparked similar debates in China.[3] Against this backdrop, traditional concepts such as public-private, state-market, or individual may be too naïve or simplistic to explore IP law developments. Likewise, a unidirectional explanation of how foreign laws and norms influence domestic law such as the legal transplant theory may need more nuanced elaboration to explain the complexity of influences of

---

[2] See, for example, Chapters 4 and 16 in this volume.
[3] See Chapters 6 and 7 in this volume.

norms or norm interaction as well as business practices in today's dynamic economies.

The fast pace of technological changes presents more complexities. The market for creative works and innovation is always undergoing changes. One result of concurrent changes in the dynamics of interdependent IP institutions is the emergences of new practices and entities that function within the traditional institutional boundaries, as well as in between. Both in Europe and in China, there are more IP rights over innovations and creations and they are privately held by so many different actors, with heterogeneous interests.[4] To manage with the complex layers of rights and fragmented titles, various types of intermediaries are seen to be emerging.[5] These intermediaries are not the traditional stake holders represented by the right holders' and users' dynamic, but at the same time, they are seen to be benefiting from IP value chains. In addition to the Internet service providers or online access intermediaries that provide technological services to allow users to access certain types of product and business offered on the Internet, rights intermediaries serve as a broker of rights and licences. Rights intermediaries engage in administration and management of rights, such as in the case of collective copyright management organizations (CMOs),[6] licensing platforms (private patent pools), standard-setting organizations (SSOs)[7] that deal with licensing policies for IP assertions involved with the standardization process, as well as private and individual non-practising entities (NPEs) with licensing programmes.[8]

---

[4]   See, for example, Chapter 3 in this volume.

[5]   Fragmentation caused by exclusive rights is, for example, noted in Lee, *supra* n. 1 at 21. See also in the area of patents, Michael A. Heller and Rebecca S. Eisenberg, 'Can Patents Deter Innovation? The Anticommons in Biomedical Research' (1998) 280(5364) Science 698–701.

[6]   Robert P. Merges, 'Contracting into Liability Rules: Intellectual Property Rights and Collective Rights Organizations' (1996) 84 California Law Review 1293–1393. See also Daniel J. Gervais, *Collective Management of Copyright and Related Rights* (Kluwer Law International 2010).

[7]   M. A. Lemley, 'Intellectual Property Rights and Standard-setting Organizations' (2002) 90 California Law Review 1889–1980. See also, N. Lee, *Standardization and Patent Law – Is Standardization a Concern for Patent Law?* (October 2004). Available at SSRN: <http://ssrn.com/abstract=610901 or http://dx.doi.org/10.2139/ssrn.610901> accessed 31 May 2015.

[8]   See, for example, G. N. Magliocca, 'Blackberries and Barnyards: Patent Trolls and the Perils of Innovation' (2007) 82 Notre Dame Law Review 1809–1838; James E. Bessen, Michael J. Meurer and Jennifer Laurissa Ford, 'The Private and Social Costs of Patent Trolls' (2011) Boston University School of Law, Law and Economics Research Paper 11–45; compare in UK, C. Helmers,

These rights intermediaries often collect the fragmented titles to a bundle and provide governance structure for their uses in the market, thus functioning as a coordinator. Some of these intermediaries are privately motivated and operate in the market, interacting mainly with other right holders or users. For example, so-called patent trolls or NPEs are entirely market-driven intermediaries that are fundamentally based on the availability injunction as remedies for patent infringement to force manufacturing entities into licensing. At least in the USA, where patent trolls originate from, and to a lesser extent in Europe, the negative impact of their conduct is felt as they are entirely indistinguishable in the law from any practising right holder asserting rights in the market. In contrast, other intermediaries that provide collective licensing, such as patent pools on technological standards, sovereign patent investment funds[9] or rights clearing houses that operate on the authority of regulations, seem to operate between the market and the authority of the administration.[10] Such types of intermediaries are likely to operate between the market and the administrative authority of states.

Following the previous Chapter 11, which provides the legal framework for CMOs in China, this chapter argues that CMOs seem to be one such organization that operates between the market and authority in China. Starting with a discussion of a recent Chinese dispute case concerning the scope of collective administration agreements as an example,[11] we compare how the relationship between CMOs and their members are regulated in China and in the EU. This chapter argues that the current Chinese CMO system seems to be failing in achieving necessary recognition by the beneficiaries of such system. The dispute also highlights the fact that a successful implementation of CMO requires alignment of the perception of CMO

B. Love and L. McDonagh, 'Is There a Patent Troll Problem in the UK' (2013) 24 Fordham Intellectual Property Media & Entertainment Law Journal 509; in contrast, A. Mayergoyz, 'Lessons from Europe on How to Tame US Patent Trolls' (2009) 42 Cornell International Law Journal 241.

[9]   D. Gredel, M. Kramer and B. Bend, 'Patent-based Investment Funds as Innovation Intermediaries for SMEs: In-depth Analysis of Reciprocal Interactions, Motives and Fallacies' (2012) 32(9) Technovation 536–549.

[10]   For example, a clearing house is envisioned in the Convention on Biological Diversity Art. 18.3. See also G. Van Overwalle, E. Van Zimmeren, B. Verbeure and G. Matthijs, 'Models for Facilitating Access to Patents on Genetic Inventions (2006) 7(2) Nature Reviews Genetics 143–154.

[11]   北京市海淀区人民法院民事判决（2013）海民初字第1195号、   *MCSC* (*Musical Copyright Society of China*) *v. Beijing October Days Culture Media Co, Ltd.* Case No. 2013 Haidan District Court in Beijing No.1195 first trial (2013) HaiMinChuZi No.1195.

by the right holders to the copyright users, in the licensing market for works. We argue that as CMOs provide governance mechanism through the exercise of IP rights, whether there is a vibrant market for copyright licences or not forms a crucial consideration for the successful operation of a CMO. Without a healthy and functioning local market for content, CMOs' role is reduced to collecting agencies for a handful of foreign authors. As discussed in the previous chapter, the third amendment of the Chinese Copyright Law has included some discussion on the scope of operation for CMOs in China.[12] The discussion is now removed from the published version of the new Copyright Law proposal.[13] We conclude that any future reform proposal should heed the fact that a successful and functional market with widely acceptable licensing practices is a crucial prerequisite for extending any operation of the CMOs such as extended collective licensing.

2.   A CASE STUDY OF MCSC

2.1   MCSC v Beijing October Day's Culture Media (ODCM)[14]

In 2010, Haidan District Court in Beijing heard a very controversial case concerning a CMO in China.[15] The Court confirmed the following facts:

(a)   In 2010, Beijing October Days Culture Media Co., Ltd (hereinafter ODCM) organized a live concert in Beijing by an artist Zheng Jun who is a famous singer. He performed 12 songs, which were covered by a contract for copyright collective administration with MCSC.

(b)   Zheng Jun was both the lyrist and composer of the 12 songs that he performed.

(c)   Prior to the concert, on 1 March 1995, Zheng Jun concluded a contract for collective management of copyrights of the *existing and future musical works* created by him with MCSC. The contract did not explicitly exclude Zheng Jun from exercising copyrights of his own musical works entrusted to MCSC.

---

[12]   See Chapter 11 in this volume.
[13]   Chinese Copyright Law (NCAC's latest revised draft, 6 June 2014) <http://www.chinalaw.gov.cn/article/cazjgg/201406/20140600396188.shtml>   accessed 1 April 2015.
[14]   *MCSC v. ODCM, supra* n. 11.
[15]   Ibid.

(d) The Chinese Regulations on Copyright Collective Management[16] was promulgated on 28 December 2004 by the State Council and took effect on 1 March 2005.

Based on the above facts, MCSC filed a lawsuit in Beijing Haidan District Court and argued that ODCM had infringed its right to perform these songs. In the process of the trial, MCSC argued that the contract between MCSC and Zheng Jun was a 'trust' contract and of an exclusive nature, and that Zheng Jun did not have the right to perform the 12 songs without its authorization, and that the concert organizer ODCM did not have the right to include the 12 songs in the concert that it organized.

2.2   Legal Framework for the Dispute

The dispute mainly concerned the validity of the copyright administration contract and the applicability of Article 20 of the Copyright Regulation to an agreement that was agreed before the Regulation entered into force. As described in Chapter 11 of this volume, CMOs are regulated through several layers.

First, there is the substantive copyright law. Article 8 of the China Copyright Law stipulates the possibility of the copyright owners to authorize a CMO to 'exercise their copyright or rights related to the copyright'.[17] Accordingly, a CMO may 'exercise the copyright or the rights related to the copyright in its own name for the copyright owner or the owner of the copyrights related to the copyright, and participates as a

---

[16]   2004年12月22日,著作权集体管理条例 (中华人民共和国国务院令第429号 2004年12月28日公布) Regulations of 22 December 2004, of Copyright Collective Management (promulgated by Decree No. 429 of 28 December 2004 of the State Council of the People's Republic of China) [hereinafter the CMO Regulation] Unofficial English translation is available online at <http://www.wipo.int/wipolex/ en/text.jsp?file_id=181505> accessed 1 March 2015.

[17]   2010年2月26日,中华人民共和国著作权法 (中华人民共和国主席令第31号 1990年9月7日公布;   根据中华人民共和国主席令第26号2010年2月26日全国人 民代表大会常务委员会《关于修改＜中华人民共和国著作权法＞的决定》修正) [hereinafter the Copyright Law] Article 8 of the Copyright Law of the People's Republic of China of 26 February 2010 (promulgated by the Presidential Order No. 31 of 7 September 1990; as amended up to the Decision of 26 February 2010, by the Standing Committee of the National People's Congress on Amending the Copyright Law of the People's Republic of China). Unofficial English translation is available online at <http://www.wipo.int/wipolex/en/text.jsp?file_id=186569> accessed 1 March 2015.

party in legal or arbitration proceedings concerning the copyright or the copyrights related to the copyright'.[18]

A second layer is found in the Regulation concerning the collective administration of copyright.[19] The article relevant to this case in particular was Article 20, which makes the nature of the agreement with the CMO *an exclusive licence*, as it prohibits the right holder from individual exercise of copyright or from entering into an alternative arrangement. Article 20 provides that:

> any right owner, after having concluded a contract for collective management of copyright with a copyright collective management organization, shall not exercise by himself or authorize another person to exercise the rights in the contract to be exercised by that organization during the term agreed with in the contract.[20]

Chinese commentators consider this is the rule that makes the CMO agreement a form of a trust agreement whereby the trustee (CMO) may exercise rights on behalf of the beneficiary.[21] Under this understanding of the article, any works that are entrusted in this manner should be subject to the fee agreement set by the CMO. As a trust agreement targets tangible property and assets, and technically copyright is an intangible right, physical inability to take possession makes it possible for the rights to be used simultaneously. Considering this, applying the rationale of trust to the CMO is debatable however. Furthermore, CMOs in other countries are subject to the rules that apply in particular to the type of business or non-profit organization that may incorporate as a legal entity. Thus, commercial laws or the regulations that are applicable to the formation of a legal entity such as an association, or market regulation on providing copyright collecting services may apply here as well.[22] Additionally, as there is a concern for the monopoly position of any given CMOs if the approval is granted to only one entity per category of works, as is the case in China[23] or through the de facto position of the market, they may be subject to anti-monopoly or competition law rules as is the case in the EU.[24]

---

[18]   Ibid.
[19]   *Supra* n. 16.
[20]   Article 20 of the CMO Regulation, *supra* n. 16.
[21]   See Chapter 11 in this volume.
[22]   Ibid.
[23]   Article 7(2) of the CMO Regulation, *supra* n. 16.
[24]   Although in this case the question of the form of the CMO as an entity was not raised. However, one may question if CMOs in China actually form a trust as

2.3   Findings of the Court

The Court decided that the defendant ODCM did not infringe the MCSC's right to exercise copyrights in the 12 songs. Its decision was mainly based on the following reasons:[25]

(a)   The establishment of MCSC was to manage copyrights to assist copyright owners, in cases where it was difficult for copyright owners to exercise their rights effectively. But they were not supposed to be used to exclude a copyright owner from exercising his own copyrights without permission and furthermore subject them to payment of royalties to MCSC.

(b)   Article 20 of the Regulations on Copyright Collective Management[26] did not apply to the contract concluded on 1 March 1995 between Zheng Jun and MCSC. The Regulations took effect on 1 March 2005 and do not specify whether they have retroactive effect and whether they are applicable to contracts concluded before they took effect in 2005.

(c)   Thus, the contract concluded on 1 March 1995 did not exclude Zheng Jun from exercising or authorizing others to exercise his own works trusted to MCSC to manage.[27]

In sum, the Court ruled that Article 20 of the CMO Regulation, which makes the contract between MCSC an exclusive licensing agreement, did not apply to the contract as the Regulation did not have retroactive effect.

3.   GOVERNANCE OF CMOs IN CHINA AND IN EUROPE

3.1   Analysis of Zheng Jun's Case in China

The above facts of the dispute between the creator and the CMO in China underscore the general misalignment of the expectations of the right holders and the role of CMOs in the Chinese copyright market. The findings of the Haidan Court highlight several uncertainties concerning the

---

the actual form of organization, which would subject the MCSC to regulation of trust in China, if any.

[25]   *MCSC v ODCM, supra* n. 11.
[26]   CMO Regulation, *supra* n.16.
[27]   *MCSC v ODCM, supra* n. 11.

role of CMOs in China. Denying the retroactive effect of the Regulation, the Court allowed the creator to exercise copyrights of his own musical works. In other words, the Court denied the applicability of Article 20, if applying it to the contract would have prevented the right holder from exercising his right. The Court further concluded that the performance of the creator implied a licence to use his works for the organizer although there was no clear written licence between the creator and the defendant, concert promoter and organizer (ODCM). The Court held that Zheng Jun had the right to use and license these musical works for his own performance, as they were outside the scope of his contract with MCSC and he had granted an implied licence to ODCM by performing the songs.

The case generated controversy among the public as it was viewed as a case of a CMO prohibiting a singer from performing his own song, which he composed. In this regard, the Court's decision seems to be defensible from the policy point of view that a CMO should always work on behalf of the right holder and in the interest of the right holder. Therefore a CMO should not prevent the creator from actively promoting the use of his work in the market. In this particular case, the fact that the contract between MCSC and Zheng Jun was concluded before the CMO Regulation took effect affected the outcome significantly. As this limited the scope of agreement between the copyright holder and the CMO, this worked in favour of the copyright holder retaining the right to perform his own work of composition and lyrics.

Exclusiveness of the agreement is an important requirement of the operation of a CMO. To administrate copyright licensing collectively, a CMO needs to be able to act exclusively and the possibility to individually exercise rights would not reduce the transaction costs. This is one of the reasons why the Regulation needs to contain Article 20. In this aspect, the findings of the Court should have limited precedential value, only applying to a CMO's contracts signed before the Regulation took effect. Otherwise the function of a CMO as an institution that collectivises copyright licences would be significantly reduced.

3.2 CMOs' Restriction on the Creator's Freedom in China and Europe

To explore the exclusive nature or 'trust'-like nature of the CMO contracts in China, it is possible to speculate if the outcome would have been different if Article 20 of the CMO Regulation were applied to the contract.[28]

---

[28]   Commentators, including one of the co-authors of this chapter, Yang Li, have been generally sceptical as to the legality of Article 20 of the Regulations itself.

It is possible, for example, to view Article 20 of the CMO Regulation as requiring of the creators too broad a scope of exclusive licence to the CMOs, including all types of uses for copyrighted work. As a result, the right holders may not be able to retain rights for individual management after the initial agreement with the CMO. As a CMO, such as MCSC, is in a monopoly position supported by the CMO Regulation, it is possible to view Article 20 of the Regulation as removing any possibilities for the creator to individually exercise the copyrights within the period stipulated in the contract. As CMOs are not entertainment or promotion agencies for artists, exclusivity of the copyright administration may force the copyright owner to lose many market opportunities. This concern highlights actually in China, as well as in Europe, that there seemed to be a general concern that CMOs may restrict freedom of contract that a creator would otherwise enjoy to commercialize their works.

CMOs' restriction on the creator's freedom to commercialize their works may be set in the form of an exclusive agreement as discussed above. In contrast, an overly broad or extensive scope of such contracts, signed with an artist in a weaker bargaining position, raises another range of issues. In earlier case law in Europe, based on the authority of competition policy, the European Court of Justice (ECJ)addressed the issue concerning the scope of contract and a CMO's relationship with its members.[29] Indeed in a contracting situation between an individual member (right holder) and a CMO, a CMO holds a superior negotiating position, unless an individual right holder is a really famous creator. As CMOs have a relatively longer history in Europe than in China, the disputes between CMOs and their members are known in the context of abuse of dominant position. In 1974, the ECJ created what could be called a necessity or indispensability test for the operation of a CMO, by ruling that 'a compulsory assignment of *all copyrights, both present and future, no distinction being drawn between the different generally accepted types of exploitation,* may appear an unfair condition, especially if such assignment is required for an extended period after the member's withdrawal'.[30] The new CMO Directive in Europe now contains articles which codify some of the ECJ practices governing the relationship between a right holder and a CMO. In Article 4, General Principles it is provided that:

> Member States shall ensure that collective management organisations act in the *best interests of the right holders* whose rights they represent *and that they*

---

[29]   ECJ, Judgment of the Court of 27 March 1974, Case 127-73, *Belgische Radio en Televisie and société belge des auteurs, compositeurs et éditeurs v. SV SABAM and NV Fonior*. ECR 1974-00313, ECLI identifier: ECLI:EU:C:1974:25.

[30]   Ibid, at para 12. Emphasis added.

do not impose on them any obligations which are not objectively necessary for the protection of their rights and interests or for the effective management of their rights.[31]

Additionally, Article 5, from paragraphs 2 to 8, of the CMO Directive contains detailed minimum rights that Member States shall provide in their law to the right holders in their agreements with a CMO. Among others, paragraph 2 highlights the freedom the right holders to choose a CMO, as there shall be no statutory monopoly of the CMO and an obligation of the selected CMO not to refuse a membership application of any creator. Additionally the right to 'grant licences for non-commercial uses of any rights, categories of rights or types of works and other subject-matter that they may choose', regardless of their agreement with a CMO, is provided in paragraph 3, and the right to terminate or withdraw some of their works is provided as a minimum freedom that the right holders may enjoy in paragraph 4. Further conditions for restriction by a CMO concerning a competing CMO are provided in paragraph 6. More importantly, Article 5, paragraph 7 prohibits the use of blanket general agreement by requiring written specific consents for each right or category of rights or type of works and other subject-matter.

Articles 4 and 5 are a codification of the principles established by previous ECJ decisions governing CMOs. While there has been no directive harmonizing Member States' regulation of CMOs, the ECJ has ruled on the activities of CMOs based on the authority of competition law.[32] The ECJ has interpreted CMOs' practices in the Member States in numerous instances. More relevant to our case analysis is the ECJ's so-called indispensability or equity test. The test puts limits on the level of restriction that any CMO pay put on the right holder. The obligations on the members that were not absolutely necessary for the attainment of the objectives of a CMO and which would encroach unfairly on a member's freedom are considered abusive in terms of Article 82 of the EC law (now §102 TFEU). In *BRT v. Sabam*, the ECJ held an unduly broad scope of contract to be abusive.[33] Similarly, in the *Daft Punk* case, the ECJ held a rejection of membership for the right holder wanting to retain the possibility for

---

[31]   Directive 2014/26/EU, 26 February 2014 on collective management of copyright and related rights and multi-territorial licensing of rights in musical works for online use in the internal market. [hereinafter CMO Directive] (emphasis added).

[32]   Treaty on the Functioning of the European Union [hereinafter TFEU] OJ C 326, 26.10.2012, pp. 47–390, §101 and T§102.

[33]   *Supra* n. 29.

individual management to be abusive and thus against the competition law in Europe.[34]

During the period of transposition of the Directive into national law, and the disputes at Court of Justice of the European Union following implementation, it is expected that several challenges such as by a CMO with territorial monopoly for certain national repertoire may surface again. However, the current level of opening of the operation of CMOs to EU-wide competition makes sense in Europe in the context of the internal market for digital content, with integrated potential for multi-territorial copyright licences within the boundaries of the Union. As the market for digital music testifies, there are users and markets for uses that call for an integrated internal market, rather than individual markets in Member States. In practice, however, the category of repertoire and works would likely lead to a de facto monopoly situation. Such a de facto monopoly decided by the market is qualitatively different from a monopoly imposed by a state's administrative authority or through statutory authority.

In sum, the CMO regulation and practices in Europe seem to suggest that right holders in the EU have come to enjoy some level of freedom of selecting a CMO in the market. CMOs' imposition of contract terms with a broad scope (blanket exclusive licence) or too general clauses is likely to be prohibited and viewed as abusive. Further, right holders at least shall be allowed to retain the right to grant a non-commercial licence. One insight that can be gleaned from the history of CMO governance in Europe is precisely its history. Until the market matured, there were troublesome concerns about abuse of bargaining power by the CMOs.

3.3 CMO and Market Considerations – Revenue Distribution

The Haidan Court's ruling in China seems to be sympathetic towards the creator, in terms of revenue distribution. As the market for copyright licensing for compositions and lyrics may be small, when a performer right holder becomes financially successful through his own entrepreneurial endeavours by giving out live concerts, such endeavours may need to be acknowledged.

CMOs in this regard may seem to be indeed like a copyright troll – waiting for the success of the creator and doing nothing but waiting for profitable uses. Once the works are used, it deducts its fee from the licensing royalties. To an extent, there is a question of fairness, if we only consider the alternative that the copyright owner can directly conclude

---

[34]   Case C2/37.219 *Banghalter & Honem Christo/SACEM* ('*Daft Punk*').

a contract with a concert promoter and collect licensing royalties from such entities, he or she may be able to retain all the royalties rightfully due to them. When indeed an individual exercise benefits the creator and right holder, collective management sounds inefficient. This, however, is a typical dilemma of CMOs as entities that operate as licensing intermediaries. CMOs are supposed to provide services when collection is difficult or licensing is difficult even for a right holder with high market demands. In this manner, the utility of CMOs cannot be simply reduced to a single static instance of licences, but based on continuous and long-term capacity and performances as rights intermediaries.

There are some criticisms in China in this regard. To take MCSC as an example, from 1992 to the end of 2011, its total revenue for 2011 reached about CNY 88.89 million, a new record and an increase of 30.69 per cent over the previous year. However, by the end of 2011, the total distributable amount still reached CNY 734,725 million.[35] It has been claimed that MCSC does not distribute royalties to copyright owners in a timely manner and impartially and that many copyright owners have never received any royalties. The number of MCSC's members as of 2013 was 7301. Considering the population in China and the numbers of creators, the criticism may have some truth.[36] The above fact shows that the collective management of MCSC highlights that distribution of revenues should be made transparent, open and efficient.

Distribution of revenues has also been a thorny issue in the CMOs in Europe. Further, there have been some claims of discrimination (that is qualitative discrimination (revenue based)) among the members of a CMO. In 1972, this was prohibited by the ECJ ruling in *Re Gema*.[37] Indeed this may have been one of the driving forces towards the CMO Directive in Europe. The new CMO Directive regulates this in Articles 10–13 concerning revenue distributions, and the requirement of transparency in reporting to the right holders as well as the public in Articles 18–22. However, it remains to be seen whether the CMO Directive will indeed bring in more 'good governance' practices for the CMOs in Europe. As it predicts competition among the CMOs within the internal market, such competition may lead to good governance practices among them as well, in an effort to attract more members, across the national borders within the EU.

---

[35]   MCSC Annual Report 2011 <http://www.mcsc.com.cn/pdf/phpYtFrR7.pdf>, accessed 3 March 2015.
[36]   Ibid. at 4.
[37]   *Re GEMA's statutes (No. 2)* (1972) CMLR D-115.

3.4   Impact of CMOs' Exclusiveness on the Market for Copyright

The Zheng Jun case in China showed the problem that may be raised by the creators in China. If it were easier to identify the right holders, users would benefit most by directly licensing from the right holders. This may be even more the case when the right holder is famous, and the repertoire or works to license are not too many – in other words when the transaction costs are nearly zero. In such situations, the exclusiveness of rights management as required by Article 20 of the CMO Regulation in China would cause more harm than benefit to the users. When right holders can directly license their works, intermediaries only add to the transaction costs of obtaining authorization from the right holders rather than reducing them. However, the mirror of this perspective may also be true – when the market is identifiable, and when the users are known, having an exclusive CMO as intermediary only creates a burden for the creators. As such, it could create a strong disincentive for copyright holders to join a CMO. Further if CMOs are not obligated to accept the right holders, it creates a real concern that those authors who are unwilling to enter into broad and exclusive agreement with CMOs may be refused.

The case in China has even led a commentator to argue that even if the Regulation were to apply to the contract, the right holder should still have the right to use his own work. This is because, according to him, 'instead of letting organizer pay royalties to MCSC and MCSC distributes no royalties to copyright owners, might as well let organizer directly pay royalties to copyright owners'.[38] Although this may seem a pragmatic solution, his advice ultimately calls for the rule of law to be disregarded, thus it is not supportable.

According to EU law, one can posit that having a national law regulating or demanding such exclusive agreement to one CMO would be likely to be held in violation of EU law, based on the authority of case law or current Articles 4 and 5 of the CMO Directive. However, as CMOs need effective authorization from the right holders, laws allowing copyright assignments for CMO or exclusive licensing would be perfectly legal. Moreover, such clauses are commonly found in contracts authorizing the management of rights with each CMO. For example, among the Performing Rights Society for Music (PRS), the UK operates on the basis of assignment, and thus right holders may no longer license the works

---

[38]   An interview with Zhongxin Zhang, Taiwan Intellectual Property Officer (interviewer, Yang Li).

managed collectively.[39] Teosto (Finland) uses exclusive licences.[40] Outside the EU, JASRAC (Japan) requires a trust agreement and the rights are assigned and held in trust on behalf of the right holder beneficiary.[41]

The rationale for a policy for using exclusive arrangements may be pragmatic. Without some level of exclusivity to manage a specific work, CMOs cannot have sufficient economies of scale to justify their function. CMOs need authorization from the right holders to collect against use of others on behalf of the right holders where right holders cannot do so. Allowing CMOs to exercise remuneration rights instead of the right holders allows CMOs to collect rights revenues and manage the rights collectively. If the option to individually negotiate with other actors than CMOs remains, CMOs may not be able to force others to pay royalties – users may shop for better royalty rates either from CMOs or others. To the extent that individual exercise of rights disperses the function of the collective management, the exclusiveness of the agreement is necessary and justifiable. However an important policy choice and difference is whether to give such exclusivity through the law as is the case of the CMO Regulation in China, or through private agreements with the CMO as is the case in Europe.

4.   CONCLUSIONS

CMOs in China has been in the text of the statutes since the 1990s but there has been hardly any activity until recently. The short history may be behind the problems that we have seen in the Haidan Court case. Additionally, we note that immaturity of the market and CMOs makes it difficult to see what the role and function of CMOs in China is. As illustrated by the case example, it seems that the creators who are the beneficiaries of the CMO agreement seem to expect from the CMOs a role

---

[39]   See, for example, PRS for Music Standard terms of assignment-writer <https://www.prsformusic.com/joinus/writer/Pages/prs-standard-terms.aspx> accessed 31 March 2015.

[40]   See, for example, Teosto's general terms and conditions <https://www.teosto. fi/sites/default/files/files/Teosto%20General%20Terms%20and%20Conditions. pdf>, accessed 31 March 2015.

[41]   See Stipulations for copyright contract of JASRAC <http://www.jasrac. or.jp/ejhp/provisions/pdf/stipulations.pdf> accessed 31 March 2015. In contrast CPRA (Japan) (Center for Performers' Rights Administration) does not use assignment agreements and it is because they do not represent performers directly but rather are a right holders' organization which has agency-type agreements. Information on CPRA (Geidankyo) is from an interview, dated 28 February 2014 (transcript on file with the author Nari Lee).

as promoter and agent as well as royalty collectors, who would actively seek out opportunities for commercializing their works and generate more profit. As the Zheng Jun case illustrates, creators as well as users of creative works seem to have different expectations of the CMOs. As their perceptions and expectations are not aligned, the role and function of CMOs is also uncertain.

As CMOs ultimately work with the notion of a voluntary contract in the market, their operation should be market oriented. We believe that any laws and regulations should not force copyright owners to conclude exclusive contracts with CMOs unless copyright owners are willing to do so. Freedom or rights that are retained by the right holders as seen in the CMO Directive in Europe may be a good example to provide for the right holders. Especially when there is a statutory monopoly of a CMO, this may even be necessary to make CMO membership attractive for the right holders. For those copyright owners who are willing to accept exclusive collective management and often lack the ability to exercise effectively their copyrights, exclusive collective management of a CMO is more beneficial for them. But those who are unwilling to accept exclusive collective management of CMOs may have the ability to exercise effectively their copyright in some special circumstances. Laws and regulations should not force them to accept exclusive collective management.

As the previous chapter briefly sketched, China introduced collective copyrights management system as part of the ongoing IP law and system reforms. The legislative reform seemed to have set the framework for the operation of CMOs in China. However, as this chapter illustrates, without a common understanding among the market participants (creators) on the nature of CMOs as well as expectations from all institutions of IP rights, CMOs may not be operationalized in full. While CMOs are intermediaries that function within the market, in China they operate between the market and authority. In China it is closer to administrative authority than may be the case in Europe. As it is an entity that functions between the market for private rights and authority, the governance of copyright through CMOs needs to be based on both market-based considerations (copyright owners as well as uses) and the overall public benefit (competitors). Regulations governing CMOs both in China and the EU seem to indicate the particular function a CMO plays in between the market and the administrative or regulatory authorities. Focusing on the relationship between a CMO and its members (or beneficiary), we note that both in China and in Europe there is a general regulatory concern about abuse resulting from statutory monopoly power of the CMO in China, or as a dominant market actor in the EU. We observe that the differences between CMOs in Europe and China seem to be mainly coming from how they are viewed in the market for copyright.

Through the example of CMOs, it is possible to see that the story of layers of norms that govern CMOs in China may not be explained with a single theory of unidirectional legal transplant. Using the perspective of legal transplant, the CMOs in China may indicate a failed transplant or a rejection of an institutional practice. As the market plays an important role in the functioning of CMOs, without an active market for copyright licensing, transplantation of the norms alone may seem to fail. The market for copyright licences, however, calls for a change in the general perception of the public that copyright owners need to be remunerated for their works and that using another's works without authorization is wrong. A moral persuasion may need to precede the enforcement of rights.

As rights intermediaries, CMOs have an important role to play for cultural industries in creative societies. However, without functioning markets there is a real danger that CMOs may be expected to function merely as royalty-collecting societies at the periphery of the market or that they may be expected to function as a quasi-governmental entity that carries out the tasks of indirect administrative enforcement of copyright. Any copyright law reforms based on the functioning of CMOs, such as introduction of extended collective licensing, particularly taking the examples from the Nordic countries, to increase or limit the scope of CMOs' activities need to consider their impact on the market of users as well as producers of creative works.[42] While their own operation and business models for revenue generation requires successfully functioning markets for copyright licences, CMOs' operations are heavily regulated. Unlike patent trolls, CMOs may require statutory approval to operate in a given market and their business freedoms with the right holders that they represent are often restricted, as seen above. In China, this aspect of CMOs seems to be further highlighted by virtue of Article 6 of the Regulation.[43]

Transplantation of the norms to govern CMOs has to take local markets into consideration more than other parts of copyright law as this is closely tied to the market. Considering this, removing a proposal for the

---

[42]   Tanja Liljeström, 'From Representation to Agency – Acquisition of Online Music Copyrights by Collective Management Organizations, and the Future of Extended Collective Licensing' (2013) Edilex Publication Lakikirja <http://www.edilex.fi/artikkelit/10761>, accessed 31 March 2015. See also Thomas Riis and Jens Schovsbo, 'Extended Collective Licenses and the Nordic Experience – It's a Hybrid but Is It a Volvo or a Lemon?' (2009) 33 Columbia Journal of Law and the Arts 471.

[43]   *Supra* n. 16.

extended collective licensing from the third draft of the third Copyright Amendment may have been rightfully justified in China. Considering the competition and maturity of the market for CMOs, transparency and impartiality of CMOs' practices – both in terms of revenue distribution, fee structure and internal governance, having a statute making copyright collective agreement exclusive – may be counter-productive in the long run. In the short term, however, one may argue that it is necessary to have such clauses for a CMO with a statutory monopoly to induce the market for copyright licences to emerge. However, that would be like putting the horse before the cart. CMOs should be created by and for the market. In a word, when the market can decide distribution of resources, authorities (legislature, administration and judiciary) should not interfere in the market, as it is the market and not the authorities that should drive the process of distribution of copyright resources.

13. A comparative study on the relationship between injunctions and FRAND statements in China and the EU

Qi-shan Zhao

1. INTRODUCTION

In recent years, intense discussions have been raised about legal disputes involving standard essential patents (SEPs). When an SEP holder has made a declaration to a standard-setting organization (SSO) stating that it is prepared to grant licences to the standard implementers on 'fair, reasonable and non-discriminatory' (FRAND) terms, two major issues arise: (a) whether or not the SEP holder has the right to seek injunctive relief or threaten to seek an injunction, and (b) if the answer is not a straight yes or no, under what circumstances the SEP holder should be permitted to seek injunctive relief.

How to deal with the relationship between injunctive relief and the FRAND commitment is not only a problem related to the bargaining powers in FRAND licensing negotiations, but also impacts market competition and industry development. This issue has attracted significant attention from Chinese and European courts and competition authorities. For example, the courts in China, Germany and the Netherlands, as well as the Court of Justice of the European Union (CJEU),[1] have recently considered this issue. Furthermore, both the Chinese and EU competition authorities have dealt with several cases related to FRAND commitments and injunctions.

---

[1]   On 21 March 2013, the Regional Court of Düsseldorf stayed the proceedings in the trial between Huawei and ZTE and decided to ask the CJEU for its determination of appropriate remedies. In November 2014, the CJEU gave its answer to the questions raised by the court. The judgment in *Huawei v. ZTE* had not yet been given at the time this chapter was written. See further *infra*, section 4.1.1.

In light of this situation, this chapter provides an initial introduction to the debates about injunctive relief and FRAND commitments in Section 2. Subsequently, Sections 3 and 4 provide an analysis of several leading cases in China and the EU, which highlight the various approaches that the respective courts and competition authorities have taken to these matters. In closing, this chapter will present recommendations for solutions in dealing with the challenges of injunctive relief for SEPs.

2. DEBATES ON THE RELATIONSHIP OF INJUNCTIVE RELIEF AND FRAND COMMITMENT

When the parties cannot reach an agreement on FRAND licensing terms for an SEP, the SEP holder may seek injunctive relief or threaten to do so. Such litigation tactics have caused a great deal of controversy. The most important reason for objecting to the grant of injunctive relief in the case of SEPs, is that if the SEP holder successfully obtains injunctive relief, the potential licensee will be put in a weak bargaining position and the so-called hold-up problem is likely to show up. Lemley and Shapiro have commented that 'the threat to obtain a permanent injunction greatly enhances the patent holder's negotiating power, leading to royalty rates that exceed a natural benchmark range based on the value of the patented technology and the strength of the patent'.[2] They suggest that problems related to patent hold-up would be alleviated if the courts would instead allow defendants the possibility to alter the design of their products in order to escape claims of infringement.[3] Similarly, Chappatte has pointed out that SEP holders are in a position to '(i) block companies from producing any products compliant with the standard, and (ii) demand royalties for its patent that are significantly higher than the royalties it may have demanded had the technology not been included in the standard or before the standard was adopted and competition eliminated'.[4]

Some scholars, however, are of a different opinion. For example, one study empirically analysed the patents related to third-generation (3G) cellular telephone technology and concluded that there is no evidence of royalty stacking resulting from patent hold-up, among the more than

---

[2]   Mark A. Lemley and Carl Shapiro, 'Patent Holdup and Royalty Stacking' (1991) 85 Texas Law Review 1991, 1993.

[3]   Ibid.

[4]   Philippe Chappatte, 'FRAND Commitments – The Case for Antitrust Intervention' (2009) 2 European Competition Journal 319, 320.

60 companies involved in the standard.[5] In another paper, Geradin pointed out that 'in contrast to the claims made by patent hold-up theorists, innovators active in standardized fields face significant risks of being under-compensated and thus may become the victims of reverse hold-ups'.[6]

In fact, patent hold-up and reverse hold-up problems may co-exist during the negotiations for an SEP licence. Due to the ambiguity surrounding the FRAND principle, the negotiating parties may not reach an agreement about FRAND terms, in spite of the fact that an SEP holder may have previously made a FRAND commitment to the SSO. Thus in some industries which face rapid technological changes and advances, such as the ICT industry, it is widely accepted that a party can 'use the SEP first and then negotiate the license'.[7] If the SEP holder and an implementer reach an impasse during FRAND negotiations, the fact that the SEP holder might be able to obtain an injunction is a significant factor affecting the parties' relative bargaining positions. On the one hand, if the SEP holder obtains an injunction, this could be hazardous to the implementer because they could lose all their investment by being ordered by the court to stop the manufacture or distribution of the relevant products or services. On the other hand, if the SEP holder is not able to obtain injunctive relief, the implementer will be able to influence and delay negotiations by taking as much time as possible to exploit the patented technologies. Obviously, either the hold-up or the reverse hold-up may have a negative impact on the implementation of the standard and industry development. Therefore, it is important to find ways to resolve issues pertaining to injunctive relief for SEPs, in order to help the successful conclusion of FRAND agreements and reduce the risks of hold-up and reverse hold-up.

---

[5] See Damien Geradin, Anne Layne-Farrar and A. Jorge Padilla, 'Royalty Stacking in High Tech Industries: Separating Myth from Reality' (14 May 2008) <http://ssrn.com/abstract=949599> accessed 31 May 2013.

[6] Damien Geradin, 'Reverse Hold-ups: The (Often Ignored) Risks Faced by Innovators in Standardized Areas' (paper prepared for the Swedish Competition Authority on the Pros and Cons of Standard-Setting, Stockholm, 12 November 2010) 1.

[7] In fact, to some extent, both the licensor and the licensee approve this 'using first' business model. On the one hand, the licensee does not expect that the long SEP negotiation blocks the marking of the new products. And on the other hand, the licensor is unwilling to price the SEP too early, for knowing how widely the SEP are used will be good for the evaluation.

3.   INJUNCTIVE RELIEF AND FRAND COMMITMENTS UNDER CHINESE LAW

3.1   The Requirements for Injunctive Relief under Chinese Law

In theory, the award of an injunction by the court may be in the form of an interlocutory injunction or a permanent injunction. Ultimately, this will depend on the length of the effective period of relief provided for by the injunction. The requirements for interlocutory injunctions under Chinese patent law can be found in Articles 100 to 108 of the Civil Procedure Law (2012),[8] Article 66 of the Patent Law (2008),[9] and the related judicial interpretation issued in 2001;[10] all of which are concerned with injunction applications before and during litigation. Under Chinese law, the corresponding concept of a permanent injunction is referred to as a 'cessation of infringement'.[11] Cessation of infringement defines a situation where an infringer will be 'forbidden from making, using, offering to sell, selling or importing the product directly obtained by the patented process, or using the patented process, or using, offering to sell, selling or importing the product directly obtained by the patented process for production or business purposes'.[12] According to Articles 2 and 15 of the Tort Law (2009), cessation of infringement (that is injunctive relief) is one of the main remedies for an infringement and/or a tort; thus, it is viewed as the most important, as well as most effective, way to protect a patent holder's right.[13] Generally speaking, in a patent infringement lawsuit in China, if the patent is valid and infringed by the defendant, the court usually approves the patent holder's application for an injunction and orders the

---

8   See《中华人民共和国民事诉讼法（2012）》第100–108条 [Article 100–108, Civil Procedure Law of the People's Republic of China (2012)] < http://en.pkulaw. cn/display.aspx?cgid=183386&lib=law> accessed 8 January 2015.

9   See《中华人民共和国专利法（2008）》第60条 [Article 60, Patent Law of the People's Republic of China (2008)] < http://en.pkulaw.cn/display.aspx? cgid=111782&lib=law> accessed 8 January 2015.

10   See 《最高人民法院关于审理专利纠纷案件适用法律问题的若干规定》 （法释〔2013〕9号） [Supreme People's Court, 'The Provisions of Applicable Legal Matter about Ceasing the Infringement of Patent Right before Litigation' (No. 9, 2013 Judicial Interpretation) < http://baike.sogou.com/v71693665.htm> accessed 10 January 2015.

11   However, in terms of theory, cessation of infringement in Chinese patent law is different from permanent injunction in the U.S patent law both in the requirement of issue and the outcome of enforcement.

12   程永顺 [Cheng Yongshun],《中国专利诉讼》 [*Chinese Patent Lawsuit*] 知识产权出版社2005年版第287页 [Intellectual Property Press]（2005）287.

13   Ibid.

defendant to cease the infringement.[14] In such circumstances, 'cessation of infringement' is more akin to an affirmation of the infringement rather than a strict limitation placed on the defendant.

Since the Patent Law and the judicial interpretation of patent infringement issued in 2009[15] lack concrete legal provisions relating to the cessation of infringement for a patent, the Supreme People's Court issued a policy paper in 2009 entitled 'The Opinion about Some Problems of the General Situation about Intellectual Property Trial Service under the Current Economic Situation', which explained the scope of cessation of infringement for the first time and emphasized the balance between different interests when deciding to order cessation of infringement:

> 15. If the cessation of the related infringement activity can cause a vital loss of balance in the interests between the parties involved, or counteract public interests, or it cannot be performed actually, the court can measure the interests on the basis of the specific conditions, and take the more appropriate alternative measures to settle the disputes instead of ceasing infringement. If patent owner was negligent of asserting his legal rights and has contributed to infringement, the court should take a careful consideration and refuse his cessation of infringement request, in order to prevent creating a serious imbalance of interest between the parties. However it will not affect the reasonable compensation in accordance with the law.[16]

Though this document is not a formal judicial interpretation and judges should not directly cite it as the basis of their judgment, it guides the patent infringement trial.

---

[14]   朱理，邵中林 [Zhu Li, He Zhonglin], 知识产权侵权责任若干问题 [Several Problems about the Liabilities of Patent Infringement] 《人民法院报》 [*People's Court Newspaper*], 2008年9月25日 (25 September 2008).

[15]   See 《最高人民法院关于审理侵犯专利权纠纷案件应用法律若干问题的解释》（法释〔2009〕21号）[Interpretation of the Supreme People's Court on Several Issues concerning the Application of Law in the Trial of Patent Infringement Dispute Cases' (No. 21, 2009 Judicial Interpretation)] <http://en.pkulaw.cn/display.aspx?cgid=125367&lib=law> accessed 13 January 2015.

[16]   《如果停止有关行为会造成当事人之间的重大利益失衡，或者有悖社会公共利益，或者实际上无法执行，可以根据案件具体情况进行利益衡量，不判决停止行为，而采取更充分的赔偿或者经济补偿等替代性措施了断纠纷。权利人长期放任侵权、怠于维权，在其请求停止侵害时，倘若责令停止有关行为会在当事人之间造成较大的利益不平衡，可以审慎地考虑不再责令停止行为，但不影响依法给予合理的赔偿。》最高人民法院《关于当前经济形势下知识产权审判服务大局若干问题的意见》（2009法发第23号）第15条 [Article 15, Notice of the Supreme People's Court on Issuing the Opinions on Several Issues concerning Intellectual Property Trials Serving the Overall Objective under the Current Economic Situation' (No. 23, 2009 of the Supreme People's Court)] <http://en.pkulaw.cn/display.aspx?cgid=116332&lib=law> accessed 7 January 2014.

According to the above document, there are four other situations in which a 'cessation of infringement (i.e. injunctive relief)' can be prevented: (i) vital interests between parties involved are unbalanced; (ii) contrary to public interest; (iii) it is unable to cease the infringement; or (iv) the patent owner has given up suing for the infringement, and has been negligent of safeguarding his right. However, only one of these four situations, namely contrary to the public interest, was referred to in past patent infringement trials.[17]

In 2008, the Supreme People's Court gave an advisory opinion to the Liaoning High Court regarding SEPs and that opinion stated that if a patentee participates in standard-setting or otherwise agrees that the patented technology may be incorporated into a standard, the exploitation of the SEP by the implementer of the standard does not constitute patent infringement under Article 11 of the Patent Law. Moreover, although the SEP owner may charge a patent royalty to the implementers of the standard, the amount of which should be significantly lower than the normal licence fee, the SEP owner cannot forbid them from using the patent.[18] Even though this advisory opinion is a case-specific decision, rather than a formally binding precedent, it has caused a sense of unease among SEP owners, especially foreign patent holders.

In a 2013 case, *Huawei v. InterDigital*, the Shenzhen City Intermediate

---

17 See广东省广州市中级人民法院（2004）穗中法民三知初字第581号民事判决书 [Civil Judgment No.581 (2004), First Intellectual Property, Civil Division 3, Intermediate People's Court, Guangzhou of the Intermediate People's Court of Guangzhou City, Guangdong Province]. In this case, the patented product was used during the construction of an airport, and since the judge thought that requiring cessation of infringement would be in conflict with the public interest, the airport was allowed to continue using the patented product after paying compensation. Also see福建省高级人民法院（2001）闽知初字第4号民事判决书 [No. 4 (2001), First Intellectual Property Judgment, Higher People's Court, Fujian]. In this case, the defendant infringed the plaintiff's patent which was used to purify the flue gas discharged by a thermal power plant. Since the patented desulphurization facilities are thought to be significant for the protection of the environment, the court did not require cessation of the infringement but demanded the defendant to pay compensation, about RMB 240,000 a year for every patent unit used by the defendant.

18 See 最高人民法院关于朝阳兴诺公司按照建设部颁发的行业标准《复合载体夯扩桩设计规程》设计、施工而实施标准中专利的行为是否构成侵犯专利权问题的函（[2008] 民三他字第4号）[Reply of the Supreme People's Court on whether the Chaoyang Xingnuo Company committed patent infringement by implementing the patents belonging to the Standard for Designing and Building as the Industry Standard 'Specification for Design of Ram-compaction Piles with Composite Bearing Base' issued by Ministry of Construction (No.4 [2008] of the Civil Division III of the Supreme People's Court)].

People's Court claimed that an SEP holder who seeks an injunction during FRAND negotiations may be considered as abusing their dominant position in the relative market.[19]

> While two parties were still in negotiations, the defendant filed an injunction against the plaintiff demanding the plaintiff stop using the SEP; an act which breached the FRAND obligations the defendant undertook during the negotiation. Since the plaintiff always acted in good faith during negotiations with the defendant, the defendant's sole aim of lodging a complaint in the US was to compel the plaintiff into accepting exorbitant licensing terms. An SEP holder has no right to forbid a *bona fide* party from utilising the SEP, and the defendant's behaviour is seen as an abuse of their dominant position in the relative market.[20]

This case suggests that an SEP holder who seeks an injunction during FRAND negotiations may be considered as abusing their dominant position in the relative market. However, this case did not discuss the requirements an SEP holder needs to overcome in order to be granted an injunction.

In July 2014, the Supreme People's Court issued a paper entitled 'An Explanation about the Applicable Legal Questions in the Trial of Patent Disputes (2)'. This paper attempted to answer this question in Article 27:

> For a patent disclosed as a non-compulsory national standard, industry standard, as well as an enterprise standard, the court shall not accept the view that the defendant is not required to seek a license from the patent owner for the implementation of standard. However, if the patent owner does not comply with the FRAND principles and negotiates with the defendant in bad faith, the court shall generally not issue a 'cessation of infringement' in favour of the SEP holder.[21]

In light of the aforementioned judicial interpretation, it is likely that the Supreme People's Court intends to establish a special rule for the cessation of infringement relating to SEPs, whereby a consideration of an SEP

---

[19]   For the details of the related case on FRAND royalty rate, please see Chapter 14 in this volume.

[20]   See Ye Ruosi Zhu Jianjun and Chen Wenquan, 'Recognizing Abuse of Market Position by Holders of Standards Essential Patents – Huawei v. US IDC Company' (2013) 03 Electronic Intellectual Property 51, 52.

[21]   See 《最高人民法院关于审理侵犯专利权纠纷案件应用法律若干问题的解释（二）》（公开征求意见稿）[Supreme People's Court, An Explanation about the Applicable Legal Questions in the Trial of Patent Disputes (2) (Draft)]. <http://www.law-lib.com/fzdt/newshtml/20/20140801084607.htm> accessed 14 April 2015.

holder's *bona fides* only need be undertaken and without regard to public interest or balance of interests concerns.

3.2   The Perspective of the Chinese Anti-monopoly Authority

The Chinese anti-monopoly authorities also pay attention to the injunctive relief problem when they deal with the relative cases. The Chinese Ministry of Commerce (MOFCOM) did so, for example, in its approval of Microsoft's acquisition of Nokia's smartphone business.

Microsoft International Holdings B.V. (a wholly owned subsidiary of Microsoft) and Nokia concluded a Stock and Asset Purchase Agreement on 2 September 2013. On 13 September 2013, Microsoft submitted an application to MOFCOM seeking an anti-monopoly review of its agreement with Nokia. On 9 April 2014, MOFCOM approved Microsoft's acquisition of Nokia's devices and services business, subject to certain conditions, some of which concerned problems related to injunctions.[22] In this case, MOFCOM concluded that the acquisition of Nokia's devices and services business by Microsoft may exclude or curtail competition in the Chinese smartphone market and decided to approve the acquisition subject to certain restrictive conditions. One of the conditions for Microsoft was that they would grant a licence on FRAND terms for the SEPs covered by the FRAND declaration and would not seek injunctions or exclusionary orders for those SEPs utilised by Chinese mobile phone manufacturers.

Nokia also made a commitment to MOFCOM that they would not use injunctions to stop the implementation of SEPs covered by FRAND commitments, unless Nokia had offered FRAND terms to a potential licensee who did not sign the contract in good faith. Whether a licensor or licensee acted in good faith, Nokia suggested, was a matter of reciprocity and intellectual property policies made by the SSOs and the development of relevant judicial interpretation. One of the factors that the antitrust authority could take into consideration is whether a licensee would allow, without unreasonable delay, an independent third party (such as a court or an arbitrator) to determine the FRAND terms and follow the determination of that third party. Since Nokia is one of the most important SEP

---

[22]   See 商务部公告2014年第24号——关于附加限制性条件批准微软收购诺基亚设备和服务业务案经营者集中反垄断审查决定的公告 [Announcement [2014] No. 24 of the Ministry of Commerce – Announcement on the Decision of Conditional Approval upon Anti-monopoly Review of the Concentration of Business Operators by the Acquisition of Nokia's Devices and Services Business by Microsoft] <http://fldj.mofcom.gov.cn/article/ztxx/201404/20140400542415.shtml> accessed 14 April 2015.

holders in ICT standards, this commitment is significant in attempting to deal with the problem of injunctions in a proper manner.

4.   RELEVANT EU CASES

In Europe, patent law is a matter for the Member States to legislate upon.[23] Accordingly, an SEP holder has to file for patent infringement or seek an injunction in the individual national courts of the EU Member States. Due to the differences between various national patent systems, European courts have not established clear, uniform rules for granting injunctions, let alone uniform rules for granting injunctive relief to an SEP covered by FRAND commitments. In recent years, the courts in Germany, the Netherlands, the UK and France have all dealt with some cases on this issue. The German and Dutch courts have taken the lead in providing answers and the former have attempted to deal with the issue under competition law, while the latter's approach is under civil law. The injunctive relief problem for SEP licensing has also attracted a high degree of attention from the European Commission (EC) and the EC has even questioned some of the decisions of the German courts.

4.1   Related Cases Judged by Courts in Europe

4.1.1   Discussion under competition law: German courts and the CJEU

German patent law allows the patentee to apply for an injunction.[24] As a general rule however, there is no discretion for the German courts to grant an injunction for a patent infringement. Therefore, if a court finds that a patent is valid and the defendant has infringed the patent, it typically grants an injunction as a matter of course. If the defendant wants to overturn the injunction, they must file the 'compulsory licence' defence, claiming that the patent owner has abused their dominant market position. If the court recognizes the compulsory licence defence, the patent holder may not prevent the defendant from using the patent.

---

[23]   This will of course change after the establishment of the Unified Patent Court. As of 10 February 2015 six out of the 25 participating Member States have ratified the Unified Patent Court Agreement (Austria, Belgium, Denmark, France, Malta and Sweden).

[24]   Section 139(1) German Patent Act: 'Any person who uses a patented invention in contravention of Sections 9 through 13 may, if there is danger of repletion, be sued by the injured party for injunctive relief. This claim shall also apply if there is a danger of first perpetration.'

Though German patent law does not provide a basis for an infringer to avoid an injunction based on an SEP holder's FRAND statement, German courts have developed the 'Orange Book' defence for SEP users. In its 'Orange Book' judgment of 6 May 2009[25] the German Federal Supreme Court held that an SEP owner may abuse its dominant position if it has refused an irrevocable, unconditional and binding offer by a potential licensee and the potential licensee has acted as if the licence agreement had been concluded, meaning he must pay the royalty fee to the patent owner or into an escrow account. Under such conditions courts may refuse to grant an injunction.[26] This decision is named the 'Orange Book' defence. Though the 'Orange Book' case involved a *de facto* standard and the SEP holder had not made a FRAND commitment to any SSOs, district courts have held that the 'Orange Book' defence equally applies to standards established by SSOs.[27]

Following the 'Orange Book' defence the Court of Appeal in Karlsruhe, in *Motorola v. Apple*, revoked the injunctive relief granted by the District Court of Mannheim to Motorola's SEP after Apple had amended its licence offer by adding a clause allowing Motorola to terminate the contract in the event Apple were to attack the validity of the licensed patent.[28] Similarly, in May 2012, the District Court of Mannheim applied the 'Orange Book' defence in *Motorola v. Microsoft*, and awarded the SEP holder an injunction, concluding that such action did not violate EU competition law.[29] In this case, the Court took the position that a potential licensee must offer a royalty that is just short of being 'clearly excessive', before the SEP holder's refusal of the offer can be considered abusive.[30] Obviously, the above two Motorola cases in 2012 expanded the 'Orange Book' defence, and raised the requirements for a defendant to challenge applications for injunctive relief from the SEP holder.

However, these judgments were questioned by another German court

---

[25] German Federal Supreme Court, 6 May 2009, KZR 39/06 (*Orange-Book-Standard*).

[26] As for the licence fee, the defendant must account for the use of the patent on a regular basis and must pay the reasonable royalties either directly to the plaintiff or to an escrow account held by a German court. Ibid., paras 32 and 36.

[27] District Court of Mannheim, 18 February 2011, doc. no. 7 O 100/10 (*IPCom v. Nokia*); District Court of Düsseldorf, 24 April 2012, doc. no. 4b O 273/10 (*IPCom v. Nokia*).

[28] Court of Appeal in Karlsruhe, February 27, 2012, doc. no. 6 U 136/11 (*Motorola v. Apple*).

[29] District Court of Mannheim, 2 May 2012, doc. no. 2 O 240/11 (*Motorola v. Microsoft*).

[30] Ibid.

in 2013 in the case of *Huawei v. ZTE*. Huawei owned SEPs which were essential to the LTE (long-term evolution) standard developed by the European Telecommunications Standards Institute (ETSI) and had given ETSI a commitment to grant licences on FRAND terms. Since ZTE developed products based on the LTE standard in Germany, it inevitably used Huawei's SEPs. Between November 2010 and the end of March 2011, Huawei and ZTE had negotiated the SEP licence. Huawei required a reasonable royalty in return, while ZTE offered a cross-licensing arrangement. Without receiving the expected royalty, Huawei, on 28 April 2011, applied for an injunction. The Court of Düsseldorf referred to the 'Orange Book' case and accordingly, ZTE could not get compulsory licence for the SEP because they had not provided an 'unconditional' offer, nor paid a royalty for previous use of the SEP. However, the court noted ZTE's willingness to negotiate in light of the position adopted by the EC in cases such as *Samsung*.[31] As a result, and in order to reconcile the Orange Book standard with the EC's position, the Court stayed the trial and referred five questions to the CJEU for its determination of appropriate remedies.[32] According to Advocate General Wathelet:

> the proprietor of a standard-essential patent may be required, before seeking an injunction against a company that has infringed that patent, to make that company a specific licensing offer. *That applies where the proprietor of the patent is in a dominant position and has made a commitment to the standards body to grant third parties a licence on fair, reasonable and non-discriminatory terms and where the infringer is ready, willing and able to enter into such a licensing agreement.*[33]

By the end of March 2015, the CJEU had not yet given a judgment in this case. However, the judgment of the CJEU, when it is given, will bind the courts of all EU Member States and will be a milestone in dealing with injunctive relief problems in RAND (reasonable and non-discriminatory terms) licences.

---

[31] *Infra*, section 4.2.

[32] For the details concerning the five questions see Case C-170/13 *Huawei v. ZTE* (request for a preliminary ruling from the Landgericht Düsseldorf (Germany)).

[33] Court of Justice of the European Union, Press Release No. 155/14 Luxembourg, 20 November 2014 http://curia.europa.eu/jcms/upload/docs/application/pdf/2014-11/cp140155en.pdf accessed 1 June 2015. See for details, Opinion of the AG in Case C-170/13 *Huawei Technologies v. ZTE* ECLI:EU:C:2014:2391.

4.1.2 Discussion under civil law: relevant cases in the Netherlands

Similar to the German courts, the Dutch courts usually grant injunctions for patent infringements provided that the infringement is affirmed. However, the courts in the Netherlands appear to deal with cases relating to injunctions and FRAND commitments on the bases of contract law and patent law, rather than competition law.

In 2010, in the case of *Philips v. SK-Kassetten*, the District Court of The Hague granted an injunction to the SEP holder, as the Court thought that the existence of a FRAND commitment does not automatically prevent the SEP holder from enforcing its patent or seeking the injunction. The court also emphasized that the standard implementer should first ask for a licence from the patentee before using the SEP, and if the patentee had rejected such requirement, the standard implementer should file a motion requesting the court to order the patentee to grant a licence on the basis of FRAND.[34]

However in 2012, in *Samsung v. Apple*,[35] the District Court of The Hague rejected the SEP holder's application for an injunction. The Court treated Samsung's FRAND commitment as a commitment to enter into an agreement and thus Apple had received an irrevocable contractual claim to obtain a FRAND licence from Samsung. Accordingly, Samsung had to negotiate with Apple in good faith, as well as giving an offer with the term of FRAND. According to this conclusion, the court ruled that seeking an injunction during FRAND negotiations constituted an abuse of rights or a breach of pre-contractual good faith.[36]

4.2 Relevant cases of the European Commission

In April 2012, the EC initiated an investigation against Motorola because they had sought an injunction against Apple in Germany. In this investigation, Motorola owned SEPs under the GPRS standard issued by ETSI and made a FRAND commitment to ETSI. Apple had agreed to the fact that the German court would set the FRAND rate; however, Motorola still applied for injunctive relief. On 6 May 2013, the EC gave its preliminary view that Motorola's attempts to be granted an injunction against Apple was an abuse of a dominant position prohibited by EU competition rules. The Commission was concerned that the threat of an injunction can

---

[34] District Court of The Hague, 17 March 2010, case/docket numbers 316533/ HA ZA 08-2522 and 316535 / HA ZA 08-2524 (*Phillips v. SK-Kassetten*).

[35] District Court of The Hague, 14 March 2012, doc. no. 400367/HA ZA 11-2212 (*Samsung v. Apple*).

[36] Ibid.

distort licensing negotiations and lead to licensing terms that the licensee of the SEP would not have accepted absent this threat. This would lead to less consumer choice.[37] The Commission also pointed out that an interpretation of the 'Orange Book' standard, whereby a willing licensee is essentially not entitled to challenge the validity and essentiality of the SEPs in question, was potentially anti-competitive.[38] On 29 April 2014, the Commission officially announced that Motorola's attempts to seek an injunction constituted as an abuse of a dominant position prohibited by EU competition rules.[39]

Furthermore, in April 2011, Samsung applied for injunctive relief against Apple's infringement of its SEP under the 3G/UMTS standard, and in December 2012, the EC initiated an antitrust investigation against Samsung. On 29 April 2014, the Commission accepted legally binding commitments by Samsung regarding SEP injunctions. According to these commitments, in the following five years, Samsung will not seek injunctions in Europe on the basis of SEPs for smartphones and tablets against licensees who sign up to a specified licensing framework. The licensing framework provided by Samsung requires:

(i)   that there is a negotiation period of up to 12 months; and
(ii)   if no agreement is reached, a third-party determination of FRAND terms by a court or by an arbitrator if both parties agree on this.

An independent monitoring trustee will advise the Commission in overseeing the proper implementation of the commitments.[40]

---

[37] European Commission, 'Antitrust: Commission Sends Statement of Objections to Motorola Mobility on Potential Misuse of Mobile Phone Standard-Essential Patents' (Brussels, 6 May 2013) <http://europa.eu/rapid/press-release_IP-13-406_en.htm> accessed 20 March 2014.

[38] Ibid.

[39] European Commission, 'Antitrust: Commission finds that Motorola Mobility infringed EU competition rules by misusing standard essential patents' (Brussels, 29 April 2014) <http://europa.eu/rapid/press-release_IP-14-489_en.htm> accessed 3 May 2014.

[40] European Commission, 'Antitrust: Commission accepts legally binding commitments by Samsung Electronics on standard essential patent injunctions' (Brussels, 29 April 2014) <http://europa.eu/rapid/press-release_IP-14-490_en.htm> accessed 3 May 2014.

5.   COMPARATIVE ANALYSIS AND CONCLUSION

Analysing the above regulations and cases regarding injunctions and FRAND commitments in China and Europe, three major issues can be discerned: (a) whether it is permissible for the SEP holder to apply for injunctive relief after having made FRAND commitments towards the SSO; (b) whether the SEP holder, having made FRAND commitments, may impact negatively the efficacy of market competition by seeking injunctive relief during negotiations, and if so, how an SEP holder should be held liable; and (c) under what conditions injunctive relief can be granted for an SEP covered by FRAND commitments.

The first issue is suitable for clarification through the relevant patent policies of SSOs. If minimum conditions or a framework about this problem have been previously established, the risk of the future legal disputes should be reduced. For the purposes and the roles that an injunction should play in the SEP implementation process, this chapter argues that with respect to those SEPs covered by FRAND commitments, only if a standard implementer (potential licensee) has failed to negotiate in good faith can the related SEP holder apply for injunctive relief. If the relevant SSO has provided for this scenario in its patent policy, members should state that the SEP holder will apply for the injunctive relief only if the potential licensee rejects in bad faith or intentionally delays the negotiation of a FRAND licence. Generally speaking, the inappropriate behaviour of implementers includes the following three circumstances: the licensee refuses to negotiate; the licensee intentionally delays the negotiation; and the licensee refuses to comply with a court judgment and the arbitration award.

The second issue attracts attention from competition authorities. In comparison to the decision of the courts, both MOFCOM and the EC focused their analysis on the effect of injunctive relief on the relevant market. Competition authorities also provide guidelines for the FRAND negotiation process, for example the commitment of Samsung established a 'safe harbour' for all potential licensees who act in good faith. Furthermore, the conditions laid down for the approval of Microsoft's purchase of Nokia provide directions for future SEP licensing and ensure a competitive market in the interest of consumers.

Finally, the third question should be made clear by the relevant judgments of the courts. In fact, how the courts in various countries treat the injunctive relief problem for SEP infringement cases is based on their own national patent law. This is why the courts in China, Germany, the Netherlands and China have reached different opinions for similar factual patterns.

In China, the Supreme People's Court intended to set up a special rule for the cessation of infringement relating to SEPs, however this idea may still have some problems. First, the basic rules of patent injunctive relief, especially the rules of cessation of infringement, are still ambiguous in Chinese law, and there is no thorough analysis of the necessity for establishing a special injunctive rule on SEPs. In addition, the related Supreme People's Court paper[41] considers only the 'bad faith' of SEP holders other than the balance of convenience or the public interest. However, the so-called 'bad faith' of the SEP holder is a very ambiguous concept; for example, what are the specific situations in which an SEP holder can be considered to have acted in bad faith and is it possible that a licensee has acted in bad faith also? So this draft seems have neglected the possibility of a reverse patent hold-up problem, which may also cause an imbalance in the licence negotiations.

The German courts seem to emphasize the good faith of the standard implementer other than the good faith of the SEP holder. According to the 'Orange Book' framework, the standard implementer has to act as a licensee in order to gain the compulsory licence defence and the courts' requirement of giving 'irrevocable, unconditional and binding royalty offer' has the potential to create some tension for the standard implementer. The 'Orange Book' framework also does not consider whether the SEP holder has given a FRAND commitment to the SSOs, and thus the FRAND commitment is weakened from preventing an SEP holder from seeking an injunction, which ultimately may reduce the value of FRAND commitment. In the case of *Huawei v. ZTE*, the Court questioned the 'Orange Book' framework and referred five questions to the CJEU for its determination of appropriate remedies. And when the judgment of the CJEU is given, the challenge to the 'Orange Book' framework will be clarified.

In the Netherlands, the standard implementer should first require a FRAND licence from the SEP holder before the commencement of litigation and then remain willing to negotiate or explain to the court why the SEP holder's offer does not comply with the FRAND commitment. Unlike the German courts, the Dutch courts have dealt with the relevant cases on the bases of contract law and patent law and they have not explained why the FRAND commitment of the SEP holder made to the SSOs creates a duty between the patentee and the patent users.

It is difficult to state which regulation of the above three countries is best. It is suggested that the various national courts, in their analysis of patent infringement injunctive relief, should focus on analysing some key

---

[41]   See *supra*, n 21.

factors during the investigation, such as the SSO policy, the expression of the related FRAND commitment and the correspondence between the two parties during the negotiations, which indicates their attitudes towards the licence. In order to give rise to a permanent injunction, the courts should further inspect what the effects of granting a permanent injunction may have on competition and the public interest.

In summary, the appropriate handling of the relationship between FRAND commitments and injunctive relief should aim at ensuring a competitive market and the facilitation and performance of licence agreements. Ultimately, all of this depends on coordination and cooperation among the SSOs, competition authorities and the courts. Though there are no easy answers to this issue, both China and Europe are grappling with this through judicial and regulatory systems and may benefit from each other's experience and insight.

14. European standards in Chinese courts – a case of SEP and FRAND disputes in China

Yang Li and Nari Lee

1. INTRODUCTION

The fact that markets in today's economy are globalized is not news. As noticed on China's opening of its economy and joining of the world trading system through World Trade Organization (WTO) agreements, more and more economies are becoming connected and interdependent. However, in contrast to the economic reality of globalization, the laws and legal system still are largely national and private rights are territorial. Despite the long history of harmonization of the laws, there is no globally uniform intellectual property (IP) law and it is not certain whether such law could emerge. Even in the EU, where there is an operational uniform title of community trademark, the effect of the rights still is most likely tied to the territories of the states that form the EU.[1] Moreover, further initiatives to create unitary titles, as seen in the EU copyright law projects or unitary patent projects seem to stir up controversies.[2]

Despite the extensive harmonization of procedural and substantive

---

[1] See for detailed discussions on EU trademark law projects, Chapter 8 of this volume.

[2] Bernt P. Hugenholtz, 'Harmonisation or Unification of European Union Copyright Law' [online] (2012) 38(1) Monash University Law Review 4–16. For a discussion of the history of EU patent law harmonization and patent exceptions, see Nari Lee, 'Adding Fuel to Fire: A Complex Case of Unifying Patent Limitations and Exceptions Through the EU Patent Package' in Rosa Maria Ballardini, Marcus Norrgård and Niklas Bruun (eds), *Transitions in European Patent Law Influences of the Unitary Patent Package* (Kluwer Law International 2015). See also H. Ullrich, 'Harmonizing Patent Law: the Untamable Union Patent' in M.-Chr. Janssens and G. Van Overwalle (eds) *Harmonisation Of European IP Law: From European Rules To Belgian Law and Practice* (Bruylant 2012).

patent norms through international agreements, patent rights are still local. Despite the territoriality of patent rights, the rights holders and the users are free to enter into commercial agreements concerning the use of the rights. Furthermore, the producers of the goods embodying the inventions are not necessarily bound by the territorial restrictions in their making, selling and offering of the products. As such, the exploitation of a patent may well be done, crossing the territorial boundaries of a right. Often, to ameliorate frictions, practices based on commercial contracts and industrial customs and standards emerge. In other words, after the initial grants of rights, contracts, industry customs and standards are adopted voluntarily by the market participants and they function as self-regulating or governing instruments to coordinate fragmentations caused by territorial rights.

The activities of the standard-setting organizations (SSOs) that set standards for the use of the standard essential patents (SEPs) are one such example of self-regulation. While the patent rights are local, SSOs are organizations often with multiple and heterogeneous participants. The guidelines and other soft law policies that SSOs voluntarily adopt are often likely to reflect such multi-territorial nature of SSOs' participants. When a dispute arises on the conditions that are set by SSOs over the assertion of SEPs, the problem would be likely to include factual considerations that arise across territories. As such, disputes surrounding SEPs force local courts to consider not only local judicial standards and doctrines, but also those used elsewhere that may be relevant to understanding complex facts of disputes.

The tendency of judges to look for doctrinal tools used in other jurisdictions to solve complex cases has been known. The tools could be specific rules developed in a foreign jurisdiction from where the system of rights may have been imported, or they may be theoretical doctrines or practical tests that are used to interpret local statutes and to solve disputes.[3] Indeed this particular type of informal norm exchanges, branded as a 'judicial globalization', has been highlighted and noted by several commentators.[4]

This chapter discusses such tendency of the courts in the interpretation of a particular licensing principle of 'fair, reasonable and non-discriminatory' (FRAND) adopted by an European SSO, the

---

[3]   See, for example, Anne-Marie Slaughter, 'Judicial Globalization' (1999) 40 Virginia Journal of International Law 1103.

[4]   Edward Lee, 'The New Canon: Using or Misusing Foreign Law to Decide Domestic Intellectual Property Claims' (2005) 46(1) Harvard International Law Journal; Pamela Samuelson, 'Intellectual Property Arbitrage: How Foreign Rules Can Affect Domestic Protections' (2004) 71(1) University of Chicago Law Review 223–239.

European Telecommunications Standards Institute (ETSI), in Chinese courts. The chapter explores in detail the dispute surrounding SEPs between Huawei and InterDigital in China, and analyses it in the context of similar cases surrounding SEPs and FRANDs elsewhere. We explore one particular principle of proportionality,[5] which seems to have been used by the courts elsewhere in rulings of similar cases to calculate royalties which the Chinese courts seemed to have used. We observe that courts seem to rule based on the consideration of similar factors to decide complex FRAND cases. We argue that there seems to be a judicial globalization, that is, a court's use of foreign-developed principles in judging local disputes with global commercial impacts, resulting from self-regulation, and that the Chinese court cases may be understood in the same vein. We conclude by arguing that this may be a next phase in the development of Chinese IP law, where the local practices of governance have to be built after the initial norms transplant.

2. TELECOMMUNICATION STANDARDS AND PATENT POLICIES FOR SEPs

2.1   Patents and Standards

As a set of product characteristics, a standard is in essence information on product features and characteristics. A standardized product means certain qualities in a product comply with standards, i.e. measurement standard, regulations on safety or health. At the same time, the standard information is also the information that enables compatibility and inter-operability, as through implementation of standards, different parts and modules of a product may be produced separately. As standards allow modular production in complex systems products, technological standards have become crucial in industries such as information and communication technology. Standards may be imposed through administrative or governmental decision making, which is often called de jure standardization. For example, in China, general standards are set by the national law,[6]

---

⁵   It should be noted that the proportionality principle used in the context of royalty calculation is distinguished from the principle of proportionality found in the context of EU law discussion, balancing the authority of EU law with that of national law measures.
⁶   中华人民共和国标准化法 (1988) (Standardization Law of the People's Republic of China (1988)). Unofficial English translation is available <http://www.sac.gov.cn/sacen/law> accessed 1 May 2015.

and administrated and enforced by the Standardization Administration of the P.R. China (SAC). Standards are further regulated by the regulation for the implementation.[7] For de jure standards, government authorities may be able to govern the assertion of intellectual property rights (IPRs) by direct regulation.

In contrast, adoption of a de facto standard, such as the Orange Book of Philips, occurs by the operation of the market – through users' agreement and their voluntary implementation of certain standards.[8] In markets for goods with a network effect, where the value of a good depends positively on the number of users of the same good, standardization might occur as the market tips towards a standard due to the positive reinforcement of consumer desires and expectations. However, as standardization often increases the value of the product, private actors strive to influence the path of standardization and capture the value of the standards through various means, including IPR assertion. Where such tendency is strong, as in the mobile telephone market, a joint effort may be made to allow market potentials to fully develop without being captured by a few dominant players, by forming pools of SSOs.[9] SSOs such as IEEE[10] and ETSI[11] may be formed entirely out of private commercial interests among the industry players with a common goal of promoting the adoption of a standard, but sometimes may become quasi-public with the support or approval of governments. The presence of these types of SSOs, changes a de facto standardization to a semi-de jure standardization as they set the standard through agreement and provides a structured self-governance through the membership rules.

---

7   中华人民共和国标准化法实施条例   (1990)   (Regulations   for   the Implementation of the Standardization Law of the People's Republic of China, Promulgated by Decree No. 53 of the State Council of the People's Republic of China on 6 April 1990 and effective as of the date of promulgation). Unofficial English translation is available <http://www.sac.gov.cn/sacen/law> accessed 1 May 2015.

8   Disputed in the German Federal Supreme Court, 6 May 2009, KZR 39/06 (*Orange-Book-Standard*). See Chapter 13 of this volume for detailed discussion.

9   See also Nari Lee, 'Patented Standards and the Tragedy of Anti-Commons', Teollisoikeudellisia   Kirjoituksia   (2006),   <http://ssrn.com/abstract=881702> accessed 1 March 2015.

10   IEEE Standards Association (IEEE SA) is a membership-based global SSO. See their patent policy on their website <http://standards.ieee.org/develop/policies/bylaws/approved-changes.pdf> accessed 1 May 2015.

11   ETSI is a recognized EU standards body dealing with telecommunications, broadcasting and other electronic communications networks and services. See for details their website and their IPR policy <http://www.etsi.org/about/how-we-work/intellectual-property-rights-iprs> accessed 1 March 2015.

2.2   SSOs' Patent Policy on SEPs

Standardization has many benefits. As noted in the White Paper by the US Department of Justice and the Federal Trade Commission (FTC), 'standards can . . . increase innovation, efficiency, and consumer choice; foster public health and safety; and serve as a fundamental building block for international trade'.[12] Similarly, in Europe the Guidelines on the applicability of article 101 of the Treaty on the Functioning of the European Union to horizontal cooperation agreements notes that standards 'normally increase competition and lower output and sales costs, benefiting economies as a whole'.[13] However, standardization also greatly strengthens the bargaining position of the patent holders during licensing negotiations if their patents are SEPs – essential to implement the adopted standard. Commentators claimed that SEPs would lead to misuse of patents or a standard capture or hold-up calling for measures to prevent such anti-competitive behaviours.[14]

After some initial disputes, SSOs now routinely adopt self-regulating IPR policies including licensing principles to coordinate the assertion of rights among the members for the sake of efficient standards adoption. SSOs often take two types of measures: (1) providing rules on SEPs' declaration and the definition of SEPs; and (2) setting licensing principles, in case of rights assertion.[15] In practice, these two are often combined – when members are making SEPs declarations, they make commitment to the licensing principle of the SSO. Largely, there are two types of licensing principles: F/RAND and RF (Royalty Free). While FRAND and RAND may be similar in the sense that they allow a certain level of royalty, they are distinguished from the RF principle, which does not allow right holders to charge royalties. Discussions about F/RAND as licensing principles for an SSO were at the centre of an enforcement action by the US

---

[12]   US Dep't of Justice & Fed. Trade Comm'n, *Antitrust Enforcement and Intellectual Property Rights: Promoting Innovation and Competition* (2007) <www.usdoj.gov/atr/public/hearings/ip/222655.PDF> accessed 17 November 2014, p. 6.

[13]   Guidelines on the Applicability of Article 101 of the Treaty on the Functioning of the European Union to Horizontal Co-operation Agreements, OJ C 11/1 (2011), para 263.

[14]   Mark A. Lemley, 'Antitrust and the Internet Standardization Problem' (1996) 28 Connecticut Law Review 1041; see also Janice M. Mueller 'Patent Misuse Through the Capture of Industry Standards' (2002) 17 Berkeley Technology Law Journal 623.

[15]   For example, ETSI's IPR Policy, *supra* n. 11 and IEEE's new policy *supra* n. 10.

FTC for the first time in 1997.[16] The US Department of Justice and the FTC dealt with them again in a White Paper issued in 2007.[17] Likewise, in Europe, FRAND terms on the SEPs were also at the core of the recent finding of abuse in the action of the European Commission in 2014 against Motorola Mobility[18] and Samsung.[19]

Although FRAND commitments have become a part of many SSOs' patent policies,[20] such policies do not typically explain what a FRAND royalty rate would be nor how it should be set.[21] As they are considered business matters, SSOs such as ETSI do not consider it is even their role to regulate specific licensing terms and the negotiations.[22] It is thus left to parties to negotiate, and when a dispute arises, the courts need to construct the precise meaning of the FRAND commitment, using their own judgement. However the courts cannot seek guidance on deciding on a royalty rate from the law either, as they are not often set in the patent law nor in the mandatory regulations. FRAND are based on the membership agreements that are made by the SSO members voluntarily, as a means of self-regulation or private ordering. Their nature in the law could be contractual at most,[23] and thus, courts may only have general principles such as a principle of fairness in civil law,[24] or a principle of equity and good faith in contract law.[25]

In other words, when there is a dispute on these licensing principles,

---

[16]   *In re Dell*, 121 F.T.C. 616.

[17]   US Dep't of Justice & Fed. Trade Comm'n, *Antitrust Enforcement and Intellectual Property Rights: Promoting Innovation and Competition* [2007] <www. usdoj.gov/atr/public/hearings/ip/222655.PDF> accessed 17 November 2014.

[18]   European Commission, Decision of 29.4.2014. Case AT.39985, *Motorola – Enforcement of GPRS Standard Essential Patents*, C(2014) 2892 final.

[19]   European Commission, Decision of 29.4.2014 Case AT.39939, *Samsung – Enforcement of UMTS standard essential patents*, C(2014) 2891 final.

[20]   *Supra* nn. 11 and 10.

[21]   Opinion of AG Wathelet, CJEU Case C-170/13 *Huawei Technologies v. ZTE* ECLI:EU:C:2014:2391, at para. 25.

[22]   See para. 4.1 of the ETSI Guide on Intellectual Property Rights <http://www.etsi.org/images/ files/IPR/etsi-guide-on-ipr.pdf> accessed 1 March 2015.

[23]   Their contractual character has been debated sometimes, but the courts and administration seem to accept it as such. However, for counter-arguments, see Jorge L. Contreras, 'A Market Reliance Theory for FRAND Commitments and Other Patent Pledges' 2015(2) Utah Law Review 479–558; American University, WCL Research Paper No. 2014-26. Available at SSRN: <http://ssrn.com/abstract=2309023 > accessed 1 March 2015.

[24]   For example, 中华人民共和国民法通则 [General Principles of the Civil Law of the People's Republic of China], article 4.

[25]   For example, 中华人民共和国合同法 [Contract Law of the People's Republic of China], articles 5–6.

it is likely to be factually as well as legally complex, as the court needs to seek guidance either from market practice or elsewhere. They may sometimes borrow from the courts in foreign jurisdictions. Furthermore, seeking information from the market presents courts with another dilemma: courts are faced with the dispute before them precisely because the market could not mediate these licensing principles. This may force them to construct a theory such as a hypothetical negotiation or use data from other parties' licensing practices. At the same time, as the market practices for standards are global, they are faced with extra-territorial market considerations as well. Moreover, despite the local nature of the rights, and local jurisdiction, courts are forced to consider foreign market conditions to determine the market practices of the principles set by multinational SSOs. As a result, courts may need to consider whether they are competent to hear the case at all, and if they are, what is the applicable law to the dispute over contractual terms that are set outside the territory.

2.3   Patent Assertions on National Standards in China

In China, as for patents included in the national standards, there are further regulatory measures with interim provisions, which took effect in 2014.[26] The Interim measures provide for a broad definition of SEP in national standards (article 4), prohibition of inclusion of patents in mandatory national standards in principle (article 14); disclosure requirement (article 5); licensing declaration, principle and their effects to assignee (article 9, article 13).[27] In particular, article 9 provides for three options for licensing principles to be made in the declaration: (1) FRAND RF, (2) FRAND, or (3) neither of the above. In theory, patent holders are free not to license by selecting the third option. However, as article 10 of the Interim measures provides a principle of non-inclusion in the national standards in case of the third option, this option seems to be highly discouraged.

Furthermore at this moment, there is a current proposal in the draft fourth Amendment of Patent law, which includes a draft new article 82 that requires a patent holder to grant licences in case of failure to disclose SEP related to national standards during the standard-setting

---

[26]   国家标准涉及专利的管理规定（暂行）自2014年1月1日起施行   [Interim Provisions on the Administration of National Standards Involving Patents] (hereinafter 'Interim measures'). Chinese text available from SIPO website <http://www.sipo.gov.cn/zcfg/flfg/zl/bmgfxwj/201401/ t20140103_894910.html> accessed 1 March 2015.
[27]   Ibid.

process.[28] In other words, the new proposal seems to create a compulsory licensing regime for the patents that are included in the national standards, whose right holders failed to disclose during the standard-setting process.

In addition to article 82 of the proposed amendment, article 15 of the Interim Measure also provides for a procedure to resolve a patent included in the mandatory national standards where the right holder chooses not to comply with the FRAND or RF FRAND. As China is a member of the WTO, a compulsory licensing, whether in the patent law or adjacent regulatory measures, needs to be TRIPs compliant, which remains to be seen.[29]

As for the non-national standards, conditions of the anti-monopoly law as well as various administrative measures would be likely to be applied, as discussed in the previous chapter.[30] Additionally, on 7 April 2015, the State Administration for Industry and Commerce published a proposal on the further regulatory provision against IP abuse, 'Provisions of the State Administration for Industry and Commerce on Prohibiting the Abuse of Intellectual Property Rights to Preclude or Restrict Competition' (hereinafter the Provisions), which comes into effect on 1 August 2015.[31] The Provisions contain a general duty of disclosure for IPRs during the standardization (article 13, para 2(1)), a definition of an SEP (article 13, para 3) as well as licensing principle of FRAND and prohibition of refusal to license, among others (article 13, para 2(2)), for a business operator with a dominant market position. As the Provisions seemed to introduce the essential facility doctrine,[32] there are some remaining questions as to

---

28 中华人民共和国专利法修改草案（征求意见稿）》条文对照 [Comparison of text: Draft for public comments on the 4th Amendment of the Patent Law], Chinese text available from SIPO's website <http://www.sipo.gov.cn/ztzl/ywzt/zlfjqssxzdscxg/xylzlfxg/201504/t20150401_1095940.html> accessed 1 June 2015.

29 Agreement on Trade-Related Aspects of Intellectual Property Rights, 15 April 1994, 33 I.L.M. 81, Article 31. This point was noted by Weijun Zhang, in his presentation, 'China IP Day IV: Changing IP Enforcement in China – a new anti-monopoly development?' Helsinki, Finland on 12 June 2015. Presentation on file with the author.

30 See Chapter 13 in this volume.

31 关于禁止滥用知识产权排除、限制竞争行为的规定 2015年4月7日国家工商行政管理总局令第74号公布 [Provisions of the State Administration for Industry and Commerce on Prohibiting the Abuse of Intellectual Property Rights to Preclude or Restrict Competition]. Chinese text available on SAIC website <http://www.saic.gov.cn/zwgk/zyfb/zjl/fld/201504/t20150413_155103.html> accessed 1 June 2015.

32 Ibid. Article 7 of the Provision. See also for a general discussion of the doctrine in the context of the US law, T. F. Cotter, 'Intellectual Property and the Essential Facilities Doctrine' (1999) 44 Antitrust Bulletin 211.

whether the Provisions are making all patents included in the national standards an essential facility in the context of anti-monopoly law in China.

3. LOCAL RIGHTS AND A EUROPEAN SSOs – FRAND IN CHINESE COURTS

In 2013, the Shenzhen Intermediate People's Court applied the FRAND standard for the first time in China in the case of *Huawei v. IDC*,[33] whose findings were affirmed in the appeal by Guangdong Higher People's Court.[34] The case itself concerned royalty calculations for Chinese patents held by IDC, which were subject to the FRAND principle of ETSI, which is a European SSO. As discussed in Chapter 13, FRAND is also an issue debated in the EU at the moment, in terms of whether the commitment may allow the courts to deny injunctive relief in the context of competition policy. Uncertainty here is clearly visible in the various litigation between the private actors, such as *Huawei v ZTE*.[35] Their impact on competition is clearly stressed by the European Commission's findings on Motorola Mobility,[36] as well as the Commission's round of public consultation in February of 2015.[37] In the US, pre-dating the Chinese decisions, there has been a US trial court decision, *Microsoft v. Motorola*, on the calculation of FRAND royalty rates with similar facts, which seemed to have influenced the Chinese court decision.[38] Similar disputes are visible in Japan

---

[33]   *Huawei v. InterDigital Communications (IDC)*, Shenzhen Intermediate People's Court, Decision of Feb. 2013, No. 2011深中法知民初字第858号. Both parties appealed.

[34]   *Huawei v. InterDigital Communications*, Guangdong Higher People's Court No. 2013 粤高法民三终字第306号, affirming. On appeal to Chinese Supreme People's Court (14 April 2014).

[35]   *Huawei v. ZTE*, 2013, District Court of Düsseldorf, 21 March 2013, 4b O 104/12. Preliminary ruling referred, CJEU, *Huawei v. ZTE, supra* n. 21. For more detail, see Chapter 13 in this volume.

[36]   European Commission, 'Antitrust: Commission finds that Motorola Mobility infringed EU competition rules by misusing standard essential patents' (Brussels, 29 April 2014) <http://europa.eu/rapid/press-release_IP-14-489_en.htm> accessed 3 May 2014.

[37]   European Commission, Directorate-General for Enterprise and Industry, 'Public consultation on patents and standards: A modern framework for standardisation involving intellectual property rights' <http://ec.europa.eu/enterprise/newsroom/cf/itemdetail.cfm?item_type=252&lang=en&item_id=7833> accessed 4 June, 2015.

[38]   *Microsoft Corp. v. Motorola, Inc.*, No. C10-1823JLR, 2013 U.S. Dist. LEXIS 60233 (W.D. Wash. Apr. 25, 2013).

as well.[39] Although the legal bases for these series of disputes are different and the outcome of the decisions is likely to be different, factual similarities concerning FRAND commitment highlight a potential for norm interaction at the judiciary.

3.1 Facts and Ruling of Chinese Courts in *Huawei v. IDC*

Huawei v. IDC is the first case that provided the position of the Chinese courts regarding the interpretation of FRAND and interpretation of foreign SSOs' policy in China.[40] Among other things, the courts determined the upper limit of the FRAND royalty for IDC's SEPs mainly *on the basis of a comparison with the royalties IDC charged other parties outside China*. The decision was considered controversial, as it was unexpected.

IDC is a non-practising entity with many patents. Among others, IDC owns many SEPs both in China and abroad, on several Chinese wireless telecommunications standards (2G, 3G, 4G and IEEE802). Several of Huawei's telecommunication products work with these standards. Both IDC and Huawei are members of ETSI. IDC has declared to ETSI in writing that it would undertake to comply with the FRAND obligation for its SEP. Between September 2008 and August 2012, IDC sent Huawei four different letters offering to license its SEPs to Huawei at what it considered the FRAND rate. In its first and second offers, the licensing rate IDC sought from Huawei for the period from 2009 to 2016 was 100 times the rate it had sought from Apple and 10 times the rate it had sought from Samsung for roughly the same period. In the third offer, the licensing rate IDC sought from Huawei had been reduced to 35 times the rate it had sought from Apple. In the fourth offer, the licensing rate IDC sought from Huawei was only 19 times the rate it had sought from Apple. Finally, in order to force Huawei to accept its licensing offer, IDC filed a complaint on 26 July 2011 against Huawei among others, with the International Trade Commission (ITC) in the USA, and the ITC initiated a section 337 investigation.[41] In these four offers, IDC did not differentiate between the SEPs and non-SEP (that is a blanket offer), and in the fourth offer, IDC insisted that acceptance of any specific offer that it made was an essential

---

[39] *Samsung v. Apple*, IP High Court, 16 May 2014, Case nos 2013 (Ne)10043, 2013(Ra)10007, 2013(Ra)10008.

[40] The Chinese courts also expressed their views about the issues of jurisdiction and applicable laws.

[41] United States International Trade Commission Washington, D.C. (2011) Investigation No. 337-TA-868 <http://www.usitc.gov/press_room/news_release/2013/er0130lll.htm> accessed 3 March 2015.

condition of the whole offer, and to refuse any specific offer was to refuse the whole offer.

On 2 December 2011, Huawei filed a complaint against IDC in the Shenzhen People's Intermediate Court to determine royalty.[42] On the same date, another case, which we do not discuss here, was filed at the Shenzhen People's Intermediate Court by Huawei, alleging anti-monopoly law violations by IDC.[43]

On 4 February 2013, Shenzhen Intermediate People's Court ruled among other things, that the royalty rate should not exceed 0.019 per cent of the actual sales price.[44] On appeal, Guangdong Court affirmed the decision of the first instance, noting that as IDC was unwilling to disclose the royalty rate with other companies, it was reasonable to base the rate in comparison to IDC's other licensees' sales income.[45]

3.2   Application of Proportionality Principle in FRAND SEPs

The Shenzhen Court seemed to have actively applied the proportionality principle to analyse what fair and reasonable licensing of SEPs means.[46] As pointed out by Robert Merges, an application of the proportionality principle in the context of intellectual IP means that:

> The size or scope of an IP right ought to be proportional to the value or significance of the work covered by the right . . . [A]n IPR must not confer on its holder leverage or power that is grossly disproportionate to what is deserved in the situation. If an IPR would effectively confer power or control over a much more vast market or set of markets than what is actually deserved, in light of the work covered by the IP right, that right must be limited in some way.[47]

The decisions of both courts seemed to have used this principle of proportionality in the determination of FRAND, reflecting the following three

---

[42]   *Supra* n. 33.

[43]   The case was reported as 叶若思 祝建军 陈文全, '标准必要专利权人滥用市场支配地位构成垄断的认定评华为公司诉美国IDC公司垄断纠纷案', 3 电子知识产权 51 [Ruosi Ye, Jianjun Zhu and Wenquan Chen, 'Recognizing Abuse of Market Position by Holders of Standards Essential Patents – Huawei v. US IDC Company' (2013) 03 Electronic Intellectual Property 51]. See also discussion of the case in Chapter 13 of this volume.

[44]   *Supra* n. 33.

[45]   *Supra* n. 34.

[46]   See also, Anne Layne-Farrar, A. Jorge Padilla and Richard Schmalensee, 'Pricing Patents for Licensing in Standard-Setting Organizations: Making Sense of FRAND Commitments' (2007) 74 Antitrust Law Journal 671–706.

[47]   Ibid, at 162.

policy considerations: preventing a total quantity control, patent hold-up, and royalty stacking.

3.2.1   The first policy consideration: the total quantity control

According to the view of the Chinese courts, technology, investment, management and labour jointly generate a product's profit. Because patented technology is only one factor, the royalty should not cover all of the product's profits. Such a royalty would not be fair and reasonable. Thus the Court held that to avoid total quantity control the royalty charged for the licensing of SEPs should not exceed the profit, which the licensee would make from his product or service.

3.2.2   The second policy consideration: anti-patent hold-up

'Patent hold-up' refers to the situation that occurs when the existence of an SEP is not disclosed during the standard-setting process.[48] This may lead to problems during the implementation of the standard. For instance, the holder of the SEP may be tempted to ask exorbitant licensing fees for the standardized technology or even block the implementation of the standard by seeking an injunction.[49] In *Microsoft v. Motorola* the Court dealt extensively with the issue of patent hold-up. It described it as '[t]he ability of the holder of a SEP to demand more than the value of its patented technology and to attempt to capture the value of the standard itself'.[50] The Court continued by pointing out that '[t]he threat of hold-up increases as the standard becomes more widely implemented and firms make sunk cost investments that cannot be recovered if they are forced to forego implementation of the standard or the standard is changed'[51] and that '[h]old-up can threaten the diffusion of valuable standards and undermine the standard-setting process'.[52] According to the Court '[i]n addition to harming firms that are forced to pay higher royalties, hold-up also harms consumers to the extent that those excess costs are passed on to them'[53] and '[h]old-up . . . harms other firms that hold SEPs relating to the same standard because it jeopardizes further adoption of the standard

---

[48]   See Nari Lee, Standardization and Patent Law – Is Standardization a Concern for Patent Law? (October 2004) <http://ssrn.com/abstract=610901> accessed 1 May 2014.

[49]   Valerio Torti, 'Enforcement of a Maximum Licensing Cap in Standardization Environments' (2013) 35 E.I.P.R. 261, 262.

[50]   *Microsoft v. Motorola, supra* n. 38 at 55.

[51]   Ibid, para 56.

[52]   Ibid, para 57.

[53]   Ibid, para 58.

and limits the ability of those other holders to obtain appropriate royalties on their technology'.[54]

Although the Chinese Courts did not use the term 'patent hold-up' literally, they did hold that the holder of the SEPs is not entitled to profit that derives from the value of the standard itself and noted that the appropriate valuation of the SEP should only be based on the value of the patent itself, because the contribution by the holder of the SEPs lies in its innovative technology, not in the standardization. The Court also noted that added value of a SEP due to the inclusion in the standard should be disregarded. This seems to indicate that the Chinese Courts actually took anti-patent hold-up into consideration when defining the meaning of fair and reasonable licensing of SEPs.

3.2.3   The third policy consideration: anti-royalty stacking

'Royalty stacking' occurs when a licensee is forced to pay excessive royalties for the use of many different SEPs. This may cause all profits for the licensee to dissipate. In *Microsoft v. Motorola* the Court considered that 'judges . . . can and should look at the overall cumulative royalty costs for a given standard and not just assess whether the terms being offered by one particular licensor are fair and reasonable *in vacuo*'.[55] As with the term 'patent hold-up', the Chinese Courts did not explicitly use the term 'royalty stacking'. However, they considered that a product that incorporates a particular standard may implicate many SEPs held by different patent owners, meaning royalty demands may come from many different parties. This indicates that the courts considered it to be necessary to avoid the problems associated with royalty stacking when calculating fair and reasonable royalties.

When viewed from the angle of policy considerations, there seems to be little difference between the approach to the FRAND issue by the Chinese Courts in *Huawei v. IDC* and the United States District Court in the *Microsoft v. Motorola* decision, using the 'proportionality principle'. The principle was used in both cases to determine the meaning of FRAND. However, upon closer inspection there seems to be a difference when it comes to application of the proportionality principle to the concrete circumstances of the case. When applying the 'proportionality principle' to determine fair and reasonable royalties, the Chinese Courts should have specifically analysed the contribution of each of IDC's Chinese SEPs to the relevant standards and especially their contribution to each

---

[54]   Ibid, para 59.
[55]   Ibid, para 69 (quoting Motorola's submission to ETSI in 2006).

of Huawei's products that use the relevant standards. However, what was disappointing was that the Court did not use the proportionality principle in practice, that is when analysing how to calculate the royalties. Specifically, the Chinese Courts did not analyse how many SEPs were implicated by the standards; how many of these SEPs were granted in China; how many of these Chinese SEPs were owned by IDC; how many specific standards IDC's China SEPs involved; and how many Chinese SEPs owned by IDC Huawei used. Based on the facts cited above, it was logically impossible for the Chinese Courts to analyse the contribution of each of IDC's Chinese SEPs to the relevant standards and the use made of them by Huawei and their importance to Huawei's products. This analysis is actually at the core of the application of the proportionality principle. In other words, the Chinese Courts did not actually apply the proportionality principle in practice, but relied on it as a theory.

3.3 Comparison: Non-discriminatory Licensing of SEPs in *Huawei v. IDC*

The Shenzhen Court in the *Huawei* case emphasized that licensors of SEPs may have different licensing models. However, they considered that a licensor, when licensing on roughly the same terms, should give all licensees a license with roughly the same royalty rate. If not, the licensing of SEPs is discriminatory. According to the Court, the royalty IDC had tried to obtain from Huawei was discriminatory. This conclusion of the Court was based on the following facts and arguments.

Based on Apple's publically available financial data, the Chinese Courts calculated that Apple's sales revenue was about 3,000 billion USD between 2007 and 2012 and the royalty rate IDC had sought from Apple was about 0.018 per cent of the sales revenue. The Chinese Court held that the royalty rate that IDC could seek from Huawei should not exceed the rate it had sought from Apple. The Court based this on the analysis by Strategy Analytics Inc. submitted to the Court by Huawei.[56] Ironically Huawei was not included in its list but most other competitors in the global mobile phones market (Nokia, Samsung, Apple, LG, RIM, Motorola, HTC and Sony) were on its list. In other words, the Court based its royalty rate on the information of the other licensees of IDC.

Although the use of comparisons can be a very useful and convenient tool to assess the non-discriminatory character of certain licensing conditions, a 'scientific' comparison requires the taking into account of

---

[56] *Supra* n. 33.

all relevant terms of the licensing agreement, otherwise it is very difficult to draw significant conclusions from the comparison. At first instance in *Huawei v. IDC*, in order to increase the persuasion of comparison, the Court held that, if the trading terms for different licensees were roughly the same, the royalty rate for SEPs should be roughly the same in order to be non-discriminatory. However, the Chinese Courts did not specify what 'the trading terms' were nor why these trading terms were 'roughly the same'.[57] In order to compare the different royalty rates the Courts should have at least made a rough estimate of Huawei's projected sales revenue for the licensing period or alternatively have used Huawei's revenue figures for the same period as covered by the licensing agreement between IDC and Apple. However, the Courts did not seem to have engaged in such exercise. When the Courts used Apple's royalty rate as a reference, they also did not review whether Apple's own royalty rate for IDC's SEPs was in conformity with the proportionality principle. If the Courts had concluded that was not the case, the Courts' conclusion about the discriminatory character of the royalty rate through comparison would likely also be untenable.

3.4 Jurisdiction and Applicable Law in the Case

The disputes in China which we examined were not about patent infringement as such but about commercial disputes on royalty rate calculation. As the licensing condition was European (ETSI), and the disputes concerning patent infringement was pending elsewhere, disputes were about the rate of royalty on the terms set in Europe, in a Chinese court. Thus before the court dealt with the question whether IDC had acted contrary to its FRAND obligations and calculated royalty rate, it had to consider whether it had jurisdiction and whether Chinese law governed the matter.

3.4.1 Jurisdiction
IDC contended that the case was a private dispute concerning the question what constitutes appropriate licensing royalties and that the Court therefore lacked jurisdiction. The Shenzhen Court, however, decided otherwise. Because IDC and Huawei were members of ETSI, IDC's FRAND commitments required it to license its SEPs to Huawei on FRAND terms. If Huawei, as a user of the applicable industry standard, could not reach an agreement with IDC, it would be forced to accept IDC's excessive licensing royalty if it were prevented from seeking relief in court.

---

[57]   Ibid.

The position of the Court provides some guidance on how to deal with the relationship between the market and court authority. The fact that Huawei and IDC could not reach an agreement on FRAND terms revealed a market failure. Under these circumstances, courts should be able to step in to determine the FRAND licensing royalty. Thus, it is not unexpected that courts are asked to step in to determine the appropriate FRAND royalty level when SSO participants fail to reach an agreement.

In the American case of *Microsoft v. Motorola*, Microsoft and Motorola also failed to reach an agreement on the FRAND rate. Microsoft sued Motorola for breach of contract in the Western District Court of Washington. The Court determined the royalty it deemed in line with Motorola's FRAND commitments.[58] It was a pity that the reasoning of Shenzhen Intermediate Court and Guangdong High Court did not touch on the question whether IDC's FRAND commitment created an enforceable contract between IDC and ETSI, and whether Huawei as merely a user of the industry standard could request IDC to license its SEPs on FRAND terms as a third-party beneficiary of the contract between IDC and ETSI.

3.4.2 Applicable law

IDC also claimed that because ETSI was located in France, French law governed the dispute. The Courts, however, held that the applicable law was Chinese law. The reasoning by the Chinese Courts gives an indication how to determine the applicable law when there was not yet a formal licensing agreement between Huawei and IDC. The Chinese Courts based their decision mainly on the following factors: (1) the case concerned a dispute about what constituted the appropriate royalty level for SEPs, not a dispute between Huawei or IDC and ETSI about ETSI's IP rights policy; (2) the SEPs at the centre of the dispute were solely Chinese patents; and (3) Huawei and IDC had not agreed on the applicable law.

The Court struggled with the determination of the applicable law because Huawei and IDC were still at the stage of negotiation and had not yet reached any formal agreement on the licensing of IDC's Chinese SEPs.[59] Although articles 41 and 49 of the Law of the P.R. China on the Laws Applicable to Foreign-Related Civil Relations 2010[60] stipulate the

---

58   *Supra* n. 38.
59   *Supra* n. 33.
60   中华人民共和国涉外民事关系法律适用法 [Law of The People's Republic of China on the Laws Applicable to Foreign-related Civil Relations, 2010]. Text available on WIPO's website <http://www.wipo.int/wipolex/en/details.jsp?id=8423> accessed 5 March 2015.

rules for determining the applicable law, their application is conditional on the parties' choice by agreement or formal contract of transfer or licence. The Shenzhen Court did not take a note of the law, but in order to determine the applicable law, the Courts creatively used a significant relationship doctrine. Considering the special circumstance that the parties had not yet concluded a licensing agreement and had not otherwise agreed on the applicable law, the Chinese Court held that the law that was most closely connected with 'subject matters of the dispute' should be applied.[61] The Court considered that, because Huawei's domicile was in Shenzhen, the place of implementation IDC's Chinese SEPs in dispute was Shenzhen and because the negotiations concerning the licensing of IDC's Chinese SEPs mainly had taken place in Shenzhen and other places in China, China was more closely connected with the dispute than France. Therefore the Court considered Chinese law to be applicable.

3.5   Proportionality Principle and Alternative Test – Hypothetical Negotiations

Determining what constitute FRAND royalties is very complicated. While the Chinese Court seemed to have used the proportionality principle as a theoretical framework for its decision, the proportionality principle is one of the many tools that scholars have discussed, such as the traditional financial analysis based on incremental value, rule of thumb of 25 per cent, *ex ante* disclosure and auctioning models, and pseudo-pool model[62] as well as the lump-sum payment such as that InterDigital used with Apple.

The Shenzhen Intermediate Court and Guangdong High Court made a very brave and admirable attempt at defining FRAND terms for the first time in China. Although the Courts' reasoning was somewhat questionable, they nonetheless resolved the case and determined the FRAND royalty rate. Perhaps with the help of more research and after reflection on the judgments of the Chinese Courts, Chinese judges will provide a more satisfactory answer of what constitute FRAND royalties the next time they are confronted with the issue.

One alternative consideration may be found in the test used in *Microsoft v. Motorola*.[63] In this case, the Court adopted a modified

---

[61]   *Supra* n. 33.
[62]   See S. Barazza, 'Licensing Standard Essential Patents, Part One: the Definition of F/RAND Commitments and the Determination of Royalty Rates' (2014) 9(6) Journal of Intellectual Property Law & Practice 465–481.
[63]   *Georgia-Pacific Corp. v. United States Plywood Corp,* 318 F. Supp. 1116 (S.D.N.Y. 1970).

version of what are known as the 'Georgia-Pacific factors'[64] to recreate a hypothetical negotiation between the parties. In *Georgia-Pacific*, the Southern District Court of New York established 15 factors to calculate 'reasonable royalties', that is damages, in a patent infringement suit.[65] The use of hypothetical negotiations between parties to establish the RAND[66] royalty rate presumes the parties make full use of the 'proportionality principle' when negotiating a RAND royalty rate and thus puts the principle into active use when calculating a RAND royalty rate.[67] The Court first made some policy considerations such as the goal of SSOs, prevention of patent hold-up, royalty stacking, and the need for reasonable royalties on patents. In particular the Court noted that a RAND commitment 'should be interpreted to limit a patent holder to a reasonable royalty on the economic value of its patented technology itself, apart from the value associated with incorporation of the patented technology into the standard'.[68]

At the same time, the Court noted that the parties in the hypothetical negotiation would use the following factors modifying the *Georgia-Pacific* factors: (1) past royalty rates negotiated under the RAND obligation or a comparable negotiation; (2) the contribution of the patent to the technical capabilities of the standard and the contribution of those relevant technological capabilities to the implementer and the implementer's products, *separating the patented technology* from the value associated with incorporation of the patented technology into the standard; (3) the presence of the alternatives that could have been written into the standard before the standard implementation; (4) the realizable profit that should be credited to the invention as distinguished from other factors; (5) the portion of the profit or of the selling price that may be customary involving RAND commitment; and (6) consideration of RAND commitment and its purpose in the agreement between the SEP owner and the implementer.[69]

After making these observations, the Court applied these considerations

---

[64]   See *Georgia-Pacific Corp. v. United States Plywood Corp*, 318 F. Supp. 1116 (S.D.N.Y. 1970).

[65]   *Supra* n. 38.

[66]   The case was about the RAND licensing principle; however, the same factors may be used in FRAND.

[67]   *Georgia-Pacific Corp. v. United States Plywood Corp*, 318 F. Supp. 1116 (S.D.N.Y. 1970).

[68]   Ibid, order 25, at para.75.

[69]   Ibid, order 35-40 st paras 100–113. Emphasis added. The factors were used again, with some modification in, *In re Innovatio IP Ventures LLC*, ND of Illinois MDL Docket No. 2303 Case No. 11C-9308, Memorandum Opinion, Findings, Conclusions and Order of 27 September 2013.

and modified the *Georgia-Pacific* factors to the specific circumstances of the case. Based on the fact that Motorola owns a portfolio of patents essential to the H.264 Standard and the 802.11 Standard, in order to determine a FRAND licensing royalty for Motorola's H.264, the Court provided background on the H.264 Standard and then examined the importance of Motorola's patent portfolio to the H.264 Standard and to Microsoft products using the Standard. To determine a reasonable royalty for Motorola's 802.11 SEP portfolio, the Court examined the development of the Standard, the relative technical value of different portions of the Standard, the patents which covered the Standard, Motorola's SEPs, Microsoft's products which used Motorola's SEPs on the Standard, and the importance of Motorola's 11 SEPs to the Standard and to Microsoft's products.[70] In short, because the *Microsoft v. Motorola* decision applied proportionality principle in detail, the result of its calculation of licensing royalty is comparatively just and tenable. The factors used in the decision are worthy of reference when thinking about the standard and calculation of FRAND, particularly in the applicability of the proportionality principle.

4.   CONCLUDING REMARKS

For complex systems products such as mobile phones, standardization is crucial. As long as standard setting is done through private actors, the rules of SSOs play a central role in the governance of various legal and technological claims over the standards. SSOs not only coordinate heterogeneous interests in terms of adoption of technical standards to bring about technical consensus, but also they play a central role in mediating IPR claims. When patent claims are asserted on a selected standard, any producers of a device compliant with the standard would need to license from the right holder, resulting in a hold-up. To an extent, some level of standard capture is unavoidable as one complex systems product such as a mobile phone or other programmable apparatus would likely implement multitudes of IPRs following technological standards. At the same time, if an SEP holder refuses to license or even to join an SSO, this would result in a patent hold-out situation, which discourages adoption of the standards. Furthermore, as the process of innovation has been highly incremental with iterations, patent and other IPR protection were sought for each increment. As a result, there has been a well-documented

---

[70]   Ibid, order 27-206.

problem of patent thickets and potential for an anti-commons problem in this area.[71]

In contrast to patent thickets and anti-commons, in standards, a presence of a single right and its assertion would be likely to have a negative impact on the adoption of the standards. This is made worse by the fact that all rights are equally exclusive and the rights are often granted without a clear hierarchy; a single claim on the core of the technology would be equally exclusive as a portfolio of patents. As such, as long as there is one SEP, a hold-up of the value of the standardization is always possible.

For an efficient adoption of standards, SSOs' requirement of FRAND commitment over SEP aims to ameliorate problems created by fragmentation. It is an example of market-oriented private ordering as it provides governance structure over the use of SEPs, through the adoption of instruments of self-regulation, that is patent policies with FRAND licensing principles. As highlighted in the Chinese case example, the problem that such instrument raises is global. The courts hearing disputes on SEPs need to balance the principle of territoriality of law and the underlying rights with the need to respect a commercial commitment affecting global businesses.

FRANDs disputes show a globalization of court practices. In the context of previous chapters exploring normative influences from Europe in Chinese IP law, Chinese disputes show a transformation of China as a norm maker. The proportionality principle used in the calculation of FRAND in the Chinese courts is an instance of foreign judicial doctrines and concepts influencing considerations of local rights. Considering the impact of SEPs on normal consumers, some level of norm and judicial harmonization may be necessary. When rights and licensing behaviours are based on 'imported' concepts, doctrinal analysis is also highly influenced by foreign considerations and principles. Even in the absence of formal harmonization of rules, judges seem to heed the decisions made by foreign courts and note the principles used. While the actual statutory bases of the dispute in *Huawei v. IDC*[72] were the principles in the Chinese civil law and contract law,[73] to give them concrete meaning, the Chinese Courts seemed to have applied another principle developed outside China. At the

---

[71]   Carl Shapiro, 'Navigating the Patent Thicket: Cross Licenses, Patent Pools, and Standard Setting' in Adam B. Jaffe, Josh Lerner and Scott Stern (eds), *Innovation Policy and the Economy*, Volume 1 (MIT Press 2001) 119–150. See also Lee, *supra* n. 9.

[72]   *Supra* n. 33.

[73]   Article 4 of General Principles of the Chinese Civil Law, *supra* n. 24; Articles 5–6 of Chinese Contract Law, *supra* n. 25.

same time, as noted in the above, the doctrines seem to have been applied in a less practical manner. This highlights the fact that often when foreign doctrines and principles are imported through judicial globalization, still local statutory and factual considerations may adapt them differently.

As the next phase of institutional adaptation following the initial legal transplant, it is important to note that such adaptations are not only made through administrative and legal reforms, but also through the interaction of the courts and the market participants with practices of self-regulation. As noted by Drahos, self-regulation by the private market participant through the exercise of their private property rights may indicate a global regulatory capitalism.[74] SSOs' patent policy, such as FRAND, is indeed one such means of transnational self-regulation, and at the same time an instrument of governmentality with a transnational impact. They also force courts to consider tests and practices of other courts ruling on such instruments of self-regulation, thus forcing a judicial globalization. As SEPs are globally used, the impact of their assertions is multi-territorial. FRAND terms are licensing principles based on contractual terms that are set by market participants elsewhere, including foreign principles. As they are enforced and given meaning locally, as we have seen with the example of China, they also highlight an important transformation in the Chinese institutions of IP – law, administration, court and market actors, to indigenize the system of IP in practice.

---

[74] P. Drahos, 'Regulatory Capitalism, Globalization and the End of History', RegNet Working Paper, No. 33, Regulatory Institutions Network <http://ssrn.com/abstract=2449920> or <http://dx.doi.org/10.2139/ssrn.2449920> accessed 1 March 2015. See also John Braithwaite and Peter Drahos, *Global Business Regulation* (Cambridge University Press 2000).

15. The emergence of non-practising entities in China

Kelli Larson

1. INTRODUCTION

Non-practising entities (NPEs), entities known for building business models solely around the exploitation and enforcement of patents mainly through licensing agreements and sometimes litigation to generate revenues, have become increasingly important actors in the patent litigation landscape.[1] Yet, what is conspicuous about the NPE phenomenon is that it does not seem to significantly occur in jurisdictions outside of the US. Some NPE activity is found in Europe, albeit on a much lower level than their US counterparts.[2] This may be due to differences between European and US industries, legal remedies and judicial cultures.[3] It may also be attributed to the current fragmented nature of the European patent landscape. The two-tiered state of national and European patent grant and enforcement systems[4] creates a prohibitive patent enforcement environment for NPEs to operate in, where the multi-jurisdictional and multi-

---

[1]   See PricewaterhouseCoopers 2014 Patent Litigation Study 'As Case Volume Leaps, Damages Continue General Decline' <http://www.pwc.com/en_US/us/forensic-services/publications/assets/2014-patent-litigation-study.pdf> accessed 15 January 2015.

[2]   Stefania Fusco, 'Markets and Patent Enforcement: A Comparative Investigation of Non-Practicing Entities in the United States and Europe' [2014] 20 Michigan Telecommunications and Technology Law Review 439.

[3]   Ibid.

[4]   Patents are territorial by nature meaning they can only be enforced in the country of grant. At the national level, competent national authorities of European Member States handle the grant and enforcement of patents, while at the European level, the European Patent Office (EPO) conducts a similar role in handling the patent applications and administrative enforcement procedures. Even when a European patent is granted by the EPO, patent owners must still validate, and if necessary, subsequently enforce their patent in each corresponding Contracting Member State where they seek protection and enforcement. See Thomas Jaegar, 'The Framework for IP Rights Enforcement in the EU' in Christoph Antons (ed),

cultural/language enforcement landscape of country-to-country patent litigation may increase the costs of extensive patent enforcements and raises legal uncertainties of patent assertions.[5]

However, the US patent enforcement landscape is undergoing a significant transformation, which may also impact upon the future effectiveness of NPE business models in their dominate market. The 2011 Leahy-Smith America Invents Act[6] (AIA) patent reform introduced various provisions not only making it more difficult for patent owners to enforce patents,[7] but also making it easier for alleged infringers to invalidate patents.[8] In addition to the AIA, a significant number of further patent reforms are being debated[9] among the Senate and House of Representatives, many

---

The Enforcement of Intellectual Property Rights: Comparative Perspectives from the Asia-Pacific Region (Kluwer Law International 2011) 48.

5   Kelli Larson, 'Legal Implications of the European and Unitary Patent Systems for Non-practicing Entity Patent Enforcement in Europe' in Rosa Ballardini, Marcus Norrgård and Niklas Bruun (eds), *Transitions in European Patent Law: Influences of the Unitary Patent Package* (Kluwer Law International 2015). The EU is currently attempting to implement the creation of a unitary patent right and a unitary patent court that would create pan-European patent protection and a centralized enforcement system, which in theory would make it more efficient for NPEs to secure broad geographical patent protection in Europe and enforce patent rights. The unitary 'patent package' is the legislative initiative that lays the groundwork for unitary patent protection in Europe. It consists of: Regulation (EU) 1257/2012 of 17 December 2012 implementing enhanced cooperation in the area of the creation of unitary patent protection [2012] OJ L 361/1 (hereinafter Unitary Patent Regulation 1257/2012); Regulation (EU) 1260/2012 of 17 December 2012 implementing enhanced cooperation in the area of the creation of unitary patent protection with regard to the applicable translation arrangements [2012] OJ L 361/89; and the Agreement of a Unified Patent Court (hereinafter UPC Agreement) [2013] C 175/1.

6   Leahy-Smith America Invents Act (AIA), Pub. L. No. 112-29, 125 Stat. 284 (2011) (codified in scattered sections of 35 U.S.C.).

7   35 U.S.C. § 299 (2012). Section 299 of the AIA created a new joinder statute restricting the ability of a patent proprietor to sue multiple unrelated defendants in one suit.

8   35 USC §§ 311, 321. The AIA created two key administrative procedures for defendants to try to invalidate patents: the Post Grant Review Process and the *Inter Partes* Review procedure.

9   This is evidenced by the fact that there has been a staggering number of patent reforms, at least ten, that have been proposed since 2011 alone directly meant to address NPE business endeavours. Some of the Acts being proposed in the US Congress include the SHILED Act (Saving High-Tech Innovators from Egregious Legal Disputes), the Patent Litigation and Innovation Act, and the Patent Transparency and Improvements Act. Furthermore, at the State level, Vermont has been the first state to create their own law (House Bill 299) meant

with the potential effect of making patent enforcement more difficult for NPEs.[10] Moreover, recent judicial decisions have also placed limitations on NPEs in enforcing patents. For example, the 2006 decision in *eBay v MercExchange*[11] significantly limited the ability of patent owners to receive an injunction barring infringing products from the US marketplace by implementing a four-part test to determine whether an injunction is warranted.[12] Consequently, both the evolving US patent landscape and the European patent enforcement landscape appear to be increasingly difficult jurisdictions for patent owners such as NPEs to operate patent enforcement businesses. As a result, NPEs may soon find it necessary to look beyond the US and Europe to other markets for opportunities to exploit and enforce patents to generate revenues. Looking to the East, China may be able to provide for one such patent exploitation and enforcement opportunity.

As China is the second largest economy in the world, many foreign companies have no choice but to invest in and transfer technology there to remain competitive. Through a method of legal transplant and independent norm making,[13] China has been trying to establish a comprehensive

---

to curb NPEs alleged 'bad faith assertions' of patent infringements. Even US President Barack Obama has become engaged in the debate on NPEs, releasing five executive actions and seven legislative recommendations designed to protect innovators from 'challenges' allegedly caused by NPEs.

[10]   For example, the Innovation Act calls for heightened pleading standards at the outset when filing for patent infringement lawsuits requiring plaintiffs to disclose information that usually occurs later in the discovery stage or closer to litigation including the identification of all ownership claims in the patent, while another provision of the patent reform would implement a fee-shifting provision making the unsuccessful party in patent litigation liable to pay the attorney costs of the successful party. § 281A H.R. 3309 – 113th Congress: Innovation Act; § 285 H.R. 3309 – 113th Congress: Innovation Act.

[11]   *eBay, Inc. v MercExchange* 547 U.S. 388 (2006).

[12]   Ibid. A patent owner must now demonstrate: (1) it has suffered an irreparable harm; (2) the remedies available at law, such as monetary damages, are inadequate to compensate for that injury; (3) considering the balance of hardships between the parties, a remedy in equity is warranted; and (4) the public interest would not be disserved by a permanent injunction. Other judicial cases which made it more difficult to enforce patents include *MedImmune, Inc. v Genentech, Inc.* 549 U.S. 118 (2007), which made it easier for alleged infringers to challenge the validity of patents while still maintaining their licence rights; and *KSR Int'l Co. v Teleflex, Inc.* 550 U.S. 398 (2007), which raised the bar for patent holders to prove their inventions are non-obvious.

[13]   Legal transplant generally consists of a borrowing or moving of legal rules or systems of law from one jurisdiction to be applied in another jurisdiction. For example see, Alan Watson, *Legal Transplants: An Approach to Comparative Law*

intellectual property (IP) system to encourage foreign and domestic investment in research and development and to help create wealth for the country and its citizens. Within a relatively short period of time, starting from the late 1970s through Deng Xiaoping's 'Open Door Policy',[14] the People's Republic of China (PRC) has been transforming China's planned economy to a market-driven economy with a shift in the development of government policy over the years to increasingly foster the development of its own domestic economy and innovative technologies.[15] China's 'Indigenous Innovation'[16] policies, which generally refer to China's self-developed and self-owned technology, began in 2006 and ever since China has been undergoing a vast and complex economic and legal transition in the development of its IP policies and laws. China is thus trying to transform itself from a manufacturing economy to an innovation and knowledge-based 'IP power' economy.[17] Subsequently, the procurement and enforcement of intellectual property rights (IPRs) in China has become an important issue to many stakeholders in and outside of China.

The vast Chinese domestic market undoubtedly holds potential licensing opportunities for Chinese and foreign companies alike,[18] which may be able to benefit from NPEs' expertise in patent enforcement, patent

---

(first published 1974, University of Georgia Press 1993). The first and second amendments to China's patent law (1992 and 2000 respectively) were made in efforts to align the country's laws more with international treaties and more with the patent laws of the US, while the third and fourth (draft) patent law amendments (2008 and draft, 2012 respectively) were more focused on the development of Chinese domestic law and to further develop the transition of the Chinese economy to a knowledge-based economy.

[14]   Kungchia Yeh, 'Foreign Trade, Capital Inflow, and Technology Transfer Under the Open-Door Policy' in Michael Ying-Mao Kau and Susan H. Marsh (eds), *China in The Era of Deng Xiaoping: A Decade of Reform* (ME Sharpe 1993) 124.

[15]   For example, see China's 'National Patent Development Strategy (2011–2020)' <http://graphics8.nytimes.com/packages/pdf/business/SIPONatPatentDevStrategy.pdf> accessed 24 November 2014; and the Further Implementation of the National IP Strategy Action Plan (2014–2020) <http://english.sipo.gov.cn/news/official/201501/t20150114_1061802.html> accessed 27 January 2015.

[16]   Stefan Luginbuehl, 'China's Patent Policy' in Stefan Luginbuehl and Peter Ganea (eds), *Patent Law in Greater China* (Edward Elgar Publishing 2004) 10.

[17]   See China's National Patent Development Strategy (2011–2020) (*supra*, n 15); see also the State Intellectual Property Office of the PRC (SIPO) website, 'Chinese National Meeting of Heads of IPR Administration Held', 15 January 2015 <http://english.sipo.gov.cn/news/official/201501/t20150127_1067461.html> accessed 27 January 2015.

[18]   Derek Bosworth and Deli Yang, 'Intellectual Property Law, Technology Flow, and Licensing Opportunities in the People's Republic of China' (2000) 9 *International Business Review* 453.

licensing and litigation.[19] Given China's 'Indigenous Innovation' goals in lessening its dependence on foreign-based technology and becoming more self-sufficient with Chinese-invented technologies, the Chinese government may be interested in NPEs emerging in China to support the country's evolving profit-driven approach to IP[20] and to help establish a patent marketplace to promote investments in technology and technology transactions.[21] China, only recently, created a state-owned and partly state-funded NPE, called *RuiChuang IPR Funds*, set up largely to aid Chinese technology companies in acquiring patents and for defensive purposes in foreign patent disputes.[22] With the further sophistication and strengthening of the Chinese patent enforcement landscape,[23] *RuiChuang IPR Funds*, also partly funded by the likes of Chinese mega companies Xiaomi and Kingsoft,[24] could easily transform from a defensive patent fund into a patent assertion and monetization fund. What is even more salient, however, is the considerable and steadily increasing number of Chinese patents available for potential assertions. In 2014, Chinese patent applications for invention patents numbered 928,177,[25] of which 233,228

---

[19] Kelli Larson, 'An Inside View to Non-practicing Entities Business Models: A Case Study' (2013) 6 International Journal of Intellectual Property Management 294–315.

[20] For example see China's 'National Patent Development Strategy (2011–2020)' (*supra*, n 15).

[21] See Anne Kelley, 'Practicing in the Patent Marketplace' (2011) 78 University of Chicago Law Review 115; and J.F. McDonough, 'The Myth of the Patent Troll: an Alternative View of the Function of Patent Dealers in an Idea Economy' (2006) 56 Emory Law Journal 189.

[22] See Jia Liu, 'The RuiChuang Patent Operation Fund Is Announced to Be Established' (translated from Chinese) Chinese website <http://www.yicai.com/news/2014/04/3749724.html> accessed 10 May 2015. See also SIPO website <http://english.sipo.gov.cn/specialtopic/number/201405/t20140516_950286.html> accessed 10 May 2015. See also Jack Ellis, 'Inside the Multi-Million Dollar Chinese Patent Buying Fund with IV Connections' (IAM Magazine, 19 June 2014) <http://www.iam-media.com/Blog/Detail.aspx?g=48293ab7-eb17-423b-8cc3-fbdac475e943> accessed 29 November 2014. In Chinese literature, *RuiChuang* includes a 'g' at the end of the word; however, in English literature the 'g' is missing (*RuiChuan*). In this chapter I use the spelling from the Chinese SIPO website *RuiChuang*.

[23] Ying Zhan, 'Problems of Enforcement of Patent Law in China and its Ongoing Fourth Amendment (2014) 19 Journal of Intellectual Property Rights 266, 268. See also Chapter 4 in this volume on the IP revisions in China.

[24] See Ellis (*supra*, n 22).

[25] SIPO website, 'Distribution of Applications for Inventions Received from Home and Abroad', of which 801,135 were Chinese domestic applications, while 127,042 were from abroad. See <http://english.sipo.gov.cn/

patents were granted.[26] By the end of 2015, the Chinese government's target is to increase the number of patent applications to a staggering 2 million.[27] This target may be attainable supported by the lucrative incentives the Chinese government offers for those filing patent applications, such as tax breaks and monetary rewards among others.[28] One does question, however, what patent holders will do with all those patents and how domestic and foreign companies operating in China will traverse this 'great wall of patents'?[29]

Given China's evolving profit-driven approach to patents, the focus for many may be on the exploitation and monetization of patents via licensing and potentially litigation.[30] However, even if NPEs pursue the Chinese market for opportunities to exploit and enforce patents, it is not certain that the 'Western' style NPE model – purchase, acquire, or file for their own patents and enforce them against alleged infringers – would necessarily be effective in the Chinese jurisdiction. China's legal system may prove challenging for NPE patent enforcement as there are concerns over the level of protection, or lack thereof, afforded to IPRs in China, particularly on matters regarding patent protection and how serious China is on the enforcement of its patent laws in practice.[31]

---

statistics/2014/12/201502/t20150204_1071541.html> accessed 8 February 2015. For more on the different types of patents in China see *infra*, n 43.

[26]   SIPO website, 'Distribution of Grants for Inventions Received from Home and Abroad' (4 February 2015) <http://english.sipo.gov.cn/statistics/2014/12/201502/t20150204_1071537.html> accessed 8 February 2015.

[27]   See China's 'National Patent Development Strategy (2011–2020)' (*supra*, n 15).

[28]   Haiyang Zhang, 'Patent Institution, Innovation and Economic Growth in China' in Ligang Song, Ross Garnaut and Cai Fang (eds), *Deeping Reform for China's Long-Term Growth and Development* (Australian National University 2014) 512–513. Incentives may be further heightened for 'home-grown' domestic innovations. See Xibao Li, 'Behind the Recent Surge of Chinese Patenting: An Institutional View' (2012) 41 Research Policy 236.

[29]   Albert Guangzhou Hu and Gary H. Jefferson, 'A Great Wall of Patents: What is Behind China's Recent Patent Explosion?' (2009) 90 Journal of Development Economics 57, 68; Albert Guangzhou Hu, 'Propensity to Patent, Competition and China's Foreign Patenting Surge' (2010) 39 Research Policy 985.

[30]   China already is the most litigious country in terms of IP. See Richard P. Suttmeier and Xiangkui Yao, 'China's IP Transition Rethinking Intellectual Property Rights in a Rising China' (The National Bureau of Asian Research Special Report #29, July 2011) 13; Susan K. Sell, 'The Geo-Politics of the World Patent Order' in Frederick M. Abbott, Carlos M. Correa and Peter Drahos (eds), *Emerging Markets and the World Patent Order* (Edward Elgar Publishing 2013) 59.

[31]   See Ying Zhan (*supra*, n 23); Peter K. Yu, 'Intellectual Property, Economic Development, and the China Puzzle' in Daniel J. Gervais (ed), *Intellectual*

In light of these developments, this chapter further considers the emergence of NPEs in China using a conceptual framework of three drivers of NPE success in the context of China: NPEs and the Chinese patent enforcement landscape; the economics of patent enforcement for NPEs in China; and NPEs and patent enforcement culture in China. A better understanding of these three drivers of NPE success in the context of China may better help determine whether an NPE business model may succeed in China in the near future. It may also reveal useful insights not only for Chinese IP policy makers, but also for businesses that own and use patents in China. Accordingly, the remainder of the chapter is as follows: Section 2 provides some general background information on the NPE phenomenon, while Section 3 considers the potential emergence of NPEs in China using a conceptual framework of three drivers of NPE success in the context of China: NPEs and the Chinese patent enforcement landscape, the economics of patent enforcement for NPEs in China, and NPEs and patent enforcement culture in China. Section 4 explores the Chinese government's decision to establish its own state-run NPE *RuiChuang IPR Funds*, while Section 5 provides some concluding remarks.

2. BACKGROUND ON THE NPE PHENOMENON

NPEs generally are described in literature as individuals or entities that create business models focused solely on the enforcement of patent rights to generate revenues.[32] NPE patent enforcement is conducted mainly in the context of creating, negotiating and executing licensing programmes for prospective licensees in order to collect revenues from licensing/royalty payments, in addition to any damages awarded from patent litigation. The NPE phenomenon is of essential research importance

---

Property, Trade and Development: Strategies to Optimize Economic Development in a TRIPS Plus Era (Oxford University Press 2007) 174; Qing Cao, 'Insight into Weak Patent Enforcement of Intellectual Property Rights in China' (2014) 38 Technology in Society 40.

[32] Christian Helmers and Luke McDonagh, 'Trolls at the High Court?' (2012) LSE Legal Studies Working Paper No. 13; Colleen Chien, 'Of Trolls, Davids, Goliaths and Kings: Narratives and Evidence in the Litigation of High-Tech Patents' (2009) 87 North Carolina Law Review 1571; David Schwartz and Jay Kesan, 'Analyzing the Role of Non-practicing Entities in the Patent System' (2014) 99 Cornell Law Review 425; Michael Risch, 'Patent Troll Myths' (2012) 42 Seton Hall Law Review 457; Larson, 'An Inside View' (*supra*, n 19).

due to the asymmetrical advantages that NPEs encompass, which allow them to fundamentally change the economics of patent enforcement and litigation.[33]

Traditional patent litigation economics is set against patent enforcement; it is expensive and risky for parties to litigate patents through courts, it may take years and cost millions of dollars to pursue a patent infringement lawsuit through to full trial, which may only provide for a small return in a judgment or settlement.[34] Thus, for a patent owner the costs of patent enforcement may be too prohibitive to endure, while for a defendant, it may be more economical to settle any infringement allegation by paying for a licence rather than litigating in court, even if the defendant strongly believes there is non-infringement. As a result, many patents may end up being unenforced simply to avoid the costly use of the patent litigation system, particularly in the US.[35]

However, NPEs change the economic dynamics of enforcing and litigating patents. As NPEs are 'non-practising' in the sense that they do not use patents to manufacture or sell products, but rather only enforce patents to generate profits, they typically cannot be counter-sued for patent infringement.[36] As a result, NPEs need not worry about indirect costs in patent litigation such as preparing and defending against a countersuit or other business disruptional impacts. Furthermore, because NPEs do not build products with their patents they are likely not interested in cross-licensing agreements as they do not require the use of third-party patents to manufacture products. In patent assertions, NPEs may use the benefit of economies of scale by enforcing the same patent against multiple alleged infringers in one lawsuit, often in the same court venue, while using contingency-fee lawyers as counsel to help reduce the direct costs of patent enforcement and further drive down the cost of enforcement per assertion.[37] These factors help to make patent enforcement highly efficient, economical and scalable for NPEs.

---

[33]   Colleen Chien, Presentation to the DOJ/FTC Hearing on Patent Assertion Entities (10 December 2012) <http://digitalcommons.law.scu.edu/facpubs/591/> accessed 7 November 2014.

[34]   The average cost of patent litigation in the US is 3–10 million dollars. See World Intellectual Property Organization (WIPO) Magazine, *IP Litigation Costs Special Edition* (2010) chs 2 and 3.

[35]   Ibid. The high cost of patent litigation may deter many from enforcing their patents.

[36]   Ahmed J. Davis and Karolina Jesien, 'The Balance of Power in Patent Law: Moving Towards Effectiveness in Addressing Patent Troll Concerns' (2012) 22 Fordham Intellectual Property Law Journal 837.

[37]   Chien, Hearing on Patent Assertion Entities (*supra*, n 33).

3. DRIVERS OF NPE SUCCESS AND CHINA

3.1 NPEs and the Chinese Patent Enforcement Landscape

Various inputs in the Chinese patent enforcement landscape may help to drive NPE patent enforcement success. Generally, China has a two-track IP enforcement system via administrative or judicial enforcement.[38] While both tracks have their advantages and disadvantages, NPEs will likely be more interested in the judicial route as monetary damages cannot be sought from administrative enforcement.[39] Besides China's dual enforcement system and abundant number of patents available for potential assertions,[40] China also has a strong and growing high-technology sector. NPEs tend to focus on the high-technology sector for their patent enforcement assertions in specific industries such as telecommunications, computer software and consumer electronics where typically many different innovations are incorporated into a single product and where the scope of the patent may be difficult to delineate.[41] In addition to having the most Internet users and the largest smartphone market in the world,[42] China's developing telecommunications and consumer electronics industries may help support NPE business models in China. China's developing high-tech sectors may help foster its patent landscape where future innovations can be invented and where further patents may be generated for potential future assertions. Industries where multi-component innovations consisting of thousands of patents are incorporated into one invention, such as many inventions in high-tech industries, potentially may create environments which are conducive for widespread infringement to occur and where it may be difficult to determine the extent of patent protection coverage on a given component of an invention. As such, NPEs may be able to benefit from China's proliferation in patenting and the potentially unclear protection

---

[38]   See Chapter 1 in this volume.
[39]   Shan Hailing, 'Cross Border Enforcement of Intellectual Property Rights in China' in Paul Torremans (ed), *Research Handbook on Cross-Border Enforcement of Intellectual Property* (Edward Elgar Publishing 2014) 76.
[40]   See SIPO website, 'Distribution of Applications for Inventions Received from Home and Abroad' (*supra*, n 25).
[41]   Chien, 'Of trolls, Davids, Goliaths, and Kings' (*supra*, n 32). For example see Patent Freedom website, 'Exposure by Industry' <https://www.patentfreedom.com/about-npes/industry/> accessed 10 February 2015.
[42]   China had approximately 649 million Internet users in 2014. See CNN website, 'China's Online Users More than Double Entire US Population' <http://www.internetlivestats.com/internet-users/> accessed 12 February 2015.

boundaries in new innovations in their patent infringement enforcement campaigns.

Another unique input in China's patent landscape is the wide use of utility model patents as opposed to invention patents.[43] Utility model patents do not require substantive examination prior to being granted in contrast to invention patents;[44] thus, utility model protection can generally be obtained much faster than invention patent protection.[45] Also, the term of protection for a utility model patent differs from an invention patent, 10 years compared to 20 years respectively.[46] Although utility model patents do exist in Europe,[47] foreign NPEs in China, particularly American NPEs, may find the use of this type of patent to be unfamiliar. Nonetheless, Chinese utility model patents may provide an opportunity for NPEs to quickly obtain and enforce patents to potentially generate revenue.

However, further practical challenges might remain for NPE patent enforcement to emerge in China. For example, civil IP damages awards are generally perceived as being low in China compared to those in industrialized countries.[48] However, the proposed fourth Amendment to China's patent law may revise damage amounts with the potential introduction of punitive damages.[49] Moreover, China's patent law includes a working requirement where a patent owner is required to exploit the patent within three years from the date the patent is granted.[50] Therefore, if an NPE cannot exploit its patent appropriately or find prospective licensees to take licences within the three-year period, the entity may potentially lose its patent. Furthermore, while injunctive relief is available,[51] it may be difficult in practice for an NPE to obtain and enforce an injunction as the 'irreparable harm' standard must be clearly proven, while the Supreme People's

---

[43]   Yifei Sun, 'Determinants of Foreign Patents in China' (2003) 25 World Patent Information 27. China has three types of patents: invention patents with a duration of 20 years, and utility model and design patents both with a duration of 10 years. See SIPO website <http://english.sipo.gov.cn/FAQ/200904/t20090408_449726.html> accessed 28 January 2015.

[44]   Art. 40 Patent Law of PRC (2008).

[45]   Art. 2 Patent Law of PRC (2008). See WIPO website 'Protecting Innovation by Utility Models' http://www.wipo.int/sme/en/ip_business/utility_models/utility_models.htm> accessed 5 March 2015.

[46]   Art. 42 Patent Law of PRC (2008).

[47]   See WIPO, 'Protecting Innovation by Utility Models' (*supra*, n 45).

[48]   YieYie Yang, 'A Patent Problem: Can Chinese Courts Compare With the U.S. In Providing Patent Holders With Adequate Monetary Damages' (2014) 96 Journal of Patent and Trademark Office Society 140.

[49]   See Chapter 4 in this volume.

[50]   Art. 48 Patent Law of the PRC (2008).

[51]   Art. 66 Patent Law of the PRC (2008).

Court has indicated an adverse opinion on injunctions, urging lower courts to use caution in issuing such injunctions in the first instance.[52] Moreover, the rule of law, as a relatively new concept to China,[53] may render the Chinese patent enforcement landscape too unpredictable and unreliable overall for NPEs to initiate patent enforcement programmes in China.

3.2   The Economics of Patent Enforcement for NPEs in China

A second driver of NPE success may be found in the economics of patent enforcement in China. If the various inputs in China's patent enforcement landscape (that is obtaining patents, proving infringement, use of the judicial system, being awarded damages and injunctions, and so on) can be attained or conducted in a cost-effective manner these factors are likely to help drive NPE success in China. From the perspective of an NPE, if the expected return on patent enforcement is higher than the costs of undertaking the enforcement, the patent enforcement ought to be taken (risk v. reward scenario). However, patent enforcement is full of risk as there is no guarantee that a return on the patent assertion will ever be realized; the boundaries of patent protection may be difficult to determine and furthermore patents may be disputed and invalidated.[54] China's single jurisdiction for patent enforcement likely favours economical patent enforcement as an infringement or injunction decision is applied to the entire country, while it may also be highly economical for NPEs to obtain patents due to the lucrative incentives the government provides for applicants to file for patents.[55] Enforcement procedures may be made even more efficient with the recently established specialized Chinese IP Courts in Beijing, Shanghai and Guangzhou to pursue patent infringement assertions.[56]

However, some aspects of China's procedural law may frustrate efficient,

---

[52]   Stefan Luginbuehl and Thomas Pattlock, 'The Awakening of the Chinese Patent Dragon: The Revised Chinese Patent Law 2009' (2011) 42 (2) International Review of Intellectual Property and Competition Law 143; J. Benjamin Bai, Peter J. Wang and Helen Cheng, 'What Multinational Companies Need to Know About Patent Enforcement and Patent Litigation in China' (2007) 5 Northwestern Journal of Technology and Intellectual Property 459.

[53]   Yahong Li, 'Pushing for Greater Protection: The Trend Toward Greater Protection of Intellectual Property in the Chinese Software Industry and the Implications for the Rule of Law in China' (2002) 23 Journal of International Law 637.

[54]   Mark Lemley and Carl Shapiro, 'Probabilistic Patents' (2005) 19 Journal of Economic Perspectives 76.

[55]   Zhang (*supra*, n 28).

[56]   See Chapter 16 in this volume.

economical patent enforcement procedures for NPEs in China. For example, prior to patent litigation proceedings, parties shall first try to resolve disputes through consultation meetings,[57] which may be time consuming for NPEs. Proving infringement may take a lot of time and resources as the Chinese legal system does not include a discovery procedure, thereby requiring NPEs themselves to collect and submit their own evidence to prove infringement.[58] NPEs may have to hire private investigators to help with the collection of evidence and have a notary public authority authenticate any evidence adduced, while furthermore there is only a two-year statute of limitation to bring a patent infringement lawsuit beginning from the date the patentee knew (or should have known) about the infringement.[59] Additionally, a major challenge lies in the difficulty of calculating patent infringement damages.[60] While the cost of defence in China is lower compared to the US due to lower legal fees,[61] patent infringement damages awards in China are substantially lower than in the US and low compared to the likely degree of harm caused.[62] Therefore, while it may be economical for an NPE to obtain counsel in a patent infringement dispute, infringers may be more willing to defend against an NPE if the cost of defence is low and the amount of statutory damages required to pay for infringement would also be low. This may reinforce a cycle of continuous infringement and make it difficult for NPEs to enforce patents in practice. However, the recent proposed Fourth Amendment to China's Patent Laws calls for an increase in patent damage awards, namely through the introduction of punitive damages.[63] Furthermore, the availability of preliminary injunctive relief (or cessation of infringement for permanent injunction) banning infringing products from the second largest market in the world would be an efficient leveraging mechanism for NPEs to use in encouraging auspicious licensing or litigation settlement terms. However, obtaining and enforcing an injunction in practice may prove to be difficult and time consuming for NPEs.[64] It is also

---

[57]   Art. 60 Patent Law of the PRC (2008).

[58]   See Bai et al., 'What Multinational Companies Need to Know About Patent Enforcement and Patent Litigation in China' (*supra*, n 52) and Chapter 4 in this volume.

[59]   Art. 68 Patent Law of the PRC (2008).

[60]   Art. 65 Patent Law of the PRC (2008).

[61]   Kristina Sepetys and Alan Cox, 'Topics in Law and Economics in China. Intellectual Property Rights Protection in China: Trends in Litigation and Economic Damages' (2009) <http://www.ipeg.com/blog/wp-content/uploads/NERA-IP-Protection_China_2009.pdf> accessed 9 June 2015.

[62]   Ibid.

[63]   See Chapter 4 in this volume.

[64]   Ibid.

unclear how Chinese judges may react to awarding injunctive relief to NPEs that do not manufacture products but instead focus mainly on licensing.[65]

3.3 NPEs and Patent Enforcement Culture in China

In efforts to promote economic development and attract foreign investment, China finally introduced its modern-day patent law in 1984.[66] While the introduction of Chinese patent law is more a history of legal transplants of a Western imported system,[67] the problem of weak IPR protection in China is a concern held not only by foreigner patent holders, but also by Chinese patent owners.[68] Problems related to ineffective patent enforcement in China may be due to a combination of various factors, including poor judicial protection, strong local protectionism or the presence of less rule of law, yet they may also be related to Chinese culture.[69] Adverse attitudes towards invention and property rights transitioned in China first with the recognition of the necessity of having a modern patent system[70] and furthermore with an effective and well-functioning patent enforcement system. However, the concepts of individual rights or ownership may still have less meaning and importance in China as the country further transitions from an agricultural to an industrial to a knowledge economy. China appears to have a different cultural concept of patent enforcement at this stage in its economic and IP system development.[71] The concept of patents as a strong valuable asset has yet to be fully embraced and respected in China, which may be reflective of the approach many Chinese have towards infringement of IPRs and the difficulty rights holders have in enforcing patents in China in practice,[72] which is not to the benefit of

---

[65] For example, court decisions in the US and the UK have limited the availability of injunctive relief to NPEs based on the argument that it is difficult for an NPE to prove 'irreparable harm' and thus a reasonable royalty should sufficiently compensate for infringement. See *eBay, Inc. v MercExchange* 547 U.S. 388 (2006) and *Nokia Corp. v IPCom GmbH & Co. KG* [2012] EWHC 1446 (Ch).

[66] Patent Law of the PRC (promulgated by the Presidential Order No. 11 of 12 March 1984).

[67] See for example, Chapter 3 in this volume.

[68] Zhang (*supra*, n 23).

[69] Ibid.

[70] John R. Allison and Lianlian Lin, 'Evolution of Chinese Attitudes Toward Property Rights in Invention and Discovery' [2014] 20 Journal of International Law 735.

[71] Zhang (*supra*, n 23).

[72] Ibid. See also Dan Prud'homme, *Dulling the Cutting Edge: How Patent Related Policies and Practice Hamper Innovation in China* (European Chamber 2012) 103.

NPEs. As China's legal IPR framework developed rather quickly, it may take time for the Chinese people to recognize the importance and value that a sound enforcement system may bring to China's economic development. With the promotion of China's Indigenous Innovation goals China's cultural acceptance of stronger patent enforcement may be slowly on the horizon. A shift in cultural attitude towards protecting IPRs in China may be evident by the recent establishment of China's state-owned NPE – *RuiChuang IPR Funds*.

4.   CHINA'S STATE-OWNED NPE – *RUICHUANG IPR FUNDS*

This section briefly considers China's decision to create a state-owned, partly state-funded NPE *RuiChuang IPR Funds*.[73] In line with the promotion and development of its IP economy and Indigenous Innovation goals it makes sense that the Chinese government would take initiatives to help protect domestic technology companies and help increase the country's global competitiveness through the monetization of IPRs. China, however, is not the first country to establish such government-supported or state-sponsored NPE. Japan Taiwan, France and South Korea have all created patent funds generally managed and funded by their governments to help protect their respective domestic companies from foreign patent infringement attacks and for patent monetization purposes.[74] While the specific business model of *RuiChuang IPR Funds* has yet to be viewed from an operational level, it is believed that the fund will focus on acquiring IP from both domestic and foreign companies, assist Chinese companies to obtain and finance patents and help provide a defensive shield to protect Chinese companies against patent infringement attacks from foreign companies or foreign NPEs.[75] *RuiChuang IPR Funds* may have also been created

---

[73]   See SIPO website (*supra*, n 22).

[74]   Miyuki Monroig and Patrick Terroir, 'Asia Drives Transformation of Patent Economy' (IAM Magazine, July 2013) <http://www.iam-media.com/Magazine/Issue/60> accessed 14 November 2015. For example, see Japanese government NPE, Innovation Network Corporation of Japan website <http://www.incj.co.jp/english/> accessed 8 May 2015; South Korean government NPE, Intellectual Discovery <http://www.i-discovery.com/site/eng/model/licensing.jsp> accessed 8 May 2015; and French government NPE, France Brevet <http://www.francebrevets.com/> accessed 8 May 2015.

[75]   Jack Ellis, 'It's Time to Talk About Patent Funds' (IAM Magazine, March 2015)   <http://www.iam-media.com/Magazine/Issue/70/Cover-story/Its-time-to-talk-about-patent-funds> accessed 5 April 2015; Miyuki Monroig and Patrick

in response to the surge of NPE business models emerging, particularly in the US over the past couple of years with the objective of trying to purchase certain patents in the patent marketplace before NPEs purchase them, which could then be used to attack Chinese technology companies. As China's patent and licensing market further develops and the Chinese government's evolving profit-driven approach to IP strengthens, it is foreseeable that *RuiChuang IPR Funds* will also begin to monetize its patents against foreign firms to generate returns from its investments. Furthermore, *RuiChuang IPR Funds* may have been established as a vehicle for further national protectionism and government-sponsored subsidization of private enterprise through an anti-trade policy.[76] *RuiChuang IPR Funds* allows the Chinese government and private industry to work together to potentially disadvantage foreign companies. In addition to, or instead of, the Chinese government placing tariffs on imported products that compete with China's domestic industries, *RuiChuang IPR Funds* may be used to assert patent infringements against foreign companies raising their operating costs relative to domestic firms. This may give Chinese firms an upper hand with greater financial resources in competing not only domestically in China, but also internationally in global trade. *RuiChuang IPR Funds* may also be used as a political tool in international trade negotiations.[77] For example, the West is pushing for stronger patent protection to be transplanted through international Free Trade Agreements (FTAs), such as the proposed Trans-Pacific Partnership (TPP) Agreement and the Transatlantic Trade and Investment Partnership (TTIP) Agreement, to less powerful signatories such as China. Both the TPP and TTIP cover trade-related issues including trade and investment related aspects of IP.[78] The

---

Terroir, 'Inside Asia's Patent Funds' (IAM Magazine, July 2012) http://www. iam-media.com/Magazine/Issue/54/Features/Inside-Asias-patent-funds> accessed 5 April 2015; Joshua Philipp, 'China's State-funded Company looks to Profit Off US Patents' (Epoch Times, 6 November 2014) <http://printarchive.epochtimes. com/a1/en/hk/nnn/2014/11-Nov/06/A5.pdf> accessed 15 April 2015; Peter Roff, 'The Frightening Emergence of Government Patent Trolls' (The Washington Times, 31 August 2014) <http://www.washingtontimes.com/news/2014/aug/31/ roff-the-frightening-emergence-of-government-paten/> accessed 25 March 2015.

[76]   Javade Chaudhri, 'Chinese Industrial Policies: Indigenous Innovation, Intellectual Property Rights, and the Trade Issues of the Next Decade' (2011) 34 Thomas Jefferson Law Review 5, 6.

[77]   For example, see Hosuk Lee-Makiyama and Patrick Messerlin, 'Sovereign Patent Funds (SPFs): Next Generation Trade Defence?' (European Centre for International Political Economy Policy Brief, 2014) <http://www.ecipe.org/app/ uploads/2014/12/PB06.pdf> accessed 8 May 2015.

[78]   Peter K. Yu, 'The Non-Multilateral Approach to International Intellectual

Chinese government might utilize *RuiChuang IPR Funds* to potentially pre-empt stringent trade provisions or for leverage in such trade negotiations, or to retaliate against nations which enforce their patents against Chinese domestic industries as a result of a trade dispute.[79]

5.   CONCLUDING REMARKS

While the world watches China's transition from a made-in-China to an invented-in-China economy, the strengthening of China's patent enforcement regime may be creating fertile ground for international patent litigation to take place and for an environment to be created which supports the emergence of NPEs in China. The vast Chinese domestic marketplace, the abundant number of patents available for potential assertions, and the availability of remedies such as injunctive relief banning products from one of the most important markets in the world appear to be attractive features that may support NPEs emerging in China. However, while some of the drivers of NPE success may be applicable in the context of China, perhaps Chinese culture has yet to place enough importance on implementing strong patent enforcement in practice for NPEs to emerge in China at this point in the development of its IP system. Furthermore, an essential driver of NPE success rests on strong remedies being available for alleged patent infringements, such as high damages awards and injunctive relief. Given the relatively low level of damages awards available and the apprehension regarding court-ordered injunctive relief in China, NPEs would likely need to find other ways to profit from patents until the licensing market develops enough where NPEs can sustain themselves from licensing royalties. Still, even if NPEs are to emerge in China in the future it is questionable whether they would take the same shape or follow similar business models as they do, for example, in Europe and the US. Given China's evolving profit-driven stance on IP, China might be interested in utilizing NPEs to further develop its IP landscape and intellectual property regime. Nonetheless, the establishment of *RuiChuang IPR Funds* by the Chinese government shows the emergence of one type of NPE in China despite concerns with China's IP enforcement system.

Property Normsetting' in Daniel J. Gervais (ed), *International Intellectual Property. A Handbook of Contemporary Research* (Edward Elgar Publishing 2015) 83.
[79]   See Lee-Makiyama and Messerlin (*supra*, n 77).

16. Special intellectual property courts in China

Mingde Li

1. INTRODUCTION

On 31 August 2014, the Standing Committee of the National People's Congress of China passed 'A Decision to Establish Intellectual Property Court in Beijing, Shanghai, and Guangzhou'[1] (hereafter cited as the Decision). Subsequently, on 3 November 2014, the Supreme People's Court of China published a judicial interpretation, 'Rules for the Jurisdiction of the Intellectual Property Court of Beijing, Shanghai, and Guangzhou' (hereafter cited as the Supreme Court Rules),[2] which specified some aspects of the Decision. This chapter will discuss the reasons for establishing the intellectual property courts, the most important points of the Decision, and the future challenges that need to be met in order to set up more intellectual property courts.

2. SPECIAL INTELLECTUAL PROPERTY TRIBUNALS IN CHINA

China established its intellectual property system initially in 1978, enacted its Trademark Law in 1982, Patent Law in 1984, Copyright Law in 1990 and Unfair Competition Law in 1993, and has amended aspects of these laws subsequently. In the initial stages of the Chinese intellectual property system, disputes concerning trademark, patent, copyright and unfair competition were adjudicated upon by a civil

---

[1] The Standing Committee of the National People's Congress of China, *A Decision to Establish Intellectual Property Court in Beijing, Shanghai, and Guangzhou* (31 August 2014).

[2] Supreme People's Court of China, *Rules for the Jurisdiction of the Intellectual Property Court of Beijing, Shanghai, and Guangzhou* (3 November 2014).

tribunal in a court or by a competent administrative agency on another level.[3]

Since 1993, China has utilized special tribunals to adjudicate upon intellectual property cases. For example, in August 1993, the Beijing Intermediate Court and Beijing High Court established their intellectual property tribunals respectively. In October 1996, the Supreme Court of China established its intellectual property tribunal.[4] Subsequently, intellectual property tribunals were established nationwide – in every high court, in many intermediate courts and in some basic courts. At the end of 2013, there were about 410 intellectual property tribunals all over China.[5]

One of the purposes for establishing the special intellectual property tribunals was to improve the trial quality of intellectual property cases. Initially, when China enacted its intellectual property laws, the country did not have adequate numbers of skilled personnel who understood the laws or could handle the disputes concerned.[6] This was due to the fact that most of the intellectual property experts or skilled personnel were in the relevant administrative agencies. The respective laws provided that if there were disputes involving intellectual property rights, the parties should either go to a competent agency or a court to seek resolution. However, some judges in the civil courts of Beijing, Shanghai and Guangzhou had tried many cases involving intellectual property rights. Accordingly, these courts gradually became competent in intellectual property law and the related trial activities and the judicial system decided to gather those judges together, in order to establish some intellectual property tribunals in some courts. This initially occurred in Beijing, Shanghai and Guangdong. During the early period of these tribunals, there were not so many intellectual property rights cases to be heard. This in turn afforded the judges of these tribunals the time to discuss, analyse and decide the cases at hand in much greater detail.[7]

If we say that the intellectual property tribunal has been a special practice in China to resolve intellectual property disputes since 1993, there is also

---

[3]   This is the so-called 'Dual Track' to resolve intellectual property disputes.

[4]   Intellectual Property Center of China Academy of Social Sciences, *A Study on the Reform of the Intellectual Property Enforcement Mechanism of China* (Intellectual Property Press 2008) 193–194.

[5]   This data is from the Intellectual Property Tribunal, Supreme Court of China.

[6]   Although China enacted its Trademark Law in 1982, Patent Law in 1984 and Copyright Law in 1990, there were shortages of skilled personnel in the beginning.

[7]   See Intellectual Property Center of China Academy of Social Sciences (*supra*, n 4) 193–194.

another special practice aimed at specifically resolving disputes concerning patents, plant varieties and the layout-designs of integrated circuit boards. In this respect, the Supreme Court of China has appointed some of the intellectual property tribunals to adjudicate upon these kinds of cases. Initially, the appointed intellectual property tribunals were at the level of the intermediate courts and high courts. However, in the last several years, some intellectual property tribunals, at the level of the basic courts, have also been appointed to resolve disputes concerning utility model patents and design patents. Thus it would appear that cases involving utility model patents and design patents are less complicated for the basic courts to resolve.

At the end of 2013, there were seven intellectual property tribunals, at the same level of the basic courts, that can adjudicate first instance cases concerning utility model patents and design patents; 87 tribunals, at the level of the intermediate courts, that can adjudicate first instance cases concerning patents (including invention patents, utility model patents and design patents); 45 tribunals, at the level of the intermediate courts, that can adjudicate first instance cases concerning plant varieties; and 46 tribunals, at the level of the intermediate courts, that can adjudicate first instance cases concerning layout-designs.[8] It should also be noted that most of the tribunals that can adjudicate first instance cases concerning plant varieties and layout-designs of integrated circuit boards are among the tribunals that can adjudicate first instance cases concerning patents. The decisions of all of these intellectual property tribunals can be appealed if the parties to a case are not satisfied by the decision of the respective tribunal. The decision made by the appeal court is the final one.[9]

This practice of establishing special intellectual property tribunals to meet the challenge of shortages in the numbers of skilled personnel appears not to be particularly Chinese because there is also an international trend towards establishing special intellectual property courts or tribunals. In 1982, the United States established the Court of Appeals for the Federal Circuit. This court specifically adjudicates upon appealed patent cases from all over the country.[10] In 1991, the United Kingdom

---

[8] Supreme Court of China, *China's Judicial Protection of Intellectual Property* (White Paper, 2014).

[9] According to the Civil Procedural Law of China there are four levels of courts: basic courts, intermediate courts, high courts, and the Supreme Court; and two levels of trial: first-instance trials and appeal trials. So the appeal court makes a final decision. Sometimes, however, the Supreme Court or the High Court may review the decision by an appeal court.

[10] Federal Courts Improvements Act of 1982, Public Law 97-164 (2 April 1982).

established the Patent County Court in London, in order to resolve patent disputes from England and Wales.[11] In 1993, the European Union (or, as it was then, the European Community) issued the 'Trademark Regulation', which requires the Member States to designate national courts hearing Community trademark cases.[12] In 2001, the European Union also enacted the Community Design Regulation, which requires the Member States to designate national courts for hearing Community Design cases.[13] In 2005, Japan established an Intellectual Property High Court and this court adjudicates upon appealed cases concerning patents, utility models, designs and computer programs from the Tokyo and Osaka District Courts. In 2008, Taiwan established an Intellectual Property High Court to adjudicate upon patent cases, including first instance cases and appeal cases. Finally, in 2014, the European Union enacted a regulation to establish a Unified Patent Court and Unitary Patent system.[14]

Although China has established about 410 intellectual property tribunals and appointed some of the tribunals to adjudicate upon cases concerning patents, plant varieties and layout-designs, there is no special intellectual property court at any level. Furthermore, due to the fact that there is no national intellectual property appeal court, the cases are appealed to different higher courts, and judicial standards are inconsistent. Accordingly, many experts have suggested that there should be a national intellectual property appeal court in China. The Outline of the National Intellectual Property Strategy 2008 responded to this suggestion and made the proposal 'to study the possibility to establish a national intellectual property appeal court'.[15] The word 'intellectual property' here means patents, plant varieties, layout-designs, trade secrets and computer programs.[16]

---

[11]   See Michael Fysh, *The Perspective of the London Patents County Court Judge* (paper to 14th Annual Conference on International Law and Policy at Fordham University School of Law, April 2006).

[12]   Art. 91 of Council Regulation (EC) No 40/94 of 20 December 1993 on the Community trade mark.

[13]   Art. 84 of Council Regulation (EC) No 6/2002 of 12 December 2001 on Community Designs.

[14]   See the website of the European Patent Office <http://www.epo.org/law-practice/unitary.html>.

[15]   State Council, *Outline of the National Intellectual Property Strategy* (25 June 2008) art. 46 <http://www.wipo.int/wipolex/en/details.jsp?id=859> accessed 21 April 2015.

[16]   During the drafting of the strategy, the intellectual property center, China Academy of Social Sciences suggested the solution to establish a national appeal court to adjudicate cases concerning technology, including patents, plant varieties, layout-designs, trade secrets and computer programs.

3. INTELLECTUAL PROPERTY COURTS

China has achieved tremendous socio-economic development in the last 30 years as a result of cheap labour, natural resources and other factors. As industry has modernized, so has the need to change the country's developmental model, which is now focused on the socio-economic development of innovative and creative industries, and the protection and utilization of the outputs of these industries. In 2007, the 17th Congress of the Communist Party proposed to 'enhance the power of self-innovation, and construct an innovative country'.[17] In 2012, the 18th Congress of the Communist Party introduced a strategy to promote innovative development.[18] Consequently, how to effectively protect the outputs of intellectual creation and innovation has become a crucial issue for China. In this respect, the Chinese government drafted its National Intellectual Property Strategy from 2004 to 2008, and enacted the Outline of the National Intellectual Property Strategy on 5 June 2008.[19] In 2012 the 18th Congress of the Communist Party stressed the need to protect intellectual property rights.[20] In 2013, the Third Plenary Congress of the Central Committee of the Communist Party further emphasized the need to utilize and protect intellectual property rights in China.[21]

In order to enforce this strategy and further utilize intellectual property, it is necessary to take some measures to effectively protect intellectual property rights. In October 2013, the Third Plenary Congress of the Central Committee of the Communist Party suggested the establishment of special intellectual property courts.[22] In June 2014, a leading group in the Central Committee of the Communist Party issued a plan to establish intellectual property courts in Beijing, Shanghai and Guangzhou. Accordingly, based on this plan, the Supreme Court of China drafted a proposal to the Standing Committee of the National People's Congress[23] and on 31 August

---

[17] General Secretary Hu Jintao, *The Political Report to the 17th Congress of the Communist Party* (October 2007).

[18] General Secretary Hu Jintao, *The Political Report to the 18th Congress of the Communist Party* (October 2012).

[19] State Council (*supra*, n 15).

[20] General Secretary Hu Jintao (*supra*, n 18).

[21] Central Committee of the Communist Party of China, *The Decisions about the Overall and Further Reforms in Some Important Aspects* (October 2013).

[22] Ibid.

[23] The draft has been discussed several times by some limited groups, and the author of this chapter participated in two of the discussions; one was held by the Supreme Court of China, and another was held by the Legal Working Committee of the National People's Congress.

2014, the Standing Committee of the National People's Congress passed the Decision to Establish Intellectual Property Courts in Beijing, Shanghai and Guangzhou (the Decision).[24] This decision can be considered a milestone for the protection of intellectual property rights in China.

According to the explanation accompanying the Decision, the purposes of establishing the intellectual property courts are to implement the strategy promoting the development of China through innovative and creative industries, to effectively protect intellectual property rights by the judicial system and to enhance the trial quality of intellectual property cases.[25] It is apparent that the establishment of the intellectual property courts is a way to address the challenges resulting from socio-economic development and to stimulate innovation and creation by offering effective protection for intellectual property rights. However, the Decision may be considered experimental, as it only created three intellectual property courts in Beijing, Shanghai and Guangzhou.

4.   JURISDICTION OF THE INTELLECTUAL PROPERTY COURTS

In light of the Decision, the intellectual property courts shall be established in Beijing, Shanghai and Guangzhou. The courts have jurisdiction to hear cases concerning patents, plant varieties, layout-designs of integrated circuit boards and technical secrets.[26] Apparently, these kinds of cases are closely related to technology, or bear the features of technology. Accordingly, the Rules further added 'computer programs'.[27]

Regarding the specific cases that can be adjudicated upon by the intellectual property courts, the original proposal by the Supreme Court only listed cases concerning patents, plant varieties and layout-designs. During the discussions, many experts proposed that cases concerning trade secrets should also be included in the list, or at least cases concerning technical secrets should be included.[28] In contrast, some other experts argued that

---

[24]   The Standing Committee of the National People's Congress of China (*supra*, n 1).

[25]   Chief Justice of the Supreme Court of China Zhou Qiang, *An Explanation on the Decision to Establish Intellectual Property Courts in Beijing, Shanghai, and Guangzhou* (27 August 2014).

[26]   See art. 2 of the Decision.

[27]   See art. 1 of the Rules.

[28]   According to art. 10 Unfair Competition Law of China, trade secret is divided into technical secret and business secret.

there is not a clear division line between a trade secret and a technical secret, and some secret information might be relegated either as trade secret or as technical secret. The Standing Committee of the National People's Congress accepted the suggestion to include technical secrets in the case list, and in a specific case the court shall discern whether the secret information is a technical secret or a trade secret.

Many experts also suggested the inclusion of computer programs in the case list because computer programs have technological features. In this respect, the Intellectual Property High Court of Japan does adjudicate upon cases concerning computer programs. Other experts, however, argued that a computer program is the expression of an idea and should be protected by copyright law and that technological inventions are protected by patent law, so it was not necessary to include computer programs in the case list. Although the Standing Committee of the National People's Congress did not accept the suggestion, the Supreme Court accepted the idea and included computer programs in the case list.

In light of the Decision, the cases that can be adjudicated by the intellectual property courts are civil and administrative cases. According to the current 'dual track' approach in China, the owner of an intellectual property right can go either to a court or a competent administrative agency after his or her right has been infringed. If an administrative agency makes a decision and the parties are not satisfied, they can sue the agency in a civil court. The Decision and the Rules provide that the intellectual property courts can adjudicate civil and administrative cases concerning patents, plant varieties, layout-designs, technical secrets and computer programs. On the other hand, because the intellectual property courts only have jurisdiction to hear civil and administrative cases, criminal cases are excluded from the case list. This is not problematic because the infringement of patent, plant variety or layout-design does not result in criminal liability in China. However, the Decision included technical secrets in the case list and the Rules included computer programs in the case list. According to the Criminal Code of China, there can be criminal liability resulting from copyright infringement and the misappropriation of another's trade secret.[29]

Furthermore, it is curious that the Supreme Court Rules provide that the intellectual property courts shall adjudicate cases concerning the identification of well-known trademarks. Prior to May 2014, once a well-known trademark was identified as being so, either in an administrative procedure or a judicial procedure, the trademark could be protected as

---

[29] See arts. 217–219 Criminal Code of China.

a well-known trademark, and the owner of the trademark could obtain a certain degree of unfair competitive advantage. This practice, however, seriously deviated from the purpose of the protection of well-known trademarks as provided for in the Paris Convention and the Agreement on Trade-Related Aspects of Intellectual Property Rights (TRIPS). Due to the fact that the basic principle for the protection of well-known trademarks is for the purposes of resolving disputes, well-known trademarks should be identified as necessary on a case-by-case basis, and following the resolution of the dispute, there should be no special protection as a well-known trademark. According to the amended Trademark Law, which came into effect in May 2014, a well-known trademark should be identified for the purposes of dispute resolution and the trademark owner shall not advertise his or her trademark as a well-known trademark.[30] This means that every court can identify a trademark as well-known if it is necessary to resolve a dispute but no special status as a well-known trademark can exist after the dispute is resolved. Accordingly, it is not necessary for the Rules to provide that the intellectual property courts can adjudicate well-known trademark cases.

5.   THE INTELLECTUAL PROPERTY COURTS AS INTERMEDIATE COURTS

On the basis of the Decision, the Intellectual Property Courts established in Beijing, Shanghai and Guangzhou are intermediate courts, so the intellectual property cases adjudicated upon by these courts are first instance cases. Consequently, if the parties are not satisfied by a court decision, they can appeal the case to the appropriate high court, such as the Beijing, Shanghai or Guangdong High Courts. According to this provision, the appeal courts for these cases are still spread all over the country and there is no central national appeal court for cases concerning patents, plant varieties, layout-designs, technical secrets and computer programs.

According to the Decision, as intermediate courts, the three Intellectual Property Courts shall adjudicate upon appealed intellectual property cases from the basic courts in the related municipality. For example, the Beijing Intellectual Property Court can adjudicate upon appeals concerning copyright (except computer program cases), trademark (except well-known trademark cases) and unfair competition (except

---

[30]   See Chapter 4 in this volume.

technical secret cases) from all the basic courts within the Beijing municipal area. This is also the case for Shanghai Intellectual Property Court. However, for the Guangzhou Intellectual Property Court, it may be a different matter because it can only adjudicate upon appeals from the basic courts within the Guangzhou Municipal area, but not from the basic courts in other areas of Guangdong Province. In contrast, the Guangzhou Intellectual Property Court has jurisdiction for cases concerning patents, plant varieties, layout-designs, technical secret and computer programs from all of the areas of Guangdong Province (except for Shenzhen).

According to the Decision, the Beijing Intellectual Property Court also has jurisdiction to hear cases resulting from the decisions of the administrative agencies under the State Council. These agencies are the Patent Review Board under the State Intellectual Property Office, the Trademark Review Board under the Administration of Industry and Commerce, and the Plant Variety Review Boards under the Administration of Agriculture and Forestry. The Patent Review Board can make decisions whether a patent should be granted or not and whether a granted patent is valid or not.[31] The Trademark Review Board can make decisions whether a trademark can be registered or not and whether a registered trademark is valid or not.[32] The Regulations for the Protection of New Plant Varieties allow the Plant Variety Review Board to make decisions as to whether a right on a related new plant variety can be granted or not and whether a granted new plant variety right is valid or not.[33] Before the Decision, these cases were adjudicated upon by the Intellectual Property Tribunals of the First Intermediate Court and Second Intermediate Court of Beijing respectively. However, after the establishment of the Beijing Intellectual Property Court, all cases resulting from administrative decisions shall be adjudicated upon by the Beijing Intellectual Property Court and resulting appeals directed towards the Beijing High Court.

One of the most promising features of the Intellectual Property Courts is that they possess trans-regional jurisdiction over the listed cases. According to the Decision, in the first three years of its implementation, the Intellectual Property Courts can adjudicate upon the listed cases from the related municipal area or province.[34] For example, if a patent owner is going to put forward a lawsuit in Beijing, he or she

---

[31] See arts. 41 and 46 Patent Law of China (2008).
[32] See arts. 35 and 44 Trademark Law of China (2013).
[33] See arts. 32 and 37 Regulations for the Protection of New Plant Varieties (1997).
[34] See art. 2 of the Decision.

can only go to the Beijing Intellectual Property Court and no other intermediate courts. This is also the case for the Shanghai Intellectual Property Court. For example, before the Decision, Beijing had three intellectual property tribunals respectively in the First, Second and Third Intermediate Courts of Beijing. The Beijing Intellectual Property Court was inaugurated on 6 November 2014 and the intellectual property tribunals in these intermediate courts were removed. In fact, most of the judges in the newly established Intellectual Property Court are from the former three intellectual property tribunals. This is also the case for the Shanghai Intellectual Property Court, which is based on the two intellectual property tribunals of the First and Second Intermediate Court of Shanghai. The Shanghai Intellectual Property Court was inaugurated in December 2014.

For the Guangzhou Intellectual Property Court, the trans-regional jurisdiction over the listed cases is different from that of Beijing and Shanghai. Before the Decision, there were several intellectual property tribunals in some of the intermediate courts in Guangdong Province, such as the tribunals in the Shenzhen, Zhuhai, Foshan and Dongguan intermediate courts, that could adjudicate upon first instance cases concerning patents, plant varieties and layout-designs. According to the Decision and the Rules, after the establishment of the Guangzhou Intellectual Property Court, all of the first instance cases in the list shall not go to other intermediate courts, but go directly to the Guangzhou Intellectual Property Court. This means that if a right owner of a patent, plant variety, layout-design, technical secret or computer program is going to put forward a lawsuit in Guangdong Province (whichever city they are in), they must go directly to the newly established Guangzhou Intellectual Property Court.

Before the Decision, the intellectual property tribunals in the Shenzhen, Zhuhai, Foshan and Dongguan Intermediate Courts had tried many patent cases. Accordingly, the judges in those tribunals are skilled in the trial of patent cases. In fact, in the past few years, the intellectual property tribunal in the Shenzhen Intermediate Court has adjudicated more patent cases than the tribunals in the Guangzhou Intermediate Court. Prior to the Rules being issued by the Supreme Court, there was a suggestion that Shenzhen should be an exception for the trans-regional jurisdiction of the listed cases in Guangdong. The reasons for this are that Shenzhen is a special economic zone. Many high tech-enterprises are located there and the judges in Shenzhen Intermediate Court are very competent. Although the Decision and the Rules show there was no such exception for Shenzhen, it turned out in December 2015 that Shenzhen is out of the jurisdiction of Guangzhou Intellectual Property Court. This means that the Intellectual Property Tribunal of the Shenzhen Intermediate Court will continue to adjudicate the listed cases.[35]

The trans-regional jurisdiction over listed cases has an important meaning for the judicial system in China. According to the Decision, the Intellectual Property Courts shall be organized by the related Standing Committee of the People's Congress in Beijing, Shanghai and Guangzhou. The chief judges, judges, and the trial committee shall be appointed and removed by the related Standing Committee of the People's Congress and the Intellectual Property Courts shall be responsible for, and report their work to, the related Standing Committee of the People's Congress.[36] Again this is not a problem for the Beijing and Shanghai Intellectual Property Courts because the chief judges, judges, and the trial committee (at the level of intermediate courts) have been appointed or removed by the Standing Committee of the People's Congress in Beijing or Shanghai. Therefore, the Intellectual Property Courts in Beijing and Shanghai can adjudicate the listed cases from the related municipality, which is in accordance with the control area of the Standing Committee of the People's Congress.

The meaning of the trans-regional jurisdiction is more important for the Guangzhou Intellectual Property Court. On the basis of the Decision, although the Guangzhou Intellectual Property Court is organized by the Standing Committee of the People's Congress of Guangzhou, the chief judges, judges, and the trial committee are appointed or removed by the Standing Committee of the People's Congress of Guangzhou; and the court is also obliged to report its work to the Standing Committee of the People's Congress of Guangzhou. The Guangzhou Intellectual Property Court can adjudicate cases from all over Guangdong Province (except for Shenzhen). This is really a breakthrough of the Judicial Organization Law of China.

Within the first three years of the Decision, the Intellectual Property Courts in Beijing, Shanghai and Guangzhou shall only have jurisdiction over the listed cases from these municipal areas or provinces.[37] After the three years has expired the situation is not clear: can the Intellectual Property Courts in Beijing, Shanghai and Guangzhou have jurisdiction over the listed cases from other provinces or municipal areas? For example, after three years, is it possible that the Beijing Intellectual Property Court

---

[35]   To author's knowledge, this exception is due to the fact that Guangzhou Intellectual Property Court has a shortage of judges to hear the listed cases from all over Guangdong Province.

[36]   See art. 6 of the Decision.

[37]   See art. 1 of the Decision.

can adjudicate the listed cases from the Tianjin municipality, Hebei Province, Shanxi Province and Inner Mongolia? If so, the trans-regional jurisdiction will be of great significance for the intellectual property judicial system.

6.   FUTURE TASKS FOR THE INTELLECTUAL PROPERTY COURTS

The establishment of three Intellectual Property Courts in Beijing, Shanghai and Guangzhou is experimental. In this respect, the Decision provides that after three years from its enactment, the Supreme Court shall report to the Standing Committee of the National People's Congress on how the Decision has been implemented.[38] Specifically, the Supreme Court shall report on how the Intellectual Property Courts have operated and on their merits, achievements and shortcomings. If the courts are found to have operated well, more intellectual property courts will be established in other cities, such as in Xi'an, Chongqing and Wu Han. In fact, in the explanation of the drafted decision, Chief Justice Zhou Qiang of the Supreme Court stated that the principle for the establishment of the intellectual property courts is to explore step by step, and move further with great caution.[39] If further establishment of intellectual property courts is to be explored, some important issues must be considered carefully.

The first issue to be considered is how to locate the intellectual property courts. The Decision established three Intellectual Property Courts in Beijing, Shanghai and Guangzhou, which are in the most developed areas in China. However, this does not mean that intellectual property courts should be established in every capital city of all provinces, autonomous regions or in every municipality directly under the State Council.[40] On the basis of the trans-regional jurisdiction, China can set up several intellectual property courts in the middle and western areas that can have jurisdiction over the listed cases from the nearby provinces or autonomous regions. In the author's view, there should be no more than ten intellectual property courts at the level of intermediate courts established, in order to adjudicate the listed cases from all over China.

---

[38]   See art. 7 of the Decision.
[39]   Chief Justice of the Supreme Court of China Zhou Qiang (*supra*, n 25).
[40]   There are four municipalities under the State Council now, Beijing, Shanghai, Tianjin and Chongqing.

The second issue is whether to establish a single national appeal court for the listed cases. According to the Decision, the three Intellectual Property Courts established will adjudicate first instance cases, which can then be appealed to the corresponding High Courts in Beijing, Shanghai and Guangdong. Consequently, if there are ten intellectual property courts at the level of intermediate courts, there will be ten high courts to accept appealed cases. Obviously this is not ideal for establishing common judicial standards because the ten high courts may have different views regarding the appealed cases.

During the drafting of the National Intellectual Property Strategy, the Chinese Academy of Social Sciences suggested a two-step solution. The first step is to direct appealed first instance cases concerning patents, plant varieties and layout-designs into five high courts, such as the Beijing, Shanghai, Guangdong, Xian and Chongqing High Courts. The second step is to let the Intellectual Property Tribunal of the Beijing High Court assume the role of a national appeal court, adjudicating the cases concerning patents, plant varieties and layout-designs from all over China. The Intellectual Property Tribunal of the Beijing High Court can be called the National Intellectual Property Appeal Court, just like the US Court of Appeals for the Federal Circuit, or the Japanese Intellectual Property High Court.[41] During the debates surrounding the Decision many experts suggested establishing a national intellectual property appeals court rather than the intellectual property courts at the level of intermediate court. However, the Decision decided to establish three intellectual property courts and leave the task of establishing a national intellectual property appeal court for future consideration. Without any doubt, China should establish a single national intellectual property appellate court, at least to adjudicate the listed cases.

The third issue to be considered carefully is whether the courts have jurisdiction over three or two subject matter areas of law – the so-called three-in-one or two-in-one competence question. According to the Decision, the Intellectual Property Courts in Beijing, Shanghai and Guangzhou shall adjudicate the civil and administrative cases concerning the listed cases, so the criminal cases have been excluded. This is the so-called 'two-in-one' approach. On the basis of the drafting Decision, the cases in the list were patent, plant variety and layout-design cases. Because there is no criminal liability for the infringement of patent, plant variety and layout-design in China, the 'two-in-one' solution is no problem.

---

[41] See Intellectual Property Center of China Academy of Social Sciences (*supra*, n 4) 233–242.

However, when the Decision was passed by the Standing Committee of the National People's Congress, technical secrets were added to the list. Again, cases concerning computer programs were added to the list by the Rules of the Supreme Court. Thus there are some problems for the 'two-in-one' solution because there is criminal liability for the infringement of trade secrets[42] and computer programs. In the drafting of the National Intellectual Property Strategy, the Chinese Academy of Social Sciences suggested a 'three-in-one' solution, meaning that the intellectual property cases, whether they are civil cases, or administrative and criminal cases, shall be adjudicated by a given intellectual property tribunal, not separately by a civil tribunal, an administrative tribunal and a criminal tribunal.[43] The Outline of the National Intellectual Property Strategy accepted this suggestion and provides that it will 'explore the possibility to set up the specialized intellectual property tribunals to adjudicate the civil, administrative, and criminal cases'.[44] Since the enactment of the Outline of the National Intellectual Property Strategy, the judicial system has enforced the 'three-in-one' approach all over China. This has achieved a great deal in creating common judicial standards over intellectual property cases. In the future, the intellectual property courts at the level of intermediate courts and the national intellectual property appeals court should adopt the 'three-in-one' approach and not the 'two-in-one' approach.

7.   CONCLUSION

When the United States established the Court of Appeals of the Federal Circuit in 1982, it set the trend in the world to establish special intellectual property courts or tribunals. The United States, United Kingdom, European Union and Japan are leading in this trend. The reason behind this is clearly that patents, designs, plant varieties and computer programs are a key competitive advantage of a country. To unify judicial standards over these kinds of cases may in turn encourage innovation and creation, and promote the social and economic development in a country.

In following this trend, China has established special intellectual property tribunals since 1993. With the change of its development model

---

[42]   According to art. 10 Unfair Competition Law of China, trade secret is divided into technical secret and business secret.
[43]   See Intellectual Property Center of China Academy of Social Sciences (*supra*, n 4) 216–221.
[44]   State Council (*supra*, n 15) art. 45.

and the upgrade of industry, China's social and economic development depends more and more on the innovation and the protection of intellectual property rights. Based on this background, China decided to establish three intellectual property courts, in Beijing, Shanghai and Guangzhou. The Decision demonstrates that China is going further in the line of a specialized intellectual property jurisdiction.

There is no doubt that China will establish more intellectual property courts in the near future, so some of the important issues described above must be considered carefully. It is apparent that the intellectual property courts, including a national intellectual property appeals court would greatly improve the judicial protection of intellectual property rights and would encourage innovation, creation and the promotion of social and economic development in China.

17. Chinese developments regarding judicial enforcement mechanisms in intellectual property law

Yajie Zhao and Niklas Bruun

1. INTRODUCTION

China's introduction of modern intellectual property (IP) legislation fulfilling the basic standards set out in the Berne and Paris Conventions, as well as in the Agreement on Trade-Related Aspects of Intellectual Property Rights (TRIPS), has been a rather recent and fast development.[1] It is common knowledge that the introduction of basic material standards in IP law does not necessarily translate into practice. There are many examples in the history of comparative law that demonstrate situations where law in books has never really become law in practice.[2] The first prerequisite for an IP system to function well is that IP protection has to be recognized, and in cases where registration is required, it must be registered. Second, the management of IP rights must be handled in an efficient manner and there must be exploitation avenues for rights, so that a process from innovation to business practice can take place. Third, in cases of infringements the protection has to be enforced.

A functioning national IP governance focuses on all the aspects of IP protection: the development of clear rules and legislation regarding material protection, the availability and access to protection, management of IP and the enforcement of IP rules.

It is clear that China has made significant progress in developing its IP system. The numbers of patent applications and IP registrations have been

---

[1] Stefan Luginbuehl, 'China's Patent Policy' in Stefan Luginbuehl and Peter Ganea (eds), *Patent Law In Greater China* (Edward Elgar Publishing 2014) 3–24.

[2] Ugo Mattei, 'Comparative Law and Economics' in Boudewijn Bouckaert and Gerrit De Geest (eds), *Elgar Encyclopedia of Law and Economics* (Edward Elgar Publishing 2000) 518–519.

increasing steadily.[3] China has a modern IP system in place and it is also heavily used. The Chinese challenges are mainly therefore related to IP management and IP enforcement.[4]

The management of IP in China is dealt with in other chapters of this volume. In this chapter we try to assess how China is responding to the IP enforcement challenges it is facing and to what extent it is transplanting enforcement models from Europe or other parts of the world to its IP system. The chapter is structured in the following way. First we give a short overview of the main enforcement challenges for the Chinese IP system. Then we will have a rather detailed look at the present structure, practice and ongoing reforms of the Chinese system. Finally we will discuss these developments from a comparative European perspective.

The Chinese challenges are both specific Chinese features in the justice system as well as more general concerns, which seem to be common all over the world. The latter ones relate to the capabilities and competence of the courts to deal with complex issues related to new technology, the duration of the court procedures and the predictability of outcomes. Specific Chinese features are related to the relative weakness of the rule-of-law tradition in China with the Supreme People's Court as both a last instance appeal court, but also as an instance issuing guidelines and guidance especially for lower courts. Furthermore, there is a strong tradition of administrative adjudication of IP disputes in China, for instance, the State Intellectual Property Office of China (SIPO) and its regional offices have a role in this administrative procedure. Also the huge regional differences regarding technological development and also relevant IP problems raise specific challenges for the Chinese IP system. Finally the system of remedies also has some very specific Chinese features.

2. DEVELOPMENTS WITHIN THE CHINESE COURT SYSTEM

Over the last few decades, China has made significant improvements in the field of IP law and its enforcement. For example, the number of IP cases has increased considerably in the last few years. The number of all

---

[3] Thomas F. Cotter, *Comparative Patent Remedies – A Legal and Economic Analysis* (Oxford University Press 2013) 336–346.

[4] Cao Jingjing, 'Dual Enforcement System' in Luginbuehl and Ganea (*supra*, n 1) 195–208.

first and second instances, and protest cases[5] for civil IP cases from 2001 to November 2006 was 64,099. The number of filed cases had already reached 66,609 during the first six months of 2014.[6] According to the Supreme People's Court's annual report of 2013, there were 114,075 first and second instances IP cases. The number of first instance foreign-related IP civil cases was 1,697, which meant an increase of 18.75 per cent compared to 2012.[7]

Within the coming three years, China will significantly enhance the implementation of Chinese IP rights via the establishment of specialized courts, as is made clear in Chapter 16 of this volume. On the other hand, China faces many challenges in harmonizing IP enforcement nationwide, especially in the field of patents.

The Chinese judicial system is under the supervision of the Supreme People's Court (SPC). The organization and administrative supervision at each level is regulated by the Court Organization Law (COL). Under the SPC, the system has three levels of local courts: 32 higher courts, 409 intermediate courts and 3117 basic courts.[8] Furthermore, there are military courts and other specialized courts.

The geographical division of the courts and their levels follow the national division and levels of local governments.[9] Generally speaking, the organization of the Chinese courts is very similar from one to another. Patent cases are normally heard in the chamber of a court (often no. 3 or no. 5).[10]

---

[5]   Protest cases are cases which are reheard by the People's Court, based on the protest procedures carried out by the People's Procuratorate. It is a legal supervision mechanism of China. When a decision contains mistakes made by the People's Court, according to the law, the People's Procuratorate can protest the incorrect decision, and require that the proceedings be reopened and the case reheard.

[6]   孙雷：《关于在北京　上海　广州设立知识产权法院的决定　探析》，《中国版权》2014　年第5期，另参见2014年知识产权上地论坛 [Sun Lei, 'Analysis on the Standing Committee of the National People's Congress Decision on the Establishment of Intellectual Property Court in Beijing, Shanghai, Guangzhou' (2014) 5 *China Copyright*, 5–9]. Published also at the Shangdi Forum of Intellectual Property 2014.

[7]   最高人民法院：　《2013年中国法院知识产权司法保护状况》，《人民法院报》，2014年4月25日 [2013 China IPR Judicial Protection in Court, *People's Court News*] <http://www.chinacourt.org/article/detail/2014/04/id/1283299.shtml> accessed 6 June 2015.

[8]   最高人民法院：《人民法院简介》 [The Supreme People's Court of China, 'Introduction of the People's Courts'] <http://www.court.gov.cn/jgsz/rmfyjj/> accessed 2 May 2014.

[9]   Shao, Wei, *Patent Litigation Practices In Mainland China* (Taiwan Ministry Of Economic Affairs, Intellectual Property Office 2011).

[10]   Ibid. 12.

The basic people's courts hear the first instance trials, unless otherwise stipulated by law.[11] They have no jurisdiction over patent infringement cases. But certain courts have been authorized by the SPC to hear first instance trials on contractual issues which involve patent matters. Due to the differences in regional development, the SPC has also authorized some basic courts to hear the first instance trials on infringement cases on utility models and designs. Examples of such courts are the Yiwu Court of Zhejiang Province, the Kunshan Court of Jiangsu and the Haidian Regional Court of Beijing, which hear first instance civil trials regarding patents of utility models and designs. Earlier, it was predicted as a trend that, in the future, with the improvement in Chinese IP legal practice, more and more basic courts would have jurisdiction over patent cases. However, after the establishment of IP courts inside China, it is unclear how this will be developed in the near future. The issue will be discussed further in Sections 3 and 4 of this chapter.

The intermediate people's courts only hear first instance trials where (1) they are stipulated by law, or (2) the cases are transferred from their related lower courts. They also have jurisdiction as second instance courts in trials that are (1) appeals of the cases that are first heard at their lower courts, or (2) protest cases that are against the lower courts' judgments, which are raised from the People's Procuratorate according to the trial supervision procedure.[12]

According to the law, patent infringement cases on innovation patents will be heard at least on the level of intermediate courts. Intermediate courts are situated in the capital cities of the provinces, the autonomous regions, and the municipalities, which are directly under the control of the central government, and function as first instance in these cases.

According to article 27 of the COL, the higher people's court of each province can only hear the trials as first instance cases if (1) this is stipulated in laws and/or regulations decree, or (2) if the cases are transferred to it from an intermediate people's court. They also hear appeals or protest cases regarding the intermediate courts' judgments. In contrast to the basic and intermediate people's courts, the higher people's courts cannot request to transfer a filed case to be heard at their higher level because the SPC does not hear any transferred case from its lower level.

The SPC is at the highest level and supervises the judicial workings of the other courts.[13] It also has the authority to interpret the application

---

[11]   Arts. 20 and 21 of the COL.
[12]   Art. 24 of the COL.
[13]   Art. 29 of the COL.

of law.[14] The SPC only hears cases as the first instance if (1) the laws and/ or regulations stipulate so, or (2) if it is considered necessary. It hears cases as the second instance that are appeals or protest cases regarding the higher courts' or special courts' judgments.

The SPC has an IP division that consists of five benches with 25 judges, one assistant and seven clerks. This division has jurisdiction over (1) civil cases on IP or competition matters, (2) administrative cases regarding licences and authorization of patents, trademarks and other IP rights. It also hears and judicially supervises the refusals of its lower courts' effective judgments of the previously mentioned two case types.[15] According to the trial supervision process, protests that are raised by the Supreme People's Procuratorate will also be heard inside this division, except the cases that are originally heard by one of the benches inside the division. The division also has authority to review the IP cases or give consultative instructions according to the requests from its lower courts. Moreover, this IP division of the SPC is responsible for research, guidance and supervision of all national IP trials and anti-trust cases; and responsible for the implementation of the national IP strategy.[16]

Apart from judicial enforcement, China has a dual enforcement system for IP protections, which offers administrative protection to its IP right holders.[17] The IP administrative protection is a legal protection mechanism that is carried out by the relevant national administrative authorities in compliance with the relevant legal procedures and measures. It deals with IP disputes, maintains the IP order and enhances IP social awareness.[18] The contents of administrative protection of IP covers, but is limited, to the following: (1) authorizations and recognitions; (2) administrative procedures regarding mediation, ruling, reconsideration, arbitration and so on; (3) investigations regarding fines and enforcement; (4) remedies; (5) sanctions; (6) legal supervision; and (7) administrative services.[19] The administrative authorities offer remedies for right holders in IP infringement cases and it is a parallel protection system compared to

---

[14]   Art. 32 of the COL.
[15]   The division has authority to deny the application of retrial and hear the retrial in the mentioned civil and administrative cases.
[16]   最高法院:《最高法院知识产权庭介绍》[People's Supreme Court, 'Introduction of the IP division of the SPC' (12 April 2010)] <http://www.court. gov.cn/zscq/zscqt/201004/t20100412_3940.html> accessed 31 July 2014.
[17]   SIPO and its 62 regional offices.
[18]   邓建志,单晓光:《我国知识产权行政保护的涵义》,《知识产权法》,2007年 第1期 [Deng Jianzhi and Shan Xiaoguang, 'The Conception of IP Administrative Protection in China' (2007) 75 1 *Intellectual Property Law* 62].
[19]   Ibid.

judicial protection. Namely, IP protection in China offers a 'dual enforcement' system.[20] Based on real needs, IP right holders can seek remedies either from the relevant State Council departments and their regional offices or from the judicial branches.

Generally speaking, compared to the judicial remedies, administrative remedies are faster for infringement cases, the procedures are less complicated and the enforcement of decisions is also more efficient. However, if one of the parties decides to challenge the administrative decision and initiates a judicial appeal in the related intermediate court, then the process would be longer. Moreover, the administrative remedies do not offer compensation to the right holders.[21] On the other hand, administrative protection still maintains its popularity because it costs less than the judicial protection, and frequently brings parties to mediation.[22]

3. THE 'THREE-IN-ONE' MODEL

The efforts to promote the transition of China to an innovative country, the requirements of an internationalized economy, the increased difficulty and complexity of the IP cases, and the need for a unified judicial implementation of IP law inside China have elevated concern regarding IP law enforcement since 2008.[23] The Chinese State Council has stated in its 12-year strategy: 'We should improve the trial system for intellectual property-related cases, optimize the allocation of judicial resources and simplify remedy procedures. We should consider setting up special tribunals to accept civil, administrative or criminal cases involving intellectual property.'[24]

The first model of the improvements, carried out by the regional courts, is the 'three-in-one' pilot tribunal in different provinces. Generally

---

20 刘峰：《我国知识产权侵权救济 '双轨制' 的正当性》,《知识产权法》, 2008 年第2期 [Liu Feng, 'The Justice Analysis On the "Dual Enforcement System" of Patent Infringement Remedies in China' (2008) 2 *Intellectual Property Law* 50].

21 Shao, Wei (*supra*, n 9) 17.

22 Luginbuehl (*supra*, n 1) 20.

23 State Council of the People's Republic of China, *National Intellectual Property Strategy Outline* (5 June 2008) <http://www.gov.cn/gongbao/content/2008/content_1018942.htm> accessed 6 June 2015.

24 State Council of the People's Republic of China, *Notice of the State Council on Issuing the Outline of the National Intellectual Property Strategy* (State Council 2008) para 45.

speaking, it is a trial model that either hears all civil, administrative and criminal IP cases in one tribunal; or hears the IP cases with a collegial panel of judges that are from civil, administrative and criminal tribunals; or is a combination of the two. The representative models are: Pudong model (January 1996), Nanhai model (July 2006), Xi'an model (December 2006), Wuhan model (April 2008), Chongqing model (November 2008), Beijing No. 2 Intermediate Court model (December 2008) and Zhuhai model (December 2009).[25]

It is not only a model for the hearing of cases, but also a matter of how to organize the court.[26] The non-unified implementation at the provincial level shows that: (1) the court level for the first instance of the 'three-in-one' model is different from one province to another – legislatively speaking, at which court level the IP tribunal shall belong to and how it shall be organized is still under discussion;[27] (2) some provinces establish a separate, qualified and specialized tribunal for IP cases, some hear the case within each of the original chambers; and (3) some models concentrate on enhancing the court in general and some focus on improving the panel of judges. Even though, at the central state level, the strategy outlines a clear aim, the implementation differs noticeably at the provincial level. How the differences will be harmonized is unclear.

From an international perspective, China's 'three-in-one' model is a unique system. Although it has been implemented in different ways, it is a common mechanism that the Chinese courts use to support and enhance

---

25   胡淑珠：《论知识产权法院（法庭）的建立——对我过知识产权审判体制改革的理性思考》,《知识产权》2010年第四期 [Hu Shuzhu, 'Discussions On the Establishment of IP Court' (2010) 4 *Intellectual Property* 37]. See also 周志伟, 戴启洪： 《我国知识产权法院设立方案探讨》, 2014年知识产权上地论坛 [Zhiwei Zhou and Qihong Dai, 'Analysis on the Establishment of China Exclusive Intellectual Property Courts', Shangdi Forum of Intellectual Property 2014].

26   This current situation is caused due to the legal reform development of China. After the open and reform policy, even though China achieved considerable improvements in the field of legal enforcement, it is still undeniable that the legal practices for hearing IP cases are limited. Hence, according to the law, the qualified court has the autonomy to organize and adjust the IP chamber according to its regional situations. The court experiments with the model via organizing different modes, and at the same time hearing cases. Thus, the three-in-one model contains two characteristics. It is an inventive case hearing model and at the same time a court-organizing model. It is a mechanism that China uses to collect practical experiences and handle real cases at the same time.

27   胡淑珠：《论知识产权法院（法庭）的建立——对我过知识产权审判体制改革的理性思考》,《知识产权》2010年第四期 [Hu Shuzhu, 'Discussions on the Establishment of IP Court' (2010) 4 *Intellectual Property* 37].

the openness of information and resources.[28] At the time of writing, China has six high people's courts, 74 intermediate courts and 80 basic people's courts applying the three-in-one model in IP cases.[29]

4. THE INTELLECTUAL PROPERTY COURTS IN BEIJING, SHANGHAI AND GUANGZHOU

On 31 August 2014, the Standing Committee of the National People's Congress of China published 'A Decision To Establish Intellectual Property Court In Beijing, Shanghai, Guangzhou' (the Decision).[30] According to articles 3 and 4 of the Decision, IP courts are intermediate courts. The IP courts are under the supervision of the SPC and the High People's Court of their respective regions.[31] Meanwhile, the jurisdiction of these three courts is stipulated in the SPC Rules for the Jurisdiction of the IP Courts of Beijing, Shanghai and Guangzhou released on 27 October 2014 (the Rules).[32]

These three courts have exclusive jurisdiction over the first instance cases within their municipal districts concerning: (1) civil and administrative cases on patents, new plant varieties, layout designs, technical secrets, and computer software; (2) administrative cases on administrative acts carried out by State Council departments or local people's governments above the county level, that involve copyright, trademark, or unfair competition; and (3) civil cases involving well-known trademarks.[33] In contrast to Beijing and Shanghai, the IP court in Guangzhou has its regional jurisdiction on the first and third type of cases within the whole Guangdong province.[34]

---

[28]   李小武：《中国知识产权法院的设立目的》, 2014年知识产权上地论坛 [LI Xiaowu, 'The Aims of the Establishment of the Chinese Intellectual Property Court', Shangdi Forum of Intellectual Property 2014].

[29]   袁定波：《设立知识产权法院意在规范市场竞争》,《法制日报》, 2014年6月9日 [Yuan Dingbo, 'Establishing the Intellectual Property Court Aims to Standardize the Market Competition' *Legal Daily* (9 June 2014)].

[30]   《全国人民代表大会常务委员会关于在北京、上海、广州设立知识产权法院的决定》, 2014 [Standing Committee of the National People's Congress, *Decision on the Establishment of Intellectual Property Court in Beijing, Shanghai, Guangzhou* (31 August 2014)] <http://npc.people.com.cn/n/2014/0901/c14576-25581035.html> accessed 6 June 2015.

[31]   Art. 5 of the Decision.

[32]   《最高人民法院关于北京、上海、广州知识产权法院案件管辖的规定》, (法释 [2014] 12号) [No. 12 SPC Rules on the Jurisdiction of the IP Courts in Beijing, Shanghai and Guangzhou (27 October 2014)] <http://www.chinacourt.org/law/detail/2014/10/id/147980.shtml> accessed 6 June 2015.

[33]   Art. 1 of the Rules.

[34]   Art. 2 of the Rules.

The Rules have excluded copyright and trademark civil cases from the first instance of the IP courts. The newly established IP courts will only function as second instance appeal courts for cases as such, unless otherwise stipulated. There are still many remaining questions in practice, which require the SPC's guidance or interpretation. Examples of such cases are the unification of jurisdiction over complicated cases that contain patent, trademark and copyright at the same time, and the standards and procedure for transferring copyright and trademark cases from the basic people's courts to the IP courts in Beijing, Shanghai and Guangzhou.[35]

The earlier authorized basic people's courts no longer had jurisdiction over the aforementioned three types of cases inside Beijing, Shanghai and Guangzhou after the Rules came into force. The intermediate courts of Beijing, Shanghai and Guangzhou have no jurisdiction on the mentioned three types of cases, but the administrative cases carried out in the municipal district of Guangzhou will still be heard at its original intermediate courts inside Guangdong. If a case whose subject matter partly falls into the three types of cases mentioned, it can also be heard in the IP courts.

The newly established IP courts differ from the already existing three-in-one model; they are 'two-in-one'. It means that the newly established IP courts hear only civil and administrative cases. Moreover, at the provincial level, the administrative cases on administrative acts, which are carried out by State Council departments or local people's governments above the county level, and which involve copyright, trademark, or unfair competition, are left out. The second instance of the aforementioned three types of IP cases are heard inside the higher people's courts in Beijing, Shanghai and Guangzhou.

In this context, China will not establish a separate high people's court for IP cases. First, if the high court does not hear the first instance of IP cases, or only hears the listed type of cases for IP courts, the number of cases for the special IP courts is not big enough for a separate high court.[36] Secondly, the establishment of a specific high people's court for IP would face other legal problems, such as how to fit it in the current court system, to which level of government it is responsible, how to manage its team of judges and so on. Thirdly, the current IP courts are still in the phase of

---

[35] 冯晓青，武志孝《我国知识产权法院与普通法院关系研究》，2014年知识产权上地论坛 [Fen Xiaoqing, and Wu Zhixiao, 'Research on the Relationships between Intellectual Property Court and General Court in China', Shangdi Forum of Intellectual Property 2014].

[36] Ibid.

gaining experience. China might establish a high people's court at a later stage.

5. THE IMPACT OF IP COURTS ON THE 'DUAL ENFORCEMENT SYSTEM'

It is difficult to say if there will be any substantive change to the dual enforcement system with administrative enforcement on the one hand and judicial enforcement on the other. The establishment of IP courts changes and unifies the jurisdiction of civil and administrative cases to the IP courts in Beijing and Shanghai, but how this will be implemented inside the whole country is not clear at this stage. The establishment of IP courts does not change any substantive law or the implementation of substantive law but it has brought about a significant change regarding the jurisdiction of administrative cases.

According to article 1(2) of the Rules, the jurisdiction of the first instance of administrative cases on administrative acts that are carried out by State Council departments or local people's governments above the county level and which involve copyright, trademark and/or unfair competition, have all been transferred to IP courts instead of the original intermediate courts. However, such unification at this stage is only limited to Beijing, Shanghai and the municipal area of Guangzhou. Administrative cases for the aforementioned matters which are carried outside of Guangzhou will be still heard at the original intermediate courts.

The Rules also stipulate the exclusive jurisdiction of the first instance IP court in Beijing in article 5 as follows:

(i) refusals of the administrative adjudications or decisions, which are made by the State Council departments, on the authorizations or acknowledgements of patents, trademarks, new plant varieties, or integrated circuit designs; (ii) refusals of the administrative decisions on the compulsory licenses, or arbitration decisions on compulsory license fees, which are made by the State Council departments, on the authorizations or acknowledgements of patents, trademarks, new plant varieties, or integrated circuit designs; and (iii) refusals of other administrative acts related to IP authorizations or acknowledgements. Reported in the annual report of the SPC, there were 2886 first-instance administrative IP cases in 2013, among which 1312 (45.23 per cent) were foreign-related cases.[37]

---

[37] 最高人民法院：《2013年中国法院知识产权司法保护状况》,《人民法院报》, 2014年4月25日 [2013 China IPR Judicial Protection in Court, *People's Court News*] <http://www.chinacourt.org/article/detail/2014/04/id/1283299.shtml> accessed 24 April 2014.

The unification of jurisdiction of administrative cases may significantly raise public IP awareness. It is possible that the establishment of IP courts will have an impact on the preference of parties for the judicial or administrative path when choosing remedies.

6. CHINESE IP JUDGES

So far, China has 7,000 judges in the higher people's courts and 36,000 in the intermediate courts.[38] In total, China has 2,700 judges for IP cases.[39]

In accordance with article 6 of the Decision, the presiding judges in the newly established IP courts will be nominated by the respective Directors' Meetings of the Municipal People's Congress Standing Committee of Beijing, Shanghai and Guangzhou, and separately approved by their respective Standing Committee of the Municipal People's Congress. The rest of the judges will be nominated by the presiding judge and approved by the respective Standing Committee of the Municipal People's Congress of Beijing, Shanghai and Guangzhou.

The Decision does not mention the specific criteria for electing IP judges. During the deliberation of this Decision, members from the deliberating group recommended to promulgate standards on electing IP judges.

First, the IP judges are facing the same problems as other judges in the judicial system. For example, the remuneration for Chinese judges is paid by their local governments. Although it has been commonly understood for many years that the remuneration of judges shall not be paid only from the local government, this problem still persists.[40] In short, the SPC has pointed out the following six common problems in the judicial system: (1) fairness and efficiency of the judgment; (2) difficulties in case filing, litigation and enforcement; (3) need for improvement in the system and mechanisms to guarantee access to an independent and fair judiciary; (4) administrative burden of courts affecting quality and efficiency;

---

[38]   最高人民法院：《人民法院简介》[The Supreme People's Court of China 'Introduction of the People's Courts'] <http://www.court.gov.cn/jgsz/rmfyjj/> accessed 2 May 2014.

[39]   刘春田：《知识产权法院的职责与使命》,《人民法院报》2014年9月3日 [Liu Chuntian, 'Intellectual Property Court's Mandate and Mission' *People's Court News* (3 September 2014)] <http://rmfyb.chinacourt.org/paper/html/2014-09/03/content_87169.htm?div=-1> accessed 6 June 2015.

[40]   Lina Wang, 'Intellectual Property Protection in China' (2004) 36(3) *International Information & Library Review* 253–261.

(5) partiality and corruption in the court officials; (6) heavy workload with increasing caseloads for some courts and poor working conditions for court personnel for the less developed regions.[41]

Stated in the strategy outline in 2008, these will also be parts of the further reforms to the judicial system. It was claimed that the Chinese courts faced a lack of judges, and many judges were short of the relevant background knowledge and experience at the beginning of the establishment of the IP system. Since the 1980s, China and its adjudicators have unified the implementation of IP law at a certain level. During the last 30 years of development, many professional judges have been trained and gained practical experience. At the same time, apart from the shortage of judges, the loss of judges has also become a problem within the Chinese judiciary.

However, there is an opposing voice nowadays. The current reform claims that professionalism as well as the unification of implementation is limited, and therefore the judicial system should aim at improving the judiciary. The judicial system is introducing '员额制' (elected judiciary/ quota system for judges). It is a system that refers to the existing judiciary, according to the workload, the size of the city and its population, economic development, and other factors to determine the number of judges inside the courts and using only qualified judges. The system is a new form of judicial mechanism consisting of judges and judge assistants.[42]

Unlike European countries, China is not introducing a pool of IP judges. The SPC published its *Guidelines on Enrolling Judges for Intellectual Property Courts* (the Guidelines) on 28 October 2014 and confirmed the application of the new mechanism. The judges are elected according to article 3. Based on the Guidelines, the newly established Beijing IP court has 25 judges in total.[43] The Guangzhou and Shanghai courts were separately established on 16 and 28 December 2014 respectively. The Guangzhou court has 13 IP judges and the Shanghai court has ten.[44]

---

[41]   Qiang Zhou, 'Report on the Work of the Supreme People's Court (2013–2014). Delivered at the Second Session of the Twelfth National People's Congress on 10 March 2014' <http://www.china.org.cn/china/2014-05/08/content_32331522.htm> accessed 6 June 2015.

[42]   郑永昶:《建立法官员额制度之构想》,《人民司法》, 2003年第7期 [Zheng Yongxu, 'The Idea Establishing the Quota System for Judges' (2003) 7 People's Judiciary 25].

[43]   北京知识产权法院:《北京知识产权法院法官信息》,审判信息网 [Intellectual Property Court in Beijing, 'Information of IP judges in the Intellectual Property Court in Beijing'] http://www.bjcourt.gov.cn/fgxx/detail.htm?court=30&channel=100606002> accessed 1 December 2014.

[44]   中华人民共和国知识产权局:《广州知识产权法院挂牌成立》, 2014年12月17日 [State Intellectual Property Office of the PRC, *The Guangzhou Intellectual*

Meanwhile, IP judges are facing other specific challenges as well. First, as stated by the presiding judge of the IP division of the SPC, Xiaoming Song, Chinese IP courts will be among the largest in the world to hear IP cases. After the establishment of specialized IP courts, it is predictable that the number of IP cases will increase. Especially in the IP court of Beijing, the number of cases, including the first and second instances, will reach more than 10,000. Considering the number of judges in the court, the Beijing court is already facing challenges, such as how to resolve the disputes properly and sufficiently and how to balance the interests of right holders and the public.[45] The growth in the number of cases is much faster than the growth in the number of judges; the current reform is ongoing under the challenge of 'too much cases but too little judges'.[46]

Secondly, the establishment of IP courts is a forerunner of judicial reform. The establishment of IP courts is not only a major reform of China's IP rights judicial protection system, in fact, it has become the experiment lab and pilot of Chinese judicial reform and bears the responsibility of the reform initiatives.[47] Meanwhile, the elected judiciary system is still different from the appointed judiciary system. However, too many extra political responsibilities and administrative expectations may actually harm judicial independence or it may weaken under the stress of too many irrelevant tasks.[48] Whether the model implemented in Beijing, Shanghai and Guangzhou can actually be introduced in the whole country is still questionable. For example, there are questions as to how to decide the number of judges in a court inside a certain region, under what

---

Property Court Is Established (17 December 2014)] accessed 24 March 2015; 中华人民共和国知识产权局：《上海知识产权法院挂牌成立》，2014年12月31日 [State Intellectual Property Office of the PRC, *The Shanghai Intellectual Property Court Is Established* (31 December 2014)] <http://www.sipo.gov.cn/mtjj/2014/201412/t20141231_1054112.html> accessed 24 March 2015.

45   袁定波：《设立知识产权法院意在规范市场竞争》，《法制日报》，2014年6月9日 [Yuan Dingbo, 'Establishing the Intellectual Property Court Aims to Standardize the Market Competition' *Legal Daily* (9 June 2014)].

46   胡道才：《员额制后，法官该如何选任》，《光明日报》2014年9月4日   [Hu Daocai, 'After the elected judiciary, how to elect judges' *Guangming Daily* (4 September 2014)] <http://www.njfy.gov.cn/www/njfy/xwzx_mb_a3914090559424.htm> accessed 6 June 2015.

47   袁定波：《设立知识产权法院意在规范市场竞争》，《法制日报》，2014年6月9日 [Yuan Dingbo, 'Establishing the Intellectual Property Court Aims to Standardize the Market Competition' *Legal Daily* (9 June 2014)].

48   李小武：《中国知识产权法院的设立目的》，2014年知识产权上地论坛 [Li Xiaowu, 'The Aims of the Establishment of the Chinese Intellectual Property Court', Shangdi Forum of Intellectual Property 2014].

standards to elect the judges from the existing groups, and how to balance the number of cases and judges.[49]

Thirdly, article 4 of the Guidelines stipulates that a person within the judicial personnel, who meets the qualifications of the Judges Law of the People's Republic of China, can be a qualified IP judge if he or she meets the following criteria: he or she (i) has the level four senior judge's qualification; (ii) has more than six years of relevant experience in trial working; (iii) holds a bachelor or above degree of law from the ordinary universities; and (iv) has strong capacities as regards presiding over trials and writing skills for legal documents. The current system does not require IP judges to have a technical background. Article 5 allows each region to decide the criteria for other legal professionals as IP judges. It has been pointed out by other judges that if, during the further reform, there is no top-level binding guidance on the ratio of judges but each region is allowed to decide the number of judges, the imbalance of different regions may lead to more difficult unification, or even to a bigger mess.

7.   THE CHINESE DEVELOPMENT IN A COMPARATIVE PERSPECTIVE

Although the European unitary patent system has not yet been implemented, its principal importance in the field of IP enforcement is undeniable in the context of broader social, political and economic concerns, especially within the European Union (EU) and the European patent system, but also beyond. Since the adoption of a unitary patent package in 2012, Chinese scholars are already taking the unitary patent as a reference point when discussing the establishment of the Chinese IP court system.[50] In the context of enhancing and governing the values of private intangible property rights, this chapter will, by using the EU as a reference point, expand the discussion to cover some features, as well as insert an EU approach as to how China is developing its IP enforcement.

The problem of achieving a consistent and efficient harmonization

---

49   刘丽:《法官员额制度研究》, 辽宁省沈阳市中级人民法院 [Liu Li, 'Studies on the Elected Judiciary System' *Liaoning Shenyang Municipal Intermediate People's Court* (19 October 2014)] <http://syzy.chinacourt.org/public/detail.php?id=6424> accessed 6 June 2015.

50   李明德:《知识产权法院与创新驱动发展》,《人民法院报》2014年9月3日 [LI Mingde, 'Intellectual Property Court and Innovation-Driven Development' *People's Court News* (3 September 2014)] <http://rmfyb.chinacourt.org/paper/images/2014-09/03/05/2014090305_pdf.pdf> accessed 6 June 2015.

within IP enforcement is something that is on the agenda – in different forms – both in China and in the EU. As a significant part of IP governance,[51] achieving a harmonized IP enforcement system becomes strategically important to regional economies inside both China and the EU. The enforcement of IP rights in different regions shall match the situation of the regional development of technology, economy and culture of the state.[52] In Europe the long existence of the European Patent Convention (EPC) has resulted in a considerable degree of harmonization in the examination and grant system operated by the European Patent Office. However, the system is not really European since the granted patents are national patents and the harmonization does not cover litigation. Patent right holders therefore still need to enforce their rights in courts in different countries.[53] These courts have very different knowledge and experience levels of IP cases.

Currently, since a European Patent under the EPC equates to a number of national patents, national courts and authorities of the Contracting States of the EPC are competent to decide on the infringement and validity of European patents. In practice, this gives rise to a number of difficulties when a patent proprietor wishes to enforce a European patent, or when a third party seeks the revocation of a European patent in several countries: high costs, risk of diverging decisions and lack of legal certainty. Forum shopping is also inevitable as parties seek to take advantage of differences in national courts' interpretation of harmonized European patent law and in procedural laws, as well as differences in speed (between 'slow' and 'quick' courts) and in the level of damages awarded.

The Agreement on the Unified Patent Court addresses the above problems by creating a specialized patent court (Unified Patent Court, or UPC) with exclusive jurisdiction for litigation relating to European patents and European patents with unitary effect (unitary patents).

The UPC will comprise a Court of First Instance, a Court of Appeal and a Registry. The Court of First Instance will be composed of a central division (with its seat in Paris and two sections in London and Munich) and several local and regional divisions in the Contracting Member States to the Agreement. The Court of Appeal will be located in Luxembourg.

---

[51]   See Chapter 2 in this volume.
[52]   See Chapter 1 in this volume.
[53]   Dietmar Harhoff, *Economic Cost-Benefit Analysis of A Unified and Integrated European Patent Litigation System* (Munich, 26 February 2009) <http://ec.europa.eu/internal_market/indprop/docs/patent/studies/litigation_system_en.pdf> accessed 6 June 2015.

The Agreement was signed by 25 EU Member States on 19 February 2013. It will need to be ratified by at least 13 states, including France, Germany and the United Kingdom to enter into force. It has been a long process to reach this state and the judges within this system have to be highly experienced and included in a pool of specialized judges from the Member States.

Even though the IP rights are still territorial, each major IP system has already implemented similar standards because of the Berne Convention, Paris Convention and TRIPS. As regards enforcement, especially in the past 20 years, every major IP system of enforcement has certain common structural features. Abstracting patent enforcement as an example: the patent systems in many countries make provision for special IP courts, awards of damages in the form of lost profits and reasonable royalties, provide one or more avenues for third parties to fend off potential liability by challenging the patent validity,[54] and apply compulsory licences for the sake of public interest and so on. Big differences occur at the application level of the common standards.

At this phase, we can already see that the enforcement problems faced in Europe clearly have some similarities with the Chinese situation. Within the EU, patent law and procedure are much more advanced in some European countries (the UK, Germany, the Netherlands) than in some of the new Member States. Inside China, nationally speaking, China is now running a triple system of IP enforcement. For the undeveloped regions, the jurisdiction follows the basic rules stipulated by the COL and the procedural laws. For its developing regions, the SPC authorizes qualified regional courts. For the developed regions, the state establishes specific IP courts. Such an arrangement can fulfil the current needs and also will not disturb the already existing court system.[55] As a matter of fact, although there is a harmonization of the material content of IP laws, there still is a lack of harmonization of enforcement.

The intellectual property court is an international trend as well as a demand by China for its own legal reform, aiming to enhance judicial independence and remove the impact of administrations.[56] How China

---

54   Cotter (*supra*, n 3) 379.
55   刘春田：《知识产权法院的职责与使命》,《人民法院报》2014年9月3日 [Liu Chuntian, 'Intellectual Property Court's Mandate and Mission' *People's Court News* (3 September 2014)] <http://rmfyb.chinacourt.org/paper/html/2014-09/03/content_87169.htm?div=-1> accessed 6 June 2015.
56   吴汉东:《知识产权法院的专门法院属性与专属管辖职能》,《人民法院报》2014年9月3日 [Wu Handong, 'The Characters and Exclusive Jurisdiction of the Intellectual Property Court' *People's Court News* (3 September 2014)]

will develop and unify the enforcement of IP further is unclear at this stage. For example, will the SPC authorize more basic courts for IP-related matters? Or will it unify the implementation of the 'three-in-one' model on a national level? Will the SPC authorize more provinces to have IP courts? It is clear at this stage that China will not establish a special IP court in each province, but there is discussion as to whether China may use the specific IP courts for the listed cases. Normal IP cases will still be heard under the already established 'three-in-one' tribunals.[57]

According to article 7 of the Decision, the Standing Committee will evaluate the progress of the establishment of IP courts in China after three years. IP courts are very important for collecting practical experience for China.[58] The presiding judge of the IP division of the SPC, Xiaoming Song, has also observed that the IP courts are facing many challenges. These include facing the challenges of legal reform, economic and technical development, and the reform of the judicial system.[59] The establishment of IP courts also raises new questions: for example, how to unify the standard at a technical level for IP cases, and whether it is necessary to establish separate IP courts at the level of higher people's courts. Even though the picture is not clear, the establishment of IP courts can be regarded as a revolutionary milestone, which shows that China is very actively striving towards the better enforcement of IP. The pilot courts in Beijing, Shanghai and Guangzhou will also offer experienced support to the further renewal of the court system.

Even though the IP systems of China and EU are not alike, the confrontation between the unified IP enforcement standards and various levels of regional developments already reveals a core problem, namely that the unified theoretical ideal is not always attainable in real and different practices.

<http://rmfyb.chinacourt.org/paper/images/2014-09/03/05/ 2014090305_pdf.pdf> accessed 6 June 2015.
[57]   Ibid.
[58]   Ibid.
[59]   袁定波:《最高法知产庭庭长详解知识产权法院制度设计走向》,《法制日报》, 2014年11月7日 [Yuan Dingbo, 'A detailed disclosure of the design trend of the intellectual property court system from the chief judge of the intellectual property chamber of the Supreme Court' *Legal Daily* (7 November 2014)].

8. CONCLUSION

The situation in China, at this stage, is very promising and it is carrying out considerable legal reform regarding IP after joining the World Trade Organization. During the adjustment process of market internationalization, law becomes a package of complicated public interests, economic reform and social welfare.[60] The country obviously is aware of the need to encourage its domestic innovation and seeks long-term economic growth instead of having a market with copies.[61]

The legal reform is a part of China's strategy aimed at creating a technology- and capital-intensive economy. Until 2020, the reform is aimed at 'establishing a comprehensive IP system', 'promoting creation and utilization of IP', 'enhancing IP protection', 'preventing abuse of IP rights', and 'fostering a culture for IP rights'.[62] It is clear from the latest annual report of the SPC that strengthening IPR adjudication was highlighted before the Twelfth National People's Congress.

The newly established IP courts inside China will train more professional IP judges and offer valuable experience for further legal reform, and the newly implemented 'elected judiciary' will significantly enhance the efficiency as well as the quality of IP cases. The reform clearly shows that China is aiming at stronger IP protection within the country. On the other hand, the stronger protection of IP may lead to a possible increase in the cost of judicial implementation and enforcement, as well as for the administration and the parties. In this regard, at least on the surface, the development in China is very similar to the European development where the establishment of the Unified Patent Court and the many efforts to guarantee high-quality judges in the new court system is a main priority on the IP Agenda in Europe.

In contrast to the EU, for China it is especially the relationship between private enforcement mechanisms in courts and administrative enforcement mechanisms involving patent authorities that is in focus. It seems clear that, after the establishment of the special IP courts, when big corporations enter into patent disputes, courts are better equipped to deal with such conflicts than administrative bodies.

Moreover, the existing triple system already indicates a considerable

---

[60] Wenqi Liu. 'Intellectual Property Protection Related to Technology in China' (2005) 72(3) *Technological Forecasting and Social Change* 339–348.

[61] Gregory K. Leonard and Lauren J. Stiroh (eds), *Economic Approaches to Intellectual Property: Policy, Litigation and Management*, (Thomson/West 2006) 11, 403.

[62] State Council of the People's Republic of China (*supra*, n 23).

gap inside China between well-developed and developing regions. Will the reform increase the gap? The regional development difference also exists in the EU. For the EU, the UPC will considerably unify the legal enforcement of patents in different EU countries and establish a more comprehensive system inside the EU. It will also enhance the efficiency of law. The establishment of the UPC will significantly reduce the diversity of judgments from the national courts. Moreover, in March 2014, the EU Council established a centre in Budapest to train judges for the UPC, to ensure the professional capacity of the IP judges. If the UPC functions properly, it could be a reference point for Chinese practice and offer practical experience for legal unification. On the other hand, the establishment of the Unitary Patent (UP) and UPC also faces many challenges, one being how to harmonize the legal reform with the economic needs of different regions in the EU.

The challenge for legal reform is not only limited to the problem of law, but may also involve other factors. Such considerations can be found both in the current practices of the EU and China. This is a common problem of legal governance. The level of protection of IP also needs the support of advanced technology and an open market.[63]

China, as a country carrying out vertical legal reform from top to bottom, has a long way to go and needs more time to mature its market. The cooperation of legal reform with political as well as economic considerations should be harmonized instead of sacrificing the effectiveness of law.[64] China is now facing challenges both in carrying out legal reform and in harmonizing its socio-economic reforms with different regimes.

---

[63] J. Ginarte and W. Park, 'Determinants of Patent Rights: a Cross-national Study' (1997) 26 Res. Policy 283–301. See also Liu (*supra*, n 60).
[64] Liu (*supra*, n 60). See also Leonard and Stiroh (*supra*, n 61).

18. Criminal enforcement of IPR in Nordic countries and China

Laura Tammenlehto and Kan He

1. INTRODUCTION

Counterfeiting and piracy are constantly expanding phenomena that result, among other things, from growth of world trade, globalization of the economy and rapid developments in IT and digital technology.[1] In the digital environment the possibilities for copying and distribution of protected materials are much more effective than before and are enabled by technological developments that allow for the production of an unlimited amount of high-quality copies. Furthermore, the Internet allows for the rapid and extensive dissemination of these copies and thus creates an environment that sets many challenges for the supervision of intellectual property rights (IPR)s.[2] The Agreement on Trade-Related Aspects of Intellectual Property Rights (TRIPS Agreement) mandates minimum regulatory measures, in order to ensure the compliance of IPRs relating to commercial activity.[3]

In the EU, the criminal enforcement of IPRs has not yet been harmonized but the protection of IPRs is delineated separately in each country based on each country's national legislation. One legislative proposal presented by the European Commission on criminal measures was aimed at ensuring the enforcement of IPR (IPRED2) in 2005.[4] This proposal

---

[1] European Commission, *Combating Counterfeiting and Piracy in the Internal Market* (Green Paper, Brussels, 15 October 1995, COM(98)569 Final) 4.

[2] Finnish Government, *Hallituksen esitys Eduskunnalle laeiksi tekijänoikeuslain ja rikoslain 49 luvun muuttamisesta* HE 28/2004 vp. 7.

[3] R.M. Hilty, 'Economic, Legal and Social Impacts of Counterfeiting' in Christophe Geiger (ed), *Criminal Enforcement of Intellectual Property. A Handbook on Contemporary Research* (Edward Elgar Publishing 2012) 10–11.

[4] European Commission, *Proposals for a European Parliament and Council directive on criminal measures aimed at ensuring the enforcement of intellectual property rights and for a Council framework decision to strengthen the criminal law framework to combat intellectual property offences* (Brussels, 12 July 2005,

followed an earlier directive that was introduced and was concerned with civil and administrative measures relating to enforcement of IPRs (Directive 2004/48/EC; IPRED1). It should be noted that in enacting IPRED1, the use of criminal measures, in both preventing and sanctioning the most serious IPR infringements, was seen as extremely necessary,[5] and IPRED1 actually contained minimum rules relating to criminal enforcement of IPRs in the drafting phase;[6] however, they were left out of the adopted directive.[7] The goal of the IPRED2 proposal was to supplement the regulation of IPRED1 with criminal measures, including punishments that would be sufficient to create necessary deterrence in the whole EU area.[8] The directive proposal was actually accepted by a vote of the Parliament on 25 April 2007, but the plenum left it on the table. Finally, the Commission cancelled it due to limitation in 2010.[9]

Nordic[10] inter-governmental cooperation in legislative matters, including in the fields of criminal law and IP law, has been intense over the last number of years. The efforts of this cooperation have been to unify the structures and services of society in all Nordic countries based on the ideologies of the 'Nordic Welfare Model' and the 'Nordic

---

COM(2005)276 Final; hereinafter European Commission, *Proposals for Criminal Enforcement Measures*).
    [5]   See e.g., European Commission, *Proposal for a directive of the European Parliament and of the Council on measures and procedures to ensure the enforcement of intellectual property rights* (Brussels, 30 January 2003, COM(2003)46 Final) 16.
    [6]   European Parliament (Committee on Legal Affairs and the Internal Market), Report on the proposal for a directive of the European Parliament and of the Council on measures and procedures to ensure the enforcement of intellectual property rights (5 December 2003, FINAL A5-0468/2003) 42–3.
    [7]   Ibid. 23. The purpose of IPRED1 has been to unify the Member States' national provisions concerning IPRs and the national procedures relating to situations of infringements, and to create a consistent European line for the measures and procedures following the infringement of IPRs.
    [8]   European Commission, *Proposals for Criminal Enforcement Measures* (*supra*, n 4) 2.
    [9]   The cancellation was published in the Official Journal of the EU on 18 September 2010: OJEU C 252/2010, p. 9.
    [10]   Commonly, the concept of 'Nordic countries' includes Finland, Sweden, Norway, Denmark and Iceland, which have many similarities in e.g. social welfare systems, taxation systems, penal and criminal policies etc. See more e.g. T. Lappi-Seppälä, 'Penal Policy and Criminal Justice in Finland and Other Nordic Countries' in Kimmo Nuotio, Sakari Melander and Merita Huomo-Kettunen (eds), *Introduction to Finnish Law and Legal Culture* (University of Helsinki 2012) 215. This chapter, however, focuses on Finnish, Swedish, Norwegian and Danish legal systems and the Icelandic one is left only to be mentioned if necessary.

Welfare State'.[11] Accordingly, criminal liability relating to the infringement of IPRs is quite similar in all Nordic countries. Furthermore, since all of the Nordic countries are signatories of the most important international conventions relating to IPRs,[12] Nordic law is harmonized to a certain degree at an international level. With specific regard to the criminal enforcement of IPRs, the most important of the international instruments is the TRIPS Agreement and provides for a minimum level of criminal sanctions to be available in the member states.[13] Due to the lack of EU-wide harmonization in the field of criminal enforcement of IPRs, this chapter will only compare the Chinese system with the Nordic countries, as opposed to conducting a comparative study concerning the whole of the EU.

2. IP INFRINGEMENT AS AN IP CRIME

2.1 The Background and Grounds for Criminalization of Severe IPR Violations in the Nordic Countries and China

It is generally accepted that criminal penalties are necessary for the protection of IPRs and a number of reasons can be offered. First of all, with penalties one points out the blameworthiness of certain acts. Second, the usage of illicit means of competition in entrepreneurship can be somewhat controlled with the threat of penalties.[14] Third, increasing the maximum penalties for severe IPR violations has enabled the usage of many coercive measures in the investigation of those offences, which ensures more effective enforcement of these criminal provisions.[15] It has become a norm now that criminal measures are an indispensable part of protection of IPRs; however, the justification or reasons for each country to introduce criminal measures may sometimes differ.

Criminal provisions relating to violations of IPRs in the Nordic

---

[11]   Ibid. 216.
[12]   M. Levin, *Lärobok i immaterialrätt* (10th edn, Norstedts Juridik 2011) 63.
[13]   C. Colston and J. Galloway, *Modern Intellectual Property Law* (3rd edn, Routledge 2010) 773–5.
[14]   Finnish Government, *Hallituksen esitys Eduskunnalle rikoslainsäädännön kokonaisuudistuksen toisen vaiheen käsittäviksi rikoslain ja eräiden muiden lakien muutoksiksi*, HE 94/1993 vp. 202.
[15]   M. Tolvanen, 'Rikosprosessuaaliset pakkokeinot aineettomiin oikeuksiin kohdistuvien rikosten tutkinnassa, estämisessä ja paljastamisessa' (2013) Lakimies 7–8, 1304; H. Olsson, *Copyright. Svensk och internationell upphovsrätt* (8th edn, Norstedts juridik 2009) 243.

countries were originally enacted several decades ago and have been somewhat modified over the years. In addition to the requirements of international conventions, the fight against organized counterfeiting and piracy has been the overarching basis for renewing, modifying and specifying legislation in this area. Due to rapid technological development, it has also been necessary to draw up more effective measures to tackle increasing problems relating to rapid and large-scale copying of protected goods.[16] Unlike the Nordic countries, where criminal enforcement of IP was introduced arising from their own needs, China has introduced and improved criminal enforcement into its IPR regime largely as a result of external pressure from developed countries and in order for China to fulfil its obligations under international treaties such as the TRIPS Agreement. The strongest pressure comes from the USA through the utilization of the Tariff Act's 301 and/or 337 investigations,[17] bilateral trade negotiations with China[18] and the World Trade Organization platform[19] to impose pressures on the government by threatening to impose trade restriction on China. The results of these efforts include lowering the thresholds for criminal liability related to trademark and copyright infringements; introducing criminal liability for the digital transmission of works; and initiating several annual campaigns against online copyright infringements and trademark infringements. With the rise of domestic demand for the protection of IPRs, technological developments and the recognition by the Chinese government of the importance of IP for the national economy, the country has amended its laws concerning criminal liability for violation of IPRs recently.

---

[16] HE 28/2004 vp (*supra*, n 2) 7; Levin 2011 (*supra*, n 12) 544–6 and 561; Swedish Government, *Regeringens proposition om skärpta åtgärder mot upphovs-rättsintrång*, Prop.1981/82:152, 11; J. Schovsbo and M. Rosenmeier, *Immaterialret* (2nd edn, Jurist- og Økonomforbundets forlag 2011) 569–70.

[17] Articles 301 and 337 of Tariff Act of USA authorized international trade representatives to investigate the situation of IP infringement in overseas countries.

[18] See Memorandum of Understanding on the Protection of Intellectual Property between China and US 1992.

[19] See Dispute DS362, *China – Measures affecting the protection and enforcement of intellectual property rights*, Report of the Panel, WT/DS362/R (26 January 2009).

2.2 The Ideology behind Criminalization of IPR Violations in Nordic Countries and China

Criminalization, in general, means declaring some act punishable.[20] Criminalization is to be based on acceptable and significant societal reasons.[21] The main purpose of criminalization is to protect the order of society, not to protect someone's private interests.[22] While considering criminalization, the legislator must evaluate whether criminalization is essential in order to protect the object of legal protection at hand, or whether an equivalent goal could be achieved with other measures that interfere less with the rights of individuals.[23] The principles of criminalization direct the application of criminal law, and they are guided by the view that the legitimacy of the criminal justice system is based on its ability to protect interests, which we consider important, from impending violations of others.[24] The principle of legality plays a significant role in the Nordic criminal law thinking.[25]

As for the object of protection, the legislature in China holds that it is the maintenance of market economy order that primarily justifies the criminalization of IPR violations. The protection of a private right is a secondary consideration.[26] That offers the guidance for policy makers that IPR violations are criminalized only when they are harming the efficacy of the market economy.

It is true that both China and the Nordic countries hold that criminalization is considered necessary due to the fact that civil and

---

[20]   I. Anttila and P. Törnudd, *Kriminologia ja kriminaalipolitiikka* (WSOY 1983) 184; N. Jareborg, *Allmän kriminalrätt* (Iustus 2001) 46.

[21]   D. Frände, *Yleinen rikosoikeus* (Edita 2005) 21–5.

[22]   M. Tolvanen, *Johdatus kriminaalipolitiikan teoriaan* (University of Joensuu 2005) 77; J. Andenaes, *Alminnelig strafferett* (5th edn, Universitetsforlaget 2004) 73–5; Jareborg 2001 (*supra*, n 20) 45–8.

[23]   Finnish Government's Constitutional Law Committee, *Perustuslakivalio kunnan lausunto hallituksen esityksestä oikeudenkäyttöä, viranomaisia ja yleistä järjestystä vastaan kohdistuvia rikoksia sekä seksuaalirikoksia koskevien säännösten uudistamiseksi*, PeVL 23/1997 vp., 2.

[24]   T. Lappi-Seppälä, 'Rangaistus kriminaalipolitiikan keinona' in Tapio Lappi-Seppälä et al., *Rikosoikeus* (University of Helsinki 2013) 69.

[25]   S. Melander, 'Criminal Law' in Nuotio, Melander and Huomo-Kettunen 2012 (*supra*, n 10) 242–3; P. Asp, M. Ulväng and N. Jareborg, *Kriminalrättens grunder* (Edita 2013) 45–6; K. Waaben, *Strafferettens almindelige del I. Ansvarslæren* (4th edn, Gadjura 1999) 72.

[26]   Tian, Hongjie, 'On Criminal Protection of Intellectual Property Rights in China' (2003) 3 China Legal Science 143–54, 144. Section 7, Chapter 3 of criminal law of PRC.

administrative sanctions are not considered sufficient to prevent illegal manufacturing and other exploitation of IPR-protected goods.[27] This actually makes the criminal enforcement of IPRs the last-resort measure. On the basis of this holding, criminal sanctions are meant to be reserved only for the most severe violations of IPRs and more lenient actions are primarily sanctioned by civil (or administrative) measures.[28] The reasons are first, an IPR is a private right that should be enforced and protected by the right holder and the use of public resources to protect private interests needs additional justification; second, the severity of criminal penalties itself determines the cautiousness of using criminal liabilities. The imposition of criminal liability involves not only a restriction on personal liberty, but also has a negative impact on a person's reputation and credibility.[29]

The viewpoints differ slightly between the Nordic countries and China regarding an acceptable level of governmental interference in IPR crimes. IPR crimes are categorized as economic crimes. In China the view is that criminal law should only be utilized as a means of enforcement by exercising extreme caution and as a matter of last resort.[30] This approach is justified by the fact that it is sometimes difficult to distinguish illegal conduct from legal conduct relating to economic activities, because these activities cover a wide scope and involve complicated social relationships.[31] It is considered that unjust intervention by the government may destroy the established social order and negatively affect the working of the market. In the Nordic countries, on the other hand, strong governmental interference in economic crime is considered essential in order to ensure the proper functioning of the market.[32]

---

[27] Olsson 2009 (*supra*, n 15) 231.
[28] Schovsbo and Rosenmeier 2011 (*supra*, n 16) 569.
[29] The destruction of reputation and trust of a person is especially true in the Eastern cultures. Normally, those who bear criminal liabilities cannot find a job or even live in their own community.
[30] Liu, Ke and Gao, Xuemei, 'Analysis about the Intellectual Property Protection under the Principle of Criminal Law as the Last Resort' (2011) 1 Law Science Magazine 125–27, 126.
[31] Ibid. 145.
[32] Finnish Government, *Hallituksen esitys eduskunnalle rikoslainsäädännön kokonaisuudistuksen ensimmäisen vaiheen käsittäväksi rikoslain ja eräiden muiden lakien muutoksiksi*, HE 66/1988 vp. 72; Prop.1981/82:152 (*supra*, n 16) 10–12.

3. IP CRIMES IN NORDIC COUNTRIES AND CHINA

3.1 The Definition of a Crime

Traditionally, in the Nordic countries the general description of a crime has been that a criminal act is an act that fulfils the essential elements defined in a criminal provision, is unlawful and indicates the guilt of the offender. According to this, the basic components of crime are essential elements, unlawfulness and guilt.[33] A finding of criminal liability requires the fulfilment of certain conditions, while on the other hand, the liability can be excluded based on certain grounds.[34] The evaluation of criminal liability begins with analysing the essential elements of a criminal provision. The essential elements are abstract precept norms, which describe the punishable behaviour and concern everybody equally. The object of evaluation of liability in criminal law is an actual act or omission and, therefore, natural phenomena and some involuntary bodily movements are delimited outside criminal liability. IPR offences are characteristically such crimes that are conducted with active acts instead of omissions.[35]

In China, a crime is defined as an act that seriously harms society, leads to criminal liability and bears a penalty in accordance with the criminal law of the People's Republic of China (PRC).[36] This definition summarizes three elements of a 'crime'. First, a crime is an act that seriously harms society. This indicates both qualitative and quantitative characteristics of a crime. Qualitatively, a crime is an act that harms society as a whole or the social community itself in addition to private conflicts between criminals and victims. Quantitatively, a crime should reach certain thresholds that are regarded as 'serious'. This 'seriousness' requirement is defined variably in different crimes. Second, a crime

---

[33] P. Koskinen, '7. Rikosoikeuden yleiset opit ja rikosvastuun perusteet' in Tapio Lappi-Seppälä et al., *Rikosoikeus* (WS Bookwell 2009) 161; D. Frände, *Yleinen rikosoikeus* (Markus Wahlberg tr, 2nd edn, Edita 2012) 8–10; P. Asp, M. Ulväng and N. Jareborg, *Kriminalrättens grunder* (Edita 2010) 33–5; L.B. Langsted, P. Garde and V. Greve, *Criminal Law. Denmark* (2nd edn, DJØF 2004) 46.

[34] T. Lappi-Seppälä, 'The Doctrine of Criminal Liability and the Draft Criminal Code for Finland' in Raimo Lahti and Kimmo Nuotio (eds), *Criminal Law Theory in Transition. Finnish and Comparative Perspectives* (Finnish Lawyer's Publishing Company 1992) 217.

[35] J. Tapani and M. Tolvanen, *Rikosoikeuden yleinen osa. Vastuuoppi* (Talentum 2013) 147–8 and 163.

[36] Art. 13, Criminal Law of PRC.

makes the committer bear criminal liability. As in the Nordic countries, criminal liability is examined first by assessing whether the essential elements in criminal provision are met. However, in each criminal provision, the element of acts and intent are specifically described. Then it would be evaluated by some additional elements such as causality and capacity to commit a crime. In certain cases, a perpetrator will not bear criminal liability. For instance, a person under the age of 14 cannot bear criminal liability and accordingly any misconduct is not a crime. Third, a crime is an act that shall be subjected to a penalty that is stipulated in criminal law.[37]

3.2   IP Crimes in Criminal Law

3.2.1   A general introduction
The starting point in all of the Nordic countries is that any violation of someone's exclusive right, direct or indirect, that is conducted intentionally or with gross negligence, can be punishable by the imposition of criminal sanctions. This formation of criminal liability makes it very difficult to specifically define the limits of criminal liability and creates some challenges to the requirement of accuracy.[38] Also the fact that the actual contents of the criminal provisions are defined through very arcane special legislation, instead of in the specific criminal provision concerned, complicates the situation.[39]

---

[37]   The penalty includes a principle penalty and a supplementary penalty. The former includes public surveillance, criminal detention, fixed-term imprisonment, life imprisonment and the death penalty. The latter includes fines, deprivation of political rights and confiscation of property. For foreigners, deportation can be applied individually or supplementarily. Arts. 32–35, Criminal Law of PRC.

[38]   The prohibition of inaccuracy is a part of the criminal law principle of legality. This prohibition is directed primarily to the legislator, and the purpose of it is to inhibit the legislator from enacting too wide and inaccurate statutes, or vague descriptions of criminal behaviour. The prohibition of inaccuracy requires that the act and the threat of penalty are expressed with such clarity that at least a person with legal training (advisably also an 'ordinary' person without legal training) is able to define in advance what kind of action is criminalized and how severely. See more Tapani and Tolvanen 2013 (*supra*, n 35) 135–6; Frände 2012 (*supra*, n 33) 37; Asp, Ulväng and Jareborg 2010 (*supra*, n 33) 62–4; Langsted, Garde and Greve 2004 (*supra*, n 33) 37.

[39]   Finnish Government's Constitutional Law Committee, *Perustuslakivalio kunnan lausunto Hallituksen esityksestä Eduskunnalle laeiksi tekijänoikeuslain ja rikoslain 49 luvun muuttamisesta*, PeVL 7/2005 vp., 3; Finnish Government's Legal Affairs Committee, *Lakivaliokunnan lausunto Hallituksen esityksestä*

The current forms of IPR crime provisions in all Nordic countries result from several reforms, and the structures of the essential elements of offences and grading of crime types have been unified and regularized.[40] The endeavour has been to increase and clarify the criminal protection of IPRs.[41] In principle, the essential elements of an offence are comprehensive, but as stated above, reading merely the section that criminalizes the action in question cannot specify the limits of criminal liability. The protection of criminal law is not determined directly in the criminal provision but through the protection of the exclusive right in question.

Unlike the Nordic countries, only specific IP violations are considered as crimes in Chinese criminal law. This offers a clear message for the public to understand the crime. However, the specific choice of IP violations may leave some serious IPR violations without criminal liability. Section 7, Chapter 3 of the PRC Criminal Law established IP crimes in four fields: namely, registered trademarks, patents, copyright and trade secrets. The definition of these crimes constitutes qualitative and quantitative parts. The qualitative part describes the characteristics or nature of the act while the quantitative part sets up a threshold for criminal liabilities and indicates the seriousness of the act. There can also be found a specific section on criminal liabilities relating to the Copyright, Trademark and Patent Law of China. However, it is argued that all of the sections of these Acts relating to criminal liability have been integrated into the Criminal law of the PRC. Therefore, in practice, it is only criminal law that is applied in each case.

3.2.2 Specific IP crimes

The starting point in all Nordic countries is that every act that violates an exclusive right of another defined in the Trademarks Act and Patents Act and that is committed with intent or with gross negligence may be punished by criminal law sanctions. There are not any specific acts defined

---

Eduskunnalle laeiksi tekijänoikeuslain ja rikoslain 49 luvun muuttamisesta, LaVL 5/2005 vp., 3–4; Asp, Ulväng and Jareborg 201 (*supra*, n 33) 64.

[40] Finnish Criminal Law Committee, *Rikosoikeuskomitean mietintö*, KM 1976:72 (Oikeusministeriö 1977) 43–5; Schovsbo and Rosenmeier 2011 (*supra*, n 16) 570.

[41] K. Nuotio, 'RL 49 luku. Eräiden aineettomien oikeuksien loukkaaminen' in Lappi-Seppälä et al. 2009 (*supra*, n 33) 1345; Olsson 2009 (*supra*, n 15) 231–2; 'Rapport fra arbejdsgruppen om en styrket indsats mod piratkopiering' (2008) 43–6 <http://www.dkpto.dk/media/49111/rapportpiratkopiering.pdf> accessed 9 June 2015.

in the legislation which could be considered as trademark crimes. The situation is the same for patent crimes.[42]

There is also no requirement for the amount of damages necessary to be inflicted on a right holder regarding the violation of their exclusive right by an act of infringement. However, if the amount of damage caused is evaluated to be significant, it can increasingly affect the punishment sentence of the perpetrator.[43] On this point it is necessary to point out that the perpetrator is, naturally, obliged also to compensate for all damages resulting from his/her actions, but this obligation does not affect the evaluation of the perpetrator's criminal liability.

Acts violating copyright are more specifically defined than violations relating to patent and trademark. In all Nordic countries, the dissemination of pirated goods and the import of pirated goods are specifically mentioned as punishable acts.[44] Also the production of a few copies for private use is not prohibited in certain limited situations.

In contrast to the Nordic countries, the violation of IPRs is only criminally punishable when these acts are done with intent in China. Negligence can never be an element in evaluating a crime. In addition, it is only parts of a violation of trademark rights that can be punished criminally in China. These include forging registered trademarks; sales of products bearing forged registered trademarks; and illegally manufacturing signs of registered trademarks and the sale of these signs. The first violation refers to the act of using a trademark identical to a registered trademark for the same type of goods without authorization from the right holders.[45] The second is defined as the act of knowingly selling the products bearing a forged registered trademark and the amount of sales is relatively large.[46] The third refers to forging or making representations of the person's registered trademark without authorization of another or selling such representations or forged signs in serious circumstances.[47]

With regard to patent, a patent infringement is never considered a crime

---

[42] Nuotio 2009 (*supra*, n 41) 1357; Schovsbo and Rosenmeier 2011 (*supra*, n 16) 571.
[43] See Finland Criminal Code 49:2, Norway: Trademark Act § 61 and Patent Act § 57, Denmark: Trademark Act § 42 and Patent Act § 57. In Sweden there are not any aggravating circumstances mentioned in the law.
[44] Finland Criminal Code 49:1 and Copyright Act § 56a, Sweden Copyright Act § 53, Norway Copyright Act § 54, Denmark Copyright Act § 77.
[45] Art. 213, The Criminal Law of PRC.
[46] Art. 214, The Criminal Law of PRC.
[47] Art. 215, The Criminal Law of PRC.

in Chinese criminal law. Criminal law only criminalizes the act of forging a patent. This refers to the act of forging another's patent and the circumstance shall be serious.[48]

In respect of copyright in China, there are two kinds of acts of violation of copyright that may be held criminally liable; namely, the crime of infringing copyright and sale of infringed copies. They are connected to each other. Under the umbrella of the crime of copyright infringement, several different acts may be liable for criminal sanctions. They include reproducing and distributing[49] literary, musical, film, television, video recordings, computer programs and other works without authorization from the right holders; publishing books that contain another's exclusive right of publishing; reproducing and distributing audio or video recordings produced by a third party without the permission of the producers and making and selling works of fine art bearing the forged name of another.[50] This crime of sale of infringed copies refers to the act of knowingly selling the infringed copies as mentioned above.

Both of the crimes require an offender to act on purpose. And more specifically, they require them to do it 'for the purpose of making profit'.[51]

In China, a requirement of either the amount of sales or the seriousness of the circumstances are necessary for somebody to bear criminal liability for IP violations and this is considered as a threshold for the

---

[48]   Art. 216, The Criminal Law of PRC. Normally, it includes the following acts: (1) labelling another's patent number on the products or the packages of the products without authorization from the right holders; (2) using another's patent number in advertising and other promotional materials, misleading others to mistakenly think that the technology involved belongs to others without authorization from the right holder; (3) using another's patent number in contract, which leads another to mistakenly think that the technology belongs to others and (4) forging or falsifying another's patent certificate, patent documents or patent application.

[49]   'Reproducing and distributing' here is a broad term, it includes the act of reproducing, distributing and reproducing and distributing. In order to adapt the law into the digital era, the judicial interpretation regards 'making works available to the public through information network' as 'reproducing and distributing' in this article.

[50]   Art. 217, The Criminal Law of PRC.

[51]   More specifically, the following circumstance can be confirmed: (1) directly or indirectly charging fees for advertising in another's works or tying works of third-party; (2) directly or indirectly charging fees for advertising service in the websites by making another's works available to the public through information network or by using infringed copies uploaded by others; (3) charging subscription fees or other fees for membership by making another's works available to the public through information network using membership; and (4) other circumstance in which making profits by using another's works.

criminalization of IPR violations. For instance, in the case of forging a registered trademark, the amount of illegal operation[52] shall be more than CNY 50,000.[53]

In comparison to the Chinese law, the fields of application of the Nordic industrial property rights crime provisions are rather wide and in theory every act that violates the special law concerning trademarks or patents and is conducted with intent or gross negligence could be punished with criminal sanctions. That is, of course, if the individual act is considered to be serious enough and it fulfils all the essential elements defined in the law. In other words, there are not some certain acts that are punishable with criminal sanctions as in China, and there is also not any definition of what amounts to 'significant damage'.

3.3   Intent

In assessing the culpability of an act, the decisive factor is the intent of the perpetrator. In the Nordic countries the foundations of culpability are intent and negligence. The starting point of the doctrine of intent is to evaluate what the perpetrator has perceived and wanted at the moment of commission of the illegal act.[54] Intent must cover all elements of a crime, that is all circumstances that are included in the essential elements of the criminal act in question.[55] In evaluating intent, the perpetrator's duty to find out about relevant facts relating to the case must be taken into consideration.[56] Defining the line between intent and negligence is very

---

[52]   The 'amount of illegal operation' refers to 'the value of counterfeited products in the process of manufacturing, storing, transporting and selling'. When calculating the value of 'counterfeited products', the actual selling price is used if the counterfeits have already been sold. When the products have not been sold, the labelling prices or the average prices of counterfeited products that actually have been sold are used. If these prices are not clear, the middle price of the genuine products will be used. See Art. 12 of the Supreme Courts of PRC and Supreme Prosecutary of PRC's Interpretation on Issues Applying laws in Handling Criminal Cases Concerning IPRs Infringement, published on 8 December 2004 and effected on 22 December 2004 (hereinafter 2004 Judicial Interpretation).

[53]   Art. 1 2004 Judicial Interpretation. Any circumstance that reaches the level of 'serious' shall be criminally punishable. The 'extremely serious' circumstances only affect the level of penalties. See the remainder of this chapter.

[54]   Koskinen 2009 (*supra*, n 33) 174.

[55]   Frände 2012 (*supra*, n 33) 107.

[56]   P. Koponen, *Talousrikokset rikos- ja prosessioikeuden yhtymäkohdassa* (Vammalan kirjap. 2004) 118. Situations in which the perpetrator deliberately avoids obtaining information (intentional unawareness) in order to avoid criminal liability have been considered to be particularly problematic. P. Koponen,

important, since it affects the determination of the sentence; more specifically, the level of knowledge determines the type of punishment and the length of imprisonment.

Similar to the Nordic countries, the culpability of Chinese offenders is divided into intent and negligence. Save for crimes related to trade secrets, all other IP crimes in China require the offender to commit the unlawful act with intent; accordingly, an offender knows that the act is unlawful. Additionally, the criminal copyright requires proving that the offender committed these acts for the purpose of making profit. This additional requirement is sometimes difficult to prove and should be eliminated in the view of some criminal law scholars. For criminal liability relating to trade secrets, negligence can also play a role in establishing liability. If the offender has a reason to know the act is a violation and continues to obtain, disclose and use another's trade secret, he or she is criminally liable.

3.4 Complicity

In the Nordic countries, the same regulation relating to complicity applies to IPR offences as to any other crime. The regulation regarding complicity varies slightly between Finland, Sweden and Denmark. In Norway the system is based on a different principle. In Finland, Sweden and Denmark complicity is based on the principle of separation of liability, which means that perpetrator and complicity liability, that is instigation and abetting, are separated from each other. In these countries, the complicity liability is to a certain point bound to the punishability of the perpetrator's actions. However, sentencing for abetting is not dependent on convicting the main perpetrator, although naturally the main crime in question needs to be determined. On the other hand, in Norway division of liability is based on the principal of joint liability, which means that every person who has contributed to the crime, is convicted as a perpetrator. The differences in the actions of the parties concerned are taken into consideration in defining and measuring the sentence.[57]

Complicity is regulated with the most accuracy in Finland. The starting point is that if two or more persons have committed an intentional offence together, each is to be punished as a perpetrator. Perpetrator liability

---

'Ongelmallinen olosuhdetahallisuus meillä ja Yhdysvalloissa – Ovatko systematiikka ja yhdenvertaisuus ylläpidettävissä?' (2007) 1 Defensor Legis 52.

[57] Finnish Government, *Hallituksen esitys Eduskunnalle rikosoikeuden yleisiä oppeja koskevan lainsäädännön uudistamiseksi*, HE 44/2002 vp. 146–50.

requires consensus or, in other words, awareness of the fact that one's own actions together with the actions of others fulfil the essential elements of a crime. In that case, liability is not limited to the consequences of one's own actions, but is extended to cover the entirety of actions. Additionally, perpetrator liability requires participation in committing a crime that is significant relative to the wholeness of the act.[58] The length of sentence of the main offence follows the penal scale defined in the criminal provision. A person who intentionally furthers the commission of an intentional act or of its punishable attempt through advice, action or otherwise, before or during the commission of the main offence, can be convicted for abetting. The abettor is convicted based on the same criminal provision as the perpetrator. Inciting an act of abetment is also punishable as abetting. For abettors the penal scale is mitigated and means that the maximum penalty is three-quarters of the maximum penalty for the main offence in question. There is no specific or automatic mitigation of the penal scale enacted in the law in Sweden and Denmark for abetting, but it is merely separated from the perpetrator liability.

In China, similar to Nordic countries, the same regulation relating to complicity applies to IPR offences as to any other crime. If two or more offenders participate in a crime intentionally, they are punished together. However, if they commit a crime based on negligence, each is responsible for his or her own act. One special regulation here is that it is considered as an organized crime if three or more offenders formulate a fixed group to commit crime.

3.5 Right to Prosecute IPR Crimes

In the Nordic countries the main rule is that the public prosecutor handles the prosecution. Usually in situations where the request of the complainant to prosecute is required, the actual prosecution is still handled by the public prosecutor. Only in specially enacted cases is the complainant allowed themselves to pursue the criminal case in court.[59] In the case of IPR violations, it is enacted that the public prosecutor is in most cases entitled to prosecute only if the complainant requests the prosecutor to do so. In Finland, the public prosecutor is allowed to prosecute *all* copyright, trademark and patent violations only on the complainant's request, or

---

[58] Ibid.
[59] A. Jokela, *Rikosprosessi* (Talentum 2008) 213–15; B. Lindell et al., *Straffprocessen* (Iustus 2005) 173–4; J. Hov, *Rettergang. II. Straffeprosess* (Papinian 1999) 240; V. Greve, 'Denmark' in C. van den Wyngaert (ed), *Criminal Procedure Systems in the European Community* (Butterworths 1993) 59–60.

if a significant public interest requires such action. In Sweden, Norway and Denmark the situation is the same regarding some IPR offences (in Sweden crimes against trademark, in Norway crimes against trademark and patent, and copyright in petty form, in Denmark crimes against trademark, patent and copyright in aggravated forms). The situation is different in Sweden regarding patent and trademark violations; in those situations both the complainant's request and significant public interest is required. In Norway copyright crimes in aggravated forms can be prosecuted by the public prosecutor without any further requirements. In Denmark the complainant can prosecute petty forms of copyright, trademark and patent crimes.

In China, in most cases, the police investigate IP crimes and then the public prosecutors prosecute IP crimes. The prosecutors have the power to examine IP crimes and decide whether the case is brought before the criminal court. The prosecutors are also obligated to prosecute an IP criminal case that is brought by the relevant administrative agencies in their investigation of an administrative violation of IPs. If such a violation is found to reach the threshold of criminal liability, the agency is obligated to transfer the case to the public prosecutors. In some circumstances, the right holders can bring criminal cases by themselves. However, this happens rarely in practice.

4.   THE PENALTIES FOR IP CRIMES IN NORDIC COUNTRIES AND CHINA

The penalties for IP crimes consist of the same elements in all Nordic countries, namely monetary retributions and custodial sentences. However, the lengths of custodial sentences vary between different countries. In Finland and Sweden fines punishing criminal actions are imposed as day fines, this means that the amount of fines is strictly limited by an actual perpetrator's income. The idea behind the system is that the amount of fines should not become unreasonable in relation to the perpetrator's solvency and the fines are defined as a certain percentage of the perpetrator's monthly income. The Danish legal system also recognizes the day fine institution but it is used only for punishing offences that are enacted as punishable under the Danish Criminal Code. Fines imposed based on the criminalization of some other law are imposed as total sum fines.[60] Therefore, fines

---

[60]   R. Tuori, 'Ylinopeussakot – Rahamassoja massamenettelyssä' (2002) 3 Defensor Legis 448.

imposed for IPR offences are defined as total sum fines, whereas fines for trade secret violations are sentenced based on the day fine system. In Norway all fines are imposed as total sum fines, and there is no day fines system in use. However, in defining the amount of the fine, factors such as income and the financial situation of the perpetrator can be taken into consideration.[61]

The length of custodial sentences is also quite similar in all Nordic countries. The maximum penalties for the most serious offences vary between one-and-a-half years' and three years' imprisonment. To be more precise, the maximum penalty for a serious IPR offence is one-and-a-half years' imprisonment in Denmark, two years' imprisonment in Finland and Sweden, and three years' imprisonment in Norway. It is worth mentioning that in Denmark the divergent section 299b of the Danish Criminal Code provides for a maximum sentence of up to six years' imprisonment for violating copyright, trademark or patent in such a way that the profits gained for oneself or another are significant or the act itself is very gross in character. This provision is reserved for situations where the conduct is so serious that the harm to society needs to be accentuated through the utilizing of criminal sanctions.[62]

As noted above, the wordings and legislative techniques for IPR offences vary somewhat between different Nordic countries. Therefore, in Norway and in Sweden it is in theory possible to be sentenced to imprisonment for a negligent IPR violation, whereas in Finland and in Denmark it is not. In practice, however, this hardly is a possibility, since the sentencing practice is proportional to the severity of the act.

Similarly in China, the penalties for the crime are a combination of imprisonment and fines. The fine is determined based on the amount of illegal income or illegal operation. It aims at depriving all amounts of economic gains of the offender based on the assumption that the main motivation for committing economic crime is to gain profits or benefits. The fines can be up to five times the amount of illegal income or half of or the same as the amount of the illegal operation.[63]

The period for imprisonment is quite long in China. There are two

---

[61]   Finnish Government, *Hallituksen esitys eduskunnalle sakkoa, muuntorangaistusta ja rikesakkoa koskevien säännösten uudistamisesta*, HE 74/1998 vp. Yleisperustelut. 2. Nykytila. 2.2. Muut pohjoismaat. Norja.

[62]   Schovsbo and Rosenmeier 2011 (*supra*, n 16) 571.

[63]   Art. 4, Supreme Court and Supreme Prosecutory of PRC on Several Issues on Application of Laws in Handling Criminal Cases Involving Infringing Intellectual Property Rights, adopted on 4th April 2007 and effected on 5th April 2007. No. 6 Interpretation of Supreme Court 2007 (2997 Interpretation).

scales for imprisonment in China: up to three years or detention between three and seven years based on the amount of illegal income or the seriousness of circumstances.[64] Fines can be sanctioned independently or with imprisonment. In certain circumstances, the offender can be sentenced to probation. However, there is no probation in the following situations: (1) committing the violation again after criminal or administrative punishment; (2) no signs of showing repentance; (3) refusing to hand in the illegal income; and (4) other circumstance.[65]

5.   LAW IN ACTION

In Finland, the Supreme Court (Korkein oikeus, KKO) recently evaluated a situation relating to a violation of copyright on the Internet. In case KKO 2010:47 (ään)[66] the defendants (12 in total) were sentenced to fines for copyright misdemeanours, abetting in a copyright misdemeanour and abetting in a copyright misdemeanour committed as a young person. The defendants had maintained a torrent file distribution network, Finreactor, through which Internet users had been able to illegally download copyright-protected material to their own computers. The actions took place between 29 August and 14 December 2004. The KKO evaluated that section 2 subsection 3 of the Finnish Copyright Act (404/1961) relating to the spreading of copyright-protected material has in legal practice been interpreted to cover situations where protected material has been offered in electronic form for the audience to copy.[67] Regarding the criminal liability of the defendants, the KKO stated that in this situation the file distribution activity should be evaluated as a whole and the actions and liabilities of the parties concerned should not be assessed as separate acts. However, the complicity of those who had maintained the network,

---

[64]   There is one exception. In respect of sale of counterfeited copies, the penalty is only up to three years when the amount of illegal income is huge.

[65]   Art. 3, 2007 Judicial Interpretation.

[66]   The Justice of the Supreme Court, who voted differently from the majority of the Justices came to the same conclusion as the majority, but with slightly different reasoning.

[67]   This has been the situation e.g. in the case KKO 1999:115, in which A had created an electronic mailbox which enabled a distribution of copyright-protected computer programs, in his computer. A had also maintained the mailbox and accepted the users of it. A had required that the other users had to download computer programs into the mailbox to be able to use the programs already available there, and had done so himself. See <http://finlex.fi/fi/oikeus/kko/kko/1999/19990115> accessed 9 June 2015.

and the users who had delivered the description and content files to the network to be distributed, as copyright misdemeanour, would be evaluated based on whether the actions of a person in question had been significant relative to the illegal distribution and copying of copyright-protected files. Also whether a person had acted by consensus with the other operators was to be considered. Therefore, acts relating to maintaining the system would also be significant and mean complicity in a copyright misdemeanour. The criminal liability of the administrators was not precluded merely by the fact that their immediate participation in distributing and copying of separate files had not been necessary due to the technical way of executing the file distribution network.[68]

The intent of the defendants was not under evaluation, since the defendants had admitted to having understood how the network functioned and having known that every user who downloaded files would also become their distributor. All defendants had also admitted knowing that at least the main part of the material distributed online was protected by copyright. In addition to these, other actions of the defendants indicated that the violations of copyright were intentional.[69]

In the judgment[70] the perpetrators were stated to have intentionally violated the complainants' copyrights by maintaining together the Finreactor service and through that participating in the manufacture of copies of protected material and distributing them among themselves and the users of the network service. The acts that were considered sufficiently significant to fulfil the essential elements of copyright misdemeanour were, for instance, supervising the content of distributed material, user administration, modifying the instructions of the network service and overseeing the technical maintenance of the network service. On the other hand, taking care of user administration, for instance, such as by giving prohibitions of operation and changing user classification, was not for everyone's part considered so significant that all user administrators would have been convicted as perpetrators. What was considered decisive in determining

---

[68]   KKO 2010:47 Pääasian perustelut, para 18, available at <http://finlex.fi/fi/oikeus/kko/kko/2010/20100047> accessed 9 June 2015.

[69]   Ibid. paras 20–22.

[70]   There is also another case relating to this same activity. The case KKO 2010:48 (ään) concerned the liability of an individual A, who was a registered user of Finreactor file distribution network. A had delivered torrent-files to Finreactor enabling other users to illegally download copyright-protected game files to their own computers from other places than from A's computer. With this action A was considered to have illegally distributed game files to the audience, and was sentenced to fines for copyright misdemeanour.

whether the defendant would be sentenced as an accomplice or as an abettor was the extent of the defendant's actions, and not so much the nature of them.[71]

The reason why the above-mentioned case was not tried as a copyright offence was most likely the fact that at the time of commission the fulfilment of copyright offence still required the perpetrator's aim to make profit also for violations committed using a computer network or computer system. The change of legislation removing the requirement of aim to make profit in computer-related violations came into force on 1 January 2006. Nowadays, a similar situation would fulfil the essential elements defined in Chapter 49, section 1 subsection 3 of the Finnish Criminal Code, and would most likely be sentenced as a copyright offence with a maximum of two years' imprisonment.[72]

In Sweden, one of the Appeal Courts (Svea Hovrätt, SH) has processed a similar, though larger-scale, case relating to Pirate Bay torrent file distribution service. In the case three[73] defendants were sentenced to imprisonment for abetting a copyright offence. The defendants had been responsible for organizing, administrating, systemizing, programming, financing and maintaining the torrent file distribution service Pirate Bay between 1 July 2005 and 31 May 2006. The case is interesting, since no one was convicted or even recognized as the actual perpetrator, but the only convictions given were for abetting.

In its judgment SH ruminated on the existence and venue of the main offence, and its effects on the liability of the abettors. The outcome was that the main offence had been committed as copyright-protected material had been illegally distributed to the audience. The main reasoning for the crime to have taken place in Sweden was that the servers, in which the decisive information relative to committing the offence were stored, were found in Sweden.[74] It also came to the conclusion that it is enough that the main offence is shown to have been committed by an unknown perpetrator in Sweden for the abettors to be convicted, since criminal liability of

---

[71] KKO 2010:47 (*supra*, n 68) paras 6, 22–3.

[72] It can be concluded from the amounts of monetary compensation the defendants were ordered to pay that the violation was not minor. See KKO 2010:47 *Tuomiolauselma*, available at <http://finlex.fi/fi/oikeus/kko/kko/2010/201 00047?search%5Btype%5D=pika&search%5Bpika%5D=KKO%202010%3A47> accessed 9 June 2015.

[73] There were in total four defendants included in the appeal case, but the matter could not be solved concerning one of them due to the fact that he was sick and was not able to participate in the hearing. See: Svea Hovrätt Deldom B 4041-09 (26 November 2010) p. 13.

[74] Ibid. p. 16.

the abettors is independent of the criminal liability of the perpetrator.[75] Relating to complicity, the SH evaluated the case to be such that every defendant's criminal liability should be evaluated separately based on the actions they had taken and that each of them should not be held liable for everything that had been done.[76] Therefore the defendants were sentenced separately to four months', eight months' and ten months' imprisonment. The choice of type of punishment was reasoned with the viewpoint of general prevention, since the sentencing practice in this field of criminality is practically non-existent.[77]

What is interesting in comparing these two cases is that in the Finnish case, the defendants were convicted as perpetrators whereas in Sweden they were convicted as abettors, even though the descriptions of the defendants' acts did not differ notably from each other. The chosen interpretive approach clearly differs between the two countries. Also interesting is that in Sweden the sentences were substantially higher and can be explained by the fact that the legislation in force at that time in Finland bound the court to a maximum penalty of fines. It would be interesting to see how this type of situation would be evaluated in Finland now that the legislation, at least in theory, enables imprisonment in these types of situations, and how the interpretation of the situation in case KKO 2010:47 would direct and affect the interpretation of similar cases in the future.

There is an upward trend concerning the number of criminal cases in China.[78] More than 80 per cent of the cases involve crimes concerning the infringing of a registered trademark.[79] The infringement of copyright stands in second place. On average, 99 per cent of the defendants in criminal cases are confirmed as guilty.[80] These statistics tell us that, first, criminal enforcement has caught the increased attention of both the rights holders and the government; secondly, public prosecutors are very cautious to prosecute these cases since they have to guarantee the success rate of the case; thirdly, the enforcers prefer to seek obvious violations such as trademark infringement. Recently, some new forms of IPR violations, especially

---

[75]   Ibid. pp. 17–18.
[76]   Ibid. p. 22.
[77]   Ibid. pp. 45–6.
[78]   All courts together in China heard 3,992 criminal cases in 2010, 5,504 cases in 2011, 12,794 cases in 2012 and 9,212 cases in 2013. See SIPO, *The Report on China's IP Protection (2010, 2011, 2012, 2013)* <http://www.sipo.gov.cn/zwgs/zscqbps/> accessed 12 June 2015.
[79]   Ibid.
[80]   Ibid.

concerning the Internet, have been incorporated into the criminal law. For instance, in the first 'deep-linking' criminal case in China,[81] the defendant was sentenced to one year and three months for copyright infringement. In this case, the defendant set up a website and connected it to a server. In the administration platform, he linked the index address of torrent files in other websites to the server. The end users could see 941 films by using the QVOD software compulsorily offered by the defendant. The defendant additionally created lists, indexes and film introductions on the website to attract users. He made more than 100,000 CNY from advertising. The court held that the act of the defendant constituted an infringement of the right of transmission from an information network in copyright law. Furthermore, the defendant showed his intent to 'make profits' by receiving revenues from advertising. Thus, he was criminally liable for the act. The significance of the case lies in the fact that it was the first time that a Chinese court criminalized indirect infringement over an Internet network.

6. ANALYSIS

Through the presentation and discussion of the above sections, it can be found that criminal enforcement in the Nordic countries and China share some common features, while also some differences exist. First, the motivation to criminalize IPR violations has in the Nordic countries derived internally from the needs of society, whereas in China the motivation has mainly been driven by external pressure. This is one of the reasons, in addition to the effects of the legal culture in general, why the criminal provisions in the Nordic countries are wide and general, and in China they are specific; China is reluctant to criminalize more IPR violations. However, it cannot be denied that both countries have modified their criminal laws in accordance with international treaties such as the TRIPS Agreement. However, in the Nordic countries the effects of the TRIPS Agreement in this specific field were not very significant, since the pre-existing criminal law fulfilled the requirements set out in the Agreement. The main difference is that the Nordic countries already have the experience, while China was a new student of IPRs before implementing the TRIPS Agreement. This is also one of the reasons for the existence of the terms 'norm giver' and 'norm taker'.

---

[81]   *Junxiong Zhang v. PRC* (2013) First Trial of Criminal Case No. 11, People's Court of Putuo District, Shanghai (张俊雄侵犯著作权案，（2013）普刑（知）初字第11号).

Second, the justification for the criminalization of IPR violations in China is mainly the necessity to maintain the order of a market economy, while in the Nordic countries it is the protection of private rights that mainly rationalizes the criminalization of IPR violations. This basic assumption may explain the difference in scope of criminal protection in China and in the Nordic countries. It is clear from the discussion above that IP crime always requires serious circumstances or a large illegal income in China, while such requirements are evident in the Nordic countries only in the most serious of situations. It is safe to say that in the Nordic countries the conduct is criminalized even if the infringing acts have been committed without any commercial interest.

Third, the intent required for the crimes is also different. In China, with the exception of trade secret crime, IPR infringements are criminalized only when the offender commits the crime intentionally. Negligence can never be enough for the perpetrator to be held criminally liable. This can also be attributed to the different justifications for the criminalization of IPR violations in both jurisdictions. IP crime is recognized as an economic crime that harms a market economy in China while in the Nordic countries it is an economic crime that also infringes private economic rights.

Fourth, the penalties are higher in China than in the Nordic countries. The main reason for this is that the whole sanctioning system in China is stricter than in the Nordic countries. One possible reason for this could also be that China has an alternative system for administrative offences. In this instance, any act that violates the social security law can be held liable in the form of fines and/or custodial sentences of up to 15 days. This law embodies all the acts stipulated in criminal law. The difference is that the act does not reach the threshold and cannot be considered as a crime. With this system, the penalty for crimes has to rise higher than the administrative sanctions, in order to be distinguished from them.

In a word, it can be summarized that the criminal protection of IPRs in Nordic countries is very wide and the sentences are rather low compared to the Chinese system, in which the criminalizations are very narrow with relatively high sanctions. However, the main reason for the low sentences in the Nordic countries is not that IPR offences are not considered to be serious offences, but the fact that the whole sanctioning system in the Nordic countries is rather lenient. This may raise the question of which system is better than the other.

Objectively speaking, the system in Nordic countries is more flexible in the way that less modification is to be expected in the future, even if the situations were to change, since the criminal aspects already cover a very wide scope of acts and the actual contents are defined through the special legislation. This leads to the situation that the content of criminalization has also changed, if the content of the private right is modified. However, this is not only a convenient feature of the system but can cause legal uncertainty, since the core elements of criminal law are not integral. In the Chinese system, there is very little room left for further inclusion of IP crimes in criminal law. However, this may exclude certain serious crimes. Basically, both of the systems have their advantages and disadvantages and are developed under the specific conditions of the countries. It is difficult to say which system is better.

However, the elements of each system may be shared between each other. For instance, it is being discussed in China whether a criminal provision that authorizes IP laws to define a crime is suitable since the criminal law itself cannot be changed often while the relevant IP law may be modified more quickly. For the part of the Nordic countries, more specific descriptions of the actual contents of the criminalizations of IP law could be used to enhance legal certainty.

7. CONCLUSIONS

The criminal enforcement of IPRs in the Nordic countries and in China has developed from very different motivations and justifications. First of all, the starting point for the criminalizations of aspects of IP law differs. In the Nordic countries, this has been considered necessary due to, for instance, pointing out the blameworthiness of certain acts and behaviour, whereas in China the criminal legislation derives more from external pressure. Also the viewpoints regarding an acceptable level of government interference and the effects of it differ slightly from each other in the surveyed countries.

The degree of criminalization varies significantly between the Nordic countries and China. The definitions of acts that are considered as IPR crimes are much more specific in China and enhance the legal certainty in the field. However, these very specific criminal provisions increase the risk that some clearly reprehensible behaviour will fall out of the scope of application of them, even though it may not necessarily have been the purpose of the legislator. On the other hand, the situation is somewhat reversed in the Nordic countries, where the purview of the criminal provisions reaches a very wide scope of actions, but the actual definition of criminal conduct certainly leaves room for improvement.

The definitions of crimes or criminal conduct more specifically are, in principle, quite the same, but defining the criminal liability in IPR offences is pursued very differently. The clearest difference is demonstrated by the level of intent of the perpetrator. In the Nordic countries intent is divided into three levels and the most problematic element is defining the line between the lowest level of intent (*dolus eventualis*) and gross negligence. This definition is in the end a significant factor in the choice of the type of punishment and in determining the level of penalty. Although violations committed with gross negligence can be punishable with criminal sanctions, the level of penalty of a gross negligent act never rises to the same level as for an intentional act. In China, on the other hand, there are only two levels of intent in the first place and negligent violations of IPRs cannot be punished with criminal sanctions at all. The level of sanctions is also noticeably higher in China than in the Nordic countries, although the penalties in use are of the same type – fines and imprisonment.

The amount of case law regarding IPR offences in the Nordic countries is very low. There are only a few cases available and it seems that even those cases are already becoming partly outdated. However, this does not preclude the possibility that both jurisdictions can learn from each other considering the social, economic and political environment.

19. Customs enforcement of intellectual property in Europe and China

Daniel Opoku Acquah and Kan He

1. INTRODUCTION

Customs enforcement of intellectual property rights ranks high in the facilitation of trade between the EU and China.[1] For the EU, the reason is simple: protecting and enforcing intellectual property rights is important not just for the competitiveness of its industry abroad, but also for the creation of jobs and the safety of its citizens.[2] For China, it is to attract foreign investment and foreign technology.[3] China is the EU's biggest source of imports and has also become one of the EU's fastest growing export markets. Both sides now trade well over 1 billion a day.[4] In 2013,

---

[1] See European Commission – TAXUD, 'EU–China Customs Cooperation' (DG TAXUD website), <http://ec.europa.eu/taxation_customs/customs/policy_issues/international_customs_agreements/china/index_en.htm> last accessed 2 April 2015.

[2] See European Commission, *Protection of Intellectual Property Rights in Free Trade Agreements* (Brussels, October 2012) <http://trade.ec.europa.eu/doclib/docs/2012/november/tradoc_150081.pdf> last accessed 2 April 2015. Also, a recent study by the European Patent Office and the Office for Harmonization in the Internal Market found that, during the period 2008–2010, intellectual property rights-intensive industries generated almost 26 per cent of all jobs in the EU. Eighty-eight per cent of EU imports consisted of products of intellectual property rights-intensive industries while its export sector accounted for an even higher share of 90 per cent. See European Patent Office and the Office for Harmonization in the Internal Market, *Intellectual property rights intensive industries: contribution to economic performance and employment in the European Union. Industry-Level Analysis Report* (September 2013) <http://ec.europa.eu/internal_market/intellectual-property/docs/joint-report-epo-ohim-final-version_en.pdf> accessed 2 April 2015.

[3] Natalie P Stoianoff, 'The Influence of the WTO over China's Intellectual Property Regime' (2012) 34 Sydney Law Review 65, 69.

[4] European Commission, *Customs: EU and China sign landmark mutual recognition agreement and intensify their customs cooperation* (IP/14/55, 16 May 2014) <http://europa.eu/rapid/press-release_IP-14-555_en.htm> accessed 2 April 2015.

the EU imported € 279.9 billion worth of goods from China and exported € 148.1 billion worth of goods to China.[5] Customs play an important role in this trade relationship by ensuring that goods flow smoothly, while also protecting citizens against unsafe, illegal goods. As China remains the main source country of infringing goods imported into the EU,[6] the border enforcement of intellectual property rights is seen as an effective means of preventing this illegal trade in counterfeit and pirated goods.[7]

The EU is a norm giver, as opposed to China which is a norm taker, when it comes to the border enforcement of intellectual property rights. The first generation of the EU's Border Measures Regulation (BMR) was adopted in 1986 in the form of Council Regulation 3842/86.[8] This Regulation later served as a model for the elaboration of the corresponding provisions of the Agreement on Trade-Related Aspects of Intellectual Property Rights (TRIPS)[9] (although the TRIPS border measures focus

---

[5] Ibid.

[6] European Commission – TAXUD, *Report on EU customs enforcement of intellectual property rights: Results at the EU border – 2013* (Publications Office of the European Union 2014) <http://ec.europa.eu/taxation_customs/resources/doc uments/customs/customs_controls/counterfeit_piracy/statistics/2014_ipr_statis tics_en.pdf> accessed 2 April 2015. This has been the situation (both in the number of cases and articles) in all of the Commission's annual customs reports since 2004. See for example: <http://ec.europa.eu/taxation_customs/customs/customs_ controls/counterfeit_piracy/statistics/archive_en.htm> accessed 28 August 2015.

[7] With respect to the EU, see the Union's Strategy for the Enforcement of Intellectual Property Rights in Third Countries (2005/C 129/03) <http://trade. ec.europa.eu/doclib/docs/2010/december/tradoc_147070.pdf> accessed 2 April 2014; Council Resolution of 25 September 2008 on a Comprehensive European Anti-Counterfeiting and Anti-Piracy Plan [2008] OJ C253/1. The EU also includes clauses on border measures in its bilateral free trade Agreements with third countries, and engages in cooperation on intellectual property in other fora such as the EU– China Customs Cooperation: http://eur-lex.europa.eu/legal-content/EN/TXT/? uri=uriserv:OJ.L_.2004.375.01.0019.01.ENG accessed 28 August 2015.

[8] Council Regulation (EEC) No 3842/86 of 1 December 1986 laying down measures to prohibit the release for free circulation of counterfeit goods [1986] OJ L347/1.

[9] Marius Schneider and Olivier Vrins, 'Regulation (EC) 1383/2003' in Marius Schneider and Olivier Vrins (eds), *Enforcement of Intellectual Property Rights Through Border Measures: Law and Practice in the EU* (2nd edn, OUP 2012) 107; see also Al J Daniel Jr., 'Intellectual Property in the Uruguay Round: The Dunkel Draft and a Comparison of United States Intellectual Property Rights, Remedies and Border Measures' (1992–1993) 25 NYU Journal of International Law and Politics 751, 754 (indicating that the Dunkel proposal on enforcement of intellectual property rights as part of the draft Agreement for TRIPS during the Uruguay Rounds appears to be derived largely from a draft agreement tabled by the European Community). The Paris Convention for the Protection of Industrial

almost exclusively on importation issues).[10] The EU and China are both Members of the World Trade Organization (WTO) TRIPS Agreement[11] and the obligations imposed by TRIPS have resulted in the incorporation of TRIPS minimum standards (including border enforcement) into the domestic regimes of both China and the EU. For China, this has meant the transplantation of Western-style intellectual property norms via the WTO and a complete overhaul of its domestic intellectual property system.[12] For the EU, TRIPS provided leverage in bilateral trade negotiations. Thus, the EU has concluded with China bilateral trade agreements outside of TRIPS that have resulted in further norm interaction between the Chinese and EU intellectual property systems.[13]

This chapter focuses on one aspect of the interaction of these norms: customs enforcement of intellectual property rights. This will be analysed from two angles: (1) how the customs authorities from both sides manage large and small consignments of imported goods[14] in the application of the customs regulations; and (2) how EU–China bilateral customs cooperation on intellectual property rights[15] further aids this interaction. This chapter concludes that even though there are differences in the scope and application of the rules on both sides, increasingly, decision making on intellectual property between the EU and China is becoming Europeanized. This is partly due to the concerted efforts on the part of

---

Property and the Berne Convention for the Protection of Literary and Artistic Works contained articles on border measures. However, these provisions lacked details and an effective and binding dispute settlement mechanism.

[10]   Art. 51 TRIPS only stipulates the obligation for Member States to have in place customs measures for imported goods that are counterfeit and for pirated goods.

[11]   China became an official member of the WTO in 2001.

[12]   See for instance Stoianoff (*supra*, n 3) at pp. 65–89. It is however important to note that the introduction of border measures to protect the interest of rightholders in China is associated with the Sino-US negotiations on protection of intellectual property which eventually led to the publication by the National Council of the 'Regulation on the Customs Protection of Intellectual Property of the People's Republic of China' in 1995 – the first effective law in respect of border measures. Since then, the Chinese Regulation has been amended on three occasions to meet the demands of the times – the latest one being in 2010.

[13]   Wei Shi, *Intellectual Property in the Global Trading System: EU-China Perspective* (Springer Berlin Heidelberg 2008).

[14]   Imports because, for instance in the EU, from 2010 to 2013, in more than 90 per cent of all cases of intellectual property infringements, customs action was started whilst the goods concerned were the subject of an import procedure.

[15]   See *supra*, nn 1 and 13. Emphasis is placed on the recent joint strategic frameworks emerging out of this cooperation.

China to meet international expectations, and also as a consequence of the strong institutional and resource base of the EU Commission, which negotiates these agreements. Despite these developments, China, as a norm taker, has been cautious in adopting these rules in ways that fit its economic, social and political interests and this therefore leaves room for uncertainty as to which direction this cooperation will take.

2. THE SCOPE OF THE BORDER MEASURES REGULATIONS IN EUROPE AND CHINA

The current European Regulation on border measures[16] (hereinafter the new BMR or Regulation 608/2013) sets out the conditions and procedures[17] for action by customs authorities where goods suspected of infringing *all* intellectual property rights[18] come under their supervision. It encompasses: (1) goods which are subject to a customs declaration;[19] and

---

[16]   Council Regulation (EU) No 608/2013 of the European Parliament and of the Council of 12 June 2013 concerning customs enforcement of intellectual property rights, in force since January 2014.

[17]   Recital 10 in the preamble to Regulation 608/2013 clarifies that the Regulation solely contains procedural rules for customs authorities and does not set out any criteria for ascertaining the existence of an infringement of an intellectual property right. This marks a slight departure from the previous regulations, which not only set the conditions, but also fixed the measures to be taken by customs when goods under their supervision are found to infringe intellectual property rights (see arts. 1 and 16 of Regulation 1383/2003).

[18]   See recital 5 in the preamble and art. 2 of Regulation 608/2013. The previous customs Regulations did not cover certain intellectual property rights. As a result, certain infringements were excluded from their scope. The new BMR covers all intellectual property rights and infringements.

[19]   This receives its basis through the explicit reference in art. 1 of Regulation 608/2013 to Council Regulation (EEC) No 2913/92 of 12 October 1992 establishing the Community Customs Code (hereinafter the Community Customs Code) and the use of terminology emanating from this instrument such as 'suspensive procedure', 'free zone' or 'free warehouse', found in arts. 84(1)(a) and 166–167 of the Community Customs Code. For example, art. 84(1)(a) defines suspensive procedure in relation to non-Community goods as those under 'external transit, customs warehousing, inward processing, processing under customs control, and temporal importation'. This ensures that customs authorities are able to take action against all goods that come within their control. It also means that the Customs Regulation should be interpreted by reference to the language of the Community Customs Code, in order to guarantee that the original meanings and requirements of the EU legislator are respected. Since October 2013, Regulation (EU) No 952/2013 of the European Parliament and of the Council of 9 October 2013 laying down the Union Customs Code (recast) repealing Regulation (EC)

(2) goods which are not subject to a customs declaration.[20] The new BMR does not, however, cover goods that have been released for free circulation under the end-use regime,[21] goods of a non-commercial nature contained in travellers' personal luggage,[22] or parallel imports and overruns.[23] The reasons for these are obvious: goods released for free circulation under the end-use regime are goods that are still under customs control.[24] For goods contained in a traveller's personal luggage, the rules apply if there are indications that the goods are connected with commercial trafficking. As to which exhaustion regime or what percentage of overruns in regard to article 1(5) applies, that question appears to have been answered in article 1(6), which specifies that '[t]his Regulation shall not affect national or Union law on intellectual property or the laws of the Member States in relation to criminal procedures.' Thus, national law should define which exhaustion regime or percentage of overruns applies.

From the Chinese viewpoint, the Regulation on the Customs Protection of Intellectual Property of the People's Republic of China (hereinafter the Chinese Regulation) stipulates that customs protection of intellectual property rights refers to 'the protection provided by customs authorities on the exclusive right to use a trademark, copyright and related rights, and patent rights over imported or exported goods that are protected by laws and administrative regulations of the People's Republic of China'.[25]

No 450/2008 of the European Parliament and of the Council of 23 April 2008 laying down the Community Customs Code (hereinafter the Modernized Customs Code) came into force. The new Regulation comes with new numbering which changes the numbering of the articles referred to in this note. However, since its substantive provisions do not apply until 1 May 2016, the numbering of the old Regulation applies.

[20] Art. 170(1) of the Community Customs Code stipulates that 'without prejudice to Article 168(4), goods entering a free zone or free warehouse need not be presented to the customs authorities, nor need a customs declaration lodged'. However, art. 168(4) provides that the 'customs authorities may check goods entering, leaving or remaining in a free zone or free warehouse . . .'. This leaves it to national law to decide, or, in the absence of such a provision, the discretion of customs authorities.

[21] Art. 1(3) Regulation 608/2013.

[22] Art. 1(4) Regulation 608/2013.

[23] Art. 1(5) Regulation 608/2013.

[24] Art. 82 of the Community Customs Code stipulates that 'where goods are released for free circulation at a reduced or zero rate of duty on account of their end-use, they shall remain under customs supervision. Customs supervision shall end when the conditions laid down for granting such a reduced or zero rate of duty cease to apply . . . .'

[25] See art. 2 Chinese Regulation.

Unlike the European situation where almost all nomenclatures are defined either in the Regulation or in the Community Customs Code,[26] the Chinese Regulation does not define 'exportation' or 'importation'. Neither are there any interpretations on the meanings of these terms by the courts or the relevant agency. Furthermore, the Chinese Regulation does not give any guidance as to what should be done in regard to parallel imports and overruns, among others. For goods contained in a traveller's personal luggage or transported by personal post, if they are exceeding the reasonable amount for personal use and allegedly infringe intellectual property, they shall fall into the scope of customs protection. Compared to the TRIPS provision on border enforcement, the scope of both the European and Chinese Regulations is broader. However, compared to the Chinese Regulation, it would seem the European Regulation covers virtually all customs procedures and situations relating to border control of goods infringing intellectual property rights that come within its external borders (whether Community or non-Community goods).[27]

3.   THE EUROPEAN REGIME OF BORDER MEASURES

3.1   Importation

In the EU, all imported goods that come within its borders that infringe local intellectual property rights can be intercepted either through *ex officio* action[28] or through an application (national or Union).[29] *Ex officio* action is where customs authorities suspend the release of, or detain, any goods which they suspect of infringing intellectual property rights which are not covered by a decision granting an application, except in the case of

---

[26]   See *supra*, nn 19 and 20.

[27]   The second and third indents of art. 4(7) of the Community Customs Code define Community goods as goods: (a) imported from countries or territories not forming part of the customs territory of the Community which have been released for free circulation; and (b) obtained or produced in the customs territory of the Community, either from goods referred to in the second indent alone or from goods referred to in the first and second indents. Art. 8 stipulates that 'Non-Community goods means goods other than those referred to in subparagraph 7'.

[28]   See art. 18 Regulation 608/2013.

[29]   See art. 17 Regulation 608/2013. For a description of the application procedure, see arts. 5–10.

perishable goods.[30] By application means an application has been filed by a right holder. These procedures apply to all categories of imported goods including goods in transit, and even those under 'special procedure' such as small consignments of goods,[31] among others. In the EU, the majority of customs actions have been initiated by a prior application of right holders.[32]

3.2 Simplified Procedure for Large Consignments of Goods

The European framework of border measures does not define large consignment of goods. The latter is thus used solely for purposes of striking a distinction between normal and small consignments of goods (which is defined).[33] The current standard is that, when customs authorities intercept goods under importation that infringe intellectual property rights (with some exceptions for small consignments of goods), the goods undergo either a simplified procedure for destruction or civil infringement proceedings (based on applicable national law).[34] The latter may happen where the declarant or holder of the goods opposes destruction. This procedure applies in all Member States.

To effect the simplified procedure, customs authorities are required to inform the holder of the decision (or in the case of an *ex officio* action, persons or entities potentially entitled to submit an application) of their suspension to release or detain the goods (with some limited information) within one working day of their action.[35] They have a similar time frame within which to communicate their action to the declarant or holder of the goods.[36] Upon notification, the holder of a decision has ten working days (or a non-extendable three working days in the case of perishable goods) within which to confirm, in writing, to the customs authorities that the goods infringe an intellectual property right and they should be

---

[30] Art. 2(20) Regulation 608/2013 defines 'perishable goods' as goods considered by customs authorities to deteriorate by being kept for up to 20 days from the date of their suspension of release or detention.

[31] Art. 2(19) Regulation 608/2013 defines 'small consignment' as a postal or express courier consignment of three units or less or having a gross weight of less than 2 kilograms. However, with this procedure, only goods which are covered by an application can be seized. For details, see *infra*, Section 3.3.

[32] European Commission – TAXUD (*supra*, n 6).

[33] See *supra*, n 31.

[34] See art. 23 Regulation 608/2013.

[35] Such as the actual or estimated quantity of the goods, their actual or presumed nature and images.

[36] See arts. 17 and 18 Regulation 608/2013.

destroyed.[37] The deadline of ten working days is extendable upon a justified request, such as the initiation of legal proceedings.[38] For *ex officio* action, the right holder shall have four working days after notification to submit an application. As soon as the application is granted, the same procedure for a holder of a decision applies.

Additionally, the declarant or holder of the goods must consent to their destruction within a non-extendable time frame of ten working days (or three working days in the case of perishable goods) of notification. Where the holder of the goods does not register his agreement or opposition to the destruction of the goods within the stipulated deadlines, the customs authorities may deem that to mean consent to destruction.[39] As a requirement, the customs authorities are supposed to grant the release of the goods or put an end to their detention immediately after completion of all customs formalities. For example, in the event that after informing the right holder, he fails to meet the deadline to confirm an infringement of intellectual property rights or consent to the destruction of the goods save for a situation where legal proceedings have been initiated,[40] customs authorities shall immediately put an end to detention of goods.

In a related manner, and only in the case of design rights, patents, utility models, topography of semi-conductors or plant varieties, even where proceedings have been initiated, the holder of the goods can seek the early release of the goods before the completion of proceedings by providing a security deposit,[41] unless the applicant for the customs action secures a preliminary injunction to restrain that process. It is uncertain why such a provision would cover only these types of intellectual property rights. However, that is certainly positive in regard to, for instance, the pharmaceutical sector where, in the form that the Regulation currently appears, generic medicines in transit in the EU could be intercepted by customs authorities on the mere suspicion that the goods may be diverted into the EU market. With this provision, the declarant or the holder of a consignment of generic medicines that gets intercepted could file for the early release of the goods with the assurance that he can prove in proceedings that the goods are not meant for the European market.

---

[37] Art. 23(1)(a) and (b) Regulation 608/2013.
[38] Art. 23(4) Regulation 608/2013.
[39] Art. 23(1)(c) Regulation 608/2013.
[40] Art. 23(1)(c) Regulation 608/2013.
[41] Art. 24 Regulation 608/2013. For example, among the conditions to be fulfilled is that the amount provided as guarantee should be sufficient to protect the interest of the holder of the decision.

3.3 Simplified Procedure for Small Consignments of Goods

The idea of including a provision that specifically permits customs authorities to destroy small consignments of counterfeit and pirated goods upon the request of the right holder is new in Europe. This provision, which is captured in article 26 of the new BMR, may be a realization (and acknowledgment) on the part of European law-makers of the recent changes in the distribution methods for counterfeit goods resulting from Internet sales. Statistics from the annual reports of the European Commission on customs enforcement of intellectual property rights have shown an increase in postal and courier traffic for counterfeit goods. The 2013 report shows that cases related to postal and courier traffic accounted for 72 per cent of all detentions[42] – indicating a 10 per cent increase over the 2010 figure, which represented 62 per cent.[43] Medicines remained, for the fourth consecutive year, the top category in terms of the number of articles detained in this stream.[44] Such a provision was therefore anticipated.[45]

However, this measure is only applicable where the goods in question are covered by a decision granting an application and where the goods are not perishable. Thus, customs authorities cannot take *ex officio* action against such goods unless they are protected in that Member State. What further makes this procedure distinctive is that, unlike the other categories, customs may only liaise with the holder of the decision where they need further information in order to determine whether an intellectual property right has been infringed. Apart from that, all other relevant decisions such as detaining the goods or destroying them are left to customs.[46] Only in case of an opposition by the declarant or holder of goods will the holder of the decision be involved and then it might be necessary to initiate legal proceedings.

---

[42] European Commission – TAXUD (*supra*, n 6).

[43] European Commission – TAXUD, *Report on EU customs enforcement of intellectual property rights: Results at the EU border – 2010* <http://ec.europa.eu/polska/news/documents/120206_statistics_2010.pdf> accessed 8 April 2015.

[44] This is the case despite the fact that there has been a decrease in the volume of medicines over the years. In 2010, medicines represented 69 per cent of total goods seized through postal or courier traffic compared to 36 per cent in 2011. In 2012, medicines represented 23 per cent in this category and in 2013 19 per cent.

[45] Schneider and Vrins (*supra*, n 9) at p. 261 indicating in their note 865 that such a procedure had been suggested by bodies like the Legal Sub-Group of the European Observatory on Counterfeiting and Piracy and the European Communities Trademark Association etc.

[46] See art. 26(2) of Regulation 608/2013, which specifies that when the procedure set out in this article is applied, art. 17(3) and (4) and art. 19(2) and (3) shall not apply.

In contrast, customs authorities do not liaise with the declarant or holder of the goods at the point of deciding whether or not to detain the goods. However, when they do detain the goods or suspend their release, they have to inform the declarant or holder of the goods within one working day of their action and that they intend to destroy the goods. The declarant or holder of the goods is given the right to be heard. Within ten working days, he will have to express his agreement or disagreement to the destruction of the goods and a failure to do so will mean his consent to their destruction. On the other hand, if the declarant or holder of the goods opposes destruction, customs would immediately inform the right holder (by feeding him with all necessary information) to initiate proceedings. If the holder of the decision fails to initiate proceedings within ten working days of notification, customs shall release the goods or put an end to their detention.

4.   THE CHINESE REGIME OF BORDER MEASURES

4.1   Recordation

Similar to the EU, Chinese customs authorities offer the right holders both *ex officio* action and *action by application*. A requirement for recordation of information on intellectual property before the Custom General Administration is necessary for the initiation of the *ex officio* action.[47] This requires right holders to file an application and offer the evidentiary documents to prove the legitimacy of their intellectual property.[48] Once the customs authorities approve the application within 30 working days, the recordation is effectuated on the day of the decision.[49] It lasts for ten years while the intellectual property is still valid and it is possible to renew the term.[50] If the status quo of the recorded information is changed, it requires right holders to notify customs within 30 days when the right holders know of the change.[51]

---

[47]   See art. 7 Chinese Regulation.
[48]   Ibid.
[49]   See art. 8 Chinese Regulation.
[50]   See art. 10 Chinese Regulation.
[51]   See art. 11 Chinese Regulation.

4.2 *Ex Officio* Procedure

After the recordation of intellectual property, the customs authorities will supervise the importation and exportation of the goods.[52] When it detects the allegedly infringing goods, it shall notify the right holders immediately in written form and wait for a response from the right holders.[53] After receiving this notice, the right holders can either apply for the detention with a guarantee within three days or not require the customs authorities to detain the goods. In the latter situation, they shall state the reasons in written form.[54] The holder or sender of the goods will also be notified by the customs authorities if right holders apply for the detention.[55] They have the right to argue for non-infringement with evidentiary documents.[56] The customs authorities shall investigate the allegedly infringing goods and determine whether these goods are infringing the intellectual property of right holders within 30 working days calculated from the date of detention.[57] If they find that the goods are infringing the intellectual property, they will confiscate, and in certain cases destroy, these goods.[58] They shall also release the goods when they find no infringement. If they cannot determine whether the goods infringe the intellectual property, they shall notify the right holders and the holders of the goods in writing within 30 working days from detention. The holders of the goods can require the customs authorities to release the goods if they offer a guarantee in this instance.[59] Right holders have to ask the court to stop the infringement or preserve the property. The customs authorities are obligated to release the goods when they receive no notice from a court after 50 working days from the date of detention.[60]

4.3 Detention upon Application

Without the recordation, right holders can apply for the detention of the allegedly infringing imported and exported goods at the port of entry or exit with evidentiary documents and guarantees when they discover

---

[52] See art. 20 Measures for Implementing the Chinese Regulation.
[53] See art. 21 Chinese Regulation.
[54] See art. 21 Measures for Implementing the Chinese Regulation.
[55] See art. 16 Chinese Regulation.
[56] See art. 18 Chinese Regulation.
[57] See art. 20 Chinese Regulation.
[58] See art. 27 Chinese Regulation.
[59] See art. 28 Measures for Implementing the Chinese Regulation.
[60] See art. 29 Measures for Implementing the Chinese Regulation.

those goods.[61] After receiving the application, the customs authorities shall examine the application and take measures to supervise the allegedly infringing products when the application is granted.[62] After detecting these goods, the customs authorities shall notify the right holders as well as the sender and holders of the goods. It is the right holders who ask the court to take measures to stop the infringement or preserve the goods as soon as possible after receiving the customs notification. The customs authorities shall not investigate the case nor inspect the goods. If the customs authorities do not receive the notice from the court to assist the enforcement within 20 working days after the date of detention, they shall release the detained goods.[63]

4.4   Procedure for Small Consignments of Goods

In the case of imported or exported goods in individual luggage and in the post, the customs authorities shall detain the allegedly infringing goods if they do not fall into the scope of personal use or they exceed an amount of personal use. However, if the passenger or holder of the post claims to give up the goods and the customs authorities approve that, this rule shall not be applied. Passengers also have the right to claim that the goods are not infringing intellectual property or the goods are solely for personal use with evidentiary documents.[64]

4.5   The Measures in Action

In recent years, 99 per cent of detained or allegedly infringed goods have come from exportation and more than 96 per cent of cases are dealt with *ex officio*, which is totally different from the situation in Europe. Around 94 per cent of cases involved the infringement of a registered trade-mark.[65] These infringements are mostly found in consumer goods such as cigarettes and food stuffs.[66]

---

[61]   See art. 12 Chinese Regulation.
[62]   See art. 15 Chinese Regulation.
[63]   See art. 17 Measures for Implementing the Chinese Regulation.
[64]   See art. 31 Measures for Implementing the Chinese Regulation.
[65]   An interview with an official at Nanjing Customs Administration. See also General Custom Administration, IP protection of Custom in China 2014 <http://www.sipo.gov.cn/zlssbgs/gzdt/2015/201506/t20150602_1126009.html>   accessed 15 June 2015.
[66]   2011 and 2012 Annual Report of Custom Protection of IPRs.

5.   EU–CHINA CUSTOMS COOPERATION – A FRAMEWORK OF NORM INTERACTION

On the bilateral front, the EU and China have cooperated on customs matters since 2004 when they signed the 'Agreement between the European Union and the Government of the People's Republic of China on cooperation and mutual administrative assistance in customs matters'. This cooperation has served as an important medium for norm interaction between the EU and China. One aspect is the establishment of a Joint Customs Cooperation Committee (JCCC)[67] to oversee the proper functioning of the agreement. To increase the effectiveness and efficiency of this cooperation and to ensure overall coherence, the Committee adopted in 2010 a 'Strategic Framework for Cooperation' for the period 2010–2012.[68] In a recent evaluation, the Committee found that the framework has been useful. It therefore came up with a new 'Strategic Framework for Customs Cooperation 2014–2017'[69] that takes into account new challenges and opportunities. Thus, the new strategy prioritizes four key areas of customs cooperation[70] and the first one focuses (of interest for this subject) on combating intellectual property rights infringements. To this end, customs authorities from both sides are to cooperate on:

1.   exchange and joint analysis of seizure statistics to detect general trends and risks, which will lead to better targeting of high-risk consignments;
2.   exchange of case-specific information on detentions through a network of customs officers in seaports and airports in the EU and in China;

---

[67]   The Committee consists of representatives of the customs authorities of the EU and China. It is an important forum enabling both sides to discuss key issues related to customs, exchange information and work towards finding common solutions to problems that need to be addressed (hereinafter, the Committee).

[68]   This is captured in the introduction to the Council of the European Union conclusions on EU–China customs cooperation 'Ensuring smooth and safe trade between the EU and China: Strategic framework for customs cooperation 2014–2017'. Available at <http://www.consilium.europa.eu/uedocs/cms_data/docs/pressdata/en/intm/142577.pdf> accessed 9 April 2015, and the 'Action plan concerning EU–China customs cooperation on IPR (2014–2017)' that proceeds from this Framework Strategy: <http://ec.europa.eu/taxation_customs/resources/documents/customs/policy_issues/international_customs_agreements/china/action_plan_eu_china_ipr_2014_2017.pdf> accessed 9 April 2015.

[69]   See ibid.

[70]   They are: to strengthen IP rights enforcement, promote supply chain security, fight against fraud, and facilitate trade.

3. enhancement of cooperation between customs and other law enforcement authorities in order to dismantle production and distribution networks of intellectual property rights-infringing goods;
4. a joint partnership between the customs authorities and the business communities in China and the EU, which will enable the right holders to understand how to best enforce their rights and how to assist Customs in targeting controls in the most optimal way; and
5. exchange of knowledge and experience of each other's intellectual property rights enforcement policies and practices.[71]

As can be seen from its scope, these are practical and robust measures that go beyond border controls to deal with the roots of counterfeiting and are aimed at disrupting the production and distribution channels of goods infringing intellectual property rights. This is aimed at providing a long-term solution to the international trade in intellectual property-infringing goods since border measures alone are inadequate. This has long been the aim and strategy of the EU.[72] It follows the same course as the recent EU action plan on intellectual property rights infringement: 'Towards a renewed consensus on the enforcement of Intellectual Property Rights',[73] which seeks to strengthen intellectual property rights in the internal market. The action plan focuses on commercial-scale infringements, which do the most harm to the EU economy. It therefore proposes new enforcement tools – such as the 'follow the money' approach,[74] which aims to deprive commercial-scale infringers of their actual or potential revenue flows. To ensure this externally, the EU–China action plan systematically requires that customs authorities from the EU and China pass on useful, agreed and well-defined information to authorities and agencies responsible for enforcing intellectual property rights (such as the police and judiciary), effectively share experiences, and discuss working arrangements and practices relating to the strengthening of cooperation between customs and other relevant authorities and agencies in charge of the enforcement of intellectual property rights. They are also to share information on detentions and seizures on a quarterly basis. Statistics from this data would serve as a tool for joint analysis by risk management

---

[71]   See *supra*, n 68.
[72]   See the EU's enforcement strategy in third countries, *supra*, n 7.
[73]   Communication from the Commission to the European Parliament, the Council and the European Economic and Social Committee, 'Towards a renewed consensus on the enforcement of intellectual property rights: An EU action plan', Strasbourg, 1 July 2014 COM (2014) 392 final.
[74]   Ibid, p. 6.

experts from both sides with a view to detecting general trends and other risk information.[75] This evaluation should be done at least every year or on a more frequent basis.

The strategy also builds on the existing network of frontline officers networking from main ports in the EU and China possibly via a specially developed IT system, allowing for direct and easy interaction to ensure successful targeting of, for example, high-risk consignments that may be coming into the EU. Importantly, the framework also enjoins both sides to exchange knowledge and experience of each other's intellectual property rights enforcement policies and practices. As the EU is known for its technical expertise and institutional advantage on customs matters, it may well be that this could lead to the gradual transfer of norms from the EU to China. As part of ensuring the efficiency of the framework, each of the points of cooperation identified comes with evaluation criteria that point to how it should be achieved. Considering these dynamic improvements, the new strategy brings, coupled with the requirement to create a working group that would oversee the operation of the Action Plan, a financing plan and a mechanism for evaluation. Therefore it can be expected that this cooperation may lead to further opportunities for norm interaction between both sides in ways that go beyond border measures.

6.   CONCLUSION

This chapter examined the interaction of norms in relation to the implementation of border measures in Europe and China. The relationship shows that the EU is a norm giver, China is a norm taker. This leads to the outcome that Chinese laws on border measures are considerably Europeanized. This is reflected not only in the similarities between the Regulations of both parties, but also in their differences. Because relations between both parties are dynamic social processes, which may both be cooperative and also contain seeds of conflict, we are confronted with some structural and functional similarities as well as differences on how the laws from both sides interact. For example, whereas both Regulations distinguish two customs procedures – *ex officio* action and through application – the forms of application as well as their meanings differ. While *ex officio* cases are not so numerous in Europe, the same cannot be said about China. Moreover, how both jurisdictions manage parallel imports and overruns, large and small consignments of import goods,

---

[75]   See *supra*, n 68.

and enforcement (amidst cooperation) are telling examples, which are discussed in this chapter.

China as a norm taker has adapted border measures into its economic, social and political environment. Even though this deepens cooperation with the EU, China is still largely constrained by its domestic interests. As China still remains the main country of origin suspected of exporting infringing intellectual property items into the EU, it remains to be seen whether the renewed EU–China customs cooperation on intellectual property rights will lead to greater convergence in law or whether there could still be some disagreements on fundamental legal concepts and practice.

Index